The Critical Theory of Axel Honneth

The Critical Theory of Axel Honneth

Danielle Petherbridge

LEXINGTON BOOKS
Lanham • Boulder • New York • Toronto • Plymouth, UK

Published by Lexington Books
A wholly owned subsidiary of The Rowman & Littlefield Publishing Group, Inc.
4501 Forbes Boulevard, Suite 200, Lanham, Maryland 20706
www.rowman.com

10 Thornbury Road, Plymouth PL6 7PP, United Kingdom

British Library Cataloguing in Publication Information Available

Library of Congress Cataloging-in-Publication Data

Library of Congress Cataloging-in-Publication Data Available

ISBN 978-0-7391-7203-2 (cloth : alk. paper) -- ISBN 978-0-7391-7204-9 (electronic)
ISBN 978-1-4985-1618-1 (pbk:alk, paper)

♾TM The paper used in this publication meets the minimum requirements of American National Standard for Information Sciences Permanence of Paper for Printed Library Materials, ANSI/NISO Z39.48-1992.

Printed in the United States of America

Contents

Acknowledgments

This book was completed with the institutional support of the Irish Research Council and University College Dublin. I would particularly like to express my gratitude to the Irish Research Council for awarding me a postdoctoral research fellowship which enabled the completion of the manuscript. I would also like to thank the anonymous reviewers from Lexington Books for constructive criticism on an earlier draft of the book and Polity Press for kind permission to publish extracts from Axel Honneth's, *The Struggle for Recognition*, Polity Press, 1995.

There are also numerous people I would like to thank for their generous support during the completion of this manuscript. I would especially like to extend my deep gratitude to Maeve Cooke, for her exceptional support and advice throughout the various stages of the work. A special thanks also to Brian O'Connor and Amy Allen for invaluable advice and for critical comments on an earlier version of the manuscript. Thanks are also due to Dermot Moran for his suggestions in the later stages of the project, and to faculty, staff, and graduate students at University College Dublin, especially postdoctoral fellows and graduates who discursively engaged with some of the ideas in the book.

Most of all, I would like to warmly thank my family and friends, particularly my parents Maureen and Geoff for their constancy and encouragement. By far the most significant expression of gratitude is dedicated to John, for his love and companionship throughout the life of this work and beyond, and for bringing new meaning to Hegel's insight that love is indeed 'a miracle, that we cannot grasp.' It is with the greatest thanks that I dedicate this book to him.

Introduction

From the beginning, Axel Honneth's project has been directed towards the key problem of reconstructing a conceptual framework that can both comprehend the structures of social domination and identify the resources for its practical transformation.[1] In this spirit, Honneth is dedicated to continuing the project of Critical Theory in its two-fold strategy of reflecting upon its own premises and pre-scientifically locating the emancipatory interest which frames its theoretical analysis.[2] In this respect, Honneth has made a profound contribution to Critical Theory, most notably in terms of defending a normative, emancipatory project and developing a comprehensive theory of recognition that can provide a framework for analyzing the distorting effects of modern social conditions on subjective experience and subject-formation.

As the leading theorist of the third generation of the Frankfurt School, Honneth has productively renewed the project of Critical Theory in ways that both continue and differentiate his own project from first and second generations. As Jürgen Habermas' successor in social philosophy at the University of Frankfurt and Director of the Institute for Social Research, Honneth has been instrumental in extending the Institute's interdisciplinary research programs, most notably around the research themes of the 'structural transformation of recognition' and 'paradoxes of capitalist modernization.' Although not formally a student of Habermas', Honneth was appointed as an assistant professor in Habermas' research group in the 1980s, and after holding positions in Berlin and Konstanz, was appointed to Habermas' chair in Frankfurt in 1996.[3] More recently, he has also been appointed to a chair in the philosophy department at Columbia University in New York, coincidently retracing the steps of first-generation members of the Frankfurt School who were offered institutional refuge at Columbia when they fled Germany during the 1930s.[4] However, while Honneth is undeniably committed to the mode of social critique originally derived from the first generation of the Frankfurt School, he also fully endorses the communicative transformation of Critical Theory first initiated by Habermas. In this sense, much of Honneth's work has been dedicated to developing an alternative intersubjective basis for Critical Theory that can safeguard its normative intent and he shares Habermas' basic intuition that such norms can be found as current practices or experiences within our social lifeworlds.

While Honneth has engaged with many of the same theoretical resources as Habermas, from historical materialism, philosophical anthropology, psychoanalysis, developmental psychology, American pragmatism, and German Idealism, he has also sought to make them his own and has undertaken a form of reconstructive criticism that has resulted in remarkably new and productive outcomes. Honneth's alternative readings of Hegel, Feuerbach, Marx, Lukács, and Mead have produced not only an alternative theory of intersubjectivity but also a theory of recognition alert to subjective experiences of social suffering, fragmentation, and alienation. One of the hallmarks of Honneth's work has also been his preparedness to engage productively with a range of alternative positions in both contemporary French philosophy and phenomenology, including the work of Derrida, Sartre, Merleau-Ponty, Castoriadis, Foucault, and Levinas in developing a multidimensional theory of intersubjectivity and recognition.[5] In this respect, in contrast to Habermas' much more critical and dismissive treatment of this line of thinkers and the circumscription of the reception of their work in terms of his own philosophy of language and theory of rationalization, Honneth's work has proven important for opening new lines of engagement with a range of traditions. This is especially the case in terms of emphasizing the more phenomenological and existential aspects of the French tradition, for example, in Sartre's work, the pre- and extra-linguistic dimensions of sociality and intersubjectivity, the importance of the asymmetricality of ethical relations highlighted by Derrida and Levinas, as well as fruitfully engaging with Foucault's analysis of power and conflictual notion of the social understood as a strategic field of struggle.[6]

However, it is not only his predisposition to an engagement with a range of alternative philosophical traditions and theoretical resources that sets Honneth apart from previous generations of the Frankfurt School, but also his political and social context. Born in 1949 in Essen, Germany, Honneth's formative years were more influenced by the social changes and new social movements of the 1960s and 1970s, rather than any direct experience of the years of German National Socialism and wartime atrocities, or the failure of the so-called revolutionary consciousness of the working classes both in the interwar years and in the face of Nazism.[7] Nonetheless, Honneth suggests that the social upheavals and transformations of his own generation, particularly within the working class population in Germany at the time, alerted him at a 'pre-theoretical level' to the existential experiences of social suffering and shame, feelings of disrespect that also resonated in his readings of the works of E.P. Thompson and Barrington Moore as explanatory factors for social conflict and change.[8]

These impulses have become guiding motifs in Honneth's work and his theory of recognition is predicated on the idea of a 'phenomenology of social suffering,' those lived experiences of disrespect that provide immanent resources within social life for the basis of social critique and transformation. In this respect, Honneth continues the guiding premise of first and second generations of Critical Theory by developing a critique of philosophical categories which is immanently connected to social diagnoses that identify an often concealed, suppressed, or ignored emancipatory interest or horizon in social reality. Honneth's primary focus has indubitably been an examination of the pathologies of individual subject-formation and distorted identity as the basis for social conflict and struggle.[9] In this sense, he has largely taken up the first generation's concerns with subjective experiences of domination, alienation, reification, and the deformations of identity development, rather than pursuing Habermas' core concerns with procedural rationality, language philosophy, and macro-social dynamics.[10] Nonetheless, Honneth shares with both generations the distinctive Frankfurt School approach by aiming to bring together the empirically orientated social sciences with philosophical critique as a means of identifying social pathologies in modern capitalist societies.[11]

However, the theoretical manner in which Honneth reconceives of both a theory of society and social change, his dedication to a fundamentally action-theoretic stance and re-orientation of the communicative paradigm, his development of a multidimensional theory of intersubjectivity and philosophical anthropology, and his more nuanced analysis of power, clearly sets him apart from members of both first and second generations of Critical Theory.

One of Honneth's primary concerns has been to fundamentally defend an action-theoretic view of the social, thereby resisting all forms of structural, functional, and totalizing social analysis. In his early critique of the first generation of the Frankfurt School, Honneth contends that their social-theoretical analysis was not robust enough to develop a reflexive critique of society in the terms originally defined by Horkheimer.[12] In Honneth's view, Horkheimer and Adorno's incapacity to adequately analyze a communicative domain of the social leads to their inability to locate a pre-theoretical resource for critique in everyday life beyond the paradigm of labor and to a one-dimensional conception of power understood in terms of the human domination of nature. Although Horkheimer and Adorno attempted to separate their critical method from the falsely universalizing influence of the model of the natural sciences, Honneth argues that they fall victim to an account of social life overly determined by the act of dominating nature by failing to develop a more complex account of social processes.[13] Despite his original insights into a dimension of 'cultural action,' Horkheimer's adherence to a philosophy of history structured in terms of the dimension of social labor prevented him from fully identifying an intersubjective dimension of social action that could provide a pre-theoretical resource for critique. Moreover, in his early work, Honneth argued that Adorno's negativism forces Critical Theory into a position in which it is no longer possible to gain access to a social-historically grounded form of reflexive critique and it is left articulating a pre-theoretical reference point that is located in the experience of modern art.[14]

Therefore, notwithstanding his attempts to reconstruct more systematically the project of Critical Theory articulated by first-generation members of the Frankfurt School, Honneth is convinced that the communicative transformation of Critical Theory initiated by Jürgen Habermas offers the most promising conceptual means by which access to a pre-scientific realm of moral critique can once again be established. In defining an emancipatory practice or experience in social reality, Honneth seeks to elaborate Habermas' early concept of 'emancipatory interest.'[15] However, following his own anthropological-theoretical impulses, Honneth attempts to reorient Habermas' original idea away from a cognitive or rational interest in emancipation towards a deeper layer of moral expectations structured into social relations of recognition. Moral expectations are then understood to be "the product of the social formation of a deep-seated claim-making potential in the sense that they always owe their normative justification to principles institutionally anchored in the historically established recognition order."[16] Although he fully endorses Habermas' attempt to locate a transcendental element of critique that arises from anthropological structures, for Honneth, a form of 'immanent transcendence' can only be identified in the deep-seated identity claims inherent in intersubjective relations of recognition.[17]

In this vein, while accepting Habermas' emancipatory aims, Honneth attempts to develop an alternative theory of intersubjectivity that extends it beyond its linguistic dimensions and provides a more comprehensive account of the normative structures that underpin the moral basis of both autonomous human action and interaction. In his early work, *Social Action and Human Nature* (1988), Honneth began to develop a comprehensive anthropological theory of intersubjectivity, not only by reorienting Habermas' communicative approach but also undertaking alternative interpretations of Mead, Feuerbach, Marx, and the tradition of German philosophical anthropology in an effort to reconstruct the intersubjective paradigm along the lines of a theory of 'practical intersubjectivity.' This early dynamic notion of intersubjectivity as indicating a 'practical involvement' with others and the world is later transformed into a comprehensive theory of intersubjectivity as recognition, one based on patterns of interpersonal relations and interaction between subjects that not only forms the basis of Honneth's conception of the social and of subject-formation but also the anthropological premise that grounds his theory overall.

For Honneth, this reconfiguration of the intersubjective paradigm also requires a consideration of an intersubjective notion of power that can account for the conflictual aspects of a more broadly conceived notion of communicative action and provide a more comprehensive critique of the structures of social domination. In his first major work, *The Critique of Power* (1991), Honneth puts Foucault's analysis of strategic interaction to work with Habermas' theory of communicative action in an attempt to develop a reflexive critique of power and domination. Therefore, despite arguing that Foucault lapses into a systems-theoretic analysis of power, Honneth suggests that Foucault's conception of the social as a domain of strategic interaction is instructive for developing an intersubjective notion of power that is lacking in Habermas' account. Significantly, this originally enabled Honneth to articulate a much broader notion of interaction and give much greater credence to social domination. In this way, Honneth develops an account of the social that perceptively analyzes a relational notion of power at a micro-level, at the level of everyday interaction in the lifeworld. Domination and power can therefore potentially be conceived in broad terms, not just at the level of systemic production, nor in terms of the colonization of the lifeworld but in everyday interactions, thus avoiding the false opposition between a norm-free domain of power and a power-free domain of communication that Honneth argues results from Habermas' theoretical presuppositions.[18]

However, at the conclusion to this early period of his work, Honneth ultimately claims that neither Foucault nor Habermas is able to provide a comprehensive action-theoretic account of the social nor the basis for a reflexive critique of power. Honneth's response to the work of both theorists is to attempt to develop an expanded notion of normative interaction that is applicable to the coordination of action in all spheres of social life, including the market and state bureaucracy. The consequence of Honneth's own reconstruction of a more broadly conceived theory of communicative action is that he also attempts to redefine the analysis and critique of power, and to incorporate a notion of conflict and social struggle as central to the paradigm of the social.

To accomplish the task of bringing together a notion of social struggle with a normative theory of society, in *The Struggle for Recognition* (1995), Honneth turns to Hegel's early Jena philosophy of recognition, which for him provides the means to reconstruct Foucault's struggle-theoretic insights in normative-theoretic terms. Through an intersubjectivistic reading of Hegel, and with recourse to intersubjective insights taken from Mead and Winnicott, Honneth develops a theory of recognition which is posited as the normative ground for a model of critical social theory. The concept of recognition is intended to provide a framework for analyzing social conditions of individual self-realization and the development of social relations and institutions. The normative foundation of recognition is grounded anthropologically and conceptualized as an originary notion of undamaged intersubjectivity which is understood to provide the fundamental preconditions for successful subject-formation and the immanent development of ethical life.

In his more recent work, *Reification* (2008), Honneth has further augmented the basic presuppositions drawn from Hegel with a range of philosophical resources, and the concept of recognition has been reconstructed into a dual category of both normative theory and ontology of primary affectivity. Moreover, in a recent series of works centered on Hegel's *Philosophy of Right*, he has introduced a historical dimension into his account of recognition and developed a more comprehensive analysis of social institutions, as well as a theory of democratic ethics and a notion of social freedom grounded in relations of recognition.[19] This extensive body of work has maintained many of the early guiding impulses but it has also resulted in both subtle forms of clarification and significant emendations.

Despite the advances in Honneth's project, the argument developed in this book is that important insights from Honneth's earlier work on philosophical anthropology, intersubjective theory, and the critique of power have, nonetheless, been lost in developing his later theory of recognition. The problem with Honneth's theory of recognition is that the theory of intersubjectivity is circumscribed only within the normative terms of recognition, and as a consequence he fails to pursue the more multi-dimensional theory of sociality and interaction explored in his early work. Like Habermas before him, Honneth therefore ends up separating power from both communicative action and forms of recognition constitutive of the subject in the context of intersubjective relations. He therefore provides an overly normativized account of intersubjectivity without fully considering the potential entanglement of recognition and power in terms of both social institutions and subject-formation, and this weakens the critical purchase of his theory. In more recent work, these problems have been further exacerbated by the shift towards an ontology of primary affective attunement as the basis for the theory of recognition and an apparent oscillation between different foundational strategies for grounding the project of critique.

However, as this study seeks to demonstrate, insights for an alternative theory of intersubjectivity that can account for both an adequate theory of power and normative forms of subject-formation can be immanently reconstructed from within Honneth's writings. This book traces the development of Honneth's work from his earliest writings to his most recent work in order to elucidate these insights and to trace their circumvention in his more mature project.

In order to achieve this aim, the critical reconstruction provided here is structured in terms of three main theoretical features in regard to Honneth's work: firstly, his reconstruction of the intersubjective paradigm; secondly, the development of a philosophical-anthropological basis for critique; and, thirdly, his attempt to provide a comprehensive framework for analyzing relations of power and domination. These three interlocking themes mutually inform one another, and the development of a critique of power can only be understood in the context of the particular constellation of philosophical anthropology and intersubjectivity operative in Honneth's work.

The aim of this study, then, is to provide a reconstruction of the development of these major conceptual elements in Honneth's project in terms of the interconnection between philosophical anthropology, intersubjectivity, and the project of critique.[20] The interpretation undertaken here proceeds by way of an immanent reconstruction of Honneth's own readings of the key theoretical figures that inform his project, while also providing a counter-interpretation of each theorist to elucidate the tensions and possibilities that arise for the project of a critical social theory. It is argued here that Honneth's interpretations of the work of Habermas, Marx, Foucault, Hegel, Mead, and Winnicott are central to his reconfiguration of the intersubjective paradigm and for the development of 'reflexive stages in a critical social theory.'[21]

Nonetheless, this reconstruction of Honneth's work is not merely a genealogical study, even though it traces Honneth's project from his earliest writings to his most recent work. Rather, this study provides a critical immanent reconstruction that seeks to uncover the difficulties encountered by Honneth in his attempt to bring together the elements of anthropology, normativity, and critique. In the five parts that structure this book, Honneth's interpretations of Habermas, Marx, Foucault, Hegel, Mead, and Winnicott are re-traced in detail to elucidate the tensions that have arisen in his attempt to develop a normative theory grounded on an anthropology of recognition. In the final part, the consequences of Honneth's particular analysis of power will also be considered alongside the justificatory measures taken to ground his project of critical theory.

This study, then, is not explicitly concerned with a detailed explication of the theory of recognition nor does it discuss Honneth's three-tiered social-theoretical model of recognition or work on democratic institutions at length. Rather, the book's aim is to elucidate Honneth's more general underlying attempt to reconstruct the intersubjective paradigm and his anthropological approach to grounding critical theory. The path this study traces through Honneth's work is therefore specifically focused on the early insights Honneth brings to the elaboration of a broad-based theory of intersubjectivity and critique of power, and the subsequent loss of these insights in his later work with the move to a theory of recognition. This reconstruction is therefore not orientated primarily around Honneth's most well-known work, *The*

Struggle for Recognition, but argues instead that Honneth's early works such as *Social Action and Human Nature* and *The Critique of Power* are central to an understanding of his project and contain important insights that are central to a consideration of his later work.

This book therefore examines Honneth's attempt to establish an anthropological ground for the critical theory of recognition, which is posited as the fundamental intersubjective basis for successful subject-formation and normative forms of socialization. The problem with this theory of intersubjectivity is that forms of sociality and subject-formation are conceptualized only within the normative terms of recognition, rather than as constituted by various modalities of interaction, including power and strategic action. Honneth therefore reduces power and domination merely to pathologies of recognition, and by so doing, confines the critique of power to the terms of unsuccessful recognition. As a result, Honneth provides an overly circumscribed account of sociality and subject-formation based on a one-dimensional theory of intersubjectivity, and this blunts the critical edge of his theory. Despite the undoubted achievements of Honneth's project, this study seeks to re-examine Honneth's contributions both to the intersubjective paradigm and to the critique of power, and to return to his early insights as the basis for a project of critical theory.

1

Honneth's Reconstruction of Critical Theory

Chapter One

The Intersubjective Grounds of Critique

From Mutual Understanding to Mutual Recognition

For Honneth, the task of Critical Theory requires more than simply mounting a critique of existing social conditions; notably, it must also carry the potential for immanently motivating social change. In the tradition of Left-Hegelian critique in which Honneth situates his own project, critical social theory must therefore consist of two fundamental elements: both a pre-theoretical resource or empirical foothold in social reality which reveals an emancipatory instance or need, but also a quasi-transcendental dimension or mode of context-transcending validity in order to provide a normative horizon from which to critically assess forms of social organization.[1] In other words, critical social theory requires a dialectical interplay between immanence and transcendence which can enable critical diagnoses of existing social conditions to be made.[2]

Honneth considers this dialectical method or form of 'intramundane transcendence' to be the defining characteristic of critical social theory in the Frankfurt School tradition, a methodological approach that Horkheimer outlined in his programmatic work of the 1930s.[3] Horkheimer extends the Left-Hegelian legacy by the particular way in which he aims to bring theory and practice together, which locates an emancipatory interest within social reality that is identifiable as the motivating factor for contesting social relations of domination. Honneth argues, however, that Horkheimer was ultimately unable to meet the requirements of his own critical method. His work is so severely limited by the Marxist philosophy of history within which it is framed that he is left trying to identify an emancipatory interest in the dimen-

sion of social labor, which is no longer empirically verifiable or anthropologically sustainable. As a result, Horkheimer is unable to realize the potential
of developing a notion of 'cultural action,' which would have alerted him to a
domain of social action in which the reproduction of society is understood
not to be the property of independent systemic processes, but is instead
"determined by the normative self-understanding of communicatively socialized subjects."[4]

Honneth therefore argues that the project of social criticism undertaken
by the first generation of the Frankfurt School can no longer be defended in
its original form.[5] In the end, Horkheimer and Adorno perpetuate a purely
functionalist analysis that provides a one-dimensional view of historical development in terms of the 'unfolding' of a form of instrumental rationality
and a form of social action associated with the human domination over
nature—a form of domination that is also directed at the inner nature of
socialized subjects. Moreover, they develop a totalizing 'logic of reification,'
one that becomes the explanatory factor in processes of socialization, social
labor, and relations of domination, which is extended beyond Lukács' original assessment of the abstraction that results from capitalist commodity exchange, into a civilizational analysis and an anthropological category.[6]
Honneth's concern is that Adorno and Horkheimer's totalizing critique and
inability to identify a communicative form of social action creates a radical
disjuncture between the form of normative critique and social reality, such
that it perpetuates the view of a 'totalizing ideology.'[7] In other words, they
leave no possibility that any form of emancipatory interest or practice might
be identified within social reality due to the distorting effects of 'cultural
manipulation' and social domination that typifies the capitalist life form.[8]

As a consequence, Critical Theory is left claiming a privileged critical
vantage-point and unwittingly divorces itself from any pre-theoretical experience according to which normative claims might be made. Honneth therefore
argues that the task for contemporary critical theorists is to maintain the
'ideal' form of immanent or reconstructive criticism that characterized the
original Frankfurt School approach, without taking on board their historical-
philosophical and sociological assumptions, which in Honneth's view, risk
constructing a form of 'elitist specialized knowledge.'[9]

In contrast, Habermas' communicative transformation of Critical Theory
is not only able to locate a form of normativity immanent to linguistic intersubjectivity, and thus avoid the impasse reached by the first generation, but
he also famously identifies two dimensions of social action—labor and interaction—that characterize the historical development of the species in terms
of two different forms of integration and processes of rationalization, thereby
avoiding a totalizing analysis. Following Habermas' communicative turn,
Honneth argues, that the task now confronting contemporary critical theorists
is determining which instances or experiences can be pre-theoretically locat-

ed within social reality that also contain 'system-bursting' potential to compel change within a given social context.[10] For the critical theorist to avoid claiming a privileged or paternalistic position, the emancipatory instance or experience that compels social change must be identified within the existing social order and must be of the same normativity or rationality that becomes manifest in new forms of social organization.[11] A pre-theoretical interest must "be regarded as a moment of socially embodied reason insofar as it possesses a surplus of rational norms or organizational principles that press for their own realization."[12] In this sense, Honneth fundamentally endorses Habermas' intersubjective reorientation of Critical Theory and seeks to identify a pre-theoretical basis for critique in intersubjective recognition relations, which are understood to provide the normative ground from which critical assessments of social life can be made.

With this in mind, Honneth attempts to develop a project of critical social theory that shifts the emphasis of normativity onto what he terms the moral grammar of social interaction, those broadly conceived communicative conditions that relate to identity and autonomy in the context of a multiplicity of everyday interactions and moral experiences. He therefore proceeds ontogenetically in an effort to uncover the normative intersubjective conditions required for successful self-realization, seeking to emphasize both the intersubjective dependency of human subjects and the conflictual nature of social interaction and subject-formation.

In this spirit, Honneth clarifies his project as an attempt to reconstitute Habermas' attempt to locate a source of inner-social transcendence in communicative action in more concrete terms, by making the Hegelian motif of a 'struggle for recognition' fruitful for social theory.[13] As Honneth suggests, the difficulty facing those who take up the inheritance of Critical Theory's Left-Hegelian tradition today is to try to find an instance in social reality that time and again contains a normative surplus that presses beyond all given forms of social organization. Honneth argues, the real challenge is to show that such an empirical reference point is "not the result of contingent conflict situations, but rather expresses the unmet demands of humanity at large…" and that "…it designates a normative potential that reemerges in every new social reality because it is so tightly fused to the structure of human interests."[14] For Honneth, a form of intramundane transcendence can be located in feelings of misrecognition, of humiliation and disrespect, which consequently, for him are regarded as the motivating factor for social change.[15]

Honneth argues that there is a certain ambivalence evident in Habermas' project, because it is not entirely clear whether the quasi-transcendental justification for critique "is to reside in the normative presuppositions of human language or in social interaction." For Honneth, "it makes considerable difference whether social interactions themselves bear normative expectations or whether it is only through language that a normative element comes into

communication."[16] Likewise, he suggests the same ambiguity seems prevalent when Habermas uses the concept of 'recognition' both for granting
social status and for supporting language-based validity claims, without ever
sufficiently distinguishing between the two.

In contrast, Honneth understands his own proposal as an attempt to dissolve such distinctions by proceeding 'social-anthropologically' from a core
of expectations of recognition that all subjects bring to social interaction—
hence dissolving the distinctions that Habermas' appears to make. Therefore,
although both theories are intersubjective, Honneth suggests they proceed
along very different axes. Habermas reconstructs a version of speech-act
theory in the manner of a formal-pragmatics; in this way his conception is
fundamentally modeled on the pragmatic, universal conditions of mutual
understanding. In comparison, Honneth understands his own intersubjective-
theoretic project as situated in the formal analysis of the forms of human self-
relation and identity-formation. Thus, the fundamental differences between
their projects can be attributed to these two very different paradigms: one is
the analysis of speech and the other is a conception of subject-formation with
anthropological orientation.

These intuitions stem from Honneth's very early studies with Hans Joas
on philosophical anthropology in *Social Action and Human Nature*. In this
work, and with particular reference to Mead and the tradition of German
philosophical anthropology, the anthropology of Marx, and members of the
Budapest School, Honneth begins to develop a broadly conceived 'anthropology of social action' that is not confined to linguistic presuppositions. In
this context, Honneth and Joas argue that "Habermas is mistaken when he
too hastily identifies the fundamental structure of intersubjectivity with
speech," and they seek to demonstrate the importance of embodied expressiveness and relationality prior to linguisticality.[17]

In his early work on philosophical anthropology, Honneth begins to think
through the peculiarities of the structure of human needs, compared to animal
instincts, and the consequences this might have for a specifically human
capacity for action communicatively construed. He therefore develops the
argument that sources of normativity are not restricted to linguisticality but
are first associated with "physical gestures or mimetic forms of expression."[18] Honneth's early observations are central to his reconfiguration of the
intersubjective paradigm and, as will be discussed further below, they are
carried through to his later work where they are reconfigured into a notion of
the subject's practical involvement or attunement with the world.

In his early work, Honneth clearly states the importance of understanding
the complexity of ontogenetic development and its irreducibility to phylogenetic processes, a commitment he maintains throughout his work. In contrast
to Habermas, Honneth proceeds ontogenetically in an attempt to avoid the
problems that Habermas' theory encounters by fusing the levels of ontoge-

netic and phylogenetic development together in an over-generalized and over-stated account of moral development articulated in terms of rationalization processes. This way of proceeding means that Habermas creates an unbridgeable gap between the level of normativity and the pre-theoretical resources in social life that give motivational authority to his account of practical reason, and it is this set of problems that Honneth seeks to address in his own reconstruction of the communicative paradigm.[19]

CRITIQUE OF COMMUNICATIVE ACTION

There are a number of difficulties with Habermas' theory that Honneth's work attempts to counter and the contrast between their approaches is instructive. Of particular importance is that even in his early work, Habermas' critical theory is based on the assumption that certain procedural rules are always already presupposed by human discourse and that these rules can be drawn on to validate moral principles, and thus normatively justify social interaction. Thus, according to Habermas' early formulation, a rational basis for social life can only be achieved when social relations are organized "according to the principle that the validity of every norm of political consequence be made dependent on a consensus arrived at in communication free from domination."[20] Habermas' theory of discourse ethics therefore assumes not only the particular capabilities of participants in discursive agreement but the exclusion of all forms of coercion. For Habermas, rational consensus presupposes an ideal speech situation as a kind of meta-norm, a situation that assumes a kind of symmetry and reciprocity, requiring all participants to adopt the standpoint of the 'generalized other.' In assuming the standpoint of the generalized other, participants must abstract from the individuality and concrete identity of themselves and the other. The moral self, in Habermasian terms, then, appears to be a "disembedded and disembodied being" who must leave behind his or her private and particular affiliations.[21] Through such a principle Habermas suggests a rational consensus can be achieved in the context of conflicting opinions and interests regardless of differing traditions, cultural perspectives or individual life histories.

In Habermas' view, differences in moral perspectives based on divergent ways of life can be made to conform with the universalist normative presuppositions of communicative rationality only if a distinction is maintained between issues of justice and questions of the good life. Accordingly, for Habermas, the consideration of particular identities and ways of life within moral argumentation is misguided; the freedom and equality of moral subjects only refers to common universal characteristics regardless of individual needs and identities. Moral judgments, then, are concerned only with right or just action, not with substantive values of the good. Norms are, therefore, considered to be obligatory for all persons universally and equally, whereas values refer to shared preferences or goods that have a teleological orienta- tion. In Habermas' view discourses pertaining to values and goods are entan- gled with an individual's or group's identity, and relate to values informing a sense of self. They relate to the questions: "Who am I/we, and who do I/we want to be?" In comparison, moral discourses are concerned with the ques- tion: "How should I/we act?" and relate to problems of what behavior can be deemed legitimate between individuals, or what norms can be considered rationally binding.[22] Habermas concludes that moral-practical dilemmas can be resolved on the basis of a universal sense of communicative reason, whereas questions relating to ethical identities can only be considered in terms of the ethical values within a particular form of life.

The consequences of Habermas' proceduralism, however, are significant. Conceived as formal pragmatics, his theory of practical reason ends up con- tributing to the very problems of ethical dislocation and meaninglessness it aims to diagnose and rectify, by emptying the category of moral reason and thereby relinquishing the very processes of intersubjective recognition it originally intended to salvage.[23] Habermas' strict separation between ques- tions of justice and the good life leaves us with the unenviable possibility, as he himself once admitted, "that one day an emancipated human race could encounter itself within an expanded space of discursive formation of will and yet be robbed of the light in which it is capable of interpreting its life as something good ... right at the moment of overcoming age old repressions it would harbor no violence, but it would have no content either."[24]

It is precisely this claim to universalizability and the abstraction from concrete life forms that Honneth problematizes. Furthermore, Honneth ques- tions whether Habermas neglects to consider the relation of his own theory to a particular version of the good life. The attempt to define the moral domain in terms of justice alone and the prioritization of this domain over questions of ethical identity tends to suggest the unacknowledged privileging and inter- nalization of certain primary goods, thereby securing in advance the neces- sity of these values as internal sources of moral motivation.[25]

In contrast to Habermas, Honneth argues that such an inarticulation about moral sources prevents us from explaining the willingness of individuals to adopt the goals of moral discourse to begin with. Rather we need to under- stand that both moral norms and ethical identities are set within an evaluative framework that alone determines the point of such moral norms and goods. Hence, Honneth suggests we need to acknowledge that the moral-practical domain is always set firmly within the ethical. This amounts to the theoreti- cal suggestion that the existence and expansion of morality is dependent upon the struggles through which subjects bring about the recognition of their gradually developing claims to identity. The foundation of a moral- practical critique, then, is to be found in the normative claims that are structurally inherent in everyday relations of mutual recognition rather than, as Habermas suggests, limited to the structures of symmetry and reciprocity inherent in language.

Honneth therefore argues that normative claims are experienced and articulated by people in everyday life as disturbances that may, or may not, make mutual recognition possible. These disturbances throw into relief, at the most basic level, the *processes* through which recognition is, or is not, achieved prior to the articulation of moral norms. Honneth argues that these are processes and conditions that individuals must feel are safeguarded even before they can attain the competency considered necessary by a theory of discourse ethics. By theorizing these conditions, Honneth wants to account for the psychological, affective, and bodily relations of recognition as modes of 'recognitive-communication,' as well as the contexts of human vulnerability and suffering and their consequences for identity formation. He is particularly interested in the potentially 'ethically' rational character of norms and values that are embodied in the basic attitudes and ways of life of members of a community. In this sense, his is a motivational theory of practical reasoning—motivational in the sense that these processes must be felt as disturbed in the first place in order that moral-practical claims can be made.

In Honneth's view, the Habermasian form of moral reasoning, as the impartial application of general principles, describes only a restricted field of moral life concerned with public institutional forms of morality, but which, according to Honneth, ignores everyday motivational contexts.[26] The universalist principle of Habermas' discourse ethics demands from interaction partners a willingness and refined ability to enable consideration of normative questions from a generalized standpoint while leaving aside their concrete relations with others in everyday experience. Even if individuals could acquire the competency needed to engage in discursive will-formation, a dilemma can be detected here. Situations requiring discursive argumentation tend to arise when, through conflict and crisis, social and political agents challenge an established background consensus from a particular point of view or experience of domination. Claims that address dilemmas in social life arise not at the abstract level of universalization but at the concrete level of conflict and resolution. Discourses therefore arise when the intersubjectivity of ethical life is endangered or disputed, yet Habermas assumes the ongoing validity of a reconciled intersubjectivity at the deepest level of his theory.[27]

The reason for this apparent contradiction, according to Honneth, can be attributed to Habermas' separation of labor and interaction, and his partial incorporation of systems theory, which results in the distinction between lifeworld and system and corresponding forms of integration and rationalization. The problem with this analysis is that it permanently decouples certain forms of action from any kind of normative integration. The consequence is that forms of (inter)action such as those associated with work and the market, are exempt from the expectation of being normatively guided or integrated, and are associated only with purposive-rational action. For Honneth, the distinction between system and lifeworld and associated forms of action and integration results in the problematic conceptual division between norm-free domains of labor, the market and the state, and a power-free sphere of communication. Although Honneth's main concern is to argue for a theory that can account for the normative values underpinning all spheres of action, just as importantly his critique of Habermas points to an inadequate and one-dimensional theory of power—one that divorces power from intersubjective socialization and communication, and narrows the critique of power largely to an analysis of systemic processes.

The advantage of Habermas' move is that a discourse-theoretical project can be used as the basis for critiquing the colonization of the lifeworld by bureaucracies and markets. However, the problem with this perspective according to Honneth is that all "occurrences and phenomena that appear as 'pathological' in social reality are thereby interpreted as consequences of an increase in organizational rationality or the autonomization of attitudes connected with the domination of nature."[28] From this perspective, in Honneth's opinion, Habermas also follows too closely the tradition of the Frankfurt School by defining the apparent 'health' or 'sickness' of a society in terms of the predominance of instrumental rationality and a notion of domination associated with the instrumental appropriation of nature. For Honneth, one of the unfortunate legacies of Left-Hegelianism is that such a model of social critique is characterized by the way in which social pathologies are consistently measured only according to the yardstick of rationality. The problem with this perspective, suggests Honneth, is that pathologies that do not pertain to the cognitive dimensions of human beings cannot come to light at all, thereby resulting in a one-dimensional philosophical anthropology and correspondingly a narrow basis for critique.[29]

As Bernstein has also suggested, part of the problem with Habermas' move to separate communicative from instrumental reason, labor from interaction, is that it results in a purification of the ideals governing communicative action. Habermas thinks he is compelled to maintain a dualism between types of action because he is concerned to ensure that such ideals are not "implicated in what they mean to resist, that a clean categorical separation between the progressive and regressive forces of modernity [can] be drawn."[30] Moreover, Habermas assumes that it is only the very ideality of communicative norms that gives them rational authority. However, like Honneth, Bernstein questions whether the meaning of such ideals can be separated from their use and their role in everyday practice in the permanent manner in which Habermas suggests. The way in which Habermas conceptualizes such ideals, suggests Bernstein, robs them of the material and temporal conditions of meaning. Consequently, the 'purification' of the material and temporal core of communicative ideals begs the question of whether they maintain a foothold in social reality. Bernstein questions, however, whether the purification of the norms of interaction proposed by Habermas can ever have motivational force. The crucial point he makes is that "what makes a norm *practical* rather than theoretical is that its authority is intrinsically motivating..."[31] If this is correct, the result of Habermas' purifying gesture is that communicative norms are in fact theoretical, not practical, and this defeats the very project of practical reason that he sets out to renew.

The proceduralism of Habermas' discourse theory and his overly cognitive account of the normative implications of linguistic action therefore means it is difficult to theorize how the initial feelings of injury that motivate moral claims are converted into claims in the first place. What we are left with, in Habermas' account, is simply the abstract claim of rightness. But for Honneth this is not enough "because, in general subjects experience injury to what we can describe as the 'moral point of view' not in terms of a deviation from intuitively mastered rules of speech, but rather as violence to identity claims acquired through processes of socialization."[32] Honneth suggests that an alternative way of renewing Critical Theory today therefore requires a reconceptualization of the pathologization of social life in terms of a theory of 'damaged recognition.' Thus, the normative criterion must shift to the intersubjective presuppositions of human identity development, rather than the intersubjective presuppositions of language.

As the following chapter demonstrates, Honneth's critique of Habermas' strict separation between instrumental and communicative action, system and lifeworld, is also reflected in his attempt to reintegrate a notion of labor back into the communicative paradigm and to give greater credence to the moral dimension of alienation in critical theory. Moreover, not only does Honneth's critique of the separation of labor and interaction seek to address the question of normativity underlying all social spheres but it also simultaneously begs the question of the need for an alternative analysis of conflict and power.

Chapter Two

Reading Marx after Habermas

Reintegrating Labor into a Communicative Theory of Society

From the outset, Honneth has been convinced that a reorientation of the intersubjective paradigm to a theory of recognition requires that the category of labor be re-integrated into the theory of communicative action rather than understood merely as a form of instrumental action. In this sense, Honneth's early interpretation of Marx and his attempt to develop a recognition-theoretic account of labor is crucial for his development of a theory of communicative action applicable to all spheres of life. Honneth's re-articulation of the *moral* dimensions of alienation and class struggle are central to his early reorientation of Critical Theory, and represent some of the defining features of his project to reconstruct the communicative paradigm as a theory of recognition.

Despite his repeated criticisms of the paradigm of production and the functionalist interpretation characteristic of Marx's later economic writings, Honneth finds in the anthropological writings of the early Marx the basis for an intersubjective account of the moral dimensions of labor and alienation. Honneth's reading of Marx appears to have been formative for the early articulation of an action-theoretic notion of personality-formation or self-realization that has become central to his reconstruction of the communicative paradigm. Importantly, though, Honneth's move does not represent a return to the paradigm of labor but rather an interpretation of Marx that is filtered through the intersubjective turn in Critical Theory undertaken by Habermas.

Although critical of Marx's reduction of the concept of work to economic categories, Honneth suggests that the emancipation-theoretic aspect infused into the economic meaning of labor still has relevance for critical social theory, albeit in a reconceptualized form. In his interpretation, Honneth highlights the more 'Hegelian' aspects of Marx, drawing out the central thematics of the externalization model of labor as critical to identity-development and alienation understood as damaged relations of recognition. Guided by expressivist motifs derived from Hegel and the romantic tradition, labor is thus interpreted by Marx as a process of externalizing human abilities as a process of self-development (*Bildung*). The central point here is that, for Marx, labor is understood not only as a factor of production but simultaneously as an expressive event.[1]

Honneth argues that with this conceptual combination of labor understood both as productive output as well as the externalization of an individual's abilities, Marx was able to frame his critique of capitalism as a whole on the expressivist concept of labor. Honneth argues that throughout both his early and late work, Marx therefore develops a critique of capitalism as a socio-economic formation that structurally prevents the self-identification of laboring subjects in their own products, and also the possibility of self-realization.[2] This amounts to the proposal that identity-formation can only be satisfactorily achieved if the individual can experience the accomplishments of his or her own labor. Marx therefore presupposes that the basic 'dignity' and 'respect' essential to every human being is fundamentally dependent on the freedom to give expression to his or her abilities and accomplishments.[3] Honneth argues that this conception of an 'aesthetics of production' thereby serves as the normative framework underpinning Marx's diagnosis of alienation and reification.[4]

For Honneth, alienated labor is then explicitly defined in terms of the life activity of the individual, rather than in terms of the social system, as typified by the later work. Correspondingly, the abolition of alienation is therefore understood as the creation of social conditions which make it possible to measure the general level of social development on the basis of the development and flourishing of single individuals.[5] In this sense, as Markus has identified, despite the logic of Marx's argument which conceptualizes alienation as an objective-structural characteristic of a historical situation, the conception of alienation understood in terms of the individual's relation-to-self leads to the explicit formulation in subjective, experiential, psychological terms, that is, as *feelings* of estrangement and suffering.[6]

In relating a theory of alienation to a philosophical anthropology in the manner of the early writings, this specific element of Marx's phenomeno-anthropology finds its way into Honneth's work, and in like manner, he also orients his analysis on the development of working subjects, avoiding a systems-theoretical analysis. In his later work, however, Honneth's version of maintaining the vital connection between an expressivist anthropology and a theory of alienation is reconstructed by means of a theory of recognition, which is also reconceptualized in terms of three different types of recognition-relations. In this way, Honneth productively brings the anthropological subject-forming elements of the early Marx together with the theory of communicative action articulated by Habermas. Honneth's particular reconstruction of Marx's anthropology, then, becomes a thoroughly intersubjectivized one, and social-theoretically is one concerned with social-democratic reforms. As a consequence, in Honneth's later work he has argued that the importance of rendering the labor process accessible to moral categories stems from the fundamental connection between work and self-esteem. Significantly, with this reformulation, the expressivist features are dropped from Honneth's later conception of labor, and the moral content becomes oriented around the way in which the labor process is organized in ways that permit the generation and sustaining of a form of self-esteem in the context of recognition relations.

Honneth's recognition-theoretic reconceptualization of the externalization model of work suggests that it is no longer the subject-object relation that is critical for self-realization, rather it is the subject-revealing capacities that work enables, the abilities that are recognized in the context of relations with others. Honneth takes as his central reference point Marx's notion that "the relationship of man to himself becomes *objective* and *real* for him only through his relationship to other men."[7] 'Externalization' is, then, not conceived as the externalizing of one's capabilities in 'object'-like fashion, as an objectification that is contemplated in a purely detached, instrumental, or disinterested manner. Rather, Honneth's intersubjective-theoretic reformulation of Marx's notion suggests that the expression of one's accomplishments as an act of 'externalization' be conceived as an act of mutual recognition, whereby an individual's capacities are recognized externally by other subjects. In this way, Honneth conceives of alienation as a social relation of damaged recognition. His aim is to make social suffering and individual pain caused by capitalist modernization accessible to theoretical reflection by way of the normative presupposition of undistorted and successful socialization.[8] Honneth therefore suggests that the category of labor must be reconceptualized to account for the potential for mutually revealing subjectivity in the context of intersubjective work relations.

Honneth therefore opens up the category of labor to the communicative paradigm in a way not possible within the parameters of Habermas' theory. By internally differentiating the concept of instrumental action, Honneth is able to remain alert to the dimension of moral conflict in social relations and experiences of alienation in the context of concrete conditions of labor. In this way, Honneth reconstructs Marx's materialist phenomenology along the lines of a 'phenomenology of social suffering,' the moral knowledge which is gained from experiences and '*feelings*' of estrangement and powerlessness.'[9] Honneth's recognitive-reconstruction of Marx's paradigm of labor, read through the lens of Habermas' theory of communicative action, is then able to provide a social diagnostic of individual pain and social suffering in the context of concrete work relations.

Honneth's critique of Habermas is based on the concern that no form of social suffering or moral experience should be *a priori* excluded from the possibility of critique. Habermas' conception of communicative action, based as it is on the categorical separation of labor and interaction, has emptied the category of work from any emancipatory potential and diminishes it as a form of human activity with any normative significance. However, Honneth argues, that a 'communicative turn' does not have to mean throwing out the possibility of a critical concept of work with the 'bathwater' of the paradigm of production. Rather, Honneth attempts to reconstruct the anthropological basis upon which *all* forms of social action can be subject to critical activity, rather than confining 'practical-critical activity' to the life-world alone. Honneth also wants to reconstruct a "thematically richer concept of work";[10] one that can contribute a solution to the problem of its overburdening in Marx's project, yet still account for its emancipatory potential in terms of freedom as individual human flourishing in the context of intersubjective relations. For Honneth, a critical concept of work must be able to differentiate between alienated and non-alienated forms of work, something that Habermas' critical project relinquishes by associating work with instrumental action.[11] This association forecloses the critique of significant forms of domination, operating on the assumption that the project of emancipation from domination associated with the forces of production has somehow already been achieved.[12]

Honneth's aim is to reconstruct the expressivist elements that characterize the early work of Marx as a critical model of self-realization (*Bildung*), and particularly to develop the materialist-anthropological premises evident in Marx's 1844 *Manuscripts* as the basis for normative critique.[13] He suggests that Habermas erroneously follows the Marx of the later economic writings by equating work with instrumental action in a totalizing and abstract manner. Honneth's argument is that the activity of working on an object, or the manipulation of nature, does not automatically have to be associated with domination or instrumental action but can potentially be an activity formative for self-realization. In this sense, Marx spoke of a 'social appropriation' of nature and conceptualized the appropriation of 'humanized objects' as one of the main dimensions of socialization through which the individual transforms personal needs and abilities into social wants and accomplishments indicative of the particular social context in which he or she is located.[14]

In this regard, Honneth's reading of Marx, particularly in his early work, outlines an alternative interpretation from the one pursued by Habermas.[15] Honneth argues that despite the undoubted achievements of the 'intersubjective turn' initiated by Habermas, the manner in which he has reconceptualized 'practical-critical activity' around processes of mutual understanding has meant the disappearance of the normative criteria for diagnosing the conflict potential still available in social labor.[16] Influenced substantially by the debates surrounding the technocracy thesis, Habermas takes so seriously the danger represented by the encroachment of technological rationalization and organization onto the social lifeworld that he concentrates his reconstruction of historical materialism on the basis of a fundamental distinction between instrumental and communicative action.[17]

However, as Honneth notes, the basis on which Habermas first articulates this distinction is important. Habermas first makes this distinction in developing his critique of positivism, before he employs it in his critique of Marx, where the distinction between 'instrumental' and 'communicative' action becomes central to differentiating the humanities and social sciences from the positivistic sciences. There he argues that, far from being an interest-free form of knowledge, positivism is falsely universalizing and anchored pre-scientifically in the act of dominating nature. The unfortunate conclusion of this epistemological distinction is that Habermas levels all knowledge directed towards the process of working on nature to instrumental action. It is also within this context that Habermas identifies and differentiates the humanities and social sciences as forms of knowledge with practical and emancipatory interests, pre-scientific interests that he argues are immanent to intersubjective understanding based on the presuppositions of language use.[18]

On these epistemological grounds Habermas begins to construct a theory of action, drawing from both linguistic philosophy and on concepts of action provided by the work of Gehlen and Mead. Consequently, Habermas models a theory of action on the 'reconstruction of communicative speech acts' whereby the basis for normative critique is constituted on the moral premise of mutual understanding, and this also becomes the defining feature of his social theory.[19] In this way, for Habermas, social acts oriented to mutual understanding become the primary form of social praxis. The notion of communicative action understood in terms of modes of reaching mutual understanding is, however, also reliant on the idea that such processes occur free from domination. Habermas, therefore, makes a formal separation between the technical rationality associated with the activity of working on nature, and the moral-practical rationality associated with communicative acts.[20] The concept of communicative action, therefore, becomes not only the central notion that describes cultural integration and social reproduction, but also the measure against which social emancipation is now evaluated. In other words, the concept of communicative action bears the conceptual load in a manner not unlike the category of labor in Marx.

Habermas inherits Lukács' reading of Marx in relation to his employment of the notion of reification and he dismisses the relevance of the concept of

alienation on the basis of his attempt to distance himself from the economic
reading of historical materialism through a systematic attack on the theory of
value articulated in Marx's later economic writings.[21] This is a reading that
also indicates a major point of difference between Habermas and Honneth in
terms of their interpretations of the Marxian notion of alienation. Honneth's
own line of critique has been articulated throughout his work with remarkable continuity. In his more recent *Tanner Lectures*, Honneth directly criticizes Habermas' conflation of the notions 'alienation' and 'objectification'
which, he argues, is a result of the adoption of Lukács' concept of 'reification.'[22]

Honneth suggests that this is a highly unfortunate conceptual strategy
which leads to a problematic conception of social processes of development.
By accepting Lukács' totalizing conception of 'reification,' Habermas is
compelled to make a differentiation between spheres that require what
Honneth refers to as a 'recognitional stance' and those in which a more
functional objectifying stance is predominant. Habermas maintains this type
of functionalist explanation in *The Theory of Communicative Action*,
Honneth argues, "in attempting to conceive 'reification' as precisely the
process through which strategic, 'contemplative' (*beobachtende*) modes of
behavior penetrate into social spheres in which communicative orientations
are 'functionally necessary.'"[23] Furthermore, this functionalist explanation is
inadequate because the "question concerning the point at which objectifying
attitudes unfold their reifying effects cannot be answered by speaking of
functional requirements in an apparently non-normative way."[24] The functionalist distinctions Habermas makes between spheres differentiated according to either communicative or reifying attitudes is not empirically plausible
and consequently cannot possibly bear the 'normative burden of proof' in the
manner Habermas suggests.

In comparison, in his recent recognition-theoretic reconstruction of reification, Honneth suggests it is possible to detect the fragments of an alternative theory of intersubjectivity within *History and Class Consciousness* that
belies the ontological conception and broadens it beyond Lukács' predominant focus on the phenomena described by Marx as 'commodity fetishism.'
In this context, reification is not comprehended as a category mistake nor a
form of moral misconduct but as a distorted form of praxis that is structurally
false. In an analysis that posits recognition as a primordial form of social
interaction, Honneth argues that recognition should therefore be understood
as the antecedent condition of reification, not its polar opposite. With this
phenomeno-recognitive reconstruction of reification, Honneth once again returns to the problematic of the moral dimension of alienation first articulated
in his interpretation of Marx. Despite Lukács' totalizing concept of reification, Honneth suggests it is possible to identify underlying strains that point
to a normative theory of interaction as the ideal against which reifying forms

of agency are judged. In this way, Honneth attempts to reconstruct recognition as a particular affective disposition to, or mode-of-being in the world, that is not sufficiently captured by Habermas' formulation of communicative or rational stances. For Honneth, the human relationship to the self and the world is primarily structured by an affirmative attitude which is prior to all other attitudes including cognitive, detached, or contemplative ones. In other words, positive acknowledgement or recognition precedes cognition.[25]

Honneth argues that having relinquished a notion of alienation, Habermas has given up this means of critiquing the increasing instrumentalization and fragmentation of labor activity itself. He therefore does not have the means to articulate ways of structuring and managing labor activity in ways that promote autonomy or render work meaningful.[26] As a consequence of rejecting both the social-diagnostic notion of alienation and the model of work as externalization, Honneth argues that Habermas therefore also neglects to consider the implications of instrumental action understood as a type of activity which may be independently controlled and organized, and may be more or less autonomous and self-managed. The problem is that Habermas only judges the moral content of interpersonal activities according to the degree to which they conform to the ideal of an uncoerced act of mutual understanding but neglects to consider the ways in which forms of work might be measured according to whether they are more or less alienating.[27] In this sense, Habermas relinquishes the basis for conceptualizing work as a self-directed activity free from domination.[28]

Therefore, despite the important gains for the theory of emancipation established by Habermas' theory of communicative action, Honneth suggests there has been an equivalent loss in terms of the importance of the category of labor. Labor becomes associated not only with a separate form of rationalization and sphere of action associated with the forces of production, but through its equation with instrumental action becomes the form of action against which emancipation understood in communicative terms is normatively distinguished.

As importantly for Honneth, though, this critique of communicative action also opens onto the dynamics of social conflict. In *The Critique of Power*, Honneth extends his critique of Habermas in relation to the notions of work and instrumental action and argues for a reconfiguration of the communicative paradigm through the reintegration of a notion of class struggle as the explanatory theory for social change. He suggests that the resources for this alternative approach were available in Habermas' own early work, and might have enabled him to develop a theory of social development understood not as a dual process of social rationalization but as a moral dialectic of class struggle.

CONFLICT AND POWER AS MODALITIES OF COMMUNICATIVE ACTION

In an effort to develop a concept of the social that can not only account for the normative potential in all forms of social action but can also more adequately comprehend structures of domination and power, Honneth maintains that Habermas' approach must be broadened to account for the communicative and conflictual relations that take place through the medium of social struggle.[29] Honneth suggests it is possible to reconstruct two competing models of society and social evolution that operate and develop at different points in Habermas' work. The first model relies upon a bifurcated account of the history of the species that separates technical-rational action from communicative action, and therefore separates processes of mutual understanding from systemic reproduction and structures of domination. In comparison, the second model, which Honneth clearly advocates as the more robust for a critique of power, is able to take account of domination more broadly conceived in regard to individual socialization and social integration, and not merely one understood as a product of systemic processes. This alternative model would, however, have required Habermas to develop a reconstruction of the philosophy of history that owes its interpretation to the reading of Marx outlined in *Knowledge and Human Interests*, rather than the theory of rationalization processes developed in his response to debates surrounding the technocracy thesis.[30]

In *Knowledge and Human Interests*, Habermas identifies not only a mechanical model of history in Marx's work, but also an alternative model that indicates a self-reflexive and self-constitutive historical process that proceeds from the dynamic of class struggle.[31] In his early work on Marx, Habermas argues that while the constitution of the species through labor takes form as a linear process of development, the struggle of social classes takes a dialogical form, understood as a "process of oppression and self-emancipation."[32] The movement of class antagonism is central to Marx's understanding of the transformation of the institutional framework of society and, therefore, the "results of class struggle are always sedimented in the institutional framework of a society, in social *form*."[33]

However, beyond this moment in his work, Honneth argues that Habermas does not himself think through all the sociological conclusions that can be derived from his interpretation of Marx.[34] As Honneth elaborates, if Habermas had followed his own communicative-theoretic insights, it would have been possible not only to develop a conceptualization that conceives of the basic conflict that propels social development as intrinsic to communicative action itself, but might also have provided an alternative theory of society. If Habermas had followed through the insights of his own early work, he might also have avoided the dualism of the systems-theoretic notion he later adopts. Rather than a conception of society separated into purposive-rational and communicative spheres, Habermas' early work therefore suggests an interpretation of society separated into social classes or groups.[35]

Moreover, if Habermas had given more credence in his interpretation of Marx to the struggle between labor and capital as a form of *moral* conflict, he might have avoided the notion of a systemic or supra-individual evolutionary mechanism and the problematic notion of a unified species-subject that arises in his work. Instead, Honneth argues, he might have successfully taken into account the role of social groups or collective actors to explain the mode by which social learning processes are attained in communicative action. In this manner, Habermas' communication-theoretic approach could have been re-conceptualized to conceive of social learning processes not in a teleological fashion, but dialectically, as the result of the struggles between social groups in relation to the form and mode of development of social institutions, including the organizational form of purposive-rational action.[36] Understood in this way, Honneth argues that the history of the species can then be understood as a basic conflict that *"dwells within the process of communicative action itself*, as an opposition of social classes brought forth by social domination"* rather than as an external conflictual dynamic between two separate processes.[37]

Honneth argues that this model provides for a much more broadly conceived action-theoretic analysis, in which the interaction between social groups, whether conflictual or consensual, becomes the framework that "regulates the institutional organization of all social domains of tasks." Therefore, with this social-theoretical formulation, Honneth suggests it is no longer feasible to maintain the idea of a separate 'subsystem of purposive rational action.' Rather, even the organization of 'purposive-rational activity' can be understood to be "co-determined by moral-practical viewpoints that must be conceived as results of communicative action."[38]

Furthermore, the reading of Marx in *Knowledge and Human Interests* might have enabled Habermas to identify the central disturbance to social development generally as "the asymmetrical distribution of the exercise of power," whereby the members of a society are understood to be unequally affected by structures of domination and the 'burdens' of social labor, rather than the autonomization of technocratic rationality.[39] Consequently, neither the organization of social labor nor the establishment of social norms can be adequately explained as the result of an agreement reached through a peaceful process of intersubjective understanding.

In Honneth's reformulation, communicative action is conceived as a conflictual process that takes place between oppressed classes over the interpretation and institutionalization of social norms.[40] Moreover, Honneth's reconstruction suggests that the paradigm of the social can no longer be based on agreement or understanding; rather the paradigm of the social is constituted by social *struggle*.[41] Such a conceptual expansion of action theory, however, is not intended to conceive of collective actors as 'macro-subjects' or 'supra-individual unities' as the bearers of social development, as Habermas' early conception would seem to suggest. The struggle for recognition Honneth conceives does not take place between two classes understood as macro-subjects, but should be viewed as taking place between "social groups whose collective identity is always fragile."[42] Moreover, these identities are constantly open to change as individuals identify with different aspects in dynamic and ongoing processes of socialization. This alternative theory of social action therefore requires a shift from a conception that primarily views individuals as the bearers of communicative action to one that gives a far greater role to social groups as collective actors.

For Honneth, 'social struggle' does not just assume the form of strategic action, nor does he mean to suggest that 'social struggle' is a basic phenomenon of all social relationships, as in the work of Foucault. Rather, his claim is that conflict occurs as a contestation over the legitimacy of existing institutionalized norms and the interpretation and introduction of new ones.[43] Marx's notion of social struggle is therefore read through a Habermasian lens as "a distorted form of intersubjective understanding." In other words, in the context of structures of domination and inequality resulting from the social division of labor, communicative action can only ever be limited and cannot claim to achieve a moral consensus free from ideological constraints.[44]

The reorientation to a conceptual model based on social struggle also suggests that the development of the human species can no longer be understood as a unilinear and uniform advance in moral learning, but rather, by conceiving processes of will-formation in terms of the struggle between social groups over the validity of social norms, Honneth is advocating an alternative *dialectical* model of moral learning processes. As Honneth explains, the ability to account for the conflictual aspects of communicative action opens up an entirely new understanding of the formation and institutionalization of social norms: we are now 'compelled to conceive the modification of institutional frameworks,' that Habermas characterizes as 'communicative rationalization' simultaneously as a process of both '*repression and liberation*.'[45]

Several important implications for critical social theory result from this modification to the conception of communicative rationalization that are significant for a reconstruction of Honneth's work. As evident in the above quote, Honneth reconceptualizes processes of communicative rationalization 'co-terminously' as a process of both 'liberation' and 'repression.' In this sense, instead of adopting Habermas' bifurcated account of rationalization, Honneth is advocating an internally differentiated notion of communicative rationalization in which both positive and negative aspects of rationalization are co-implicated.[46]

This is an originary moment in Honneth's reconceptualization of Habermas' notion of communicative rationality, suggesting not only that *all* areas of social life are organized by communicative norms, but also that a notion of communicative rationality does not rely on an idealized version of social evolution in which moral progress is separated out from technological progress. Furthermore, such a conception not only signals a departure from Habermas' view of rationalization processes, but gestures towards an account that is more evocative of Adorno's work. That is, that there is a duality *within* reason in which both the achievements and deformations of modernity are attached to the movement of history, that both progressive and regressive forces are co-implicated in the same process of rationalization.[47]

The question is: does Honneth himself retain this central insight in the later development of his theory of recognition? In other words, does Honneth transform these early communicative-theoretic insights into an account of recognitive reason that accounts for both positive and negative, emancipatory and repressive, recognitive and misrecognitive processes, as internal to one and the same process of development? Or, does his later attempt to outline the *formal* conditions of recognition undermine the sensitivity he initially gives to the co-implication of action types, of the interplay of recognition and power?[48]

It is possible to see in Honneth's early work how a recognitive-communicative theory based on the notion of social *struggle* already begins to take shape at both ontogenetic and phylogenetic levels: at the level of ontogenesis, Honneth begins to conceptualize a theory of subject-formation through recognitive relations with reference to the early Marx, in which one's self-accomplishment through labor is a central component; at the level of phylogenesis, struggle is conceptualized as the central dynamic of social change and development that gestures towards a dialectical notion of moral learning processes (although at this stage only vaguely conceived). In this sense, Honneth's theory of modernity, which is central to his reconstruction of Habermas' communicative paradigm, begins to be conceptualized in terms of the expansion of recognitive relations based upon the increase of possibilities for freedom experienced as mutually recognitive flourishing.

In this respect, while giving far greater credence to conflictual elements, Honneth follows Habermas in terms of emphasizing the positive accomplishments of modernity. His historical reconstruction in terms of a dialectic of moral learning processes is understood as the expansion of the potential for the human capacity for freedom as self-realization in the context of recognitive relations, an account of moral learning that is also able to address experiences of fragmentation and alienation through labor. Honneth's understanding of modernity as the enlargement of recognitive-relational capacities, therefore, provides him with the framework against which the achievements and pathologies of modernity can be assessed.

Honneth's alternative reconstruction of Habermas' early work offers a much richer action-theoretic approach to critical theory that not only accounts for structures of domination at the level of systems, but also gestures toward an intersubjective-theoretic notion of power. As a result of his bi-level concept of society, Habermas offers a time-diagnosis that accounts for social pathologies only at a systemic level, those caused by what he terms the 'colonization of the lifeworld.' The advantage of Honneth's critique and alternative account of the social is that he is able to take consideration of social pathologies that cut across the division Habermas makes, those that occur within the social framework more generally. In articulating a basis for critique, Honneth is therefore able to account for relations of power and conflictual forms of interaction that potentially give far greater theoretical credence to the broad spectrum of *experiences* of domination.

However, despite the critical potential of Honneth's insights, a potential ambiguity can already be detected between various aspects of his reconstruction of Habermas' work. For although Honneth advocates an agonistic conception of communicative action at the level of social theory, the notion of open and continuous struggle is somewhat contradicted by the underlying assumptions of an 'undamaged notion of intersubjectivity' that we can already detect as the underlying presupposition for a theory of recognition. In his early reconstruction of Habermas' project, however, it is clear that Honneth favors an account of the social that emphasizes the conflictual and agonistic elements of communicative action.

On the path to developing the theory of recognition, Honneth also undertakes a reconstruction of Foucault's work in order to provide an alternative notion of 'struggle' as a counterpoint to Habermas' view of the social as a paradigm of mutual understanding. In *The Critique of Power*, Honneth perceptively draws on the work of Foucault to develop a relational account of power that is not to be found in the work of either Marx or Habermas. The intersubjective-theoretic notion of power outlined in Honneth's interpretation of Foucault has significant implications not just at the level of social theory, but also for the philosophical anthropology that grounds his work as a whole. Many of the potential strengths, but also missed opportunities, in regard to Honneth's reworking of the intersubjective paradigm and the 'critique of power,' also stem from his reading of Foucault's work.

Unfinished Studies on a Theory of Power

Chapter Three

The Social as a Field of Struggle

Foucault's Action-Theoretic View

In *The Critique of Power*, Honneth traces the theoretical transitions between the work of Horkheimer, Adorno, Foucault, and Habermas, as a contribution to what he terms "reflective stages in a critical social theory."[1] With this methodology Honneth understands the theoretical history he presents as a 'reflective learning process' at the level of theory that has a teleological orientation. Significantly, for Honneth, in this trajectory Foucault is posited as the heir to Adorno, and his work is considered to provide a theoretical development in terms of the project of a critical theory in the Frankfurt School tradition. In this sense, Honneth's own self-understanding is that the studies in *The Critique of Power* represent a critico-reflexive process with systematic intent that begins with Horkheimer and Adorno, progresses with Foucault's work, and culminates in Habermas' theory of communicative action, which represents a theoretical advance over previous models of critical social theory.[2]

The aim of Honneth's theoretical reconstruction is to develop a comprehensive theory of the social and social action that can provide a framework for analyzing social relations of power and domination.[3] In this respect, despite his full endorsement of Habermas' intersubjective-theoretical turn, Honneth is also critical of the way in which Habermas develops a functionalist analysis of modernity. The consequence of Habermas' analysis of social development, explained in terms of a partial systems-theoretic process of social differentiation, is that it substantially diminishes the role of social action. In particular, Honneth is therefore critical of Habermas' overly dualistic and compartmentalized accounts of both power and communicative action and the resulting separation of spheres of social action.

In comparison, certain currents in Foucault's work represent an attempt to conceptualize what Honneth has termed a 'struggle-theoretical intuition' that offers an alternative to Habermas' systems-theoretic analysis and gestures towards a conception of social development as "a process of differentiation mediated by social struggles."[4] Moreover, Foucault's account of the social as a field of agonistic struggle provides an important counterbalance to Habermas' account of the social in terms of consensus and mutual understanding. For Honneth, Foucault's intersubjective notion of power in terms of the 'practical intersubjectivity of struggle' provides an alternative to Habermas' restrictive account of power rendered in either systemic terms, or otherwise as a distorted form of communication. Honneth's unique achievement is to bring together through reconstructive critique the insights contained in Habermas' 'intersubjective-theoretical turn' with Foucault's motif of the struggle-constituted notion of the social.[5]

Honneth's immanent critique of Foucault in *The Critique of Power* is important not only in terms of the project of articulating the centrality of struggle to the paradigm of the social, but also to the articulation of an intersubjective-theoretic notion of power that is central to the development of a theory of intersubjectivity. The argument here is that Foucault is a central but under-acknowledged nodal point in the conceptual history of intersubjectivity that Honneth traces throughout his own work. Moreover, Honneth's reconstruction of Foucault's work remains significant in the stages towards the development of the theory of recognition that deserves further scrutiny.

To be sure, in Honneth's view, the action-theoretic account of power within Foucault's work is ultimately cancelled out by what Honneth identifies as a countervailing tendency towards systems-theoretic explanations typified by the analysis in *Discipline and Punish*. Moreover, in Honneth's final analysis, the engagement with Foucault's work only convinces him that the centrality of a notion of 'struggle' for a critical social theory can only be achieved by replacing Foucault's notion of power/struggle with a notion of recognition/struggle, a morally motivated concept of social struggle drawn from Hegel's early writings.

Nonetheless, the insights taken from Foucault's work form an important contribution to Honneth's working out of the 'struggle-theoretic intuition' that is later incorporated into the theory of recognition. Thus, a reconstruction of Honneth's immanent critique of Foucault enables an examination of the importance this work plays in Honneth's trajectory of reflective stages in critical theory. However, this immanent reconstruction also enables us to question whether or not Honneth retains the insights he begins to uncover in relation to a theory of power, both in terms of a theory of intersubjectivity and a theory of society with the move from Foucault to Hegel (via Habermas). As several writers have noted, Honneth's move from Foucault to Hegel seems to leave behind the more agonistic elements that were so central in his early work on Foucault. As Sinnerbrink has suggested, by foregrounding the morality rather than the politics of recognition in his later work, the action-theoretic model of the social as a field of social struggle that was a crucial inspiration for Honneth's intersubjectivist theory seems to recede in subsequent work.[6] It can also be argued that despite Honneth's early engagement with Foucault, he overlooks important insights disclosed through the notion of productive power in terms of the later development of the theory of recognition. The question remains, might the theory of recognition have benefited from a more sustained consideration or extension of the positive or 'constructive' elements of power and its implications for the theory of recognition?[7]

The argument here is that despite his very astute critique of Habermas' overly dualistic account of power, in the end, Honneth himself does not provide a fully articulated, alternative *theory of power*, and that indications towards such a theory in Honneth's work remain undeveloped. Although Honneth goes on to develop his own program of critical social theory in *The Struggle for Recognition*, the argument here is that he misses the opportunity to develop his original insights in relation to a programmatic *theory of power*, and that the beginnings of such an alternative account can already be found in his reading of Foucault's work in *The Critique of Power*.

POWER AND SOCIAL STRUGGLE: HONNETH'S READING OF FOUCAULT

In the interpretation provided in *The Critique of Power*, Honneth identifies three differentiated phases in Foucault's work: firstly, an initial semiological-structuralist phase of the 1960s in which Foucault conducts an historical analysis of discourse in the manner of an 'ethnology' or 'archaeology.'[8] In Honneth's reading, this semiological-structuralist phase gives way to a second phase in the 1970s with the shift from the theory of knowledge to the theory of power. In this second phase, Honneth identifies an action-theoretic view in Foucault's conception of the social, one constituted by social struggle, as well an intersubjective theory of power and conflict. Finally, in an inversion of the first action-theoretic model of power, Honneth argues that a third approach appears that represents a turn to the totalizing theory of power as social control, an approach that views modernity as merely a process that establishes the augmentation of social power according to a social-theoretic model of total institutions. However, in contrast to Honneth, the argument advanced here is that the action-theoretic approach and the analysis of total institutions should not be viewed as linear and separate phases in the strict sense, but represent two aspects of a complex notion of power that is interspersed throughout Foucault's work from the 1970s onwards.[9]

Nonetheless, one of the most original aspects of Honneth's interpretation of Foucault is the reconstruction of the theory of power from an action-theoretic point of view built upon a concept of 'struggle.' In this sense, rather than emphasizing the Nietzschean characteristics of Foucault's work, for example, as a doctrine of dispositions, Honneth suggests that it is possible to reconstruct the traces of a model of action in Foucault's work that contributes to a theory of society. In this reading, the uniqueness of Foucault's model of power is that he transforms Nietzsche's naturalistically informed theory of power into one conceptualized in terms of the production of "positive as well as negative aspects."[10] In Foucault's hands, Nietzsche's conception of "the world as an interplay of forces" forming multiple configurations of power, ceaselessly organizing and reorganizing themselves as the fundamental disposition he called 'will to power,' becomes an action-theoretic notion of power in which the social is viewed "as an uninterrupted process of conflicting strategic action" among situated individuals and groups.[11]

This action-theoretic view contains the intuition that 'struggle' and conflict are in fact constitutive of the social itself. Honneth suggests the threads of this 'struggle-theoretic' idea and the action-theoretic notion of power are dispersed throughout Foucault's work of the 1970s, pronouncements made primarily in the selected interviews in *Power/Knowledge*, but also perceptible in *Discipline and Punish* and *The History of Sexuality: Volume One*.[12]

However, as other writers have noted, this originally Nietzschean hypothesis of 'struggle' which is central to Foucault's genealogy of power, can already be identified in the 1971 essay "Nietzsche, Genealogy, History," which "described the field of history in terms of a struggle (*lutte*) among contingent forces."[13] There, Foucault outlines the project of genealogy or 'effective history' "as the history of disparate, chance events" in an effort to critique unilinear conceptions of history and in particular Enlightenment theories of moral progress. As Hanssen suggests, by

> characterising genealogy as the assessment of differential force relations, Foucault in fact rescripted the odious master-slave dialectic with which Nietzsche's *Genealogy of Morals* opened, abstracting from its racist overtones and logic of ressentiment, determined as he was to expose a more general *agonistic* play of forceful differences, "the endlessly repeated play of dominations." Dismantling humanistic conceptions of historical progress, he unravelled the vicissitudes of a history of cumulative violence.[14]

This also implies that there are two countervailing tendencies that ebb and flow throughout much of Foucault's work. For on the one hand, Foucault's work offers the fragments of both an intersubjective-theoretic notion of power and action-theoretic insights into an agonistic conception of the social. However, on the other hand, Foucault also portrays human history as merely the "accumulation of violence or domination" or the "augmentation of power." Constantly throughout his work, then, the notions of contingency and chance, and open and continuous struggle, appear to be cancelled out by the presupposition that all human history is the history of domination and the totalization of power. Consequently, as Hanssen suggests, Foucault's notion of differential struggle seems to capture "a quasi-transcendental negative logic ... not unlike Adorno's negating force, even as it [transpires] as an immanent transitive force *in* history." [15]

According to Honneth, Foucault only begins to articulate an action-theoretic account of the social once he abandons his initial semiological-structuralist framework upon encountering conceptual difficulties in the meta-theoretical conclusions reached in *The Archaeology of Knowledge*. At this point, Foucault comes to realize that there is an immanent connection between the discursive formations that produce knowledge in a given period, and non-discursive factors, such as "an institutional field, a set of events, practices, and political decisions..." [16] With this realization, Foucault moves to supplement the axis of knowledge with one of power, and to reconceptualize the relationship between the material and the discursive in the new formulation of the power/knowledge nexus. [17] Honneth argues that *The Archaeology of Knowledge* represents the end of a first phase in Foucault's work, and marks a shift into a second, action-theoretic phase of his work with the incorporation of an intersubjective-theoretic notion of power. In Honneth's schema, this second stage precedes and is further distinguished from a third phase represented by the socio-historical studies on the totalizing aspects of power.

However, it might be alternatively suggested that rather than signifying the move to the first of two differentiated phases and corresponding theories of power, it is precisely at this point that Foucault's work begins to develop two parallel currents that continue to overlap, both of which remain present throughout his genealogical project and both of which contribute to a complex notion of power.

In contrast, instead of identifying two *parallel currents* in Foucault's work, Honneth identifies a second and distinct action-theoretic *phase*, in which Foucault begins to identify the centrality of non-discursive practices to the construction of knowledge. In other words, according to Honneth, Foucault begins to articulate the relationship between power and knowledge, and the reciprocal interplay of forms of knowledge and power in the constitution of the social only at a distinct phase in his work. This interrelation is captured by Foucault's well-known statement that "power and knowledge directly imply one another; ... there is no power relation without the correlative constitution of a field of knowledge that does not presuppose and constitute at the same time, power relations." [18] Honneth argues that once Foucault abandons his more structuralist-orientated analysis of knowledge and begins to examine the social and institutional conditions of the production of knowledge, he begins to articulate a social-theoretical framework that is pivotal for the remainder of his work. It is in this context that, for Honneth, Foucault's action-theoretic view of the social begins to emerge.[19]

The outlines of this action-theoretic or struggle-theoretic notion of the social begin to take form particularly in Foucault's pronouncements articulated in the interviews between 1972-1977, collected in the volume *Power/Knowledge*.[20] It is in this work that Honneth suggests Foucault most clearly defines an action-theoretic approach and it is worth considering the details of Foucault's analysis as they pertain to Honneth's own attempt to reconstruct an alternative notion of social struggle and power.

In one of the many interviews in *Power/Knowledge*, Foucault suggests that in relation to the articulation of a theory of power there is:

> ...a refusal of analysis couched in terms of the symbolic field or the domain of signifying structures, and a recourse to analysis in terms of the genealogy of relations of force, strategic developments and tactics. Here I believe one's point of reference should not be to the great model of language (*langue*) and signs, but to that of war and battle. The history which bears and determines us has the form of a war rather than that of a language: relations of power, not relations of meaning. History has no 'meaning,' though this is not to say that it is absurd or incoherent. On the contrary, it is intelligible and should be susceptible of analysis down to the smallest detail—but this in accordance with the intelligibility of struggles, of strategies and tactics.[21]

Here, we find the suggestion that history does not reveal purpose or meaning, but rather, represents a struggle over interpretation, a struggle between various knowledges, and a battle for the production of particular discourses of 'truth.' Moreover, although Honneth does not discuss this point, the notion of 'struggle' is also employed by Foucault as a genealogical device for unearthing 'subjugated' knowledges and for 'remembering' historically, the polymorphous nature of social struggles that he suggests have been subsumed by the dominant, 'universalizing' narratives of liberalism and Marxism. In this sense, Foucault's preoccupation with the mutually constitutive notions of power, force, and war can be read both as the *struggle* over knowledge production and as a critical reconstruction of the historical knowledge of struggles; that is, as a retrieval of the 'memory' of power/struggle not just in terms of the paradigm of class, but in terms of the 'polymorphous' nature of historical struggles and the "memory of power as real struggle or war" that differentiates it from the accounts offered by both Marxism and liberalism.[22]

Foucault therefore begins to define his analysis in opposition to 'classical' political science and Marxist social theory, both of which he suggests are deficient in terms of analyzing the 'mechanics of power.'[23] In this context, he questions why western political and social-theoretical discourses have continued to view power as "juridical and negative rather than as technical and positive." According to Foucault, both conceptions of power are unable to explain modern forms of social integration because they remain trapped within conceptual categories that explain premodern forms of power. As he remarks in one of his polemical flourishes; "We need to cut off the King's head," and disavow ourselves of a conception of power tied to the problem of sovereignty.[24]

In both *Power/Knowledge* and *Society Must be Defended*, Foucault argues that the juridical or liberal conception of political power and the Marxist conception have in common what he terms 'economism' in the theory of power.[25]

In the case of classical political theory, Foucault suggests that "power is regarded as a right which can be possessed in the way one possesses a commodity, and which can therefore be transferred or alienated, either completely or partly, through a juridical act or an act that founds a right," in the manner of exchanging contracts.[26] "Power," then, "is the concrete power that any individual can hold, and which he can surrender, either as a whole or in part, so as to constitute a power or political sovereignty." In this way, Foucault suggests, power "is modeled on a juridical operation similar to the exchange of contracts," and therefore, that all liberal conceptions of power speak of power as either a possession or a transference of rights, and are analogous with commodities and wealth.[27]

Furthermore, Foucault argues that premodern forms of power, bound as they are to a theory of sovereignty, presume that power is not only descending, "exercised from the highest to the lowest levels," but that the notion of sovereignty is viewed as inseparable from the general 'mechanics of power,' that is, the relationship of power with sovereignty is considered to be "coextensive with the entire social body." In this way, power is always "transcribed ... in terms of the sovereign/subject relationship."[28]

For their part, Foucault suggests that the problem with Marxist conceptions of power is that they are bound to 'a statist model of thinking' as well as being defined in a similar manner in terms of political sovereignty. Foucault argues that this mode of analysis, dependent as it is on the idea that power is acquired and possessed by the state apparatus, also represents power as an entity that is essentially repressive and acquired by force.[29] Furthermore, Foucault suggests that the Marxist conception of power is conceived in terms of the "economic functionality" of power. It is always defined as secondary to a prior determining material realm which reduces the analysis of the social field of power to the economy.[30] The notion of power is then understood only in relation to the perpetuation of relations of production and the reproduction of a class domination made possible by the development of productive forces and the way they are appropriated.[31] For Foucault, the problem with the Marxist concept of 'class struggle' is that the emphasis in the analysis is placed on "investigating 'class' rather than 'struggle.'" Rather, for

Foucault, the primary social-theoretic problematic is not "the sociology of classes, but the strategic method concerning struggles."[32]

In contrast, then, Foucault suggests power should not be regarded as a phenomenon of domination, whether of domination of one individual over others, or of one group over others, or one class over others. Rather, power must be analyzed:

> as something that circulates, or … that functions only when it is part of a chain… Power is exercised through networks, and individuals do not simply circulate in those networks; they are in a position to both submit to and exercise this power. They are never the inert or consenting targets of power; they are always its relays. In other words, power passes through individuals. It is not applied to them.[33]

In response to both the Marxist and juridical or liberal conceptions of power, then, Foucault attempts to outline a strategic model of power based on horizontal networks or intersubjective relations and the notion of social struggle.[34]

It is here that the implications for Honneth's reading become clear. For although in some places in his work Foucault seems to lean towards naturalistic or instinct-theoretic characteristics (for example, 'the will to knowledge'), Honneth suggests that Foucault's emphasis on social struggle is rendered more 'meaningful' when read as describing an action-theoretic view of the social.[35] From an action-theoretic view, Honneth reads Foucault's notion of social struggle as a strategic model of power that is understood to provide alternative understandings of both the subject and the means of social power. Power, then, is not viewed as a 'fixable property' or a possession but rather "as the in-principle fragile and open-ended product of strategic conflicts between subjects."[36]

Significantly, Foucault also defines power in terms of its *relational character*. As Foucault further explains, "power is not something that can be possessed, and it is not a form of might; power is never anything more than a relationship that can, and must, be studied only by looking at the interplay between the terms of the relationship."[37] In contrast to the notion of power understood in the juridical terms of sovereignty, this relational concept of power "describes the phenomena of power … in the historical terms of domination and the play of relations of force."[38]

Understood by Foucault as a 'multiplicity of force relations,'[39] Honneth suggests this somewhat Nietzschean formulation conceals an action-theoretic model of relations as the basis of his theory of power whereby "strategic action among social actors is interpreted as the ongoing process in which the formation and exercise of social power is embedded." Social power, then, can be understood not as a one-sided appropriation or exercise of rights but is acquired and maintained "in the shape of a continuous struggle of social actors among themselves."[40] As Foucault himself proclaims in *Society Must be Defended*, the "relations of force and the play of power" are "the very stuff of history. History exists, events occur ... to the extent that relations of power, relations of force, and a certain play of power operate in relations among men."[41] In this sense, it can be argued that Honneth's reading of Foucault accurately portrays an actionistic notion of power that Foucault himself more explicitly articulates in his later published work. Hence, Honneth correctly argues that despite the mechanistic language that Foucault uses to describe this relational notion of power, "we may assume an action-theoretic model of relations as the basis of his theory."[42]

As Honneth suggests, this action-theoretic model of the social is also evident in fragments in the social-historical studies of the 1970s, *Discipline and Punish* and *The History of Sexuality: Volume One*. Here, Foucault clearly articulates a relational account of power, locating power at the "everyday level of social life," as a "microphysics of power" that traces the formation of power "back to the strategic exchanges in everyday conflicts of action."[43]

Foucault more explicitly draws out the action-theoretic notion of power in certain passages in *The History of Sexuality*, where he articulates the notion of power in the context of concrete action. Suggesting that "power comes from below," he goes on to explain that it can be understood as:

> the multiplicity of force relations immanent in the sphere in which they operate ... the process which, through ceaseless struggles and confrontations, transforms, strengthens or reverses them; as the support which these force relations find in one another, thus forming a chain or system, or on the contrary, the disjunctions and contradictions which isolate them from one another. [44]

In Honneth's view, this 'struggle-theoretic' notion of the social suggests "a nexus of strategic relations between individual or collective actors," that is, a notion of the social "as an uninterrupted process of conflicting strategic action," or a perpetual state of war.[45] In many such passages, Honneth notes that Foucault's conception of the social at times seems to imply a version of the Hobbesian notion of an original state of war of all against all, in which social struggle arises from an originary notion of self-interest, rather than merely conflicts over interests that arise from historical conditions.[46]

Nonetheless, it can be argued that at its core Foucault's work is suggestive of an intersubjective and practically engaging notion of power, a relational view of power that constructs the field of social action.[47] Honneth's action-theoretic interpretation of Foucault is borne out by Foucault's own remarks in the later summary of his position in "The Subject and Power," where he outlines his notion of power as a theory of interaction or a relational theory of power.[48] There he states: "Power exists only when it is put into action,"[49] and "what characterizes power is that it brings into play *relations* between individuals (or between groups)."[50] In fact, Foucault suggests, 'power' is not the property of an individual or group, rather, "power designates *relationships* between partners to interaction."[51] In this sense, Honneth remarkably intuits from Foucault's earlier texts the outline of an intersubjective-theoretic concept of power, or what Honneth terms, the "strategic intersubjectivity of power."[52] It is an intersubjective account of power in which subjects "exercise their action" on other subjects, actors act on the actions of other actors.[53]

This intersubjective account of power can be traced through Foucault's own work, evident in statements where he suggests there is "no absolute outside" to power and that power is what *constitutes* the social.[54] This relational notion of power comes to the fore in "The Subject and Power," where Foucault also suggests that power is only enacted by and between *subjects*, indicating a further refinement of the theory of power in his work. In this late essay, he describes power as a mode of interaction that develops historically with modernity with the creation of freedom and particular forms of subjectivity.[55] The notion of subjectivity in the context of freedom is articulated with the suggestion that power can only be analyzed by taking as its starting point forms of resistance. Here, Foucault is at pains to distinguish forms of power from forms of domination. Using the example of slavery in this context, he suggests, that power is only operative when there is minimally a chance of freedom. In other words, power does not exist in the context of physical compulsion or violence, but only where there is the possibility of resistance.[56] From this perspective, then, power is never pure domination as it can be viewed in the Weberian tradition. Rather, for Foucault, power always implies resistance such that the dialectic of 'power and resistance' constantly enacts social struggle.

In the "The Subject and Power," then, Foucault begins to suggest that power *always already* implies freedom. Foucault therefore seems to shift from his earlier view that power can only be explained in antagonistic terms and argues that perhaps the notion of 'agonism' might be more appropriate, in that:

> The relationship between power and freedom's refusal to submit can therefore not be separated. The crucial problem of power is not that of voluntary servitude (how could we seek to be slaves?). At the very heart of the power relationship, and constantly provoking it, are the recalcitrance of the will and the intransigence of freedom. Rather than speaking of an essential freedom, it would be better to speak of an 'agonism'—of a relationship which is at the same time a reciprocal incitation and struggle; less of a face-to-face confrontation which paralyses both sides than a permanent provocation.[57]

In this context, Foucault seems to reorient the notion of 'conduct' as acting upon the actions of others in specifically action-theoretic terms; not evoking an all-encompassing notion of 'government' or 'discipline,' but of an *agonistic* relational dynamic 'grounded' in a notion of freedom.[58]

Furthermore, Foucault suggests, a relationship of power can only be articulated when "'the other' (the one over whom power is exercised) be thoroughly *recognized* and maintained to the very end as a person who *acts*; and that, faced with a relationship of power, a whole field of responses, reactions, results, and possible inventions may open up."[59] The significance of this passage is two-fold: firstly, Foucault seemingly suggests that his theory of interaction presupposes a minimal account of intersubjectivity or 'recognition,' at least in the sense that one's partner to interaction is recognized as a subject who acts; secondly, here Foucault clearly identifies the action-theoretic perspective at work in his own theory of power, one that suggests the 'creativity' of action, the 'productive effectiveness' that power relations enable. Foucault clearly outlines an action-theoretic view when he states: "what describes a *relationship* of power is that it is a mode of action which does not act directly and immediately on others. Instead it acts upon their actions: an action upon an action, on existing actions or on those which may arise in the present or in the future."[60]

In rejecting an account of power that designates it as a property or right, Foucault suggests he has been interested in studying not the 'what' or 'who,' but the 'how' of power. In this sense, Foucault argues for a form of analysis that extends the relations between "theory and practice." That is, an analysis grounded in 'practice' or the 'practices of power,' one which "consists of taking the forms of resistance against different forms of power as a starting point," that is, to analyze "power relations through the antagonism of strategies."[61] In this sense, Foucault has in mind an agonistic form of power, a theory of power, as Honneth suggests, that is based on "a model of action built upon a concept of 'struggle.'"[62]

However, as Hanssen has argued, even in "The Subject and Power," the terms of Foucault's account seem to militate against one another. For as the above passages indicate, right until the end, Foucault "remained equivocal when it came to circumscribing the relation between 'agonism' and 'antagonism.'" Indeed, in speaking of the 'antagonism of strategies,' a state of permanent provocation, Hanssen suggests, "one might be inclined to conclude that 'agonism' described an 'ungrounded ground,' an infinite contestation in freedom, yet one whose practical articulations invariably took the form of adversarial antagonisms, rather than, say, dialogical cohabitation."[63]

Despite this equivocation, the double presence of an 'agonistic' form of power and one informed by a notion of the 'antagonism of strategies' are clearly evident in Foucault's later work, where it is apparent that his theory of power is multifaceted and cannot be reduced to strategic action alone. Foucault's work provides an intersubjective-theoretic view of power as a reciprocal interplay of social forces, and the implications of this action-theoretic account of power are important in another respect: it suggests that an *a priori* notion of interaction cannot be posited as mutual, communicative, or recognitive as Honneth and Habermas presuppose. Even if we assume a minimal theory of interaction as the starting point for a theory of the social, the modalities of that interaction may be imbued with multiple action types, including power or strategic action. Foucault, then, articulates a theory of intersubjectivity that points to the constancy of the conflictual nature of sociality and subject formation, rather than assuming that social sociability can be insulated or separated out from forms of unsocial sociability, or that we can assume an *a priori* ethical form of intersubjectivity that can be insulated from power.

Foucault's 'micro-analysis' of power enables a consideration of power as a modality of everyday relations and forms of interaction. Power, then, is not just understood in systemic terms as something imposed externally or 'from above.' Rather, it is internal to the social itself, in terms of intersubjective and network-like relations. From Foucault's perspective, "power relations are rooted deep in the social nexus, not reconstituted 'above' society ... to live in society is to live in such a way that action upon other actions is possible—and in fact ongoing." In fact, emphatically he maintains that a "society without power relations can only be an abstraction."[64]

Here, then, Foucault outlines a theory of power that lends itself to Honneth's own critique and provides the basis for reconstructing an alternative theory of power. Firstly, Foucault articulates power not as a symbolic medium confined to the sub-system of the state, but the activity that produces the social itself. In comparison to Habermas' systems-theoretic view of power, Foucault describes struggles as 'immediate': "In such struggles people criticize instances of power which are closest to them, those who exercise their action on individuals."[65] Nonetheless, in "The Subject and Power" Foucault does seem to concede some ground to the action-theoretic views of Arendt and Habermas, granting a role to communicative relations in his social-theoretical framework that he had otherwise dismissed, acknowledging that communication is also a means of "acting upon another person or persons." Moreover, he even seems prepared to consider that an intersubjective notion of power is also a means of grounding an alternative politics by "acting in concert" to "accomplish things."[66] When pushed in a late interview, Foucault also concedes that Arendt's notion of power as consensus might act as a "critical" or "regulatory principle."[67] Thus, rather than excluding consensus or agreement from his considerations on power, Foucault here distinguishes more clearly between different levels or degrees of power, domination, and 'government,' arguing that power does not entirely overlap with consensual agreement and that power as 'government' involves some form of intersubjective reciprocity, that is, the "question of government" requires that interaction partners recognize one another as "persons who act."[68]

In this respect, although Foucault argues that power is not a function of consent, "not a renunciation of freedom, a transference of rights, the power of each and all delegated to a few," he also acknowledges that this "does not prevent the possibility that consent may be a condition for the existence or the maintenance of power." The "relationship of power," he argues, *can be the result of a prior or permanent consent, but it is not by nature the manifestation of a consensus.*"[69] In an effort to more readily distinguish power from violence, Foucault therefore seems to be prepared to consider that his own notion of power as 'enabling and positive' might have some affinities with the Arendtian concept of power, particularly in terms of the way in which he understands power relations as a form of action that modifies the action of others. Moreover, in articulating a theory of action as 'conduct in freedom' in this manner, Foucault also begins to consider the importance of the subject's relation-to-self as integral to the way in which power operates.

In "The Subject and Power" essay, Foucault elaborates and extends the concept of productive power. The 'technique of government' is here defined as productive in the sense that it is a mode governing 'the conduct of conduct.'[70] Power not only structures the field of the social as an ensemble of actions, but is also conceived as producing subjectivity:

> The form of power applies itself to immediate everyday life which categorizes the individual, marks him by his own individuality, attaches him to his own identity, imposes a law of truth on him which he must recognize and which others have to recognize in him. It is a form of power which makes individuals subjects. There are two meanings of the word *subject*: subject to someone else by control and dependence, and *tied to his own identity by a conscience or self-knowledge*. Both meanings suggest a form of power which subjugates and makes subject to.[71]

In Foucault's conception, there appears to be no consideration of an *a priori* self-perception, only the total *social* construction of the self. The subject is one who is 'marked by' or 'tied to' an identity or knowledge of self that can only be intersubjectively constituted. However, according to Foucault, 'self-realization' in the context of others is one formed by relations of power, not simply mutual agreement or recognition. It can also be surmised from the above text that the notion that power is productive is operative at two levels in Foucault's work: both in terms of a theory of society, in that it is *constitutive of the social; and a theory of socialization*, in terms of the production of individual identity or processes of subjectivation. In fact, in "The Subject and Power," Foucault makes the qualification that despite his earlier focus on the analytics of power, what he has really always been tracing is the history of subjectivity, the process by which modern individuals are *made into* subjects.

The above passage is also central to understanding Foucault's account of action, an account of action conceived prior to identity. In this sense, Foucault is at pains to avoid an account of action that is necessarily grounded on identity, given that for him, all processes of subject- or identity-formation are simultaneously processes of subjectivation, that is, they are subject to power as much as they are defined in the condition of freedom. It is also here, brought together in the concept of 'subjectivation,' that the two currents that can be identified in Foucault's work can be seen to be operative in the one complex notion of power. For Foucault, power is both subjugating and enabling and subject-formation or subjectivation is always double-sided; it is dependent on power relations as much as it occurs in the condition of freedom and agency. In the above text, Foucault also clearly defines a notion of intersubjectivity as 'mutually constructing subjectivity'; subjectivity is produced or constructed in the context of relations with others, not merely affirmed or acknowledged. In this sense, Foucault speaks about the 'bestowal' of identity through intersubjective relations, and the construction of the subject in relations of power. In order to understand this claim it is necessary to remember that power cannot be reduced to domination but must be understood as a potential or capacity, as constitutive rather than repressive. The above passage also suggests, then, that the act of 'recognition' is always power saturated and involves a 'politics of truth' rather than simply neutral affirmation.

In his own work Honneth disassociates the notion of power from the act of recognition, and in contrast to Foucault, conceptualizes intersubjectivity as 'mutually revealing subjectivity.' In Honneth's own reading of Foucault, despite acknowledging the potential of a productive notion of power, he goes on to reduce his interpretation to a totalizing disciplinary mode of power. He frames his reading of *Discipline and Punish* and *The History of Sexuality: Volume One*, in terms of the three concepts 'norm,' 'body,' and 'knowledge,' of which the concept of 'norm' appears to be the most significant. Honneth is therefore skeptical of the way in which Foucault develops the notion of productive power in the context of a critique of socialization in terms of 'normalization,' or disciplinary power, particularly in *Discipline and Punish*. However, as will be discussed in the next chapter, the basis for this conception of 'norm' or 'normalization'—and of Honneth's own skepticism—can only be understood by tracing what Honneth views as Foucault's subsequent attempts to account for the ways in which seemingly disparate and fragmented instances of social action come to form an order or system of power, and why Honneth views these problems as insurmountable in the context of developing a normative critical theory.

Chapter Four

Regimes of Discipline

Foucault's Domination-Theoretic View

Honneth traces the shift from an action-theoretic view to a systems-theoretic account in Foucault's work in terms of a chronological trajectory that signals a movement away from his original intersubjective-theoretic insights. From the basis of the strategic model of action as a field of open conflict and struggle, Honneth reconstructs the steps Foucault takes in developing an analysis of the formation and reproduction of power structures, or totalizing systems of power in the social-historical studies *Discipline and Punish* and *The History of Sexuality: Volume One*. In his analysis, Honneth follows the moves Foucault makes in developing a 'decentered' notion of power that connects similar outcomes of action from multiple contexts, if only momentarily, into a centerless system in network-like fashion. This 'decentered' concept is constructed as a critical alternative to 'statist' conceptions that are based on the notion of a single center of power. In this way, Honneth suggests that to his credit, Foucault is consistent in conceiving social systems of power as open and fragile structures that are continuously exposed to "a renewed process of testing through social conflicts."[1] Thus, maintaining the Nietzschean-inspired thread of a contingent and 'dynamic model of competing forces,' Foucault describes social systems of power in multidimensional fashion as a combination of "innumerable points of confrontation, focuses of instability, each of which has its own risks of conflicts, of struggles, and of at least a temporary inversion of power relations."[2]

In this respect, Honneth suggests that Foucault's approach marks a sharp contrast not only to Althusser's one-dimensional notion of the 'ideological state apparatus,' but also to Adorno's conception of power. It is in this respect that Honneth considers Foucault's work to represent a 'progression' from the theory of society provided by Adorno, who ignored the dimension of "social action by seeking to understand social structures in general as coagulated forms of an activity of control directed at both inner and outer nature."[3] In Honneth's view, Adorno neglects to consider a struggle-theoretic dimension of social action, and therefore assumes that power is merely the function of "the goal-directed activity of a centralized administrative apparatus."[4] In comparison, Honneth suggests that in Foucault's analysis, an order of control can only be said to develop 'horizontally' rather than hierarchically, as a combination of strategic conflicts on the level of everyday action that share a common objective. This analysis is in keeping with Foucault's general concept of the social as constituted by intersubjective relations, a 'horizontal' view of the social that, it can be argued, in many ways Honneth also shares.[5]

However, Honneth suggests that if society is understood as "a continual stream of conflicts,"[6] the burden of proof still falls to Foucault to establish how power becomes even temporarily stabilized to form an order of domination. In Honneth's reading, Foucault's response to the problem of articulating the means of the 'stabilization' of social struggle is to substitute it with the notion of 'institutionalization.'[7]

However, for Honneth, one of the central difficulties with Foucault's work is that he does not countenance the possibility of the notion of institutionalization as the outcome of a normatively achieved consensus because for Foucault moral attitudes and legal norms are nothing but *normalizing* procedures that function as a form of social control. For Honneth, the way in which Foucault conceptualizes the social in terms of strategic interaction means the idea of a cessation of conflict due to normatively achieved consensus remains an impossibility. Honneth argues that Foucault's conception of the 'social' as an unending process of struggle now starts to raise difficulties when he attempts to define the institutionalization of social power. In Honneth's view, the problem of defining a means of stabilization or momentary cessation of conflict arises for Foucault because of the way in which he understands the relation between strategic action and power in the first place.

Honneth argues that in attempting to consider how the stabilization of conflict may occur long enough to establish any form of social power, Foucault begins to confront the limits of his own thinking. Having previously conceptualized the social as constituted *only* by social struggle in the form of strategic action, Foucault summarily dismisses the concept of any other forms of social action. Significantly, here Honneth emphasizes the problems that arise as a result of conceptualizing the social in terms of only one dimension of social action, a problem that shall be returned to below in the context of Honneth's own work. Here he argues that the consequences of the neglect to conceive of the social as constituted by multiple forms of (inter)action, now prevents Foucault from adequately understanding the very form and manifestation of social power, and his theory of power flips over into a theory of social control and domination.

In Honneth's view, if in the first instance, Foucault had considered that the social might be constituted by multidimensional forms of interaction, including communicative as well as strategic action, he would at this point be able to understand the formation of power as the result of agreement or normatively motivated consent. However, according to Honneth, because on the whole Foucault only countenances a conception of the social as a perpetual condition of struggle as strategic action, he begins to encounter difficulties when he attempts to define the 'institutionalization' of social power. As Honneth can be read to suggest, Foucault's reductionistic account of social action as *always already* strategic leads him to conclude that legal norms and moral attitudes are nothing other than 'cultural deception,' 'mere illusions' that hide the 'strategic objectives' intrinsic to all social action, therefore merely masking the inherent social conflict that is the 'essence' of all sociability.[8]

For Honneth, the neglect to consider a normative dimension is a major conceptual shortcoming in Foucault's work that undermines the very basis of social critique, and he considers it to be a methodological weakness that cannot be resolved immanently from within the parameters of Foucault's own thought. Moreover, for Honneth, in terms of developing a theory of the social based on the notion of struggle, the pressing question that arises from this refusal of any dimension of normative consensus is: "how the ... aggregate condition of a structure of power, whose prerequisite should be precisely the interruption of the process of conflict, [can] be derived from the social condition of an uninterrupted struggle [?]."[9]

Honneth suggests that the way in which Foucault implicitly addresses this problem, as an inversion of the Parsonian approach to the problem of social order, leads to a second complex of reflections in Foucault's work through which he attempts to further develop the conception of power, and which consequently illuminate the core of his social theory. However, rejecting that the stability of social order can be explained by theories of violence or ideology, and unwilling to draw on a theory of values or notion of normative agreement, Foucault is then compelled to explain even the momentary stabilization of conflict in terms of an analysis of the employment of ever more effective means for the preservation of power. In other words, Foucault analyzes the employment of power in increasingly systemic terms.

Foucault explicitly develops this line of thought further in opposition to conceptions that explain the acquisition of power through either physical violence or ideology, both of which he suggests only understand power as repressive. He argues that a repressive notion of power is completely unsatisfactory when it comes to explaining forms of social integration. As he ex-

plains in *The History of Sexuality*, the idea that power is repressive assumes
that power:

> only has the force of the negative on its side, a power to say no: in no position
> to produce, capable only of positing limits, it is basically antienergy. This is a
> paradox of its effectiveness: it is incapable of doing anything, except to render
> what it dominates incapable of doing anything either, except for what this
> power allows it to do ... All the modes of domination, submission, and subju-
> gation are ultimately reduced to an effect of obedience. [10]

In comparison, here, Foucault again mobilizes the unique conception of power in terms of 'productive effectiveness.' Foucault therefore transforms
Nietzsche's conception of the 'will to power,' with its sense of production of
creative energy, and makes it into the basis of an analysis of a specifically
modern form of power. The key to Foucault's conception of power is then
the idea that technologies of power "*create* rather than repress the energy of
social action,"[11] a notion of creative production and self-production that, as
we shall see below, is central to understanding the theory of power in the
context of his later work.

   However, in Honneth's view, central to the notion of 'productivity' in the
context of the social-historical studies *Discipline and Punish* and *The History
of Sexuality* are Foucault's understandings of the *connections* between the
notions of 'norm,' 'body,' and 'knowledge.' For Honneth, the conception of
'norm' or 'normalization' becomes the key to understanding Foucault's notion of the 'productive effectiveness' of power. In this context, against the
argument that power represses the objectives of strategic opponents of action, the notion of productive power refers to the reutilization of modes of
behavior through continual disciplining. For Foucault, 'normalization' or
'norms of conduct' therefore refers to 'rigidly reproduced patterns of action'
that are in effect techniques or instrumentalizations of power. [12]

   Moreover, according to Honneth's reading, Foucault posits a peculiar
form of social behaviorism, in that techniques of power do not compel 'nor-
malized conduct' by means of the influence on or control of psychic processes, but rather are completely directed to the disciplining of the body. Foucault's shift of focus towards the body is indicative of his move away from
the earlier semiological-structuralist analysis of knowledge. It is no longer
the cultural modes of thought through which power is assumed, but rather
through the body and life processes.

   Honneth here is referring to Foucault's studies in both *Discipline and
Punish* and *The History of Sexuality*, where his analysis of power is directed
towards the ways in which power acts upon the body as either disciplinary
techniques or bio-power to either: (1) 'discipline' motor and gestural movements, or (2) to regulate and control the organic processes of birth, death,
procreation, and illness. [13] Foucault therefore understands processes of social

integration in terms of the ability to control and coordinate bodily behavior and to regulate bodily processes.[14] The theory of power is therefore fundamentally connected to the governance of the conduct of human bodies, not simply as a measure of repression or control, but fundamentally in terms of the productivity of bodies, the production of action, and the 'creation' of particular life processes.

For Honneth, this social-behavioralist explanation is indicative of the structuralist heritage of Foucault's analysis of discourse and a consequence of his strict avoidance of all psychological explanations. Honneth is critical of Foucault's neglect to consider "individual psycho-dynamics ... onto which, as always, such disciplining processes radiate back."[15] The subjectless system of signs is therefore merely replaced by the subjectless system of power. In Honneth's view, Foucault erroneously does not understand the human body as a combination of physical and psychical processes, but exclusively as a "physical process of an ever-more-perfect directing of sequences of bodily motions."[16] In other words, the body becomes the site of social power. As a result of this localization, social power is no longer mobilized in terms of intersubjectively constituted struggle, but only constituted through technologies that control, mold, or fashion it—in other words, it becomes an instrument of 'government.'[17]

Foucault briefly outlines the second aspect of the 'productive effectiveness' of power on the human body in *The History of Sexuality*, in terms of control of biological behavior or 'power over life,' which he terms 'biopower.'[18] Here the theory of power is applied to an analysis of the 'biological' control of populations through administrative regulation of organic life processes (birth, death, illness, procreation).[19] Together the techniques of disciplining bodies and administering the life cycle of populations is considered to form the quintessential system of power that is characteristic of modernity.[20]

In Foucault's analysis, these techniques of social power upon bodies are made possible by new methods of data collection in regard to individuals and the production of specific forms of *knowledge* that mutually reinforce these specific techniques of power.[21] It is within this context that Foucault picks up the original threads of his critique of scientific knowledge, and the analysis of discourse is reformulated in terms of what he conceives to be a symbiosis between 'power/knowledge.'

For Foucault, this model of 'power/knowledge' is central to a revision of critical theory. Foucault's questioning of the neutrality of the various sciences, and suggestion that these forms of knowledge are associated with new power practices that respond to particular social, economic, and political aims, also brings him within the vicinity of the Frankfurt School. This is an association with which he notably also self-identifies in his later work, when in the context of discussing the 'critical tradition' he suggests it is a "form of philosophy that, from Hegel, through Nietzsche and Max Weber, to the Frankfurt School, has founded a form of reflection in which I have tried to work."[22]

In this sense, as Honneth and other writers point out, Foucault shares some fundamental agreements with Horkheimer and Adorno, laid out, for example, in *The Dialectic of Enlightenment*.[23] This is most obvious in relation to their critiques of the instrumental character of western rationality, and the forms of domination it gives rise to, as well as their shared suspicion about the objectivity of scientific knowledge. In this sense, it might be further argued that there are particular affinities between Foucault and Adorno in relation to their critiques of modernity, most notably, that both share a reading of modernity as conterminously constituted by conditions of power and freedom, and both also underscore the divergent, discontinuous aspects of history.[24] In addition, both share a particular concern for the ways in which the increase of technical rationalization leads to the subjugation of individuals, especially in terms of techniques of power enacted upon the body.[25]

However, Foucault is more Nietzschean than Horkheimer and Adorno, and at a fundamental level, he rejects the idea that scientific knowledge can ever produce discernible truths. In fact, on the contrary, he suggests that science is not discernible from ideology, maintaining that the production of knowledge is always bound up with historically specific regimes of power, regimes that form discursive truths with a normalizing function.[26] For Foucault, "the problem does not consist in drawing the line between that in a discourse which falls under the category of scientificity or truth, and that which comes under some other category, but in seeing historically how effects of truth are produced within discourses which in themselves are neither true nor false."[27]

Furthermore, with the new combination of power as a disciplinary force and its systematization, Foucault's account marks a sharp contrast to Habermas' (early) analysis of knowledge, with its distinction between various forms of knowledge-constitutive interests. Thus where Habermas makes a distinction between the sciences with an interest in the domination of nature, and the critical and hermeneutic sciences that he claims have an emancipatory interest, Foucault argues that all forms of knowledge (including the human and natural sciences) have an inherent interest in power. Honneth suggests, however, that Foucault's critique of the sciences in terms of a theory of power/knowledge has the unfortunate consequence of entangling his own critical enterprise in a contradiction because without a valid basis from which to justify his own analysis, it is also open to the same criticism that it is merely another "reflexive form of strategic action."[28] Foucault's own preference for a conceptualization that highlights "a multiplicity of rationalities and strategies of power," Honneth argues, turns out to be conceptualized in a one-dimensional manner. Or perhaps, it would be more accurate to suggest, that Foucault conceives of one rationality—technical rationality—that is located in a variety of sites or social bodies.

As a consequence of conceptualizing social power in terms of the differentiating production of knowledge in this manner, Foucault also makes a corresponding conclusion that for Honneth moves it toward a systems-theoretic analysis. With the interconnections between the concepts of norm, body, and knowledge, Foucault understands the productivity of power not just to refer to the situated governance of bodily processes and the action of individuals in differentiated social sites or subsystems, but also to a cumulative learning process whereby he understands the accumulation of knowledge to enable the optimization of social power.

In his historical investigations, Foucault understands the accumulation of knowledge to be acquired systematically through the disciplinary regulation and evaluation of modes of conduct by procedures of examination, normalizing judgment, and surveillance. As Honneth points out, and as indicated above, the exercise of power is no longer the prerogative of social groups or individual actors but is instead the domain of social institutions such as the school, hospital, prison, and factory. With this move, Foucault now conceives of institutions as "highly complex structures of solidified positions of social power." Honneth argues that a significant shift of emphasis, then, appears in this phase of Foucault's work whereby the "frame of reference for the concept of power has, therefore, secretly been shifted from a theory of action to an analysis of institutions."[29]

Honneth argues that from this point on, the analysis of power becomes one-dimensionalized and examined only from the perspective of 'power-wielding' institutions, rather than from the point of view of social actors or 'those subject to power.'[30] Moreover, for Honneth, because Foucault bases his social theory initially on the notion of an 'uninterrupted string of strategic conflicts,' he excludes at the conceptual level any possibility of *mutually* overcoming the ongoing process of struggle in a provisional end-state of stabilized power, either by means of 'mutual agreement' or 'a pragmatically aimed compromise.' As a consequence, Honneth argues that Foucault can only understand the institutionalization of power in terms of a one-sided form of domination, as a permanent use of *force*.[31]

Thus, Honneth argues, that an internal 'rift' develops in Foucault's work between the initial action-theoretic premises of a social theory based on an ongoing process of social struggle and the conception of the 'unlimited' optimization and effectiveness of disciplinary power that is self-producing and reproducing, and based in the notion of social institutions. In Honneth's view, the action-theoretic and intersubjective impulses that can be found in Foucault's work quickly become subsumed when he moves to an analysis of the way in which connected positions of power arise out of a process of perpetual conflict and come to form an order of domination. Thus, for Honneth, the original notion of power as a notion of 'practical intersubjectivity of social struggle' is unexpectedly cancelled out by the idea of power-wielding institutions, undermining the action-theoretic potential of Foucault's work.

It is precisely this problematic that later compels Honneth to look for other avenues via Hegel's early writings through which to reconceptualize the 'struggle-theoretic intuition' that he first detects in Foucault's work. He pinpoints Foucault's failure to maintain the action-theoretic stance in his work to the problem of conceptualizing the social as a constellation of perpetual, strategically oriented, rather than morally motivated, struggle. Thus, although one current of Foucault's work well conceives the social in action-theoretic terms as an open-ended field of struggle, in Honneth's view, this current is undermined because, in *Discipline and Punish* and *The History of Sexuality: Volume One*, he restricts interaction to modes of strategic conflict that are ultimately overly subject to a systems-theoretic logic. Hence, Foucault's concept of the social for Honneth also remains too open-ended; not only does it evoke a notion of 'force' in the form of 'perpetual battle' but it remains difficult to consequently formulate an understanding of the stabilization of power without recourse to an order of domination secured through totalizing institutions.

However, it can be argued here that Honneth reads Foucault's work simply in the form of a chronological trajectory, as the loss of an initial action-theoretic insight, rather than maintaining that an ongoing complexity of the two tendencies remains throughout his work. Rather it can be argued that Foucault continues to conceptualize two sides to power, both domination-theoretic and actionistic, and that he develops not just an interpersonal notion of power but also an analysis of power and institutions. The retention of the action-theoretic stance in Foucault's work is borne out by his later return to these insights in the essay "The Subject and Power," as we discussed above and to which we shall return below, where he extends his action-theoretic analysis particularly in relation to the notion of 'conduct in freedom,' while alongside this notion, maintaining a more systematizing view of power in terms of 'government.'[32] This seems to suggest it might be more fruitful to read Foucault's work in terms of the double-presence of these two currents that continue to indicate a certain complexity that is internal to the notion of power that runs throughout his work.

For Honneth, though, the true extent of the systems-theoretic thread in Foucault's analysis is tellingly revealed in the detail of his empirical investigation of the emergence of the modern prison. Honneth argues that the model of strategic action and social struggle then seems to disappear completely "behind the systemic process of the continuous perfecting of technologies of power."[33] This unexpected shift away from the initial action-theoretic approach which represented for Honneth a theoretical advance over the work of Adorno, now reverts to a systems-theoretic response which, he suggests, brings his work curiously back in line with Adorno's social-theoretical conclusions.[34]

This is most obvious in the manner in which Foucault describes the changes to forms of punishment and penal reform in terms of a cumulative increase in the effectiveness of social control. In this way, the gradual shift away from the classical system of punishment exemplified for Foucault by torture and physical force (so vividly described in the introductory pages of *Discipline and Punish*) towards seemingly more 'humane' forms of punishment, represented by the introduction of the prison sentence, merely indicate the perfectibility of processes of social control. Honneth suggests that the new techniques of disciplinary power exercised by modern institutions, of which the prison with its 'panoptic' forms of surveillance is exemplary, represent for Foucault nothing less than the continual 'augmentation of power.' Judged historically, as Honneth understands Foucault to be suggesting in *Discipline and Punish*, modern instruments of social control are therefore considered to represent an *increase* in the effectiveness of power extended throughout the entire social body, compared to premodern forms of domination that are singularized around one particular social site in terms of the 'sovereign.'

Thus, for Foucault, penal reform, which arises in the context of moral arguments about the humanization of punishment, is merely the ground for a thoroughly rationalized form of social control that ensures a systematic increase of power. In this context, it can also be said that Foucault's critique of the philosophical roots of penal reform stands in for a greater critique of the philosophical ideas of Enlightenment humanism and the legal and political frameworks to which they give rise. For Foucault, the form of 'humanism' that develops with modernity is a new form of 'pastoral care,' a form of humanism that 'cultivates and encourages freedom' and individualization. However, it is also by way of this very freedom that new forms of 'governmental technologies' are able to govern every aspect of social life, even the most intimate.[35] In this sense, Foucault maintains that the development of modern democratic parliamentary systems and a juridical framework that guarantees a system of rights is *underwritten* by a system of disciplinary techniques, or 'micro-power.' Thus, he argues, "the development and generalization of disciplinary mechanisms constituted the other, dark side of these processes."[36] In a passage that is evocative of *The Dialectic of Enlightenment*, Foucault suggests:

> The real, corporal disciplines constituted the foundation of the formal, juridical liberties. The contract may have been regarded as the ideal foundation of law and political power; panopticism constituted the technique, universally wide-

spread, of coercion. It continued to work in depth on the juridical structures of society, in order to make the effective mechanisms of power function in opposition to the formal framework that it had acquired. The 'Enlightenment,' which discovered the liberties, also invented the disciplines.[37]

Rather than perfectibility in terms of moral progress, for Foucault, the philosophical ideals of the Enlightenment instead reveal the perfectibility of the history of violence and power. As Honneth suggests, it is through the daily disciplining of the body that, for Foucault, "the true face of history is revealed." It can be traced "in the petrified violence of the prison cell, the ritual drill of the barrack square and the mute violences of school routine rather than the moral proclamations of the constitutions and eloquent testimonies of the history of philosophy."[38]

In Honneth's reading, Foucault arrives at this conclusion because he assumes that the distinctively modern institutionalization of power, as a series of disciplinary technologies rather than struggles, becomes ever more effective due to the historical process in which originally independent institutions become linked into a mutually reinforcing relay of coordinated institutions. Therefore, although they become decentralized, they also become more totalizing, and able to extend into far greater areas of social life. In this way, what were previously autonomous organizations are interwoven in a way in which the exchange of information and circulation of knowledge could occur and henceforth secure the exercise of power into a total system.[39]

Although the economy remains only a background factor for Foucault's analysis, he assumes that the process of capitalist modernization requires new, more extensive and continuous forms of social power secured through new disciplinary techniques and institutions.[40] He therefore concludes, that the historical conditions that drive the systematization of social power arise with the development of the productive forces and the increase and movement of populations that are mobilized with capitalist development in the eighteenth century. Consequently he conceives of the manifestation of a new autopoetic system of power, which independently of any social group or individual, applies disciplinary techniques to bodies and populations and thereby ensures social control. The accumulation of knowledge/power is therefore conceived as a "trans-subjective learning process" that is transferred to the level of systems.[41]

Honneth argues that this systems-theoretic response makes it clear that Foucault ultimately conceives of social change in terms of a theory of the social evolution of power at the level of systems. Social domination is not therefore the outcome of conflict between social groups but the result of a "systemic process of adaption."[42] In Honneth's view, this can be the only explanation for the apparent disappearance of the dimension of social struggle at this point in Foucault's work. As a consequence, the concept of ongoing conflict and struggle between social groups appears to recede, and no consideration is given to the politicization of bodily representations and identities, nor struggles over biological processes and life processes that may not be completely subordinated to the logic of the institutionalization of disciplinary techniques. Rather, Honneth suggests, Foucault ends up presenting an image of a 'one-dimensional society' in which social conformity is ensured by a totalizing system of integrated disciplinary institutions, or a 'disciplinary regime.'

In this sense, Honneth argues that Foucault shares with Horkheimer and Adorno a conception of modern power that trivializes the differences between totalitarian and democratic societies, and in fact, presents fascism and Stalinism merely as the perfectibility of forms of technical rationality and power perceptible in western liberal-democratic societies. Thus, for Honneth, the negative and totalizing conclusions of Adorno's philosophy of history and Foucault's social theory share much in common.

In particular, in line with Adorno, Foucault understands the experience of modernity as one of the 'unparalleled growth of power and violence' associated with the increase of technical or 'instrumental' rationality. Like Adorno, Foucault's project is defined by an attempt to expose the falseness of the claim that the history of modernity is a history of progress and emancipation. In this sense, both have a corresponding commitment to uncovering what they consider to be the subterranean history of the European Enlightenment, the history of a rationalization process that enables the augmentation of power. In a passage that sounds like Foucault's evocation of the 'dark side' of history, we read in the *Dialectic of Enlightenment*: "Europe has two histories: a well-known written history and an underground history. The later consists in the fate of human instincts and passions which are displaced and distorted by civilization."[43]

In an essay included in *The Fragmented World of the Social*, Honneth argues that both Adorno and Foucault articulate the historical increase of technical rationality primarily in terms of its effects upon the body; for both writers, the history of modernity is the history of the *suffering* of the body.[44] In fact, Honneth argues, this is "the inner affinity in their critique of the modern age."[45] Both understand the process of civilization as the process of increasing technical rationalization and its power-effects in terms of the fashioning and destruction of the body. For Adorno, however, the suffering of the body is equated with domination over nature, particularly the repression of needs, desires, and the imagination; whereas for Foucault, the body becomes the locus of social control through more and more specialized and differentiated modes of discipline and training.[46]

Moreover, both understand processes of social control to be enacted by modes of subjectivation that mark and produce particular forms of identity. The 'civilizing process' (Elias) is understood in terms of the manner in which

the individual is trained, disciplined, produced, and controlled to ensure social integration through conformity. Thus, Honneth argues, both writers
"place a coercive model of social order at the basis of their social theory."[47]

However, despite the similarities in their negative critiques of modernity
and their agreement about a new order of social coercion, Honneth goes on to
argue that the manner in which Adorno and Foucault both reach these conclusions differentiates them markedly in their final approaches. In this slightly later essay, Honneth emphasizes further than in *The Critique of Power*, the
differences between Adorno's and Foucault's critiques of human subjectivity, and offers a more sympathetic reading of Adorno in terms of his theoretical sensitivity to social suffering and the internality of the subject.

Honneth finds problematic Foucault's assumption that techniques of power are enacted *only* on the body and his presumption that psychic processes
are merely a by-product of disciplinary procedures on the body; in other
words, that the internality of the subject is only constructed externally as a
series of effects on the body. Honneth suggests that Foucault therefore views
"individuals as formless and conditionable creatures," as empty subjects,
with no psychic individuality and chance for successful personality development.[48]

In this respect, for Honneth, Foucault's approach marks a sharp contrast
to the tradition of Critical Theory, which for Honneth, must be grounded on a
notion of social suffering if it is to explain the basis for an interest in emancipatory reason.[49] Adorno, for example, directs his critique at the level of
psychic influence and control by the cultural manipulation of the mass me-
dia. Fundamentally, however, he views this predisposition to coercion as the
result of an historical process attributable to capitalist modernity which de-
stroys the *psychic* capacities of individuals and hence their ability for self-
determination. Therefore, where Foucault conceives of the conditionability
of individuals as an 'ontological' condition, Adorno understands this social
constructivism as a social-historical condition in which the "psychic strength
for practical self-determination" has been destroyed by the combined and
increasing instrumentalization of inner and outer nature that is attributed to
the long 'civilizing process,' which particularly accelerates with the advent
of modernity. Adorno also grounds his critique in a normative framework of
an aesthetic concept of successful ego-identity based on the notion of freedom as the flow of communication between the "outer sensory impressions
and inner sensibility of the subject."[50] As a consequence, as we see in *Dialectic of Enlightenment*, the notion of suffering is broadened to account for
the dimension of the psychic suffering of individuals, as well as the "destruction between the individual and the body" as a result of the "irrationality and
injustice of rule as cruelty."[51]

This reading of Adorno is central to Honneth's later re-engagement with
the work of first generation Critical Theory in terms of the sensitivity to

social suffering caused by social pathologies of reason that provides its critical-normative impulse. In a much later essay, "A Social Pathology of Reason: On the Intellectual Legacy of Critical Theory," in which Honneth articulates and by implication self-identifies with this particular heritage of Critical Theory, he cites Adorno's fundamental conviction to this impulse, with a passage from *Negative Dialectics* whereby "the moment of the flesh proclaims the knowledge that suffering ought not to be, that things should be different." [52] Thus, like Adorno, for Honneth the experience and identification of human suffering is central for mobilizing critique, for it is only through social suffering that "the interest in the emancipatory power of reason" is kept alive. [53]

For Honneth, Foucault's notion of the subject is too heavily influenced by his structuralist background, whereby the subject is denied all intentionality and is understood to be nothing but the product of "the anonymous rules of discourse or ... violent strategies of domination." However, if the individual is denied any intentionality or agency, and the subject conceptualized as entirely the product of disciplinary power, Honneth argues that Foucault presents "nothing in his theory which could articulate [the suffering of the human body] as suffering." Without a normative basis that can provide a ground against which injustice and suffering can be judged, according to Honneth, "then the psychic suffering of the subject can no longer be interpreted as the silent expression of the rape of the human body." [54]

Notwithstanding the merit of Honneth's own normatively inspired critique, it can be argued that in some of Foucault's later work, a normative dimension is revealed that is more or less obscured in his earlier social-historical investigations with their apparent totalizing preoccupation with techniques of power. [55] Significantly, in the later work, Foucault also moves from a predominantly Nietzschean-inspired genealogical critique towards a more sustained engagement with Kant's "What is Enlightenment?" essay through which he identifies with a "more profound understanding of belonging to modernity." [56] In this context, Foucault articulates the project of critique in terms of a "permanent critique of ourselves"—a "mode of reflective relation to the present." [57] In this respect, Foucault appears to realign himself with a particular reading of the critical tradition and modernity. However, for Foucault, modernity represents not so much a particular historical period but rather a critical or 'limit' attitude—the attitude of modernity—"a way of thinking and feeling; a way, too, of acting and behaving that one and the same time marks a relation of belonging and presents itself as a task." [58] Thus, modernity for Foucault represents not only a particular relationship to the present, but it also compels us to create a particular mode of relationship with ourselves and to others, and to work "upon ourselves as free beings." [59]

Moreover, and in contrast to Honneth's interpretation, it can be argued that Foucault's interest in the subject and a more 'reciprocal' relation between self and society not only points to a more complex theory of power, but also contributes fruitful insights towards an historical anthropology. As shall be discussed in the following chapter, in a cursory way, Honneth does acknowledge that Foucault's attempt to historicize the individual's relation-to-self makes a contribution towards a philosophical anthropology at the level of individual development.[60] However, the philosophical anthropology that underpins Foucault's own project, together with insights gleaned from his genealogical critique, also begin to raise significant questions for Honneth's own interpretation of Foucault and for his project more generally.

Foucault's project is overwhelmingly motivated by an attempt to address the question of the present in terms of the contingency and unpredictability of the human condition, and to conceptualize ways in which individual self-realization is possible in the condition of an interplay of both power and freedom. It is this sense of the radical contingency and indeterminacy of the human condition, in addition to Foucault's complex analysis of power, that opens up questions concerning Honneth's critical project.

Chapter Five

Intersubjectivity in the Condition of Power

Re-reading Foucault

In order to examine the implications of Foucault's theory of power for Honneth's work, not only in relation to a theory of society but also for a philosophical anthropology, it is necessary to return to Honneth's early work undertaken in *Social Action and Human Nature*, a work written prior to *The Critique of Power*. However, in so doing, an alternative reading of Foucault's work will be offered in a way that opens onto questions for both Honneth's own anthropology of intersubjectivity and his analysis of power. This re-examination of Foucault's work, in the light of a more complex reading of his action-theoretic understanding of power, leads to the suggestion that there was a missed opportunity on Honneth's part for a potentially more fruitful engagement with Foucault's work, not only for further developing his own 'critique of power,' but especially for outlining a more multidimensional theory of interaction and intersubjectivity.

HONNETH'S EMERGENT ANTHROPOLOGY OF SOCIABLE SOCIABILITY

In addition to the reflective stages of critical theory mapped out in *The Critique of Power*, Foucault also features in Honneth's earlier studies in philosophical anthropology conducted as a series of lectures with Hans Joas, and published as *Social Action and Human Nature*.[1] The collection of studies in philosophical anthropology can also be understood as 'reflective stages' or 'traces' in a theory of intersubjectivity, a learning process at the level of

theory that is explicitly anthropological in orientation. In this reflexive-theo-
retical examination, Honneth and Joas begin with the intersubjective-theoretic insights of Feuerbach and Marx, and move through various studies and
contributions to a philosophical anthropology of intersubjectivity in Western
Marxism, and then to anthropologies of social action drawing in particular on
the work of Mead and the German tradition of philosophical anthropology,
and finally to studies in 'historical anthropology' exemplified by Elias, Foucault, and Habermas.

In this context, philosophical anthropology is not viewed as a foundational science, but rather as a form of autonomous self-critique on and of the
social and cultural sciences that is reconstructive in method. The studies
provided in *Social Action and Human Nature* are therefore intended as a
'contribution' to the project of theoretical self-reflection, a "discussion of
anthropology with systematic intent."[2] In a similar manner to *The Critique of
Power*, Honneth and Joas view Habermas' attempt to reconstruct historical
materialism as a theory of social evolution by way of a theory of communicative action, as a development at the level of theory that provides the most
advanced form of self-reflexivity.

For Honneth, all social philosophical research requires a form of anthropological reconstruction. In *Social Action and Human Nature*, this reconstructive enquiry takes place at two levels: (1) an examination of the conditions of the species' history, and (2) individual development—both of which
reveal certain constants or enduring conditions. However, Honneth and Joas
caution against any claim that anthropology in this sense be understood as
presuming an ahistorical view of human cultures, nor that it is attempting to
provide "an inalienable substance of human nature."[3] Rather, for Honneth
and Joas, philosophical anthropology can only provide a reflection upon the
human condition in the form of reconstructive method, as an historical enquiry into "the unchanging preconditions of human changeableness."[4] In
other words, philosophical anthropology takes changefulness itself to be a
social constant but also seeks to confirm what is constant in human changefulness.[5]

A 'naturalistic' perspective is present throughout Honneth's work, and is
initially drawn from the work of Plessner and Gehlen, and particularly from
George Herbert Mead. The work of Gehlen is viewed as instrumental in
contributing to the understanding that the "human being [has] a unique unspecialized nature and [creates] its own environment in the forms of systems
of action, which [change] over time."[6] In *Social Action and Human Nature*,
this perspective is pivotal to outlining a philosophical anthropology of social
action grounded in a theory of intersubjectivity. It can therefore be said, that
the enquiry into the 'unchanging preconditions of human changeableness'
undertaken in *Social Action and Human Nature* is reconstructed around two

central constants in particular: not only the enduring capacity for social action, but also the enduring precondition of intersubjectivity.

Furthermore, Honneth is concerned with ways in which both the external and internal natural worlds might be shaped in a non-instrumental fashion, and for him, this means the fashioning of nature not only intersubjectively but also sociably. For Honneth, the reconstruction of philosophical anthropology as a learning process at the level of theory, therefore, also means that it always has *normative* implications. Significantly, from this point onwards, Honneth bases his critical-philosophical project on the reconstruction of *normative anthropological* premises, which he reconstructs as unchanging preconditions of human life. The consequence of this theoretical method is that not only does Honneth assert that intersubjectivity and the capacity for (free) social action are unchanging conditions of human nature, but also that *particular forms or modalities* of intersubjectivity and social action can be identified at an anthropological level. In this sense, Honneth locates what he terms "anthropologically rooted possibilities for species development," in a particular 'positive' or 'ethical' conception of intersubjectivity, maintaining that certain modalities of *social* sociability can be said to form an *a priori* form of intersubjectivity.[7]

From the very early work on philosophical anthropology, Honneth has been intent on establishing the normativity 'naturally' inherent to intersubjective relations, which initially with Joas, he traces back to its materialistic manifestation in the work of Feuerbach. In the first instance, therefore, the work of Feuerbach and Marx are foundational for this anthropological project. For Honneth, Feuerbach is not only central to establishing the relationship between anthropology and historical materialism, but also crucially he is credited with being "the first to take into consideration both epistemologically and substantially the significance of the specifically human structure of intersubjectivity." That is, he reveals "an *a priori* intersubjectivity of the human being."[8]

In tracing the modalities of intersubjectivity and social action from Feuerbach's *a priori* intersubjectivism up to the point of Habermas' theory of communicative action, Honneth is clearly led to a theoretical decision that locates normativity within an originary mode of social interaction. Drawing on these insights, in *Social Action and Human Nature*, Honneth and Joas state that the importance of the theoretical goal of an anthropological grounding of historical materialism is, therefore, "the *normatively* orientated determination of the *natural basis* of specifically human sociality."[9] Thus, Honneth not only grounds intersubjectivity at an anthropological level as a precondition of human nature but at the same time makes a fundamental claim that locates *normativity* within this same *a priori* characteristic. Honneth therefore posits as a natural fact that humans have a predetermination towards interacting intersubjectively in a manner that *always already* has a normative orientation.

Moreover, in Honneth and Joas' reconstruction of philosophical anthropology, several studies in what they term 'historical anthropology' also assume a significant position. Not only Habermas, but also Elias and Foucault are credited for contributing to an historicization of anthropology that highlights the ways in which these "natural preconditions of social action [can be traced] in such a manner and to such a degree that their historical and cultural plasticity becomes evident…" In this sense, they argue that a reflexive philosophical anthropology must take account not only of the organic bounds of the human being, but also of "the historical process through which human nature has shaped itself within [these] organically set bounds."[10] The interpretations of Elias, Foucault, and Habermas can therefore be read as contributing important insights to a historically sensitized philosophical anthropology of intersubjectivity.

Honneth's understanding of philosophical anthropology is therefore alert to the ways in which historical and cultural processes have shaped and changed subjectivity, especially the fashioning of subjectivity of and through the human body, and it is in this sense that Foucault's work is of interest as a contribution to 'historical anthropology.' Honneth and Joas argue that an 'anthropologically oriented historiography' enables us to take account of "all changes that the human being has historically experienced in his bodily demeanor, in his modes of mental and emotional experiencing, in his patterns of social action, and in his motivations."[11] However, within the context of *Social Action and Human Nature*, Honneth and Joas amplify the historicist impulses of both Elias and Foucault while downplaying the power-theoretic dimensions of their work. This set of interpretations immediately circumscribes the work of both Elias and Foucault to the bounds of Honneth's own project of establishing the normative precondition for human intersubjectivity.

Despite this circumvention and domestication of Foucault's power-theoretic stance, his work nonetheless operates on two levels that are important for Honneth's project: (1) a theory of society and (2) at the level of philosophical anthropology, where Foucault figures predominantly on the path between Elias and Habermas in articulating themes central to an 'historical anthropology.' This points to the double presence of Foucault's work in Honneth's attempts to develop both a theory of society in terms of social struggle in the tradition of Critical Theory, and a philosophical anthropology of intersubjectivity that underpins his project.

Furthermore, it can be argued that Foucault's work contributes several important insights to the project of a philosophical anthropology that extend beyond Honneth's own interpretation: firstly, to an understanding of the 'historical and cultural plasticity' of the 'natural conditions of social action';

and, secondly, to the insight that power is an anthropological constant, a modality of all social action and interaction. Foucault's work therefore raises the question of whether forms of unsocial sociability might also be taken to be an enduring modality of human intersubjectivity, that power might also be an enduring condition of human interaction; a point that Honneth overlooks, but an insight, significantly, that Kant also built into his own version of practical reason, albeit, in responding to it transcendentally. [12]

The argument developed here is that Honneth does not fully acknowledge the implications of these power-theoretic dimensions for a theory of intersubjectivity in his engagement with Foucault's work. Given Honneth's aim to develop an intersubjective-theoretic notion of social action and his attempt to provide a comprehensive 'critique of power,' Foucault's work offers important insights that Honneth might have considered more fully in the path towards developing a theory of recognition. The implication of Foucault's work is not only that power is a modality of *all* social action and interaction but that it is an *a priori* modality of intersubjectivity and social action—that intersubjectivity also exists in the condition of power. Furthermore, if we read a more dynamic complexity between the totalizing and actionistic aspects of Foucault's work, we can also glean important insights in relation to the notions of identity, action, and contingency that later become significant for examining Honneth's theory of recognition.

FOUCAULT'S ANTHROPOLOGY OF UNSOCIAL SOCIABILITY

As demonstrated above, both actionistic and power-saturated currents can be found in Foucault's work as early as the essays "Discourse on Language" and "Nietzsche, Genealogy, History" and this current in various manifestations can be traced throughout Foucault's work to "The Subject and Power" and late interviews, as well as the later two volumes of *The History of Sexuality*.

In this respect, despite his protestations to the contrary, it can be argued that throughout his work, Foucault outlines a philosophical anthropology that accounts for both positive and negative modalities of human interaction that contribute to a theory of intersubjectivity and social action; an anthropology that also illuminates forms of unsocial sociability, including force, antagonism, violence, and war, but most fundamentally, of power.

To be sure, the anthropology of force and violence that Foucault outlines is a thoroughly historicized one. In "Nietzsche, Genealogy, History," which is one of the programmatic statements detailing Foucault's genealogical project and underlying philosophical anthropology (an essay to which Honneth gives scant attention), he argues that "[n]othing in man—not even his body—is sufficiently stable to serve as the basis for self-recognition or for under-

standing other men."[13] However, despite claiming in the above text that there
are no 'constants' in history, Foucault nonetheless proceeds by arguing in the
same essay that history can only be traced through the constant effects of
power and violence *on the body*. Thus, Foucault's disclaimer reads somewhat
as a contradiction in terms, when at the same time as he proclaims that
genealogy or 'effective history' is 'without constants,' he evokes the body as
a permanent surface through which history's changeable inscriptions can be
read or traced. As Foucault explains:

> The body is the inscribed surface of events (traced by language and dissolved
> by ideas) the locus of a dissociated self (adopting the illusion of a substantial
> unity), and a volume in perpetual disintegration. Genealogy, as an analysis of
> descent, is thus situated within the articulation of the body and history. Its task
> is to expose a body totally imprinted by history and the process of history's
> destruction of the body.[14]

In this manner, Foucault employs the Nietzschean notions of descent (*Herkunft*) and emergence (*Entstehung*) to contest the notion of "uninterrupted
continuities in history," and to reconstruct history as an analysis of "events"
and "singularities."[15] Evoking the notion of 'origins' in the sense of a "myri-
ad number of 'events'," *Herkunft* is intended to signify multiple lines of
'descent,' and the "complexity, contingency and fragility of historical forms
and events to which 'traditional' history has attributed stability."[16] Rather
than repeating what he considers to be philosophical anthropology's erroneous pursuit of pre-historical origins, genealogy as *Herkunft* and *Entstehung*,
Foucault argues, reveals the historicity of emotions, instincts, values, morals,
and the "laws of physiology"; "it introduces discontinuity into our very being."[17]

   At the same time there is an ambiguity in Foucault's formulations, for
despite speaking of *Herkunft* or descent as another way of understanding
origins, as a haphazard series of events, as a means of following or maintaining "passing events in their proper dispersion,"[18] merely as a "series of
accidents," Foucault explicitly identifies the body as "the domain of *Herkunft*," whereby "the body manifests the stigmata of past experience..."; it is
the body that becomes the pretext of ... insurmountable conflict."[19] However, "to speak in this way" as several interpreters have suggested, is to suggest
"that there is a body that is in some sense there, pregiven, existentially
available to become the site of its own ostensible construction."[20] It is precisely the evocation of a body that is destroyed and imprinted by history that
in fact suggests that the body constitutes a materiality "preconditional to
history" and "prior to discursive constructions."[21]

   Moreover, Foucault continues to speak of 'emergence' in terms of the
'constancy' of domination and struggle, of a single history or 'a single dra-
ma' that is staged as an "endlessly repeated play of dominations."[22] He

therefore offers his own particular account of the 'unchanging conditions of human changeability' in terms of particular modalities of social interaction, those of force/power. In this sense, 'changeability' of the human condition, at this stage in Foucault's work, is always associated with 'force,' 'struggle,' 'violence,' and 'domination,' (although later becomes identified primarily in terms of power/struggle), whereby he suggests that "[e]mergence is always produced through a particular stage of forces."[23] Genealogy, then, for Foucault, must delineate this modality of interaction, 'force,' and "the struggle these forces wage against each other ... It is in this sense that the emergence of a species ... and its solidification are secured."[24]

Thus, it has been argued that although Foucault "rejected the origin of pristine nature just as much as Hobbes' idealized *status naturalis*, he still operated with a notion of 'force'—an ungrounded ground of sorts—which appeared to be at the root of history."[25] Quoting Nietzsche at length, Foucault goes on to to define the 'engine' of social change in terms of force/struggle when he proclaims that: "[I]n fact, the species must realize itself as a species, as something—characterized by the durability, uniformity, and simplicity of its form—which can prevail [only] in ... perpetual struggle."[26] However, this perpetuity of struggle is not morally motivated struggle, nor does it have a teleological orientation, nor can it be retraced or reconstructed as a "history of morality in terms of linear development."[27] Rather, Foucault proclaims:

> Humanity does not gradually progress from combat to combat until it arrives at universal reciprocity, where the rule of law finally replaces warfare; humanity installs each of its violences in a system of rules and thus proceeds from domination to domination.[28]

In this very Nietzschean vein, Foucault therefore displays his skepticism about placing too much faith in the notions of progress and moral development, with particular reference to the double-sided nature of the experience and processes associated with modernity.[29] He suggests, therefore, that the genealogist can only reconstruct an ethics in the interstices; ethics is not a 'common space' but a non-place, in which the genealogist analyzes good and evil. It is in this sense that Foucault begins to articulate the idea of a form of ethics that is always defined in relation to the limits of power and power formations.

To be sure, in this context, Foucault can barely hide the anthropological 'constants' that form the presuppositions of his historical analysis. In "Nietzsche, Genealogy, History," the human self-image that underpins his historical-anthropological analysis is outlined in terms of notions of violence, force, domination, and power, anthropological images that run throughout his work. However, these images are reconstructed genealogically rather than teleologically, and highlight the indeterminacy and multiplicity of types of human interaction.

In *The Critique of Power* and *Social Action and Human Nature*, Honneth predominantly concentrates on the processes of subjectivation in terms of Foucault's images of power and control depicted in *Discipline and Punish*.[30] However, as a consequence, Honneth does not fully consider the complexity of Foucault's theory of power, or the anthropological images depicted across the broad spectrum of Foucault's work. It is not just the counter-anthropological images of force, violence, and power that throw Honneth's anthropology of intersubjectivity and (inter)action into relief, but also the radical contingency and indeterminacy of the human condition and the fragmentary forms in which a history of interaction and intersubjectivity might be reconstructed.

In other words, Foucault's own version of anthropological 'constancy,' in the manner outlined above, also has a second critical importance. It begs the question of assuming an originary 'recognitive' or ethical mode of intersubjectivity, and questions whether this one dimension of intersubjectivity can be reconstructed teleologically as a moral learning process in the way Honneth suggests. As Foucault suggests: "[w]hat is found at the historical beginning of things is not the inviolable identity of origin; it is the dissension of other things. It is disparity."[31]

In this sense, Foucault points to the radical indetermination and contingency of the human condition. To be sure, this is an historicization of philosophical anthropology that Honneth recognizes on one level, but he does not really consider the implications of Foucault's *genealogical method of history* for an historical anthropology, and the radical indetermination this suggests for a philosophical anthropology of forms and modalities of action. In other words, the question Foucault's genealogical method poses to Honneth's anthropology of recognitive intersubjectivity is that there may only be "the iron hand of necessity shaking the dice-box of chance."[32] Foucault's genealogical critique points to the 'deviations' and 'reversals,' the 'errors' and 'false appraisals,' to the absences and haphazardness in charting history. In comparison, then, to Honneth's reflexive reconstructions of a theory of intersubjectivity as a moral learning process with teleological intent, Foucault argues that 'effective history' is an approach "that severs its connection to memory, its metaphysical and anthropological model, and constructs a countermemory."[33]

While not wanting to suggest that Honneth abandon a notion of 'moral history,' there are some important critical insights gleaned from an account of the *negative* history of intersubjectivity and struggle to be found in Foucault's work, rather than *only* a moral, progressive one. In other words, the critical insights raised by Foucault point to a fragmentary reconstruction, 'a moral history in fragments,' that acknowledges the power-theoretic dimensions in this reflexive reconstruction, the moments when intersubjectivity is not 'moral,' but characterized by various modes of unsocial sociability, including hostility, violence, force, and power. These are 'fragments' towards a theory of intersubjectivity that Honneth does not incorporate into his final project due to the particular teleological orientation that he reconstructs as a moral learning process at the level of theory. However, it might be argued alternatively, that a 'learning process' is not necessarily teleological in orientation, and at the level of normative theory, a critical departure from theoretical one-sidedness need not result in the exclusion of important critical insights.

RE-READING FOUCAULT: POWER AND STRUGGLE AS RELATIONALITY

To be sure, the genealogical method mapped out in essays such as "Nietzsche, Genealogy, History" represents a period of Foucault's work more inspired by Nietzsche's naturalistic tendencies than action theory, and these elements undergo a transformation in Foucault's later work, represented by essays such as "What is Enlightenment" and "The Subject and Power" which bring Foucault's work closer to Honneth's action-theoretic concerns. Nonetheless, an actionistic current can be traced through Foucault's work from the beginning of the 1970s, and his consideration of action in the condition of contingency bears central insights for a theory of intersubjectivity, and for the project of critique more generally.

The anthropological image power/force remains a constant one underlying Foucault's studies including *Discipline and Punish*, *Society Must Be Defended*, and *The History of Sexuality: Volume One*. However, these explicit formulations of power as force, as Hanssen also notes, shift slightly in his later work. In "The Subject and Power," for example, the anthropological images that Foucault foregrounds are those of interaction, relationality, power, and struggle. Here, Foucault goes to greater lengths to develop a theory of power that is clearly distinguished from a theory of domination. At certain places in the "The Subject and Power," we find the suggestion of an enduring relationship between power and freedom, rather than power and force or violence. In fact in a late interview, Foucault emphatically exclaims, "one cannot impute to me the idea that power is a system of domination which controls everything and which leaves no room for freedom."[34] It might even be suggested that in his later work, despite its elusive quality and normative slipperiness, freedom is now named as the condition "or even precondition that make power relations possible in the first place."[35]

The importance of recognizing the continuing presence of two currents in Foucault's work—both action-theoretic and systems-theoretic dimensions—becomes evident in several of Foucault's later essays written in relation to

Kant's "What is Enlightenment [*Aufklärung*]?" essay.[36] In "What is Critique?," Foucault draws together both a discussion of the mutuality of governmentalization and self-governance, and the project of genealogy, in a provocative analysis of the notions of 'enlightenment,' 'modernity,' and 'critique' inspired by the Kantian response to the question "What is *Aufklärung*?" What Foucault finds so unique, in his notably sympathetic reading of Kant's essay,[37] is an analysis that depicts the coterminous increase of forms of governmentalization *and* individual autonomy, *both* brought together, he suggests, in a new form of 'self-governance.' In this sense, 'self-governance' has two sides: it simultaneously designates a sense of obedience (to a sovereign) at the same time as it enables critique and reflexivity. In this sense, it evokes the question 'how to govern' as much as 'how not to be governed.' In other words, Foucault suggests that Kant's questioning of the limits of knowledge, contains the double-sided question: "what are the limits of governmentality in the context of freedom?"

Foucault argues that Kant's notion of critique is therefore an attempt to ground obedience on autonomy, or in his own terms, to recognize that the constant interplay of power and freedom is an enduring human condition. Foucault perceives this unique combination in the motto that begins Kant's thesis, '*Sapere Aude*,' 'dare to know,' have the courage to use your own understanding, or 'the audacity to know.'[38] However, Foucault argues that for Kant, this motto stands alongside "another voice, that of Frederick II, saying in counterpoint, 'let them reason as much as they want as long as they obey.'"[39] In this sense, Foucault searches for a way of defining freedom within limits, or as Schmidt suggests, of illuminating a means of 'desubjectivation' within the play of power and truth.

Furthermore, Foucault argues that a slippage has occurred between the concepts '*Aufklärung*' and 'critique,' both since and because of Kant, that has resulted in the question 'What is *Aufklärung*?' being posed in terms of the limits of knowledge, or the legitimacy of historical modes of knowing. In comparison, Foucault suggests that the entry into the question of '*Aufklärung*' should not be that of knowledge, but rather that of power: that is, what are the limits of power or governance? For Foucault, the question is then not one of legitimacy, but of 'eventialization.' With this term, Foucault refers once again to the genealogical method, pointing out that it is only by way of such a historicophilosophical investigation that the relations 'among power, truth, and the subject' can emerge. By employing the concept of 'eventialization,' Foucault wants to reminds us, that a historicophilosophical approach does not analyze "universal truths to which history ... would bring a certain number of modifications."[40] Rather, we are reminded not only of ruptures and discontinuities, but that we also have "to deal with something whose stability, whose rooting, whose foundation is never such that one cannot in one way or another, if not think of its disappearance, at least mark that through which and that from which its disappearance is possible."[41]

Here Foucault approaches the question of enlightenment in terms of power and 'eventialization,' in a way that more clearly elucidates the connections between the social-historical studies of disciplinary power and governmentalization, as well as the more programmatic statements about an internal relationality between power and resistance, throughout interviews and essays of the 1970s and 1980s until his death in 1984. Drawing the two elements more clearly in relation to one another, in "What is Critique?," Foucault argues:

> ...it is not a matter of making power understood as domination or mastery by way of a fundamental given, a unique principle of explanation, or of a law that cannot be gotten around; on the contrary, it is always a matter of considering it as a relation in a field of interactions, it is a matter of thinking it in an inseparable relation with forms of knowledge, and it is always a matter of thinking it in such a way that one sees it associated with a domain of possibility and consequently of reversibility, or possible reversal.[42]

Importantly, as the above passage indicates, Foucault argues that where power is perceived as a 'singular effect,' we have to recognize that it is produced by a field or 'game of interactions'; a field of interactions "with its always variable margins of noncertitude."[43] There can be no closure or totality because the relations that constitute a 'singular effect' "are perpetually being undone in relation to one another." There is only "perpetual mobility, an essential fragility, or rather an intermingling, between that which accompanies the same process and that which transforms it."[44] Foucault therefore often defines 'relations of power' as "strategic games between liberties" and it is in this respect that he also speaks of strategic games as resulting "in the fact that some people try to determine the conduct of others."[45]

This analysis of enlightenment and critique accords not only with Foucault's arguments about power and resistance—one term always implies the other—but also further highlights Foucault's constant reference to power as strategy, or strategic action. However, the evocation of the notion of 'strategy' or 'strategic action' here should not be viewed as denoting the sole characteristic of Foucault's theory of power.[46] It is important to emphasize that Foucault does not reduce power to 'strategic action' in the sense understood by Habermas and Honneth, but that as Ingram points out, he distinguishes between different degrees of power, domination, and governance. The notion of the 'strategic intersubjectivity of struggle' should therefore not be viewed as necessarily antithetical to Habermas' nor Honneth's theories of communicative or recognitive-communicative action. As Nicholas Smith points out, in this sense, Honneth's critical interpretation of Foucault in *The Critique of Power* also relies on a distinction which is vulnerable to the very same criticisms in relation to a dualistic notion of power and communicative action that he seeks to resist, and which as we have discussed above, he strenuously criticizes in relation to Habermas' theory of communicative action. As Smith argues, the very same "objections which Honneth [makes] against the idea of separate *spheres* of purposive/strategic action and communicative action" also apply to "the separation of action *types*; normatively motivated consent may also have a strategic component, and vice versa." Furthermore, Honneth's interpretation of Foucault circumscribes his theory of social action only to one, normative dimension rather than articulating a multidimensional theory of action. As Smith argues, "Honneth's general thesis that Foucault's critique of power inadequately theorizes problems of social integration seems to presuppose that the only adequate concept of social action is one that addresses itself to that problem."[47]

Rather, as Rouse and Wartenberg have pointed out, Foucault's notion of power in terms of the 'strategic intersubjectivity of struggle' needs to be understood in an open and dynamic way, as "power always mediated by 'social alignments,'" or in Elias' terms, social 'figurations.'[48] In this sense, power as governance "even between equals" always "involves some reciprocal give and take," and strategic relationships, as Ingram reminds us, can be perfectly reciprocal and not necessarily opposed to communicative action. Thus, contra Habermas and Honneth, Foucault appears to mean something quite different by his employment of the term 'strategic action': "it is a way in which certain actors modify the actions of others," not by *force*, nor ideologically, but rather by an interplay of power and freedom. As discussed above, 'power' for Foucault "is less a confrontation between two adversaries … than a question of government."[49] Thus, Ingram argues that Foucault's notion of 'strategic action' suggests that: "strategic reciprocity is prior to strategic manipulation, but also that 'strategic' actors … actively and freely contribute to structuring the field of possible responses. Strategic power and consensual freedom thus constitute one another and both are necessary features of social relationships."[50]

As Schmidt and Wartenberg suggest, in Kant's essay, "Foucault found an account of enlightenment which never lost sight of the interplay between critique and power."[51] In this sense, they suggest that Foucault's return to the question 'What is Enlightenment?' is an attempt to "understand the character and the significance of [the] complex interplay between 'power and capabilities.'"[52] Accordingly, they argue that Foucault's essay on Kant makes clear the intention of the earlier works, such as *Discipline and Punish*, that seem to concentrate more on the 'intensification of power relations' in the study of disciplinary society. However, in the later work, including a 1983 essay on Kant and volumes two and three of *The History of Sexuality*, the emphasis shifts to illuminating further the ways in which self-formation through the development of individual capabilities might take place in the context of history, a history that is conterminously one in which power is further intensified. However, Schmidt and Wartenberg argue that in this sense, it is evident that power always appears in two forms in Foucault's work: it both dominates and enables.[53] Thus, for Foucault, "the acquisition of capabilities and the struggle for freedom" constitute the permanent conditions of modernity.[54] That is why, as Ingram suggests, Foucault characterizes "freedom as an 'ascetic task' of self-production that is both discipline *and* limit."[55] For Foucault, "modernity does not 'liberate man in his own being,' it compels him to face the task of producing himself."[56] In this sense, Foucault posits freedom—or the compulsion to be free—as both an "irresistible 'limit' on our transgressive practice" as much as it is an enabling condition.[57] The crucial insight of Foucault's work is to understand the 'interplay of power and capabilities'; this is the double-sided nature of power, which lies at the heart of Foucault's project.[58]

This codetermination of power, as that which both 'dominates' and 'enables,' is crucial for Foucault because he also dismisses the idea that there is a state of pristine nature or an originary moment—an assumed precondition of either freedom or recognition—that can act as a means to ground critique. In this manner, Foucault considers the question 'What is Enlightenment?' to invoke not a consideration of 'What is Man?' but more properly, 'What am I?' That is, searches Foucault, "What is it that I am, the me which belongs to this humanity, perhaps this fragment, to this moment, to this instant of humanity which is subjected to the power of truth in general and of truths in particular."[59] In a late interview, he suggests, there "does not exist a [reconciled] nature or human foundation" against which freedom can be judged or to which we might return if only 'repressive mechanisms' were removed so that "man can be reconciled with himself, once again find his nature or renew contact with his roots and restore a full and positive relationship with himself."[60] Rather for Foucault, self-formation always takes place in the condition of relations of power. Thus, he insists on thinking about '*practices* of freedom' rather than the work on the self being considered as a kind of liberation, as though a predetermined inner-self is being 'revealed' or 'set free.' In this sense, 'practices of freedom' are moral actions that construct the subject in freedom, both despite and because of the condition of ongoing practices of power.[61]

For Foucault, there can be no *a priori* notion of the subject, rather, the subject constitutes him/herself historically in different forms and by different practices in relation to different games of truth and applications of power. In this sense, the subject constitutes or invents him/herself in an active fashion. However, Foucault tirelessly stresses that these practices are never something that the individual invents by him/herself; they are patterns "suggested and imposed on him by his culture, his society and his social group."[62] Foucault, therefore, always returns to the idea that we constitute ourselves as free subjects only ever in the context of relationships of power. For Foucault, power is only ever a relationship, a "relationship in which one wishes to direct the behavior of another," whether this is a juridical relationship or a relationship of love, by material means, or by verbal communication.[63]

It is in this sense that the notions of 'governmentality' and 'government' come to play an important role in understanding the two currents in Foucault's work. For between 'games of power' and 'states of domination' stand the unfortunately termed 'governmental technologies.' In this context, for Foucault, the notion of 'governmentality' means to refer to:

> the totality of practices, by which one can constitute, define, organize, instrumentalize the strategies which individuals in their liberty can have in regard to each other. It is free individuals who try to control, to determine, to delimit the liberty of others and, in order to do that, they dispose of certain instruments to govern others. That rests indeed on freedom, on the relationship of self to self and the relationship to the other.[64]

For Foucault, governance and self-governance can only be understood in this mutually constitutive manner, a point he suggests we can trace back to Kant, who first established an internal connection between authority or obedience and freedom. For Foucault, an increase in freedom also leads to an increase of governmentality, for "the more that people are free in respect to each other, the greater the temptation on both sides to determine the conduct of others." As compared to the juridical concept of the subject, the notion of governmentality in Foucault's view "allows one ... to set off the freedom of the subject and the relationship to others, i.e., that which constitutes the very matter of ethics."[65]

In a late interview, Foucault therefore protests that an apparent contrast between his early and late writings has been exaggerated, and that what he has always been studying is the means of 'governing' the subject. In the final books on the history of sexuality he suggests that he intended to "show how governing the self is integrated in a practice of governing others," and that from his earliest to his latest work he has always been interested in the question of "how an 'experience' made up of relations to self and others is constituted."[66] The association of power only with its strategic dimension has therefore both circumvented and limited Foucault's own intersubjective-theoretic insight into power, and has dominated subsequent interpretations from those sympathetic to post-structuralism, as well as those working within the tradition of Critical Theory.

In this sense, contra Habermas and Honneth, it is not so much that Foucault does not consider any forms of interaction or intersubjectivity other than strategic ones, but rather to emphatically maintain that no relationship is completely free of power in the sense of the attempt to direct action, whether it be the attempt to effect recognition, even in relations of friendship or love.

For Foucault, the problem with Habermas' theory of communicative action is that he conceptualizes, even as an ideal, a "state of communication which would be such that the games of truth could circulate freely, without obstacles, without constraint and without coercive effects." This, says Foucault, "seems to me a Utopia. It is blind to the fact that relations of power are not something bad in themselves, from which one must free one's self."[67]

In other words, and following Foucault here, it can be argued that communicative relations always coexist within relations of power, that (mutual) recognition may only be enacted within the context of power relations and may also contain an element of strategic intent. Furthermore, it might be suggested that a normative notion of recognition cannot be directly tied to an originary ethical moment of intersubjectivity, but that the normativity of recognition might always exist within the context of power relations or strategic forms of interaction. It can also be argued that the attempt to enact recognition might simultaneously constitute normativity *and* an action-theoretic notion of power, if by 'power' we understand recognition as an attempt to determine that the actions of the other be affected in such a way that he or she is compelled to enact recognition.[68] According to this reading, recognition like linguistic communication is not neutral; it entails the ability to ensure the conduct of the other is changed, directed, or motivated in a particular way. In Foucault's interpretation, power, then, works both ways—it is an enabling relationship—not necessarily one of domination but rather of (en)action. The problem, then, is not to try to dissolve or separate power relations from recognitive-communicative relations, rather according to Foucault the problem is "to give one's self the rules of law, the techniques of management, and also the ethics, the *ethos*, the practice of self, which would allow these games of power to be played with a minimum of domination."[69]

It can therefore be argued that the power-theoretic insights contained in Foucault's work have important implications for Honneth's theory of recognition, particularly as they pertain to subject-formation and a theory of intersubjectivity, even in terms of its anthropological determination. These are implications that Honneth does not engage with in his early work, despite his initial interest in Foucault's struggle-theoretic notion of the social. Moreover, the insights contained in Foucault's genealogical critique in regard to contingency and indetermination challenge Honneth's notion of social progress understood in terms of the immanent expansion of ethical life and ever more inclusive forms of social recognition. Exchanges of recognition are fragile and uncertain, and recognition may be enacted in the context of relations of power as much as relations of freedom; recognition may not merely enact forms of positive affirmation but exchanges may involve compromises, negative constructions, or even maintain power relations.

In this sense, while many of Foucault's assumptions are at times one-sidely totalizing and problematic from the point of view of a normative critical social theory, his work does provide insights into a theory of action that recognizes, firstly, the contingency and fragility of human interaction and, secondly, the ways in which intersubjective 'recognition' is often fraught and imbricated in networks of power. The important point to consider is that, for Foucault, action is conceived prior to the recognition or affirmation of identity. Rather, it seems that action, freedom, and power imply one another and cannot be neatly separated.

In *The Critique of Power*, Honneth notes in closing that the task of critical social theory today is to develop an alternative version of a communicative theory of society that understands social organizations as "fragile constructions that remain dependent for their existence on the moral consensus of participants."[70] Although Honneth devotes his mature project to establishing the *morality* of recognition, one of the major questions in this reconstruction is whether or not he gives due consideration to the problem of grounding critical social theory on the fundamental presupposition of an undamaged notion of intersubjectivity; in other words, does he adequately account for the *fragility* of intersubjectivity. It is precisely this question that will be addressed in the following chapters.

3

Honneth's Intersubjectivist Reading of Hegel

Chapter Six

From the Contingency of Struggle to the Primacy of Recognition

In *The Struggle for Recognition*, Honneth begins to develop his own distinctive version of social philosophy, establishing the normative ground for a critical social theory on the basis of a theory of recognition, which is also considered the fundamental intersubjective basis for successful self-realization. Honneth therefore moves from the struggle-theoretic intuitions of Foucault presented in *The Critique of Power* to an intersubjective-theoretic interpretation of Hegel in *The Struggle for Recognition*. With his particular reading of Hegel, Honneth attempts to redefine the modern notion of freedom in thoroughly intersubjective terms, whereby freedom can only be understood and enacted in relation to an other. The concept of recognition that Honneth reconstructs from Hegel's work has an important double meaning: it is simultaneously able to account for both expanding conditions of individuation or self-realization *and* more encompassing forms of socialization and social institutions. This normative foundation is grounded anthropologically by undamaged intersubjective conditions, which provide the fundamental preconditions for undistorted identity-formation and self-realization, as well as the development of ethical life.

Central to an understanding of Honneth's move from Foucault to Hegel is a critical examination of the intersubjectively constituted philosophical anthropology that provides the foundation for his theory of recognition. The problem with this anthropological construction is not merely the fact that as some critics have noted, Honneth grounds the theory of recognition with recourse to a rather one-sided or 'positive' philosophical anthropology, but that intersubjectivity is reduced to only *one* of its forms or modalities.[1] One of the main problems with Honneth's attempt to draw a theory of recognition from Hegel's early work is that the terms 'intersubjectivity' and 'recognition' are mutually defining and used interchangeably without question.[2] The unfortunate consequence of this theoretical move is that intersubjectivity is equated with recognition *in toto*.

One of the aims of the following discussion is to uncover why this is a problematic equation and to trace the manner in which it becomes the foundational principle of Honneth's mature critical social theory. It will be argued here that this fusion or elision of conceptual categories begins with Honneth's reading and appropriation of Hegel in *The Struggle for Recognition*, but that it becomes even more pronounced once he moves to 're-actualize' Hegel's theory of recognition with recourse to the social psychology of G. H. Mead, and the psychoanalytic work of Donald Winnicott. Of equal importance will be to examine the way in which Honneth shifts from his studies of Foucault's account of struggle and power to a Hegelian-inspired notion of morally motivated struggle. In addition, then, to questioning how a (Jena) Hegelian-inspired notion of struggle and conflict differs from the Foucaultian one Honneth was originally pursuing in *The Critique of Power*, this chapter will also consider the consequences of a Hegelian-derived philosophical anthropology for a theory of intersubjectivity.

From the outset it is therefore important to note that for Honneth, the *concept* of recognition is one characterized by affirmative, reciprocal, or mutual recognition and is based on a "notion of an original intersubjectivity of human life."[3] In his interpretation of Hegel, Honneth conceptualizes mutual recognition as an originary condition, a pre-existing 'nexus' of ethical relations that constitutes the social. In this schema, struggle itself is not a (co-) constitutive condition but is in fact viewed "as a *disturbance and violation* of social relations of recognition."[4] In this way, Honneth posits 'recognition' as a primary, first-order category, constitutive of sociality and posits struggle as a secondary moment of transgression, or destruction of primary affirmative sociality. Honneth's presupposition is not only that human beings are inherently social but also that recognition forms a primary relationality that is prior to any other modality, a primary form of relationality that is always already positive or normative.[5] He thereby reconstructs Hegel's model of struggle as one motivated by 'moral impulses' rather than self-interest, fear, self-preservation, or power. With this move Honneth attempts to transform Foucault's notion of power/struggle into a concept of recognition/struggle, whereby recognition is conceived as the ethical ground of all sociality and conflict.

My argument is that Honneth's move is not entirely successful, and that important insights from the earlier work are lost in developing the foundations for a normative social theory based on Hegel's early work. The question that arises in this context is, therefore, what happens to the theory of power sketched in *The Critique of Power*, within the reconfigured notion of recognition/struggle in Honneth's later work? Does Honneth smuggle it into the couplet recognition/struggle without acknowledgement, or does he strip the 'struggle for recognition' of a theory of power by reconfiguring struggle and conflict in purely moral terms?

The following discussion will trace Honneth's reading of Hegel in terms of its primary purpose of establishing an 'originary notion of intersubjectivity.' It will seek to elucidate answers to these questions by tracing the movement of Honneth's own work as it unfolds in his reading of Hegel in *The Struggle for Recognition*. The reconstruction undertaken here has a double hermeneutical purpose. The aim is to provide an immanent reconstruction of Honneth's own reading of Hegel, while at the same time, offering a immanent counter-interpretation of Hegel's work. The purpose of this methodology is to indicate the ways in which Honneth offers a masterful but quite idiosyncratic reading of Hegel's work and to uncover insights contained in Hegel's work that Honneth overlooks in developing an intersubjective theory.

LOVE AND RELATIONALITY IN HEGEL'S EARLY JENA PHILOSOPHY

Among the characteristics that distinguish Honneth's interpretation of Hegel is that it is reconstructed in relation to very specific texts of the early Jena period, primarily the *System of Ethical Life* (1802/3), *First Philosophy of Spirit* (1803/4) and *Realphilosophie* (1805/6).[6] This focus entirely on texts written in Hegel's *early* years in Jena has important consequences, particularly as Honneth argues that Hegel's early Jena theory of recognition can and should be separated out from the project undertaken in the *Phenomenology* and beyond.

In *The Struggle for Recognition*, following Habermas, Honneth makes a strong distinction between the texts of the early and mature Hegel. Although Honneth shifts from this view in his later works, where he provides an intersubjective interpretation of the *Philosophy of Right*, even then he attempts to apply the intersubjective theory evident in the early Jena texts to his interpretation of the later work.[7] However, in *The Struggle for Recognition*, Honneth is at pains to emphasize that it is only in the early texts written at Jena, most notably in the *System of Ethical Life*, that Hegel offers a theory of the 'Absolute' or ethical life in intersubjective-social terms, before he turns in the later Jena years to a conception of the 'Absolute' as *'Geist'* with its associated 'metaphysical' and 'idealist-monological' connotations. Both Honneth and Habermas argue that in the early writings, Hegel presents an intersubjective concept of Spirit in which intersubjectivity is not merely viewed as an initial stage which is then sublated in Spirit's movement towards the Absolute, rather intersubjectivity *is formative of Spirit itself.*[8]

Moreover, Honneth is convinced, like Habermas before him, that by the time Hegel writes the later *Phenomenology of Spirit* (1807), he has entirely abandoned the intersubjective premises that showed such promise in the early Jena lecture notes, and that in his attempt to outline the journey of self-consciousness, the intersubjectivity-based theory becomes subsumed by Hegel's philosophy of the Subject. In other words, for Honneth, it is only in the early Jena work that Hegel offers a theory of intersubjectivity from the ground up, so to speak, as a primary rather than secondary category.

In seeking to establish a primary notion of intersubjectivity, like Ludwig Siep, Honneth fundamentally claims that 'love' rather than struggle is the structural core of recognition.[9] In *The Struggle for Recognition*, in articulating what he refers to as the 'structure' of recognition relations, Honneth makes the very strong claim that 'love' is "both *conceptually* and *genetically* prior to every other form of reciprocal recognition."[10] In this context, Honneth goes on to claim: "Hegel was … right to discern within [love] the structural core of all ethical life."[11] Moreover, this conceptualization of a primary form of 'affective' recognition as 'positive affirmation' is further confirmed in his more recent work *Reification*, where he outlines an ontology of 'affectivity' or 'primary affective attunement,' to which we will return below. The centrality of the notions of 'love' and 'affectivity' therefore remain at the core of Honneth's concept of recognition, which he then moves to combine with a theory of social struggle, now with recourse to Hegel's work rather than Foucault's.

Following Siep's lead, Honneth begins *The Struggle for Recognition* with a comparison between Hegel and the philosophies of Machiavelli and Hobbes. The importance of beginning with Hegel's debate with Hobbes is to highlight two distinct accounts of the social, and hence two quite divergent foundations for modern social philosophy. Honneth is particularly interested in establishing how Hegel offers a ground-breaking account not only of social and of political life, but also the appropriation of Hobbes' notion of social struggle as morally motivated struggle, as an immanent dialectical movement within ethical life. The main point of Honneth's discussion is to demonstrate the way in which Hegel is able to appropriate Hobbes' model of interpersonal struggle but in a way that turns it against its own atomistic presuppositions about 'human nature,' and thereby develop an alternative basis for social theory. In other words, it designates a shift from an individualistic based model to an intersubjective one, which is located in a moral order for which 'love' is the ultimate intersubjective ground. Consequently, while incorporating the notion of social struggle in his own work, Honneth argues that Hegel also reconstructs it as a moral category, not one compelled by self-interest or self-preservation.

In Honneth's view, Hegel's original achievement is to be able to bring together the classical notion of an ethical totality of society, inspired by the 'intersubjective' notion of the '*polis*' drawn from his reading of Aristotle and Plato, with a negative, agonistic process of development with the incorporation of the concept of 'struggle for recognition.' Therefore, the notion of ethical life that is developed through Hegel's early work is understood as the outcome of morally motivated interpersonal struggle and conflict, of recurring negations that expand the "moral potential inherent in 'natural ethical life.'"[12] Thus, in contrast to Hobbes and Machiavelli, Hegel is able to develop both a theory of the 'State' as immanently constituted rather than as an externally imposed institution that establishes social order, *prevents* conflict, and legitimates sovereign power. So too, ethical life is self-constituting, developing from within an intersubjectively constituted lifeworld and integrated by what Hegel terms '*Sitte*,' 'mores' and 'customs,' or for Honneth moral 'attitudes' that are 'acted out intersubjectively.'[13] Therefore, where Hobbes fundamentally rejects Aristotle's conception of humans as naturally social beings, Hegel instead begins with a philosophically inspired notion of an organic and ethical whole. Honneth understands Hegel to mean by this an ontological substance or ethical social fabric, and particularly emphasizes the Aristotelian nature of Hegel's organic conception of ethical life, as well as the search for a unifying principle, which Hegel at this stage identifies with love.[14]

Hegel's influences during his early Jena period are multiple and complex, and include the work of Aristotle and Plato, English political economy, Hölderlin, Fichte, Schelling, and the looming shadow of Kant with and against whom Hegel's work constantly moves. Both Hölderlin and Schelling provided Hegel with a means of articulating the notion of a primary unity underlying all relations, not just between subjects, but also between subject and object.[15] The division between subject and object then already presupposes an original unity or holism in which oppositions are already united, a primordial *relatedness*. Inspired by Hölderlin, and in a critique of Kant, Hegel begins to conceptualize a 'unifying force,' or 'being,' that unites the Kantian oppositions between form and content, concept and intuition, subject and object, nature and freedom, "in such a way that each remains what it is yet merges with the other in inseparable unity."[16] Initially, for Hegel, following Hölderlin, this 'unifying force,' which is posited as the highest ideal of a free life, is 'love.' 'Love' is a 'principle of unification' that is posited as an alternative to both Kant's 'transcendental unity of apperception' and Fichte's 'absolute ego,' with its separation and positing of an 'Absolute I' as the ultimate ground for the 'Not-I.'[17] While providing a metaprinciple for the synthesis of opposites,[18] in Hegel's formulation, 'love' "cannot be grasped by the understanding," and it "cannot be commanded."[19] For Hegel, the "opposition of duty to inclination has found its unification in the modifications of love."[20]

Thus, from the first *Fragments on Love* and the *Spirit of Christianity*, we see 'love' becomes the central unifying concept in Hegel's thought. As Henrich explains: "Once Hegel adopted the concept of love as the basic principle of his thinking, the system came forth without interruption."[21] However, as Henrich suggests, 'love' was later replaced by the notion of 'life,' and later in *The Phenomenology* with that of Spirit [*Geist*] with its much broader and richer implications, where Hegel also begins to formulate the Absolute as "substance that is also Subject."[22] In this way, Hegel draws deeply on Hölderlin's notion of unification through love but makes it his own as a means of conceptualizing 'life.'[23]

However, as Henrich maintains, Hegel did not simply adopt Hölderlin's unification philosophy of love *in toto*, and the differences between the two are instructive. Hegel's conception of 'being' or 'totality,' even when he employs the term 'love' to encapsulate this unity, does not assume a sense of 'original being' or 'primordial unity'; it is not posited as a origin to which we hope to return. Hegel does not, then, conceive of a totality that precedes opposition, rather unification *is the very relation itself.* As Henrich explains: "This is Hegel's distinctive idea, that the *relata* in opposition must, to be sure derive from a whole. However, the whole is only the developed and explicit concept of the *relata* themselves."[24]

In comparison, a duality operates in Hölderlin's thought whereby 'love' is the unifying force *both* to a lost origin or primordial unity (the 'infinite') as well as the *telos* or desire for unification with the finite. However, for Hegel 'love' is conceived merely as "the unification of subject and object."[25] Thus, as Henrich so well encapsulates: "Hegel must constantly conceive all structures which Hölderlin understood as deriving from original Being, as *modes of relation which coalesce. The event of coalescence itself, and not a ground out of which coalescence derives,* is for Hegel the true absolute, the 'all in all.'"[26] Moreover, Hegel conceives of the unity as the *relata* of oppositions in terms of a movement or 'unfolding' that is future orientated, and already in the writings on Christianity, where we see him employ the idea of spirit for the first time, he introduces a notion of historicity and worldliness with the notions of 'fate' and 'tragedy.'[27] At the time of writing the *System of Ethical Life*, Hegel further conceptualizes this sense of unfolding unity or conflict between oppositions in terms of a notion of 'productivity.' In this sense, upon his arrival in Jena, Hegel's work also expresses the influence of Schelling's philosophy of nature and he begins to employ Schelling's notion of 'potencies' or 'levels' ['*Potenzen*'][28] as a means of conceptualizing various forms of opposition in 'relation,' and to conceptualize the development towards unification as a series of stages or dialectical movement towards 'Absolute Ethical Life.'

However, in the first part of *The Struggle for Recognition*, Honneth is less concerned with a detailed analysis of Hegel scholarship or with an exegetical account of Hegel's texts, and more intent on articulating his own social philosophy and notion of primary intersubjectivity. In this sense, Honneth leans quite heavily on the Aristotelian elements in his interpretation of Hegel as he begins to fashion the notion of an 'originary intersubjectivity' that becomes the cornerstone of his work.

Honneth begins his textual reconstruction of Hegel's early work with an analysis of the essay on *Natural Law* written in 1802/3, and published in the *Critical Journal of Philosophy*, that Hegel co-edited and co-wrote with Schelling.[29] Hegel is critical of the presuppositions in theories of 'natural law' that begin from a conception of human nature that presuppose that the individual is primary and prior to the social. From this presupposition, Hobbes conceives as 'natural' a state of affairs which posits that isolated and atomistic individuals can only form society by means of externally constructed institutions and laws, rather than conceiving of sociability itself as a natural state that immanently and simultaneously expands capacities for individualization *and* socialization. As mentioned above, Hegel questions not only the atomistic conception that characterizes the social theory of Hobbes but also equally the forms of transcendentally derived moral law that he associates with both Kant and Fichte, whereby practical reason is separated from human need and inclination. Hegel considers problematic all conceptions of natural law that are based on either antagonistic anthropological or formal transcendental presuppositions because they can only ever conceive of the social as an aggregate of isolated or egotistic individuals, not as a moral unity.

In contrast, Hegel at this stage in his work, is able to infuse the 'philosophy of unification' by which he has constructed a concept of ethical totality, with an intersubjective political and institutional model, adopted from the model of the city-states of antiquity from his reading of Plato and Aristotle.[30] Both Plato and Aristotle conceptualize the polis in organicistic terms, "where the whole cares for each part and each lives for the whole."[31]

It is also fair to say that the essay on *Natural Law* bears Schelling's influence, where Hegel conceptualizes his own version of Schelling's 'philosophy of nature' in terms of the 'Aether,' that 'primordial matter' or 'absolute being' which is not merely 'mirrored' in individual subjects but is "of the very essence of the individual, just as much as the aether which permeates nature is the inseparable essence of the configurations of nature … is not separate in any of them."[32] In this way, Honneth claims that Hegel is able to construct a counter-model to the Hobbesian concept of social life as 'the unified many,' as an aggregate of isolated individuals, with a model that develops sociability from an ethical substratum or original substance that develops dialectically to form a more expansive ethical whole.[33] This is what Hegel is referring to, suggests Honneth, when he quotes Aristotle in the essay on *Natural Law*, pronouncing that: "The Nation [*Volk*] comes by nature

before the individual. If the individual in isolation is not anything self-suffi-
cient, he must be related to the whole nation in one unity, just as the other
parts are to their whole."[34] Honneth therefore considers Hegel to be articulating an Aristotelian derived notion of ethical life unified in a primordial
ethical substratum or substance.

However, where Hegel conceives this totality as a relationality and movement between universal and particular, state and individual, subject and object, Honneth interprets and reconstructs Hegel's early works solely in strong
intersubjectivist terms as a theory of recognition. This reading is quite an
extrapolation from the letter of Hegel's own texts, and as we will question
later, it is not clear that such a strong intersubjectivist reading can be substan-
tiated. The 'holistic' picture offered in many of Hegel's early pronouncements is also at times difficult to reconcile with the strong intersubjective
theory that Honneth reads into the text. It is evident as we discussed above
that Hegel's notion of unification should be distinguished from Hölderlin's
notion of 'Being' and is grounded in what Henrich has described as the very
'coalescence of relation.' However, this 'coalescence of relation' cannot be
reduced to interpersonal relations between subjects defined as recognition
alone, nor does it refer to a form of originary intersubjectivity or lost unity.
Rather, as I shall discuss further below, Hegel can be read to offer a more
multidimensional theory of relationality and intersubjectivity that need not be
reduced to the primacy of recognition as a first-order category, nor to strictly
interpersonal relations. Nonetheless, it is within these central pages of his
interpretation of Hegel that Honneth begins to fashion a deep ontological
notion of 'originary intersubjectivity' that becomes the founding idea of his
own theory. Here we can read into Honneth's interpretation of Hegel a clear
outline of the founding philosophical principle that encapsulates his own
theory:

> ...every philosophical theory of society must proceed not from the acts of
> isolated subjects but rather from the framework of ethical bonds within which
> subjects *always already* move. Thus, contrary to atomistic theories of society,
> one is able to assume, a kind of *natural basis for human socialization*, a
> situation in which *elementary forms of co-existence are always present*.[35]

In asserting this statement of his own position, Honneth moves from a discussion of the essay on *Natural Law* to the text that is to become central to
his own formulation of a theory of recognition as originary intersubjectivity.
Having attempted to establish that Hegel's social philosophy is founded on
an Aristotelian inspired notion of a pre-existing ethical social fabric in which
subjects are always situated, Honneth now moves to fundamentally connect
this structure to the notion of recognition. With this fundamental move, we
see Honneth diverge from simply establishing a theory of intersubjectivity in

the more promising mode of Hegel's early work as simply a theory of 'relatedness' and instead make an irreducible link between recognition/intersubjectivity. Honneth's interpretation immediately bestows upon intersubjectivity a pre-given ethical content or determinate form as a *particular type* of intersubjectivity—it assumes a taken-for-granted ethical or normative foundation built into the very fact of relatedness or intersubjectivity as a kind of primordial unity. Thus, rather than forms of intersubjectivity being conceived as all those modes of interaction that precede recognition, recognition is understood by Honneth as a primary category, conceived as first nature.

To make this structural and conceptual connection between intersubjectivity and recognition, Honneth moves to the *System of Ethical Life* (1802/3), written at about the same time as the *Natural Law* essay, where he suggests Hegel is more able to articulate exactly what form this inherent ethical potential must take if it is to be presumed to 'always already' exist within the structure of intersubjective relations. Moreover, Honneth argues, Hegel also needs to explain further exactly how agonistic processes actually contribute to the expansion of ethical social bonds, rather than their diminishment. Honneth claims that Hegel is able to accomplish this dual task only once he renounces his earlier critical stance towards Fichte, and moves to rework Fichte's theory of recognition for his own purposes.[36]

For Honneth, the *System of Ethical Life* is the pivotal text in which Hegel moves to address the issues arising from the above-mentioned combination of Hobbesian, Aristotelian, and Fichtean themes. The manuscript, which Hegel himself left untitled and unfinished, is the earliest surviving draft of Hegel's 'Identity-System.'[37] One of the unique aspects of the text besides it Schellingesque form is that in direct contrast to Hobbes, it depicts a realm of 'natural' or pre-State ethics that is not repeated again in Hegel's later work. This latter aspect is central to Honneth's interpretation and reconstruction of an anthropological account of 'recognition' and an ontological conceptualization of ethical intersubjectivity in Hegel's work.

HEGEL'S *SYSTEM OF ETHICAL LIFE*

The *System of Ethical Life* is divided into three sections: (1) Absolute Ethical Life on the Basis of Relation; (2) The Negative, or Freedom, or Transgression; (3) [Absolute] Ethical Life [*Sittlichkeit*]. Hegel begins the *System of Ethical Life* by establishing that his aim is to develop in systematic terms what he considers to be the 'inner truth' and essence of 'Absolute Ethical Life' or *Sittlichkeit*. He does this using a mixture of methodological principles drawn from Schelling and somewhat Kantian inspired terminology, as a series of three 'stages' or 'levels' [*Potenzen*][38] of dialectical movement or 'subsumption' between what he terms 'intuition' and 'concept.' Within each of the three sections, (although this is less obvious in the second section), there is also a series of subdivisions or internal 'levels' indicative of an internal progression. Each section is therefore also organized internally as a series of reciprocal movements or 'subsumptions' between 'intuition' and 'concept,' and between various '*Potenzen*,' or 'stages.' Hegel begins by stating it thus: "Knowledge of the Idea of the absolute ethical order depends entirely on the establishment of perfect adequacy between intuition and concept, because the Idea itself is nothing other than the identity of the two."[39]

However, for Hegel, ethical life is not merely the *relation* between 'intuition' and 'concept,' or 'particular' and 'universal,' or between 'subject' and 'object' but rather their synthesis into a unified whole. Furthermore, for Hegel, the 'Ideal' of Ethical Life "is not transcendent…but is the inner truth and essence of reality."[40] In order to reach the level of 'Absolute Ethical Life' the subsumption of 'intuition' and 'concept' must move through a series of embryonic forms of ethical 'relation,' of unifying moments and negations before their synthesis is complete. Therefore in the first instance, Hegel examines (a) the concept subsumed under intuition, and (b) intuition subsumed under concept. However, ethical life understood only as a series of 'relations' based on opposites is incomplete. As Hegel wishes to demonstrate both these understandings of ethical life are inadequate. They both presume a split between 'universal' and 'particular' whereby one of the *relata* remains always dominant to the other, where one is always subsumed by the other. For Hegel, this ends in a series of lifeless abstractions with no unifying 'spiritual bond.'[41]

In the first level of the text, 'Absolute Ethical Life on the basis of Relation,' Hegel begins the dialectical movement between 'concept and 'intuition,' not with subject/subject relations but with the subject/object relation, a factor that Honneth overlooks. The first level of the text is conceived as 'natural ethical life,' and within the schema borrowed from Schelling is conceptualized as the 'subsumption of concept under intuition.'[42] The *System of Ethical Life* therefore begins with the individual subject as 'naturally determined,' as a sensuous being conditioned by need, desire, and enjoyment. Hegel here initially relates 'intuition' to feeling, and conceives of this initial level as the level of 'practice,' depicting the active subject purely in relation to the objects of his/her environment and the attempt to address basic need. The subject is primarily 'driven' by desire and enjoyment the paradigms of which Hegel states are "eating and drinking."[43] Here then, notably, Hegel does not begin his text with intersubjective relations, but as with the texts that follow the *System of Ethical Life*, with the existence of the individual in his/her sensuous desiring state in relation to the consumption of objects. Although not yet couched in the language of consciousness as with the later Jena texts, the primary form of relation is nonetheless depicted initially as a relation between subject and object, a relation that can only be unified in

Hegel's schema, by the annihilation or destruction of the object in the satisfaction of need whereby the subject is the 'subsuming power.'

In addition to 'need' at this level there is also a second form of 'practical intuition,' associated with the 'possession' of objects—that of 'labor'—which Hegel conceives as the 'subsumption of intuition under concept.' 'Labor' is distinguished from basic need by means of the 'tool,' which introduces a 'universalizing' element into the relation between subject/object, and distinguishes human from animal desire. Labor signifies that immediate desire is suspended and that gratification is delayed enabling 'possession' rather than immediate annihilation.[44] Labor, then moves individuals to become 'social creatures' and to mutually shape one another and their environment, through both the laboring process and through formative educative processes or '*Bildung*.'[45] Thus, for Hegel, 'labor' represents an 'absolute exchanging' whereby every subject "makes its particularity into universality", and this represents the first dialectical movement between universal and particular.[46] So, it might be said that the subject's first experience of itself and of the world is in fact formed in relation with objects and although 'socialized' through the transformation of desire and need in labor, is not strictly grounded in primary relations of recognition. Within the stage of 'Natural Ethical Life,' the subject is understood to move through a series of relations with objects, until in a third level he/she leaves the level of natural determination and enters what Hegel depicts as the first form of social relation.

As Whitebook notes, though, this means that 'desire,' which he argues has the connotation of a 'drive' or 'carnal phenomenon,' appears before the specifically human desire to be recognized by another. This indicates that Hegel intended to demonstrate "how the specifically human form of desire emerges out of an initial biological appetitive striving," and cannot be understood as a taken-for-granted phenomenon.[47] That is, the desire for recognition is not primary, rather the individual is 'educated' to social sociability, so to speak, out of his/her initial interactions with objects, and the frustration caused by the constant annihilation of the object in the cycle of need and the satisfaction of need. In this sense, Whitebook suggests, Hegel is neither a theorist of "first nature nor of second nature, but of the transition of the former into the latter."[48]

However, instead Honneth posits recognition as a primary, first-order category and begins his exegesis only at the point where *intersubjective relations* are first conceptualized by Hegel in relations of 'love.' It is at this point that Honneth begins his reconstruction of Hegel's text, without acknowledging the first forms of 'relation' between subject and object that are primary to Hegel's text, and this has important consequences for the assumption central to his work that humans are intrinsically recognitively sociable and ethical. As Honneth is only interested in the forms of interpersonal social relationality as *mutual* recognition, he also focuses his reconstruction almost entirely on the first and second 'levels' of the text, and mostly leaves to one side a discussion of the third level of 'Absolute Ethical Life' and the State. Moreover, as Honneth is only interested in identifying the theory of intersubjectivity as recognition that he reads into the text, he abstracts completely from the epistemological and methodological framework in which Hegel's philosophical presentation is based, arguing that the social-philosophical content of the text can be extracted and disconnected from its methodological context.[49] In Honneth's intersubjectivist rendering of the *System of Ethical Life*, he suggests Hegel begins by offering a counter-image to Hobbes' *Leviathan*, that is "not with a struggle of all against all" but with a philosophical account of "elementary forms of interpersonal recognition."[50] Honneth begins his reconstruction of Hegel, therefore, at the very first point in the text at which recognition is introduced. It is here that we encounter forms of relationality within the 'family' and 'love' between the sexes, and it is also within this level that we encounter 'language' for the first time.

Hegel continues to conceptualize this form of socialization as a 'relation' that is only relative, in terms of 'feeling as subsumption of concept under intuition.' Hegel's own presentation of the first form of social relations is very specific, and takes the form of the institution of the 'family.' This initial form of recognition consists of 'the sexes who are constituted in difference': although they are constituted in 'relation,' "one [is] the universal, the other particular; they are not yet equal."[51] For Hegel, this relation, "this being of oneself in another" therefore belongs to 'nature,' not ethical life. It is an 'ideality of nature' that "remains in inequality and therefore in desire in which one side is determined as something subjective and the other as something objective."[52] Therefore, 'love' between the two sexes for Hegel is an inadequate form of 'relation' that is not yet unified and properly 'ethical.' The 'difference' between the sexes in the love relation is only unified and mediated through the 'externalization' of their relationship in a child. It is only through the mediating third term of the child that Hegel conceives that individual subjects assume 'absolute identity' with one another, and by which their "unity therefore [becomes] real immediately"; they become "one—a living substance."[53]

Furthermore, it is in the 'labor' of raising and educating children that the family as a unit is seen to develop beyond the basic cycle of need and the satisfaction of need. It is in the relationality of the family members as a unity that represents for Hegel the first form of 'natural ethical life,' that moves beyond mere 'intuition' to 'concept.' This movement from 'feeling' to 'thought' in the educative process of children is, however, not conceptualized in terms of mutual recognition as such.[54] Rather, for Hegel: "This is the real rationality of nature wherein the difference between the sexes is completely extinguished, and both are absolutely one—a living substance."[55] Thus for Hegel, the concept of 'love' presented here has moved beyond the idea of love represented in the earlier *Fragments on Love* as "a miracle, that we cannot grasp," and now becomes a 'rational' form of relationality that is expressed and unified in the labor of educating or socializing the child to humanity.[56] Therefore, although the child is a social creature, he/she is not born into a state of desiring recognition but must be educated to sociability and ethical life.

In contrast, Honneth understands this primary form of intersubjectivity between both sexes, and between parents and children, as a form of socialization that enables the developing 'individualization' of subjects through the reciprocal recognition of "each other ... as living emotionally needy beings."[57] Honneth therefore already reads Hegel here through a particular psychoanalytic, more precisely, Winnicottian lens, whereby individuals are assumed to have a predisposition to mutuality and ethical intersubjectivity, rather than conceiving it as the end result of a learning process.

Importantly, Honneth suggests this initial form of recognition, which he later develops as providing the necessary social environment for individuals to develop the basic self-confidence and successful relation-to-self they need, is a crucial first phase of recognition that must be experienced for subjects to be able to participate in public life. However, this is not a claim or formulation that can be found in Hegel's own text. For as we have seen, Hegel conceptualizes the expansion or development of ethical life as a series of 'levels' or 'stages' indicative of a dialectical movement between 'concept' and 'intuition.' Rather, Hegel merely points out, as he had done in his study on the *Spirit of Christianity*, that 'property' (as a form of exchange) cannot be easily reconciled with the same kind of relationality as that represented by the 'private' relations of the family. He merely points out the different forms of 'relating' or 'relatedness,' but does not bestow any necessary precondition between the different experiences of 'relatedness' expressed by 'love' and 'law.'

Therefore, within Section One of *System of Ethical Life*, entitled "Absolute Ethical Life on the basis of Relation," we also encounter a second level, Part B: "Infinity and Ideality in Form or in Relation" which is still conceptualized as a form of 'natural ethical life.' Here Hegel moves to a discussion of property and possession, both in relation to ownership of property and as the result of 'surplus' labor, and the expanded interaction *between* families as social units. At this level, we see the emergence of institutional arrangements necessary for shared common life, although these are still considered by Hegel to be forms of 'natural ethical life' and not yet fully established political and institutional forms of the State. It is within this second level that is further divided into a series of 'subsumptions' or dialectical movements, that recognition is mentioned for the second time within the text, as the basis of legal 'right.' Here, 'property,' 'possession,' and labor in the context of public life is mediated by legal right, and the economic system of 'value' and 'exchange,' expressed in the 'abstract equality of things,' is mediated by 'contract,' both of which are underwritten by formal, mutual recognition.[58]

Whereas the first form of interpersonal recognition is characterized in Honneth's terms by 'affectivity' and individual need, the second form is based on 'legal right' and the universalization of mutual recognition through the abstract relation represented in contract and exchange. The particularity of the family is now superseded by the public interaction between family units, or their (male) individual representatives. The concept of 'legal right' requires an *a priori* underlying trust in relations of mutual recognition. The 'ideal' of possession itself can only be realized by mutual recognition of the other's 'right' to own or possess goods and property. However, as Honneth explains, Hegel still considers legal relations as merely a form of 'natural' as compared to 'absolute' ethical life because it is still characterized by 'the principle of singularity.' That is, legal relations represent a form of sociality whereby individuals are integrated "only abstractly via negative liberties, that is merely on the basis of their ability to [accept or] negate social offers" of exchange and contract.[59] Therefore, as Honneth reconstructs it, although legal relations represent a universalistic form of social integration, relations of right provide only a 'formal' and 'empty' notion of freedom that cannot provide intersubjective recognition of the particularities of the individual subject.[60]

However, there is a third sub-level within this Second Part that Hegel differentiates as 'the level of indifference,' that mediates between the previous two levels of (a) property/possession and surplus labor on the basis of legal relations; and (b) abstract relations based on value, exchange, freedom, and contract.[61] This sub-level concerns the relation between members of social classes within the broader context of the social division of labor and embryonic forms of political community. Furthermore, Hegel distinguishes the two previous sub-levels as characterized by individuals as 'property owners' or possessors of 'things'; they are recognized in relation to their 'possessions' in their capacity as right-bearing individuals. In the third sub-level, by comparison, the individual is recognized as a 'human being' as such, not only in relation to his or her possessions. Therefore, "[j]ust as he was recognized previously only as possessing single things, so now he is recognized as existing independently in the whole." Thus, Hegel means to say that the individual is now recognized as "absolute abstraction" as a "person" and as a "living being."[62]

In other words identified outside legal relations of property the individual is now considered as "absolute subjectivity." However, as 'absolute concept' the 'person' also exists as a free being, and Hegel suggests that being conditioned by freedom, the individual can just as easily be posited in terms of "non-recognition."[63] In the condition of recognition, therefore, Hegel at this point also introduces a concept of 'power' as a form of relation: "At this [level] a living individual confronts a living individual, but their power of life is unequal. Thus one is might or power over the other. One is indifference, while the other is [fixed] in difference."[64] For Hegel this form of relation, like recognition, is still a 'relative' one, not yet an 'absolute' one or unified in 'Absolute Ethical Life.' It is also within this context that Hegel for the first time discusses the relation of 'lordship and bondage.' Hegel explains, "This relation in which the indifferent and free has power over the different is the relation of lordship and bondage [Service]."[65] For Hegel, 'lordship' and 'service' arise whenever there is a 'plurality' of individuals: it is "the very concept of the plurality relation." And, on this count, Hegel claims such a relation is 'natural' because this is the manner in which individuals initially 'confront one another' as 'persons' in their particularity.[66]

However, in the dialectical movement of the text, the levels of 'personhood' and 'inequality' and 'power' are also eventually mediated by the relational unity of the 'family' as a whole. Coming almost full circle then, the family is considered to be both the 'unit' in which individuality exists between household members as 'persons,' and also the 'unifying' element between them. In this way, Hegel suggests that in the relationship between 'families,' which he envisages as being united in the '*Volk*,' the "forgoing particularity is transferred in the family into the universal."[67]

Whereas Hegel from this point moves to the above-mentioned discussion of a third sub-level and a discussion of social class, power, and recognition of an individual as 'a living human being' based solely on a subject's 'personhood,' Honneth instead abstracts from Hegel's text at this point and moves to the middle section on "The Negative, or Freedom, or Transgression" to discuss Hegel's interpretation of 'crime.' Honneth's method for working backwards against Hegel's text is partly motivated by an attempt to overcome the schematic presentation of Hegel's work and also to try to reconstruct the logic of Hegel's presentation. However, this reading also lends itself more suitably to Honneth's own methodological purpose, which is to extract a third form of recognition based on the notion of 'honor' from within Hegel's discussion of 'crime,' and to make clear how acts of 'crime' and 'punishment' assume and reveal a pre-existing form of 'undamaged intersubjectivity.' Honneth argues: "there is good reason to believe that Hegel granted criminal acts a constructive role in the formative process of ethical life because they were able to unleash the conflict that for the first time, would make subjects aware of underlying relations of recognition."[68] In other words, for Honneth, Hegel's discussion of crime demonstrates the normativity that underpins all social life, including pathological forms of relationality or interaction.

Hence, where Hegel in the *System of Ethical Life* includes a discussion of 'power,' Honneth leaves this modality of relation out of his discussion of Hegel's text, and moves to a discussion of a third form of recognition in relation to Hegel's discussion of 'crime' and criminal acts as a response to a lack of 'honor,' or 'inadequate recognition' in terms of an individual's specific traits and abilities. As a consequence, Honneth leaves power out of the equation and only makes an explicit link between recognition/struggle in his discussion of crime, and of intersubjective relations of recognition not of power-oriented ones. Henceforth, Honneth speaks only of 'inadequate' or 'unsatisfactory recognition' but not power. Honneth's avoidance of a theory of power in this context means that he conceives subject-formation and intersubjectivity in overly normativized terms from the ground up, as *a priori* relations of recognition.

In contrast to Honneth, though, the very interesting point that arises, if we follow the progression of Hegel's text as outlined above, is that Hegel in fact conceptualizes *both* 'recognition' and 'power' (on the same level of 'Natural Ethical Life') as forms of 'relation,' both of which are considered only 'relative' and 'natural' forms of interrelatedness. In comparison to the 'abstract' and 'ideal' notion of equality established in legal recognition, Hegel states that the relation of "lordship and bondage ... is immediately and absolutely established along with the inequality of the power of life ... in reality what we have is shape and individuality and appearance, and consequently difference of power (*Potenz*) and might."[69] Both forms of relation are considered inadequate because neither yet represents 'Absolute' or 'unified' forms of ethical life. In other words, from the perspective of our discussion and in contrast to Honneth's reconstruction of Hegel, 'power' is not excluded from Hegel's own discussion of natural forms of 'relation' and recognition, nor is it considered pathological.

THE NEGATIVE, CRIME AND RECOGNITION

However, wanting to avoid associating recognition with power, and the 'lordship/bondage' relation, Honneth instead moves to an analysis of 'crime' and recognition. In his interpretation, Honneth relies upon a reading and explanation of 'crime' taken from Hegel's earlier Frankfurt texts, namely, those collected in the *Early Theological Writings*. He argues that in the Frankfurt texts, Hegel conceived of criminal acts as reactions to the "abstract and one-sided form of relationality in legal relations."[70] Honneth suggests that a connection can be made between criminal acts and the previous stage of natural ethical life because each form of conflict is interpreted as a negative response to the abstract freedom that subjects had previously been granted in legal relations of recognition. Therefore, Honneth argues that Hegel's understanding of the 'criminal act' in the *Early Theological Writings* can be interpreted as a response to the fact that the individual is integrated only negatively into the collective life of society as subjects of abstract right.

In other words, Honneth presumes that what Hegel is actually suggesting in the *System of Ethical Life* is that the motivation for the criminal to act 'negatively' can only be understood as the experience of not being adequately recognized. The feeling of being only 'negatively integrated' into society, therefore, already presupposes a notion of 'incomplete recognition' as the motivating source for 'criminal' acts. Honneth therefore suggests that we can only make sense of the *System of Ethical Life* if we read it through the frame of the earlier Frankfurt Writings. Although this connection is not made in the *System of Ethical Life* itself, Honneth suggests that we can read a connection between 'crime' and 'recognition' in the same way in which 'crime' is depicted in the *Early Theological Writings* as demonstrating the individual's relation to an ethical whole. Honneth claims that there is no other way of understanding the logic of Hegel's 1802/3 text if we do not understand the middle section on 'crime' or 'transgression' as a model for depicting the way in which individuals are inadequately or negatively integrated into the community and thereby as presupposing forms of mutual recognition. In this reading, individuals who commit acts of 'crime' consider themselves to be inadequately or only negatively recognized, and by way of conflict or struggle, leave the state of existing recognition relations, in order to have their individual identity more adequately recognized, returning to the community (in the act of the 'crime' being 'punished') in a form of reintegration which occurs only by means of expanded and more encompassing recognition relations for both assailant and victim.

Honneth does, however, admit that Hegel does not provide the same arguments about the motivational source for criminal acts in relation to legal relations in the *System of Ethical Life*, in the manner that he suggests can be found in the *Early Theological Writings*. In this sense, it is purely an extrapolation to suggest that the account of conflict and relationality in the chapter on 'The Negative' in the *System of Ethical Life* can in fact be completely attributed to a reaction vis-à-vis established relations of recognition.

Nonetheless, Honneth suggests that if we map this reading on to the 1802 text, we can compensate for Hegel's neglect to provide a reason for the motivation behind 'criminal acts,' and can thereby "trace the emergence of crime to conditions of incomplete recognition."[71] In this way, for Honneth, 'criminal acts' as depicted in the *System of Ethical Life* have a two-fold potential for learning: (1) Through their destructive acts subjects come to know more about their own distinctive identity; (2) In the same way, subjects also learn of their mutual dependence and their reliance on recognition relations as the basis for ethical life. Honneth, therefore, concludes that social conflict contains "a moral-practical potential for learning."[72] This account reduces crime purely to a pathology of recognition, and neglects to consider the multitude of other motivational factors contributing to crime, including negative feelings, revenge, resentment, and power. Crime is depicted in almost functionalist terms, merely as the means by which originary relations of recognition are revealed, as a 'disturbance' of already existing recognition relations.

Moreover, Honneth's reading also reduces Hegel's middle chapter to an account of only one form of struggle or conflict, that of 'crime' as it emerges within the context of legal/property relations, although these relations are, as we have seen above, not yet state sanctioned and are still considered by Hegel to be forms of 'natural ethical life.' In this reading, Honneth reads *all* the various 'negative acts of destruction' that Hegel depicts through the prism of mutual recognition, and thereby suggests that all forms of 'crime' depicted indicate that the motivation for acts of crime can be traced back to 'incomplete forms of recognition.'[73]

The forms of 'negative' interaction Hegel discusses in the intermediate chapter are divided into three levels: (a) includes 'havoc' or barbarism, physical harm, annihilation, or destruction, (b) refers to legal relations between property owners and refers to acts of theft and robbery, and (c) includes interpersonal struggles for 'glory' or 'honor,' the relation of lordship and bondage, oppression and murder, revenge, battle, duel, war, and slavery, or 'service.' In Honneth's reading the first form of negative interaction Hegel mentions in Level (a) 'acts of destruction and 'annihilation' do not seem to make sense within the aforementioned schema of recognition relations. That is, acts of annihilation only make sense upon Honneth's reading because they occur "outside the social condition of legally recognized freedom."[74] Therefore because such 'negative' acts do not fit the model of responding to previously established forms of recognition, Honneth can only perceive Hegel's intent to mean that they must occur only where legal relations of recognition do not exist. Furthermore, Honneth points out that, for Hegel, such acts or forms of interaction are not properly considered to be crimes at all, because 'crime' is defined only in relation to negative forms of interaction that occur where there is a presupposition of legal relations of mutual recognition. Honneth is therefore more interested in the second form of 'negative' interaction mentioned in Level (b) in regard to theft between property owners, and bases his account of crime more precisely beginning at this point, where legal relations are more explicitly described by Hegel as being understood as recognition relations.

Initially, then, what Honneth terms 'crime' in his reconstruction of Hegel refers to 'theft' or 'robbery' between property owners, where legal relations have already been established and recognized.[75] In an act of theft of property, Hegel suggests that it is not the 'object' that is injured in the act of theft, rather it is the individual property owner who is injured when something in 'his' possession has been stolen. In such an act the individual qua property owner is said to be injured in 'his' entirety as a 'person.' Importantly, this is the place at which Honneth suggests the first account of 'struggle' occurs in the *System of Ethical Life*. It is within the context of 'personal injuries' of property theft, which at this stage occur outside a state-sanctioned legal and penal system, that subjects respond to defend themselves and hence a struggle ensues between victim and assailant.[76] At this point a subject's only 'appropriate response' to the threat or injury of theft is to defend himself against the assailant. Hence, what ensues, as the injured party's form of resistance towards the perpetrator, suggests Honneth, is the "first sequence of actions that Hegel explicitly calls a 'struggle.'"[77] Honneth describes this form of interaction, of struggle between 'persons,' as defined by their rights-bearing status. The result of the struggle must end in the favor of the victim whose entire identity is considered to be at stake in the struggle, whereas the assailant has only risked his personal interest. It is by way of struggle in the context of theft, or 'crime,' that for Honneth has a two-fold function in relation to recognition: firstly, it brings to light underlying recognition relations upon which the system of property relations is founded, and therefore of the recognitive relations of social life more generally; secondly, it is the vehicle by which subjects articulate their unmet claims of identity, and hence is a form of 'mediated agonism' which provides the catalyst for expanding recognition relations.

However, 'theft' is only one form of conflict or transgression in Hegel's schema. Honneth moves from a discussion of what he terms 'crime' in the context of property relations to a discussion of what he identifies as a third form of social conflict explicitly extracted from Hegel's text—that of the 'struggle for honor'—and it is in this way that he constructs the third form of recognition-relation that completes his three-tiered model of recognition. Hegel's own discussion in the third part of the chapter on 'The Negative' is wide-ranging and discusses numerous responses to forms of interaction that result from battles over honor. As commentators such as Siep have suggested, this is the 'Hobbesian' moment in Hegel's work where he incorporates conflicts or struggles over 'glory' into his overall schema. Siep suggests that the struggle for honor depicted in Hegel's *System of Ethical Life* can in some senses be said to resemble Hobbes' concept of a struggle between individuals for self-preservation and power. However, the difference is that with Hobbes the individual stands in a negative relation to the State, whereas for Hegel, this relation is a positive one, which he goes on to articulate in the third section of the *System of Ethical Life*. The State is, therefore, conceived as an accomplishment of developed ethical relations not an external restraint imposed against individual wills.[78]

Honneth, though, relates Hegel's fragmentary comments on 'honor,' to what he perceives to be a third, embryonic theory of recognition. Hegel's discussion of 'honor' is viewed as the 'universalizing' or 'unifying' form which is the "'indifference' or totality of the previous levels of negation."[79] In this sense, argues Honneth, Hegel appears to be attempting to unify particular forms of injury with injury to the 'whole,' implying that injury to one is also injury to the other. Hegel suggests:

> Through honor the singular detail becomes something personal and a whole, and what is seemingly only the denial of a detail is an injury of the whole, and thus there arises the battle of one whole person against another whole person. [80]

Honneth infers from Hegel's brief comments that 'honor' therefore implies the necessity of an 'affirmative relation-to-self,' which requires recognition of the other. Honneth therefore 'psychologizes' his interpretation of 'honor' and understands it as a particular "type of attitude to oneself." For Honneth, 'honor' is "a stance I take towards myself when I identify positively with all my traits and particularities."[81] In Honneth's reconstruction, the presupposition that individuals require intersubjective recognition of their identity is said to motivate subjects to struggle for their 'honor.' Struggles over 'honor' are perceived to be an attempt by individuals to "convince the other that their own personality is at stake." However, individuals are only able to demonstrate the depth of the injury to their 'whole' person if they are prepared to risk their lives in the ensuing struggle. Honneth reads this to mean that "only by being prepared to die do I publicly show that my individual goals and characteristics are more significant to me than my physical survival."[82]

It is at this point Honneth suggests that we can understand why a life-and-death struggle occurs because in such forms of social conflict, which result from personal insult, the "whole [of a person] is at stake."[83] This reading of 'honor' and the 'struggle for honor' is employed by Honneth not only as providing a third form of recognition-relation in terms of individualization and recognition of a person's particular traits and abilities, but following Andreas Wildt, also presupposes a form of ethical life based on underlying 'affective' relations of 'solidarity.' This is how Honneth attempts to explain the transition from 'natural' to 'Absolute Ethical Life,' by means of what he perceives to be 'affective' relations of recognition that go beyond 'merely cognitive' recognition and legal relations. Honneth understands this 'affective' form of recognition, or 'solidarity,' to be a third form of recognition-relation that reintegrates and reunites individuals who have been isolated in legal relations, creating the foundation of ethical community in which, to quote Hegel, the "individual intuits himself in every other individual."[84]

As Honneth is only interested in constructing a theory of intersubjectivity from Hegel's text, remarkably here he limits his discussion to the interpersonal relations between subjects as a form of affective intersubjectivity, and does not countenance the relationality between the universal and particular, the individual and the whole, or the individual and the State, and this results in a rather one-dimensional account of the concept of 'relationality' operating in Hegel's work. As Jean-Philippe Deranty has noted, Honneth's particular interpretation of Hegel purely in terms of an intersubjective model based on the 'nexus' between subjects is somewhat unrepresentative of Hegel's position. Moreover, it also has the result of 'flattening out' the notion of social integration by reducing it to 'horizontal' interpersonal relations between subjects rather than also accounting for 'vertical' relations between individuals and institutions, and individuals and the State.[85] Honneth's reconstruction remains 'external' to Hegel's text in this regard, as in many others, and instead he focuses his attention on the form of social integration that he perceives in Hegel's reference to the reciprocal 'intuition' between subjects as the basis of a form of ethical relation formative of ethical life.

In keeping with his primary concern to develop a theory of intersubjectivity as recognition, Honneth's conclusion from his interpretation of the middle chapter on 'crime' is, therefore, that it offers the key to understanding Hegel's theoretical aims in the *System of Ethical Life*.[86] Honneth suggests that there is a progression between the three stages of conflict presented in the middle chapter, and that we can interpret this progression, which ends with the account of injury or insult to 'personhood' or 'honor,' as indicating that "the identity claims of the subjects involved gradually expand." On this basis, therefore, Honneth suggests, "this rules out the possibility of granting a merely negative significance to the acts of destruction that Hegel describes."[87] Rather, Honneth reads the various forms of 'negative' interaction positively, and as a progression providing the transition from natural to absolute ethical life, by way of a theory of recognition.

For Honneth, the unique place of the *System of Ethical Life* in Hegel's *oeuvre* is the fact that two 'natural' forms of recognition are counterposed as a whole to various kinds of struggle that are summarized in the chapter on 'crime.' Furthermore, there is only one single stage of struggle in various manifestations that Hegel positions between 'natural' and 'Absolute Ethical Life' as a whole, whereas in the texts following the *System of Ethical Life*, the struggle for recognition leads from one stage of ethical life to the next. Honneth argues that although this model is difficult to justify both methodologically and social-historically, this structure provides Hegel with a means of directly countering Hobbes' presuppositions by beginning his social-theoretical account with a "'natural' state of conflict-free ethical life in a unified manner,"[88] and thereby accounting for social conflict only as a secondary condition. Notably, then, Honneth understands Hegel's great advance in comparison to Hobbes to be the positing of a primary form of intersubjective ethical life, and the designation of struggle as always a secondary condition or mode of interaction. By so doing Honneth immunizes what he terms 'crime' or criminality and conflict, from a discussion of power and domination. Instead, 'crime' is only understood in terms of inadequate recognition relations and as such Honneth separates the 'negative' from normativity, reducing the theory of intersubjectivity purely to normative forms of interaction.

Honneth's reading of Hegel thereby provides the counter-model to that of Kojève: where Kojève reads Hegel's account of social relations in the *Phenomenology* as beginning with a 'Fight,' and understands the originary modality of intersubjectivity as power and domination, Honneth turns this interpretation on its head, and while incorporating a secondary element of struggle, posits as primary an ethical form of intersubjectivity as recognition.[89] Honneth's reading is based on an anthropological conception of recognition that he reads as underlying Hegel's work as a whole, which he goes on to interpret as grounded in primary love-relations. In Honneth's schema, the first form of social relation is love—social relations begin with and are grounded on love, not violence, power, or conflict—and each stage of recognition is a necessary precondition for the next.

However, there is another way of reading Hegel's representation of the two different levels of 'relation' that he presents in the *System of Ethical Life*. If we take Hegel's work in the manner in which it is presented, it can alternatively be read as an exposition of forms or modalities of 'relation,' not all of which are internally connected to an underlying primordial concept of recognition. To be sure, Hegel conceives of them as various modalities of 'relation' that are only 'relative' and not yet fully unified, and therefore must be sublated and superseded in the unifying 'concept' of Absolute Ethical Life. However, it is not clear at this stage of his work that Hegel equates 'struggle' with 'recognition' *per se*, or that struggle is conceived as only a reaction to inadequate forms of recognition.

The middle chapter, 'The Negative, or Freedom, or Transgression,' is very difficult to read only as representing forms of 'struggle' that are internally and directly motivated and linked by recognition relations as a whole. In fact, one of the most interesting aspects of the text is precisely that recognition and struggle are not internally linked, and that various forms of struggle and relation are presented that are not directly attributable to recognition. The intermediate chapter on 'The Negative' could alternatively be read not as an expansion or 'disturbance' of established recognition relations but as competing with such recognition relations, as forms or modalities of power and struggle which exist along side recognition relations, all of which are overcome by the third form or level of Absolute Ethical Life in the State. This intermediate stage moves through different forms of 'negative' interaction, some of which destroy relations, others which create relations of power, and others that compel struggle, violence, or revenge. There is no justification in the text itself for the middle chapter to be understood as transgressions *of recognition per se*, only that various forms of struggle are an inevitable, although inadequate, condition of social life. However, Honneth reads Hegel's text as depicting all forms of struggle as internally related to and motivated by the desire for recognition, thereby immediately equating them in the couplet *recognition/struggle.*

One of the most interesting aspects of Hegel's early text that is not repeated in later work is that he conceptualizes many different types of 'relation' both as a methodological principle and in terms of social relations. In this sense, if we follow the logic of Hegel's argument, recognition itself is viewed merely as a form of intersubjectivity or 'relation' that is in fact, also inadequate as the unifying element of ethical life (and this also accords more with the position that he ends up articulating more explicitly from 1806/7 onwards). In the *System of Ethical Life*, recognition is an important aspect within the initial natural stages of ethical life; however, based on the text itself, it not clear that *all* forms of relation and interaction in the text can be reduced to recognition alone. It is also not easy to make a claim for three distinct forms of recognition as internally linked in a progressive and expanding theory of ethical life from within the basis of Hegel's own text. Again, different forms of 'recognition' are presented but they are not internally linked as the sole progressive element of ethical life whereby one form of recognition leads inevitably or necessarily to the other. Rather, as we have seen, the progression in the text moves dialectically between different forms of 'relation,' between 'universal' and 'particular,' or 'concept' and 'intuition.'

Honneth admits that it is difficult to fully substantiate to what extent the history of ethical life can be reconstructed in the *System of Ethical Life* "in terms of the guiding idea of the development of relations of recognition," nor that it is possible to adequately "distinguish various forms of intersubjective recognition" in the text.[90] However, he argues there are enough fragments that can be pieced together that suggest a three-tiered model of recognition: (1) familial relations of 'love' or affective recognition in which individuals are recognized as beings with concrete needs; (2) legal relations in which individuals are recognized in abstract terms as beings with rights and responsibilities; (3) 'affective' relations of solidarity within the State within which individuals are recognized in their particularity as beings with specific traits and abilities.[91]

The teleological theory of social recognition that Honneth reconstructs from Hegel's 1802 text also requires a corresponding three-tiered notion of personality-formation to fully augment his theory of self-realization. Honneth admits that the early Jena text does not provide an adequate corresponding theory of subject-formation to accompany the developmental stages of social recognition. It is only once Hegel moves to develop a philosophy of consciousness within the later Jena work that a more differentiated theory of subjectivity and identity-formation can be seen to develop that can go some way to accomplishing this task in Honneth's reconstruction.

Furthermore, within the *System of Ethical Life*, Honneth acknowledges that the notion of 'struggle' is not explicitly granted a '*constructive* role in the formative process of ethical life.' In other words, 'struggle' and 'recognition' are linked *negatively* rather than positively in the early Jena text.[92] Honneth wishes to understand the movement of recognition as a movement towards increasing 'universalization,' whereby the moment of struggle is responsible for the expansion of recognition-relations to a new level. However, Hegel's account of 'crime' in the *System of Ethical Life* cannot achieve this task for Honneth because the various forms of struggle depicted are not internally tied to recognition in the manner required to indicate an internal *positive* progression in recognition-relations and corresponding conditions for increased individualization.

Nonetheless, as we have discussed above, the *System of Ethical Life* remains the pivotal text for Honneth's reconstruction of Hegel, especially in terms of its reference to a 'natural ethical realm' and ontological account of intersubjectivity, which enables Honneth to establish a primary notion of ethical intersubjectivity that becomes the basis of his own work. The consequences of this reading of *System of Ethical Life* means that from this point onwards, for Honneth, intersubjectivity is equated with recognition, as a normative first-order category. However, in order to further develop 'struggle' as a secondary modality of social interaction that is central to the conceptualization of social change and the expansion of ethical life, Honneth needs to supplement his account with the particular formulation of the '*struggle for recognition*' found in the middle texts of the Jena period, namely, the *First Philosophy of Spirit* (1803/4) and *Realphilosophie* (1805/6). Despite the fact that a strong intersubjective theory is never again to be found in the later texts, Honneth argues they enable him to more explicitly conceptualize an internal positive relation between social conflict and ethical development, and thereby move to the defining conceptual configuration of his theory that is encapsulated in the couplet recognition/struggle.

Chapter Seven

The Normative Ground of Conflict and Sociality

Hegel's shift to the *First Philosophy of Spirit* in 1803/4 represents two significant alterations to the theory of recognition in Honneth's view. Firstly, he argues that Hegel's original intersubjective insights completely recede with the move to a philosophy of consciousness and the introduction of the notion of Spirit.[1] Secondly, the concept of recognition is significantly reworked so that the notion of struggle becomes immanently configured with recognition. As a result the notion of recognition is reformulated as a 'struggle *for* recognition' with its own inner logic and dynamic.[2] From Honneth's perspective, conflict comes to be defined in 1803/4 more explicitly as morally motivated, because the movement of Spirit is structured in such a way that it can only be completely realized by way of mutual recognition. In Honneth's view, therefore, the 1803/4 manuscript enables a crucial link to be made between ethical intersubjectivity and social conflict:

> The turn to the philosophy of consciousness enables Hegel to clarify what motivates struggle in the first place—motives located in the interior of the human spirit, which is supposed to be structured in such a way that for its *complete realization it requires recognition* by others that can only be acquired *through conflict.*[3]

In this sense, Honneth suggests that Hegel's turn to the philosophy of consciousness in the *First Philosophy of Spirit* provides a means to clarify the motivational source for social conflict that remained unclear in the *System of Ethical Life*. In the later text, social conflict takes on a positive connotation as the process by which full recognition can be achieved. In the 1803/4 text, following Siep, Honneth argues that struggle is no longer represented as a form of 'transgression' but from the outset is understood as a struggle *for* recognition. In other words, in the later text, the relation between struggle and recognition is reversed: "struggle no longer negates recognition but, instead, makes it its goal."[4] Struggle therefore becomes fundamental to the achievement of more encompassing recognition relations rather than their diminishment. As Honneth notes, the notion of the 'struggle for recognition' is no longer understood as an agonistic process that immanently develops from within primary intersubjective relations to form the State or *Sittlichkeit* but instead is now internal to the process by which Spirit is formed.

This link between social struggle and recognition is further systematically reconstructed in Hegel's second 'Philosophy of Spirit' or *Realphilosophie* (1805/6), which becomes the programmatic text for Honneth in terms of establishing recognition as the normative ground of all sociality and conflict.[5] It is clear that in both the 1803/4 and 1805/6 texts, Hegel is attempting to work through the difficulties inherent in the concept of recognition and the manner in which ethical life is conceived. According to Honneth, despite the fact that the philosophy of consciousness overwhelmingly structures Hegel's work at this point, the *Realphilosophie* is also the text in which Hegel makes the strongest programmatic statement about the nature of recognition as a 'social fact.'

However, Hegel's shift to the philosophy of Spirit clearly begins to cause some difficulties for Honneth's attempt to extract an intersubjective concept of recognition from Hegel's early work. In particular, Hegel's move to the totalizing model of Spirit has ramifications for the way in which conflict is perceived. The notion of struggle becomes functionalized in the shift to the category of Spirit and as a consequence Hegel is no longer interested in an agonistic concept of social conflict but in a notion that emphasizes the individual's integration into the community. Honneth is at pains to avoid both Hegel's integrationist approach to social action and also a model of social struggle that is primarily associated with labor and the master/slave dialectic as represented in the *Phenomenology*. Rather, Honneth continues to look for a way of extracting a notion of struggle from Hegel's work that is immanently associated with recognition in intersubjective terms. In other words, a notion of struggle that for Honneth both reveals underlying mutual recognition relations and provides the means to expand existing recognition relations.[6]

In the *Realphilosophie* (1805/6), Hegel begins by tracing the concept of Spirit in terms of the theoretical and practical categories firstly, of mind or 'Intelligence' and secondly, of 'Will.' Thus the categories of Spirit now completely replace the earlier notion of 'Natural Ethical Life,' and in the manner of the final system, the text is divided in a manner that approximates the categorical divisions of 'subjective,' 'objective,' and 'absolute Spirit' as represented in the *Encyclopaedia*. Thus, Hegel no longer begins with elementary forms of ethical relation but with individual 'intelligence' through which he traces Spirit's gradual realization within the framework of the philosophy of consciousness.[7]

However, despite the monological framework of the philosophy of consciousness and the stage structure of the categories of Spirit, Honneth argues that the *Realphilosophie* is still unique in its construction compared to the later texts. What is decisive for Honneth is that although recognition and the 'struggle for recognition' are not conceptualized as the basis of absolute Spirit, recognition is still built into the first formative stage as the basis of intersubjective relations, and in this way the 'struggle for recognition' is still understood as the 'driving force' of the 'development of ethical life.'[8]

In the *Realphilosophie*, the entire process is aimed at establishing the stages that a subject must pass through before she can be said to attain full 'rights,' and as a consequence also be fully integrated into institutional social life, or what Hegel terms here, "actual Spirit."[9]

In the first instance, Hegel outlines the 'cognitive process' of consciousness from sensate immediacy to understanding, and from intuition to representation, in other words to 'language' ('memory' and 'naming') via the faculty of the imagination.[10] In bringing the object to the understanding, individual consciousness is the dominating force and comes to comprehend itself by positing itself as 'negativity,' whereby it too comes to understand itself as an object: "The understanding is reason, and its object is the I itself."[11] Here Hegel means to say that the intelligence only comes to know itself through its own activity.[12] In the act of imagination which connects sense-certainty and understanding, intuition, and language, the intelligence becomes aware of itself in the act of moving from particularity towards universality.[13]

However, for Hegel, the cognitive experience of consciousness in language must be extended in a second stage beyond theoretical to practical production. In the first stage of theoretical knowledge, the experience of consciousness is constituted "in terms of imagery, in memory, knowing itself, not as content but as form."[14] This second stage of practical experience in which individual consciousness further discovers itself through self-objectification is conceptualized by Hegel in terms of the 'realization of' the individual 'will.' The 'will' is understood as a practical 'drive' that is distinguished from 'desire' precisely because it creates its own content; it is the active 'I' that produces and transforms the world as much as it transforms and shapes individual consciousness. It is 'free of external determination' and wants to 'assert' itself upon the world and make itself its own object.[15] The individual will is expressed through 'the work of the I' and begins with self-objectification through labor.[16] For Hegel, "labor is one's making oneself into a thing..." It is the "unity of the I as objectified."[17] The individual consciousness can only have practical experience of the world by producing products that have a tangible existence 'for-itself.'[18]

Once again, it is by means of the tool and the transformation of the natural world in production that individual consciousness approaches universality. The tool represents the movement from passive appropriation of nature to active creation and universalization. However, in the act of working on and transforming the natural world, Hegel conceives of the 'will' as a 'practical force' that is divided into male and female characteristics. Hegel understands the active force that harnesses 'Nature' for human purposes, and thereby ensures freedom from natural determination, in terms of a feminine power, or what he terms 'cunning.'[19] In this way, nature is utilized and instrumentalized, employed for human purpose and brought under rational control: "...Between myself and the external [world of] thinghood, I have inserted my cunning—in order to spare myself, to hide my determinacy and allow it to be made use of."[20] In this way, Hegel conceptualizes a (theoretical) splitting of the will into male and female characteristics: one which he conceives of as universal, the other as particular, as the 'arousal' of the drive, an "evil...subterranean knowing..."[21]

However, what Hegel means to suggest with this rather idiosyncratic notion of the splitting of the will, suggests Honneth, is that neither 'intelligence' nor 'will' is adequate alone because the subject is still only able to grasp itself as an object, as 'thing-like.' In order to overcome this 'thing-like' relation to itself individual consciousness must be confronted with another consciousness. It is, therefore, with this problematic notion of the splitting of the will into male and female characteristics that Hegel conceptualizes "the confrontation of one being with another" in the relation of 'love' between sexual partners.[22] It is at this point in the text that Hegel introduces the cognitive act of reciprocal acknowledgement or 'recognition' *for the first time*. For Hegel this is initially a cognitive act in which two independent egos come to know themselves in one another: "each knows itself in the other, each has renounced itself" in love.[23]

As Honneth suggests, the extension of the 'will' into the love relation between the sexes is an advance over the instrumental activity associated with labor precisely because it requires "the reciprocity of knowing oneself in another."[24] In this way, subjects come to know themselves in relation as mutually desiring beings who also wish to be reciprocally desired.[25] In the love relation, each individual must come to trust the other and to know 'itself likewise in its other' as a being who is also trusted. In this way, 'love' is defined by Hegel as,

> the element of [custom or morality], the totality of ethical life (*Sittlichkeit*)—though not yet it itself, but only the suggestion of it. Each one [here exists]

only as determinate will, character, as the natural individual whose uncultivated natural Self is recognized."[26]

Honneth reads into Hegel's conception of love as it is presented here, a more explicit formulation than that found in the earlier Jena texts, with regard to the necessity of primary recognition for successful individualization. Although now framed within the philosophy of consciousness, Honneth suggests one can extract a meaning, in terms of a theory of subjectivity, "according to which the volitional subject is to experience itself for the first time as a needy desiring subject only after having had the experience of being loved." This in turn, provides Honneth with the 'theoretical' premise "that the development of a subject's personal identity presupposes, in principle, certain types of recognition from other subjects."[27]

Honneth argues that the implications of Hegel's thesis go much further than general theories of socialization. In Honneth's reading, Hegel's theory of recognition does more than make a necessary link between successful identity formation and the experience of recognition. It provides the basis for developing a comprehensive social theory from a recognition-theoretic point of view. Honneth makes two programmatic claims that are fundamental to the construction of his own three-tiered theory of recognition, and to his claim that love is the structural core of ethical life. Firstly, he surmises from Hegel's minimal account of love as a relation of recognition that love is a form of mutual recognition that constitutes: "a necessary precondition for every further development of identity." In other words, the very nature of identity-formation cannot proceed without experiencing a successful primary love-relation, which for Honneth "reaffirms[s] the individual in his particular nature of his urges and thereby grant[s] him an indispensable degree of basic self-confidence."[28]

Secondly, Honneth claims that private relations of love are not only formative of ethical life, they are a necessary precondition for participation in public life and political will-formation. This is, in fact, not a claim that Hegel is making; however, he does seem to be suggesting that initial relations of recognition are formative of ethical life, even if at this stage they are only embryonic.[29]

Once again, these are presuppositions that are very difficult to identify within Hegel's own work. Moreover, such strong formulations in regard to the conception of 'love' means that recognition becomes overburdened by one of its determinations as a stipulated precondition or primary form of intersubjectivity. This interpretation of Hegel, it might be argued, is read through a particularly Winnicottian lens that provides a particular reconstructive basis for Honneth's intersubjective theory. Furthermore, once augmented in his later psychoanalytic reconstruction of 'love' as foundational for a theory of recognition, this conceptualization results in the loss of some of

Honneth's original insights in regard to subject-formation, social conflict and power.

In addition to the link between successful identity formation and the experience of recognition as a precondition for public life, Honneth suggests Hegel's concept of recognition here also contains an implicit 'obligation to reciprocity' that Honneth argues is fundamental to individualization. This further claim is central to Honneth's own thesis: "that an individual that does not recognize its partner to interaction to be a certain type of person is also unable to experience itself completely or without restriction as that type of person."[30] It is an obligation that is mutually necessary if not enforceable and in Honneth's view is required for the mutual affirmation of subjects. Honneth extends his psychoanalytic reading of Hegel at this point, arguing that the idea of ethical life is dependent on individuals acquiring an "inner-psychic representation" of it that can only be experienced through the "feeling of being loved." Moreover, in terms of the 'subject's formative process,' love is essential for providing "the emotional conditions for successful ego-development: only the feeling of having the particular nature of one's urges fundamentally recognized and affirmed can allow one to develop the degree of basic self-confidence that renders one capable of participating with equal rights, in political will-formation."[31]

However, in Hegel's own analysis, as with the earlier texts, love must become 'actual' or 'objective' in the 'products' that result from the unity of sexual partners. This mediation and unification is accomplished firstly, through shared labor and family property and possession, and secondly, the raising of children, "...in whom the two see their love—their self-conscious unity as self-conscious."[32] As with the *First Philosophy of Spirit*, the 'child' is viewed by Hegel as the means by which the love relation between the parents is 'actualized,' and furthermore, in which they see themselves as 'superseded' and recognized as an 'achieved unity' or 'totality.'[33] The child must be socialized and educated to achieve universalization; however, this process is not pre-given nor taken-for-granted, it is achieved as the outcome of a learning process.[34]

However, in order to move beyond the private sphere of the family, Hegel now needs to posit a first step towards institutional social life by conceptually moving to a broader social context where individuals experience themselves as subjects with intersubjectively guaranteed rights. Hegel introduces broader social relations in the context of competition, and the 'struggle for recognition' is introduced here as a response to the exclusion immediately experienced as a result of property relations. In both the 1803/4 and 1805/6 texts, Hegel's discussion of recognition and the struggle for recognition takes place explicitly and entirely within the context of property relations and 'possession' as a legal 'system' that is underwritten by recognition.[35] As in the *System of Ethical Life*, possession is therefore considered to be an 'extension' of the individual, it represents his singularity, so that if injury or theft is aimed at the possessions of an individual, it is 'his' entire personality that is in fact injured. Any offense therefore aimed at the individual's possessions is, also according to Hegel, an offense against the individual's integrity, it is 'an offense of his honor,' and results in a struggle.

The cause of the initial offense and hence what drives the 'struggle for recognition' is the very exclusivity of the concept of property/possession, which by its very nature represents a contradiction in the fundamental exclusion of the other from (common) possession.[36] The 'struggle for recognition' appears as a conflict that occurs because in the context of possession or property relations, one consciousness feels ignored or excluded by another consciousness. As Hegel depicts it: "each appears in the consciousness of the other as someone who excludes him from the whole *extension* of his singular aspects."[37] However, this singularity of possession and exclusion of one individual to another in relation to property is also an 'absolute contradiction' because each individual can only be sure of his existence, can only "validate the totality of his particularity vis-à-vis the consciousness of the other."[38]

To avoid the contradiction whereby each negates the totality of the other yet is dependent on the other for the recognition that can validate its particularity, each must enter a life-and-death struggle.[39] However, the life-and-death struggle also contains a paradox, because if the other consciousness with whom the subject struggles is ultimately annihilated, then recognition is also suspended. To overcome this contradiction, Hegel therefore argues that the particularity of one of the partners to interaction must be sublated in order to gain recognition because "...its getting recognized is its existence."[40]

What is significant from Honneth's perspective is that in the *Realphilosophie*, in contrast to the earlier texts, the 'struggle for recognition' is explicitly conceptualized as an alternative to Hobbes' account of the 'state of nature.'[41] In comparison to the earlier *System of Ethical Life*, in which it could only be inferred that Hegel's work was a response to Hobbes, in the *Realphilosophie*, Hegel explicitly reconstructs the plural relation of families as a first instance of collective social life that is seemingly characterized by competition in the context of property rights in a manner reminiscent of Hobbes.

Hegel's concept of recognition, as Ricoeur suggests, should be understood as a moral rejoinder to the challenge launched by Hobbes' naturalist interpretation of the political, and in order to do this, Hegel's main aim is to rethink the theory of the 'state of nature.'[42] As discussed above, Hegel is critical of Hobbes' concept of the social contract, which is constructed *a posteriori* as the necessary outcome of what he conceives as the 'state of nature' or 'war of all against all.' However, Hobbes' thesis in regard to the 'state of nature' is not based on the observation of empirical fact but rather a thought experiment, a speculative thesis about what the state of social life might be like without government.[43] Hobbes therefore approaches the problem backwards, according to Hegel, by beginning with the foundation of the State and speculating that political order is founded by purely non-ethical motives. As Hegel notes, in this scenario individuals have no rights or obligations to one another; the only possibility for 'interrelation' therefore lies in leaving the 'state of nature.' The problem with this construction, from Hegel's perspective, is that the notion of right is being externally attributed and it is therefore difficult to deduce exactly: "What right and obligation is for the individual in the state of nature?"[44]

In contrast, following on from his earlier work in the essay on *Natural Law*, Honneth argues that Hegel attempts to provide an alternative view of the original social contract and a concept of right that develops from what he perceives to be originary moral motives that underlie social life.[45] Hegel offers a counter view in the *Realphilosophie* that has empirical rather than theoretical connotations:

> Right is the *relation* of persons, in their *behaviour*, to others. It is the universal element of their free being—the determination, the limitation of their empty freedom. I need not spell out this relation or limitation for myself and produce it; rather, the object, in general, is itself this creation of right, i.e., the *relation of recognition*.[46]

In this way, Hegel offers a significantly altered conception of the intersubjective relations under 'the artificial conditions of the state of nature' when he introduces the recognition relation into the text in the context of 'right' and property relations.[47] Moreover, Hegel immediately extends the concept of recognition just introduced in a passage that will become one of the most programmatic statements for Honneth's own work:

> In recognition (*Anerkennen*), the Self ceases to be this individual; it exists by right in recognition, i.e., no longer [immersed] in its immediate existence. The one who is recognized is recognized as immediately counting as such (*gettend*), through his *being*—but this being is itself generated from the concept; it is recognized being (*anerkanntes Seyn*) ... Man is necessarily recognized and necessarily gives recognition. This necessity is his own, not that of our thinking in contrast to the content. As recognizing, man is himself the movement [of recognition], and this movement itself is what negates [*hebt auf*] his natural state: *he is recognition*; the natural aspect merely *is*, it is not the spiritual aspect.[48]

Honneth's interpretation of these central passages in Hegel's *Realphilosophie* provides the foundational basis for his own theory of recognition. He argues that the above passage represents for Hegel "what it means to integrate the obligation of mutual recognition into the state of nature as a social fact."[49] Honneth develops his own foundational intersubjectivism out of

Hegel's analysis of (mutual) recognition as a primary form of interrelation that is the basis for all other possible interaction. Despite the monological characteristics that result from the framework of the philosophy of consciousness as a whole, these dimensions of the *Realphilosophie* provide Honneth with an anthropological concept of recognition that is more clearly defined than any of the earlier texts. Here it is evident that Honneth's own concept of recognition takes the form of a strong intersubjective anthropology and together with his analysis of the 'natural ethical realm' in the *System of Ethical Life*, recognition comes to be bestowed simultaneously with the double role of both a normative and an anthropological concept. It is this double determination that forms both the uniqueness and yet many of the difficulties with Honneth's position.

Moreover, for Honneth, Hegel's anthropological presupposition that 'man is recognition' has major consequences for the conceptualization of social conflict and the manner in which the 'struggle for recognition' is conceived. In a central passage in *The Struggle for Recognition*, Honneth states:

> In order to show, as against the dominant intellectual tradition, that subjects can, on their own, reach a conflict resolution based on law (as formulated in the social contract) even under conditions of hostile competition, theoretical attention must be shifted to the intersubjective social relations that *always already guarantee a minimal normative consensus in advance*; for it is only in these *pre-contractual relations of mutual recognition—which underlie even relations of social competition*—that the moral potential evidenced in individual's willingness to reciprocally restrict their own spheres of liberty can be anchored.[50]

Honneth goes on to conclude from this presupposition that:

> with regard to the social circumstances characterizing the state of nature, one must necessarily consider the additional fact that *subjects must in some way, have already recognized each other even before the conflict*.[51]

It is within these central pages of interpretation that we see two of Honneth's own fundamental theoretical presuppositions defined. The first presupposition to be established is the inextricable link Honneth makes between a normative theory and philosophical anthropology grounded in the concept of recognition. Secondly, we see the theory of social struggle elided into the configuration recognition/struggle, whereby recognition is established as the *a priori* normative basis for *all* forms of sociality. Consequently, a two-tiered model of social (inter)action is formed whereby all other forms of interaction are secondary to ethical intersubjectivity as recognition, including social struggle and power. From this point onwards, the notion of social struggle is always already posited as a secondary form of interaction that is further conceptualized by Honneth as always immanently motivated by a normativity pre-established in recognition relations. Negative feelings are therefore understood by Honneth to merely represent inadequate acknowledgment by one's partners to interaction and are always an expression of ethically motivated intersubjectivity. Henceforth, intersubjectivity is directly equated with recognition. As a consequence, we see the insights that were evident in Honneth's earlier work on Foucault recede from view, both in terms of the implications for subject-formation, social interaction and conflict, and a multidimensional theory of intersubjectivity more generally.

These presuppositions are given further weight in Honneth's interpretation of the remaining parts of Hegel's *Realphilosophie*, particularly where Hegel once again introduces the 'life-and-death' struggle as a response to the negative feelings of being excluded and ignored in the social context of property relations. As with the earlier Jena texts, Hegel's conception in the *Realphilosophie* is that individuals come to the knowledge of their dependence upon one another—to the knowledge of recognition—only by their relations with others being 'disturbed' or injured through crime and conflict over property/possession. Correspondingly, in contradistinction to Hobbes, Hegel therefore also moves to define conflict that occurs in the context of property relations as motivated by 'struggles for recognition' rather than 'glory' or self-preservation.[52]

Hegel's analysis of the concept of recognition underlying property relations and the conflict that arises from the exclusionary nature of such relations leads Honneth to develop two further lines of argument that are central to his theory and his attempt to establish the ethical ground of social conflict. Firstly, Honneth argues that in reconstructing Hegel's attempt to depict the intersubjective basis of the social contract as a counter-position to Hobbes, it is possible to establish the crucial presupposition that "all human co-existence presupposes a kind of basic mutual affirmation between subjects" that is based in an *a priori* 'relationship of recognition.'[53] The fact that individuals react negatively to the social situation of being ignored, rather than out of fear or self-preservation, demonstrates for Honneth that:

> *Built into the structure of human interaction* there is a *normative expectation* that one *will meet with the recognition of others*, or at least an implicit assumption that one will be given *positive* consideration in the plans of others.[54]

In this respect, Honneth suggests that it is only by means of social conflict that subjects come to fully understand their dependence on one another. Rather than acting as isolated individuals, Honneth therefore suggests that "in their own action-orientation" subjects must "have already *positively* taken the other into account, *before they become engaged in hostilities*."[55] The above passages clearly indicate the extent of Honneth's anthropological claim and attempt to establish positive affectivity as the primary form of intersubjective relation. As discussed above, this further suggests that negative feelings are always understood in moral terms as a lack of recognition, and are separated out from other modes of interaction that might be motivated by strategic concerns, resentment, or power. In this way it might be argued that Honneth 'purifies' intersubjectivity as recognition as a primary form of intersubjectivity, and conceptualizes it in a manner that immunizes it from other forms and modalities of relation.[56]

However, Honneth goes even further in cementing the primacy of recognition and makes a strong social-ontological claim, arguing not only that subjects must have accepted one another in advance as partners "to interaction upon whom they are willing to allow their own activity to be dependent" but that both parties must have "already mutually recognized each other even if this social accord may not be thematically present to them."[57] In other words, Honneth argues that mutual recognition occurs 'behind the backs' of social actors, so to speak, whereby a primary affective form of recognition forms the very underlying ontological fabric of social life. These passages are fundamental in defining Honneth's concept of recognition as an ontology of 'affective attunement,' and the secondary relation between struggle and recognition that is carried through to his later work where conflict and struggle become even further de-emphasized.

Secondly, in analyzing Hegel's depiction of the 'life-and-death' struggle in terms of the primacy of recognition, Honneth extends Hegel's basic sketch in a manner that offers a significant reconceptualization compared to previous interpretations. If taken at its most basic, Honneth argues that all that can be inferred from Hegel's account of the 'life-and-death' struggle in the *Realphilosophie* is that there is "a constitutive link between the intersubjective emergence of legal relations and the experience of death." The most prominent existential interpretation of this presupposition was popularized by Kojève's reading of Hegel's *Phenomenology*. According to this view, the notion of the 'life-and-death' struggle is understood to elucidate the inevitability of death as the driving factor behind intersubjectively secured freedom and the possibility of shared social life, based on the reciprocal acknowledgement of individuals in their finitude as vulnerable beings.[58]

However, Honneth wants to extend the interpretation of the 'life-and-death' struggle much further in order to reconstruct the full implications of Hegel's idea in a recognition-theoretic direction.[59] Honneth's alternative reading emphasizes the morally motivated nature of social conflict and the normative expectations that subjects bring to all interaction, rather than the mutual acknowledgement of human finitude as the factor compelling subjects to acknowledge the fragility of partners to interaction. In this way, Honneth argues that normative expectations are intrinsic to recognition and that, in fact, recognition provides the *ethical ground to social conflict*. As

such, according to Honneth's reading, the 'life-and-death' struggle is structured by underlying normative relations of recognition that mean individuals
react to situations of conflict from a moral basis that enables each individual
to respect the integrity and vulnerability of the other and brings to light their
mutual dependency. The very actuality of conflict is what makes subjects
aware of the *a priori* relations of recognition that structure all social interaction.

The fundamental notion of the ethical ground of social conflict outlined
by Honneth here becomes the basis for the concept of the 'struggle for
recognition' that is central to his own work. Significantly, in his analysis of
the 'life-and-death' struggle Honneth avoids discussing the most well-known
account of 'struggle' found in the *Phenomenology*, despite comparing his
own interpretation to those like Kojève whose interpretation is centered on
the 1807 text.[60] For Honneth, it is not an *existential* condition that brings to
consciousness prior relations of recognition, rather it is the acknowledgement
of the intrinsic *moral* worth and vulnerability of the other who is dependent
on recognition for her very self-realization. In comparison to Kojève, then,
who as we saw above posits as primary the originary 'Fight' or struggle from
death as the ground of freedom, Honneth in a manner that is more akin to the
philosophical ethics of Levinas, here bases his analysis on the *a priori* normative expectations that he argues subjects bring to interaction.[61] Honneth
argues that interpretations of Hegel such as those offered by Kojève offer a
monological account of the subject who is only confronted with her own
freedom when faced with the inevitability of death.

The important point to make is that Honneth's analysis of Hegel's 'life-
and-death' struggle in *The Struggle for Recognition*, enables him to offer an
alternative interpretation of the development of the concept of 'right' as
developing immanently from within recognition relations. It is the conflict
arising in the context of legal relations, particularly in regard to broken
contracts, that leads to a struggle for recognition.[62] It is in fact the legal
enforcement of the contract and coercion of individuals who do not honor
contractual agreements that leads individuals to respond by attempting to
damage existing recognition relations because their particularity has not been
acknowledged.[63] This additional case of the struggle for recognition furnishes Honneth with the conception required to expand the struggle for recognition beyond 'love' to relations of right.

RECOGNITION AS THE SOCIAL FABRIC OF ETHICAL COMMUNITY

For Honneth, Hegel's analysis of recognition and the struggle for recognition
in the *Realphilosophie* remains inadequate beyond this point in the text. He

suggests that Hegel is unable to satisfactorily account for a third form of recognition that can address the need for recognition of individuals' unique traits and abilities, a form of recognition which cannot be met within the realm of the law nor can it satisfactorily establish a recognitive account of *Sittlichkeit*.[64] The missing account of recognition of 'individual uniqueness' can only be found in the ethical community within the State. Honneth argues that a third form of social recognition must extend beyond rational achievement to emotional concern for fellow members of the community and individual self-realization.[65] To address this lack in Hegel's later text, Honneth reads it back into the account given in his interpretation of the *System of Ethical Life* in order to account for a third form of recognition.

In the earlier *System of Ethical Life*, as discussed above, this task was fulfilled by a notion of 'solidarity,' which Honneth argued was possible to identify within Hegel's Schelling-inspired category of 'mutual intuition,' as indicative of an affective form of recognition in which the individual "intuits himself in every other individual." Honneth maintains that the earlier use of Schelling's notion of 'intuition' (as a form of knowledge) indicates that Hegel intended to construct an additional form of recognition that has the capacity to once again reunite individuals who have been isolated in the context of abstract legal relations into the 'affective' bonds of an ethical community.[66]

However, in the *Realphilosophie*, ethical life is no longer conceived in the same manner as the *System of Ethical Life*. In the earlier text 'Absolute Ethical Life' was considered to develop teleologically out of an immanent potential contained within social life. However, in the later text, the stage considered as 'intersubjective' ethical accomplishment in 1802 is instead understood as the process by which Spirit returns to itself.[67] As a consequence, Hegel conceives the completion of Spirit's externalization to have occurred with the objectification of itself in the production of state institutions, including the system of law, representing the stage of 'objective Spirit.' In addition, Spirit is conceptualized in terms of a third and 'absolute' stage, which includes the 'State' and the self-reflexive mediums of 'art, religion, and science.' However, within this altered framework, the 'State' and ethical life are no longer understood as the accomplishment of intersubjective relations. Rather, they are formed by the self-manifestation of Spirit, and this radically changes the way in which ethical life is conceived.[68]

As a self-reflection of Spirit, the State is now seen as an all-encompassing substance that acts in the place of Spirit, not as the accomplishment of intersubjective relations *per se*. As a result of this non-intersubjective reformulation, ethical life is now constructed as the relationship between individuals and the State, rather than interpersonal relations between individuals, and this in turn sets up an 'asymmetrical dependence' between the State and the social subjects within it.

Honneth argues, therefore, that Hegel loses sight of the 'recognition-theoretic insights' that were evident in the early Jena text, and limited by the framework of the philosophy of consciousness, ends up constructing a 'substantialistic' model of ethical life as a result of the way in which he works with categories that entirely conceive individuals as a "superordinate instance of the State."[69] In this context, Honneth draws on the work of Michael Theunissen, whose essay "The Repressed Intersubjectivity in Hegel's Philosophy of Right" is particularly influential. Theunissen argues that as a result of his metaphysical commitments, Hegel undermines his own intersubjective insights, and limits general social relations of recognition to abstract right and property but not to the general structure of ethical life.[70] Moreover, the result of 'objective Spirit' being identified with 'absolute Spirit' is the conceptualization of a monological subject, the "ultimate subject" that is at the same time ethical substance, and this not only denies the independence of individuals but also undermines intersubjectivity.[71] As Theunissen demonstrates, Hegel ends up "repressing" a properly intersubjective theory of ethical life for a "state-theoretical actualization of ethical life" that conceptualizes the State as an all pervasive substance which the individual internalizes as "its very own essence," thereby shifting the ethical relation from an interpersonal one to one whereby individuals are related and connected only by means of ethical substance. As a consequence, Hegel understands this relation as a relation of substance to itself, whereby individuals are merely accidents of substance.[72]

Nonetheless, despite Honneth's reservations about the political implications of Hegel's later project, in more recent work including *Suffering from Indeterminacy* (2000), *The Pathologies of Individual Freedom* (2010), and *Das Recht Der Freiheit* (2011) he moves beyond an outright rejection of the later Hegel with a reinterpretation of the *Philosophy of Right*.[73] Influenced by more recent readings of Hegel's theory of recognition in this regard, such as that proposed by Robert Williams,[74] Honneth emphasizes the continuities of the Jena Hegel of 1802, and underscores the basic idea that social relations are both the essence of individual well-being as well as the basis of their suffering. Honneth's basic thesis is that subjects can only achieve self-determination and self-realization through intersubjective relations, which intrinsically contain basic normative expectations, the denial of which causes subjects to 'suffer from indeterminacy.' Honneth now contends that the basic premises of the young Hegel are maintained in the *Philosophy of Right*: most notably that subjects are always already bound to each other by intersubjective ethical relations and that 'normative principles of communicative freedom' are incorporated in practice and embodied in those shared social mores and behavior, or '*Sitte*,' that become 'second nature.'[75]

As such, neither abstract right nor externally imposed forms of morality and conduct can secure the social conditions of freedom, nor prevent individuals from suffering from indeterminacy. As early as the *Differenzschrift* of 1802, Hegel had established that individual freedom is an 'indeterminacy' and that the "true ground upon which freedom is existent" is the "relation of will to will."[76] In order, then, to participate in a 'truly free community of living relations' the individual must relinquish individual freedom. In other words, Hegel's argument is against individualistically derived notions of freedom (as in the English tradition) and he attempts to counter such notions with an intersubjectively derived notion of freedom.

In recent work, Honneth further extends this reading and 'reactualization' of the *Philosophy of Right*. He offers a critical appraisal of what he terms the 'pathologies of individual freedom' that he argues result from those contemporary notions of social justice that are based predominantly on a notion of individual freedom.[77] Honneth argues that such pathologies are caused by an over-emphasis on individual freedom at the expense of a form of 'communicative freedom,' one that is intersubjectively realized through social cooperation and participation in recognitively anchored institutions.

Notably, Honneth develops this form of intersubjectively guaranteed freedom into a concept of 'social freedom.' Although not a term explicitly used by Hegel, 'social freedom' is a term employed by Honneth (following Frederick Neuhouser) to designate a form of freedom that can only be 'actualized' or 'realized' in basic modern social institutions, more specifically for Honneth, the institutions of family or love relations, the market, and democratic politics. Social freedom is then understood as central to an account of democratic ethics, or the shared co-operative values and practices of ethical life [*Sittlichkeit*] which are grounded in relations of reciprocal recognition. Honneth is therefore interested in the inherent 'ethicality' of social institutions and develops an account of institutions as derived immanently from within modern societies that are always already constituted normatively. Freedom guaranteeing institutions and norms are therefore not understood as being externally constructed or applied but as developing immanently from within the structure of originary recognitive relations; in other words, institutions are understood as 'crystallizations' of recognition relations that develop out of normative patterns of social interaction and the history of social struggles. In this respect, Honneth brings together his early interpretation of Hegel's Jena theory of recognition, together with a reading of *The Philosophy of Right*, as central to a theory of freedom guaranteeing social institutions and a democratic ethics in which the notion of social freedom forms the core of his account.[78]

As was the case with the Jena texts, Honneth offers an especially strong intersubjective reading of the *Philosophy of Right* that can only be sustained by remaining somewhat external to Hegel's own text.[79] In these most recent texts on Hegel, Honneth reconstructs the notion of freedom in the *Philosophy of Right* in terms of a theory of social action or cooperation, and recasts it in social-ontological terms as those habitual attitudes or rational practices of communicative or social freedom that are intrinsic to ethical life, somewhat in the sense of a 'second nature,' underpinned by primary relations of recognition. [80]

It might, however, be questioned whether Honneth continues to provide an overly normative account of the role of institutions, particularly in processes of subject-formation, and whether he adequately addresses the power-wielding and constitutive role of institutions in social life. In contrast, Emmanuel Renault draws on Foucaultian and Weberian stances in developing an alternative account of institutions and their relationship to forms of recognition. Renault argues that Honneth too one-sidedly conceives of institutions as embodying intersubjective values, and therefore understands them primarily as 'expressions' of recognition. [81] Honneth then understands institutions not as arrangements which produce recognition or deny recognition in and of themselves, but as the institutionalization of recognitive relationships which themselves belong to a pre-institutional level. [82] He therefore neglects to adequately consider the ways in which institutions are constitutive of recognition, or how power is operative within recognitive relations not only between individuals, but also between individuals and the state. In this respect, although in his latest work Honneth is dedicated to an analysis of institutions rather than simply interpersonal relations of recognition, it can be argued that his analysis of institutions remains underpinned by the original intersubjectivist account of the normativity inherent to social relations of recognition and this continues to provide the ground for his latest work.

Honneth's specific interpretations of Hegel, beginning with the 1802 *System of Ethical Life* through to the 1821 *Philosophy of Right*, lay the foundation for a strong defense of the intersubjective paradigm based on recognition. Initially, Honneth preferences the *System of Ethical Life* as the most promising for the development of an originary form of ethical intersubjectivity which he reconstructs as an anthropological and ontological theory of recognition that remains pivotal to his work. However, as we have discussed, there was also the possibility to read the *System of Ethical Life* in terms of a more general theory of intersubjectivity or 'relatedness' that was not yet overly determined by any one form of sociability, neither with love nor power. At this point in Hegel's work, although conceived as an 'ethical relation' the notion of intersubjectivity is not overly determined by the form or *modality* of the relatedness. Instead, it is more akin to a basic 'being-in-the-world' conceived as a primary relatedness to both other subjects and objects. [83]

However, as discussed, Honneth conceives of this relatedness or primary intersubjectivity solely in terms of interpersonal relations of recognition, thereby equating all forms of intersubjectivity with 'recognition,' a form of relatedness that is intrinsically normative. However, if Honneth had interpreted Hegel's early attempts to develop a theory of 'relatedness' more open-ly, without making the immediate association between a primary form of relatedness and recognition, he might have avoided not only reducing Heg-el's notion merely to forms of interpersonal relations between subjects but, more importantly for our purposes, also avoided fusing a theory of normativ-ity with an anthropology of intersubjectivity as recognition. If we read the shifts across Hegel's texts discussed by Honneth, we might also draw a different conclusion to Honneth. The fact that Hegel does not retain the notion of a 'natural ethical realm' and an originary form of intersubjectivity in the shift from the *System of Ethical Life* to the later Jena texts in fact may indicate a crucial insight on Hegel's behalf: that ethical intersubjectivity cannot be posited as a natural, first-order category but that it may in fact only be the result of a learning process, and one that is highly uncertain and contingent.

However, as we have seen from the above discussion, the consequence of Honneth's particular reconstruction of Hegel and the subsequent centrality of these formulations to his own work mean that intersubjectivity is reduced to recognition alone, and this closes down Honneth's earlier insights in regard to the broadening and deepening of the theory of intersubjectivity. As a result, Honneth posits normativity in what he regards as the *certainty* of recognition. In this sense, intersubjective relations and identity-formation are conceptualized only within the normative terms of recognition, rather than as co-constituted by a variety of modalities of intersubjectivity and forms of interaction, including power and strategic action. Moreover, by positing rec-ognition as primary and prior to all other forms of interaction, Honneth confines the understanding of social struggle and conflict to the normative terms of recognition alone, rather than theorizing a multitude of possible motivational factors, only one of which might be recognition. Finally, Honneth reduces power and domination merely to a pathology of recognition thereby reducing the critique of power to the terms of unsatisfactory recogni-tion alone, and this one-dimensionalizes both a theory of power and the possibility for critique.

Honneth's reconstruction of Hegel provides him with the ontological and anthropological basis for a theory of recognition that has become the defin-ing feature of his work. However, in order to make Hegel's recognitive insights relevant for contemporary social philosophy, in a second step Honneth needed to separate Hegel's idea from the premises of the philosophy of consciousness in which they are conceived and attempt to 're-actualize' Hegel's idea in non-metaphysical terms. Initially, in order to achieve this task, Honneth turns to the social psychology of George Herbert Mead in order to create a contemporary theoretical basis for further developing the theory of recognition and the recognitive spheres of love, rights, and achieve-ment. However, Honneth's work on recognition has also developed in multiple new directions since writing *The Struggle for Recognition*, even if the basic premise and debt to Hegel remain the same. Nonetheless, the full extent of Honneth's attempt at a 'systematic renewal' of the foundations of contemporary critical social theory cannot be fully comprehended without also examining his accounts of sociality and subject-formation with recourse to G. H. Mead and the psychoanalytic object-relations theory of Donald Winnicott, which also initiate further clarifications and reformulations in regard to the theory of recognition evident in his more recent work.

4

Intersubjective Dependency and Socialization: Mead and Winnicott

Chapter Eight

Practical Intersubjectivity and Sociality in Mead

Honneth's alternative reading of George Herbert Mead was originally central to his attempt to extend and enrich the intersubjective paradigm beyond Habermas' linguistically conceived theory of communicative action. As demonstrated in the preceding chapters, Honneth resolutely attempts to reconstruct a broad-based theory of intersubjectivity that is explored in a variety of different registers, one that can be traced from the early work on philosophical anthropology to the studies in *The Critique of Power*, and the major interpretations in *The Struggle for Recognition*. Within this theoretical genealogy, Mead's work is fundamental to Honneth's early attempts to develop both a strong theory of intersubjectivity and subject-formation, and to provide the anthropological foundations upon which he attempts to ground his theory of recognition.

Mead's work figures predominantly in this theoretical enterprise in both the early and middle writings to date: firstly, in *Social Action and Human Nature* where Mead is said to offer a theory of 'practical intersubjectivity' commensurate with Honneth's early concerns to ground historical materialism in an "anthropological reconstruction of the specifically human capacities for action."[1] Secondly, in *The Struggle for Recognition*, Mead provides a means to reconfigure Hegel's theory of sociality and the 'struggle for recognition' in post-metaphysical terms, and to provide the theory of personality-formation that was missing in Hegel's work. From the perspective of this study — to trace the theory of intersubjectivity elaborated throughout Honneth's work—the intent of this chapter is to investigate the ways in which Mead's work either enriches or diminishes the theory of intersubjectivity expounded by Honneth.

Mead's work initially enables Honneth to draw out quite strongly the naturalistic, embodied, and more materialistic aspects of intersubjectivity that are central to his work with Joas in *Social Action and Human Nature*. In their early work together, Honneth and Joas' reconstruction of Mead is explicitly positioned as an alternative to Habermas' paradigmatic interpretation. Significantly, Mead's work forms the philosophical core of both Habermas' intersubjective paradigm and Honneth and Joas' alternative notion of 'practical intersubjectivity.'[2] Whereas Habermas employs Mead as a proponent of a linguistically determined theory of communicative action and intersubjectivity, Honneth and Joas argue that Mead provides a means of avoiding a strict separation between communicative and instrumental action, and articulates a theory of intersubjectivity that is not divorced from human interaction with physical objects.[3] Honneth and Joas' collaboration produces an immensely rich study on the various traditions of philosophical anthropology—one that not only accounts for the organic conditions of human action but that stresses the inseparability of communicative and instrumental forms of action, and embodied and linguistic forms of intersubjectivity.[4]

However, this emphasis clearly shifts in Honneth's later re-interpretation of Mead undertaken in *The Struggle for Recognition*. In the later work, the strong intersubjective premise remains central but Honneth now enlists Mead to provide a 'post-metaphysical' justification of Hegel's thesis of the 'struggle for recognition.' Mead is also employed in the context of recognition-theory to provide an outline of the theory of personality-formation missing in Hegel's account of recognition and to elaborate a notion of (psychic) conflict that might explain the motivational source for the subject's struggle for recognition. Consequently, the early primary focus on the materialistic and organic aspects of interaction recede into the background and the reconstruction of Mead in *The Struggle for Recognition* focuses on interpersonal forms of interaction, drawing out the more normatively oriented aspects of Mead's account of socialization that were absent in the earlier work. Nonetheless, the philosophical anthropology first elaborated in *Social Action and Human Nature* continues to underpin Honneth's entire project. It is therefore important firstly to analyze this early work in order to trace the background to Honneth's anthropological approach and the strong intersubjectivism that remain central to his project.

TOWARDS A THEORY OF PRACTICAL INTERSUBJECTIVITY

Honneth's studies on philosophical anthropology in *Social Action and Human Nature* are central to an understanding of his project overall, particularly his engagement with the German anthropological tradition, where Gehlen provides an important basis for establishing an 'anthropology of social action.' In the German tradition of philosophical anthropology from which Honneth and Joas draw, Gehlen's work was instrumental in outlining a concept of 'human nature' in which the organic conditions of the human being were conceived in relation to a theory of action.[5] According to Gehlen, compared to other animals the human being is born prematurely and debilitated by a short gestation period, which leaves her ill-equipped to survive at birth without prolonged social nurturing. Gehlen therefore takes as his starting point the idea that in biological terms 'the human being is a defective life form'; an organism that is biologically unspecialized and poorly adapted to the natural environment. His fundamental argument is that this biological under-specialization, which is specific to the human being, is compensated for by the human capacity for action. The 'organic deficiency' of the human being has, therefore, created the unique capacity for cultural development and social action by which humans shape their own nature, the natural environment and the social world more generally.

However, Honneth and Joas argue that despite Gehlen's perceptiveness in outlining an anthropology of action, which is structured on the human being's organic deficiency and the placticity of human nature, he does not avoid reinstating his own solipsistic tendencies and continues to ground his anthropology on the notion of the solitary subject. In *Social Action and Human Nature*, therefore, Mead is positioned as a corrective to Gehlen's 'individualistic model of action' but he is also the central figure around which the argument of the work pivots. Mead's theory of intersubjectivity enables Honneth and Joas to reconstruct Gehlen's anthropological insights into 'an anthropology of intersubjective action,' or notion of 'practical intersubjectivity' upon which they structure their entire project.[6] Mead provides a model of action that can account for both the organic conditions of human action and the sociality of action. Moreover, his model of action is able to avoid reproducing a dualism between types of action, most notably between instrumental and communicative action.

Honneth and Joas argue that this unique aspect of Mead's work has often been overlooked due to his reception strictly as a theorist of symbolic interaction. Instead, they hold that Mead's work should be understood as being fundamentally based on the model of the 'organism-environment,' which significantly they claim "does not at all accord central importance to the form of interaction, but rather to human beings' manipulation of physical objects."[7] It is Mead's particular 'socialized' view of the manipulation of objects that forms the central core of Honneth's and Joas' reconstruction in *Social Action and Human Nature*, and which leads them to develop the core concept of 'practical intersubjectivity.' They argue that the over-identification of Mead's work with behaviorism, as much as with symbolic interactionism, has also lead to misreadings that give the impression he held a restricted view of action as interaction and denied the importance of the natural basis of human forms of action, including both human needs and the natural environment. Honneth and Joas argue that exactly the opposite is the case, and that Mead's work is dedicated to developing a model that emphasizes the natural conditions of human action and to overcoming the mind-body dualism prevalent in the anthropological and philosophical traditions.[8] The roots of this endeavor can be traced back to Mead's early studies in German Idealism, especially his interest in Hegel and Fichte, which led him to "place the question of the constitution of self-consciousness at the center of his early enquiries."[9] However, rather than taking Hegel's speculative philosophical route, Mead instead proposes a 'behaviorist' explanation of 'mind' or 'spirit' drawing on the natural sciences.[10]

Mead has both an epistemological and practical interest in the explanation of self-consciousness. His work is primarily concerned with the question: under what conditions does self-consciousness emerge?[11] Initially, Mead understood consciousness as something personal and private but as his work progressed he increasingly approached this problem in terms that emphasized the 'sociality' of inner experience and human action, and as a consequence greatly enriched the 'organic model of action' that he took over from John Dewey.[12] Mead soon took the view that the key to unlocking the psychological problem of self-consciousness lay in the interactive context in which the individual is involved. His major contribution towards a theory of intersubjectivity is contained in the notion of gestural communication, which includes both vocal and non-vocal forms of interaction. He further argues, however, that we only become truly self-conscious in the processes of linguistic articulation and disclosure: in the situation "in which speech or hand movements appeal to our eye or ear as well as others."[13] This was Mead's breakthrough in theorizing the 'social self': to initiate the transition to a paradigm of symbolically mediated interaction. As far as Mead was concerned, irrespective of "the metaphysical impossibilities or possibilities of solipsism, psychologically it is non-existent. There must be other selves if one's own is to exist."[14] In place of the introspective model of self-consciousness, Mead offers a model in which the subject can view herself as an object from the second-person perspective of her partners to interaction.[15] This provides the basis not only of an alternative theory of self-consciousness but also a model of perception in which even the constitution of physical objects is conceived as fundamentally social.

For Honneth and Joas, then, Mead's work is of central significance because it unites three key premises: 'the human body, human praxis, and intersubjectivity.' In *Social Action and Human Nature* they are interested not only in Mead's theory of sociality but also his alternative theory of the social constitution and manipulation of physical objects, which is able to avoid the "classical dualism of consciousness and object."[16] Their central motivation is to develop an 'anthropology of action' beginning with the model of the "organism that secures its survival in its environment through its behavior."[17]

For Honneth and Joas, Mead's reputation as a 'behaviorist' is rooted in this endeavor and is fundamentally defined by the attempt to detail the 'genesis and function' of inner experience in terms of a theory of action. Mead's theory of the 'psychical' is articulated in terms of a philosophical anthropology, and based on the functional nature of human cognition and action for the reproduction of the species.[18] Mead is at pains to point out, however, that this functional approach does not entail the denial or neglect of inner experience; rather it proposes that inner experience can only be analyzed as expressed in external behavior or observable activity. This is clearly outlined in Mead's definition of 'social psychology,' which:

> is behavioristic in the sense of starting with an observable activity—the dynamic, on-going social process, and the social acts which are its component elements—to be studied and analyzed scientifically. But it is not behavioristic in the sense of ignoring the inner experience of the individual—the inner phase of that process or activity. On the contrary, it is particularly concerned with the rise of such experience within the process as a whole. It simply works from the outside to the inside instead of from the inside to the outside, so to speak, in its endeavor to determine how such experience does arise within the process. The act, then and not the tract, is the fundamental datum in both social and individual psychology when behavioristically conceived, and it has both an inner and outer phase, and internal and external aspect.[19]

This passage outlines some of the fundamental premises of Mead's social psychology. Most noticeably it designates from the outset a particularly strong model of socialization that determines psychic life in terms of social processes and functionality in outward behavior. As indicated in the above passage, Mead understands psychic life only as 'inner *phase*' of a social act as though there is a seamless flow between external and internal life; this assumption that inner life is socially integrated in an unproblematic fashion is a questionable set of assumptions that will be discussed further below. The above passage also elucidates the second fundamental thesis underpinning Mead's work: a theory of action. This is a basic premise that drives Mead's work from some of his earliest essays where the pragmatist concerns of John Dewey are particularly influential. The axes of Mead's work pivot around both an organic theory of action as much as a functionalist understanding of action in terms of problem-solving, which he later brings together with a theory of intersubjectivity.

Mead begins applying Dewey's functionalist concept of action to the problem-complexes of philosophy in the article, "Suggestions Toward a Theory of the Philosophical Disciplines" (1900).[20] There he takes on board Dewey's critique of the 'reflex arc concept' in psychology, which is based on an understanding of a 'stimulus-response' model of action between organisms.[21] According to Dewey, the response and stimulus must be understood as an 'organic circuit,' or what he terms 'mutual adjustment' in a coordinated process, where both forms of experience contribute to and mediate towards reaching an end to an action; the response therefore must be understood as enlarging or transforming the initial component or phase in an action complex, rather than as different existential components.[22] This organic model of action is therefore more about reciprocal adjustment, of functional moments within an ongoing process of coordination, rather than a dualism between different of types of experience.[23]

In these early essays, Mead extends the theories of both Dewey and William James regarding the fundamental nature of subjectivity and its constitution in relation to the meaning and function of objects in the context of action. As Dewey had already claimed, objects derive their meaning within our actions or 'interactions' with them. These meanings are maintained and the function of objects 'unquestioned' only if our actions proceed unproblematically. Following Dewey, Mead highlights the functionalist basis for a theory of action using the well-known example of a child reaching for a burning candle. Action situations are organic and unquestioned or unreflected upon as long as they remain unproblematic and proceed as expected. It is only when an action becomes problematized that the subject becomes reflexively aware of the genesis and function of a particular action.[24]

The child's actions become problematic when the objects with which she interacts can no longer be taken for granted and provoke uncertainty or conflicting reactions, for example, producing a tension between delight and pain. We begin to reflect on the meaning of the objects involved due to the creative responses that we are called to make in the action context, and this in turn throws our subjectivity into relief. For Mead, in such problem-contexts 'old universals' are called into question and the reflexive capacities of the subject are called upon to solve the problem arising from interrupted action sequences.[25]

Mead therefore understands the 'psychical' or 'subjective' component of experience to be the problem-solving element within an action-complex; it is that phase of action that enables objects to be reconstituted with new meanings that no longer render them problematic and which facilitates the completion of the act.[26] He asserts that the functional character of psychical consciousness or subjectivity "confines its reference to this function, which is that of reconstruction of the disintegrated coordination."[27] As a consequence of these speculations, Mead suggests we can differentiate between 'subjective and objective elements of experience' in functional rather than metaphysical terms.[28] "It is in this phase of subjectivity," suggests Mead, "with its activities of attention in the solution of the problem, i.e., in the construction of the hypothesis of the new world, that the individual qua individual has its functional expression or rather is that function."[29]

These formulations, however, raise a number of questions. Firstly, the understanding of the human individual purely in terms of this reconstructive function, as the above passage indicates, renders the individual in completely functional terms.[30] Subjectivity appears to be rendered in terms that reduce it to only a problem-solving function in action; to a phase that merely reconstitutes the frame of reference in which action can be completed. Secondly, this reconstructive concept of subjectivity at first sight seems to be plagued by the same problem as Kant's transcendental ego: that is, how can we be cognitive of our individual subjectivity when the ego that 'stands over against the world' is also the same ego that is situated in the world among other objects?[31] As Habermas suggests, whose interpretation in this context is paradigmatic: How can the individual be posited simultaneously as both a "*world generating* and *autonomously acting subject*"?[32]

Mead's attempt to address both of these apparent difficulties is addressed by the introduction into his work of a distinction between the terms, 'I' and 'me,' taken from the work of William James—terms that later become central to Honneth's theory of recognition.[33] With this conceptualization, Mead suggests a distinction can be made between the 'I,' or the self as subject, and the 'me' which refers to "the self functioning as object";[34] whereas the 'me' signifies "the individual as an object of consciousness," the 'I' is suggestive of "the individual having consciousness."[35] As Mead explains, the subject always acts, then, in relation to two different but interconnected 'fields' of action: an empirical self that is both an object in the world, and at the same time a subject whose function it is to reconstruct the world of objects that has disintegrated in the context of her action.[36] It is not the 'me,' then, that performs a reconstructive and reorganizing function; the 'me' instead "performs a mediating role within an ongoing process of experience or action."[37] According to Mead the outcome of this reconstructive phase is not only a new world of objects but also a new individual. Mead claims therefore that subjectivity, or the psychical phase, is not a separate domain but an immediate and direct experience.[38] It is not a 'permanent phenomenon' or a 'property of subjects' but is fundamentally embedded in the context of action.[39] This conceptual distinction between the 'I' and 'me' later becomes crucial to Honneth's reconstruction of moral conflict in *The Struggle for Recognition*.

For Mead, self-consciousness can only emerge in a social group and is fundamentally socially constituted by taking on the perspective or role of other members of the group: "There is no self before there is a world, and no world before the self…The reference to a self takes place through individuals taking the attitude of the other."[40] Ultimately, the capacity for taking on the role of the other is developed through vocal gesture or speech, which enables the individual to call out in herself the same responses that she generates from other individuals in the social group.[41] As Honneth and Joas maintain, the concept of 'role' becomes fundamental for Mead's philosophical anthropology and it is the capacity for 'role-taking' that provides the fabric of mutually binding behavioral expectations and social cooperation.

What is unique to Mead's approach, however, and fundamental to Honneth and Joas' reconstruction, is the vast depth and reach of intersubjectivism that characterizes his theory. For Mead, even the constitution of physical objects is based on the same intersubjective conditions that are acquired in socialization by role-taking.[42]

This strong intersubjectivism in Mead's theory can be traced through two processes in regard to the constitution of physical objects: one is the subject's ability to combine multiple perspectives in determining an object. In other words, the subject must be able to take a decentered perspective in relation to an object, without losing sight of the original image or perspective she has of it.[43] This capacity is acquired in the same way that human subjects learn to take the attitude or role of the other in subject-formation. The ability to change perspectives in relation to objects is akin to the way in which different 'me's' must be unified in the process of socialization. The same process applies to the constitution of objects whereby the subject adopts the perspective of the 'generalized other,' enabling her to achieve a "comprehensive view of the object."[44]

The second premise central to Mead's theory of the intersubjective constitution of physical objects is the cooperation between the distance and contact senses, or between hand and eye. For Mead, the transfer of data from the distance senses to the contact senses also presupposes the capacity for role-taking. For Honneth and Joas, the remarkable aspect of Mead's philosophy of perception is that even the cooperation between hand and eye is grounded in the same fundamental *a priori* stratum of intersubjective action, that is below or prior to linguistic interaction.[45] Mead had already laid the groundwork for this broad-reaching and temporally prior stratum of intersubjectivism with the notion of gestural communication, which he argues precedes vocal communication and provides the basis for intersubjective action.[46] This strong theory of intersubjectivity is the key to understanding Honneth's interest in Mead and the fundamental premise of his own project, which is carried through to *The Struggle for Recognition*.

The crux to understanding Mead's theory of the constitution and perception of objects can again be attributed to his theory of role-taking. Mead explains that the imputation of interiority to the object can be understood in terms of the same process of role-taking that individuals acquire in socialization. In other words, in the same way that an individual takes the role of another subject she can also take the role of the object, and it is this capacity for role-taking that gives the object an 'interiority' and 'identity.'

Furthermore, Mead understands this interaction with objects as a cooperative process. The interiority of the object arises "from the co-operation of physical things with ourselves in our acts." He suggests it can be thought of as a reciprocal process in which "we are seeking the sort of resistance that we ourselves offer in grasping and manipulating things." Significantly, Mead understands this as a cooperative interaction between subject and physical object. He explains: "we seek support, leverage, and assistance from the object."[47] Similarly, in another fragment, Mead uses the example of an axe to clearly indicate the sociality underpinning what might otherwise be thought of as instrumental action: "In balancing an axe, for instance, one is establishing a co-operative relationship with it and to this extent putting one's self inside the object. Similarly the log which one cuts will cooperate at a certain point. The process is essentially social."[48]

In these passages we can see the way in which Mead brings together the defining features of his theory: his theory of social action and theory of intersubjectivity are brought together with his theory of perception in a way that conceives of a cooperative relation with objects and the environment. In this way, Mead makes a case against theorizing any dualism between instrumental and social action, and seeks to combine the two in an 'anthropology of action.' Mead makes clear that the ability to be able to 'transfer' a counter-pressure to objects is an ability that must already have been acquired in socialization, where the capacity to be able to take the role or the attitude of the other is paramount. As Honneth and Joas suggest, this implies that the "knowledge gained from social experiences is a precondition for the synthesis of 'things' out of chaos of sense perceptions." Moreover, the flip-side of the subject's ability to make sense of the world through the constitution of objects also enables "the human organism's delimiting of itself from other objects and its self-reflexive acquisition of a sense of itself as a unitary body. The self develops, then, in a process that is continuous with the formation of 'things' for the actor."[49]

For Honneth and Joas, Mead's philosophical anthropology and theory of intersubjectivity, his notion of a cooperative relation with the world and theory of the constitution of physical objects furnishes them with the central notion of 'practical intersubjectivity' which structures their entire project. Their central premise is that the concept of 'practical intersubjectivity' provides the fundamental basis for 'an anthropology of social action': a theory of action that takes account of the natural conditions of the human being and begins with the notion of the 'organism-environment.'[50] However, it is a concept that is also based on the fundamental sociality of all action, even that which might otherwise be considered instrumental. As Joas further explains, in comparison to other models of intersubjectivity, the notion of 'practical intersubjectivity':

is oriented neither to the *contemplative model* of a mere encountering of the other (as we find in the works of Feuerbach and Buber), nor to the *linguistic* model of understanding the other through language and action. Rather ... *practical* intersubjectivity [refers] to a structure that arises and takes form in the joint activity of human subjects to achieve ends set by their life needs, a structure into which the corporeality of these subjects and external nature readily enter.[51]

Honneth and Joas therefore explicitly differentiate their reading of Mead and the concept of intersubjectivity from Habermas' model of communicative interaction. In *Social Action and Human Nature* they are at pains to emphasize the non-linguistic aspects of Mead's theory of intersubjectivity and communicative action. By this account, 'linguistic intersubjectivity' is only one component of a broader approach and "is reconstructed by Mead from the structure of gestural communication, which is connected more closely with the body, and founded in cooperative action."[52] The significance of Mead's account for Honneth and Joas is that he defines a deep stratum of intersubjectivity that is prior to vocal communication.[53] With the notion of gestural communication, Mead makes a case for the inseparability of bodily *and* linguistic forms of action and communication, and thereby provides the basis for Honneth's early attempts to broaden the theory of intersubjectivity beyond the limits of the linguistic paradigm. For Mead, bodily forms of interaction form a part of an 'organic circuit,' a significant phase of action in addition to linguistic ones. Gestural communication, then, not only forms an essential phase in the phylogenetic development of the species but bodily and pre-linguistic forms of communication form a continuum with linguistic forms of communication. Moreover, Mead offers a theory of action in which subject and object are conceived in a cooperative reciprocal relation, rather than on the basis of a dualism between instrumental action and social interaction.

Although some aspects of Honneth's anthropological studies on embodied forms of intersubjectivity are re-integrated into his major work, *The Struggle for Recognition*, they take on a less prominent role and are confined to preliminary forms of affective intersubjectivity and the specific interpersonal love relations between subjects. Notably, as other commentators have identified, the early attempt to develop an 'anthropology of action' that explicitly avoids a dualism between types of action, and keenly pursues a more materialistic approach, gives way in Honneth's later work to a theory that is exclusively based on interaction between subjects.[54] However, the original notion of a more fundamental and temporally prior stratum of intersubjectivity, one below linguistic communication, is one that continues to inform Honneth's project throughout, and is significantly reconceptualized in an alternative register in his later work *Reification*.

THE RECOGNITIVE SELF: HONNETH'S REINTERPRETATION OF MEAD IN *THE STRUGGLE FOR RECOGNITION*

In contrast to the earlier reading contained in *Social Action and Human Nature*, in *The Struggle for Recognition* Honneth resolutely reconstructs Mead as a theorist of recognition. Honneth argues that the social psychologist intended "to make the struggle for recognition the point of reference for a theoretical construction in terms of which the moral development of society is to be explained."[55] He begins his second reconstruction of Mead with an examination of the early writings in an effort to retrace what he claims is an outline towards a theory of recognition. In this sense, Honneth begins his interpretation in the same place as *Social Action and Human Nature*: with a discussion of Mead's attempt to provide an understanding of self-consciousness in a way that could avoid the speculative approach of German Idealism. As discussed above, Mead's solution to this problem is to bring the functionalist approach to problem-solving in action together with a philosophical anthropology that emphasizes the organic conditions of human action. In *The Struggle for Recognition*, Honneth only briefly acknowledges the genealogy of Mead's functionalist approach to this issue. He points to the fact that Mead assumes that the 'psychical' or self-consciousness is revealed only in those instances in which actions are problematized, when the subject is compelled to creatively solve problems encountered in action.[56]

However, Honneth argues that Mead quickly recognizes that this early definition of the psychical provides an inadequate means of gaining access to the subjective world. His early work on the psychical indeed reveals the problem-solving abilities of individuals that primarily result in a redefinition of objects in an action-complex. However, as Honneth points out, Mead is unable to adequately explain how the individual actually comes to perceive herself as a subject in this context. The missing link here is the absence of a fully theorized concept of reflexivity: although the subject becomes aware of herself when the instrumental action she is engaged in becomes problematized, her awareness is primarily attuned to the re-constitution of objects in that situation, rather than reflecting upon the creative *subjective* source of the solution to the problem.[57] In other words, although the objects in the action-complex are reconstituted, the subject has not become an object to herself.

Notably, at this point, in stark contrast to the early assessment of Mead's philosophy of perception and constitution of physical objects that predominated the reading in *Social Action and Human Nature*, in *The Struggle for Recognition*, Honneth by-passes the earlier attempt to avoid a dualism between types of action, and this has significant consequences for his work.[58] Instead, he moves directly to a discussion of Mead's theory of social interaction and the sociality of subject-formation, focusing on Mead's slightly later essays that place an emphasis on the 'sociality of action.' Mead, he argues, is able to construct a more suitable model of the psychical or subjectivity only once he takes into account the 'reflexivity of action' and structures it upon a theory of 'human interactive behavior.'[59] For Honneth, the key to Mead's breakthrough was to underscore the importance of meaning in the behavioral expectations of partners in interaction and the subject's awareness of the social meaning of her own actions. Consciousness of subjectivity emerges only once the subject can comprehend the meaning of her own actions in the same way as they have meaning for her partners in interaction.

Central to Honneth's re-interpretation of Mead in *The Struggle for Recognition* is a particular focus on the conceptual distinction between the 'I' and 'me' as separate phases of consciousness. For Mead, the emergence of an originary relation-to-self is only possible when the actor becomes conscious of herself as a social object. The self is never the current agent of one's own behavioral expressions; the self is only glimpsed as a reaction to what one's partner to interaction perceives. Thus, it is not the 'I' that can be glimpsed but the 'me' that reflects the other's image of me: "The observer who accompanies all our self-conscious conduct is then not the actual 'I' who is responsible for conduct in *propria persona*—he is rather a response which one makes to his own conduct."[60]

The relation between the 'me,' as the set of attitudes and responses representing others, and the 'I,' as the element of self associated with inner impulses and spontaneity, can be viewed like a relationship between two partners to dialogue: "If the 'I' speaks, the 'me' hears. If the 'I' strikes, the 'me' feels the blow."[61] The 'I' is the "subjective world of experiences to which one has privileged access." It is that element of self which is always over against the 'me,' reacting to the attitudes of the community as they appear in experience.[62] In this way, the spontaneously acting 'I,' which always precedes consciousness, continually comments on the behavioral expressions incorporated within 'me.'[63] The 'me' can be regarded as giving form and 'structure to the 'I.' However, over against the 'me' is the 'I' who reacts to the attitudes of others, and in so doing can exert influence over and change the organized set of attitudes that constitute the 'me.'[64] It is important to point out, though, that the *only* self a subject can know is the 'me'; the 'I' is a phase of the self that can never be directly known in consciousness. In other words, "[f]or the 'I' to become known, it must become an object, a 'me,' thereby losing its status as a 'I.'"[65]

THE INTERNALIZATION OF PERSPECTIVES AND THE PROCESS OF RECOGNITION

Honneth's discussion of Mead's theory of the 'I' and 'me' has a very specific purpose in *The Struggle for Recognition*: it provides the means for "a naturalistic justification of Hegel's theory of recognition."[66] The basic premise of recognition in this reading of Mead is that self-consciousness is dependent not only on the existence of the other but more importantly on the *ability to take the other's perspective*. Moreover, Honneth argues that like Hegel, Mead conceives of the development of self-consciousness as proceeding from the external social world to inner experience. Remarkably, Mead's notion of subject-formation—understood as the internalization of the other's perspective—is recast by Honneth as a *process of recognition*.

However, in *The Struggle for Recognition*, Honneth's primary focus is not devoted to Mead's epistemic theory of the formation of self-consciousness, but rather a reconstruction of his 'practical' theory of self-formation or 'practical relation-to-self'—which he also claims is central to Hegel's theory of recognition.[67] Following Habermas, Honneth argues that Mead's intersubjective theory of self distinguishes two possible ways that the subject can take up a relation to itself. As Habermas contends, Mead's analysis in many places suffers from a lack of definition between the epistemic self-relation of the knowing subject and the practical relation-to-self of the acting subject: the first indicating the cognitive element of self-reference, the second, the practical one, referring to the way in which one 'behaves' or 'conducts oneself.'[68] This conceptual lack of clarity is largely due to the fact that Mead begins with self-knowledge as "a problem-solving practice and conceives of the cognitive self-relation as a function of action."[69] This functionalism remains the defining feature of both epistemic and practical forms of self-relation, with the ability to take the perspective of the other in the latter form largely confined to the process of a reorganization of attitudes and means of controlling one's own behavior.

However, Honneth does not take sufficient account of the functionalism evident in Mead's concept of self-relation and instead reconstructs his interpretation in particularly normative terms, thereby uncritically reabsorbing Mead's functionalism into his own work. His main concern is that Mead's theory of intersubjective subject-formation provides the means to reconstruct Hegel's basic insight in naturalistic terms. On this basis he turns his attention to the core premise of his later reading of Mead, which is that it provides a theory of recognition that explains "those forms of practical affirmation by which [the subject] gains a normative understanding of itself as a certain kind of person."[70] Honneth argues that after his early focus on constructing a cognitive conception of the formation of self-consciousness, Mead moves in later articles to reconceptualize the 'I' and 'me' in normative terms where he is concerned primarily with 'practical identity-formation.'[71]

Honneth argues that Mead's social psychology advances to another level once he takes into account the issue of the subject's moral and practical identity-formation. In Honneth's reading, the categories of the 'I' and 'me' are expanded once Mead brings into focus the normative dimension of inter-

action and individual development. Although the practical and cognitive processes exhibit the same structure, now it is moral behavioral responses which
ego takes on board. In this second, practical form of self-relation, the actions
by which the subject affects itself as it affects the other contain the normative
set of behavioral responses and attitudes of the community within which the
subject interacts. The subject then influences herself with the moral values of
the other and applies them to her practical self-relation. In so doing, both the
structure of this practical 'me' and the function of the self-relation are altered: "The 'me' of the *practical* relation-to-self is no longer the seat of an
originary or reflected self-*consciousness* but an agency of self-*control*."
Honneth's and Habermas' readings of Mead concur on this point: "Self-
reflection here takes on the specific tasks of mobilizing motives for action
and of internally controlling one's own modes of behavior."[72] The 'me' in
this context is a 'conservative force' that keeps in check the creative resistance of the 'I,' in this way ensuring conformity with the intersubjective
behavioral expectations of a given society.[73]

Honneth suggests the genesis of this second version of moral self-development can be found in one of the last essays published by Mead, in the
series on the social formation of self-consciousness.[74] In "The Social Self,"
Mead begins to acknowledge that the subject cannot only be thought of as
solving problems encountered in action merely on a cognitive level, but that
conflict occurring in action often has a moral content that also requires resolution. In this essay, Mead pens one line in particular that is noteworthy for
the way in which he suggests subjects learn to internalize moral norms to
take on a second-person perspective towards their own conduct in childhood:
"Thus the child can think about his conduct as good and bad only as he reacts
to his own acts in the remembered words of his parents."[75] In this instance,
we might say, that the child learns to apply not only the parents' normative
expectations but also *prohibitory* responses to her own thoughts and actions.

Honneth argues that Mead structures his notion of identity-formation on
this premise, which is now expanded to include "normative action-con-
texts."[76] Over the course of an individual's life, she not only must acquire the
roles of speaker and listener through interaction with concrete reference persons, but also takes on board the moral values of an increasing number of
interaction partners which she consequently incorporates into her own practical self-image.[77] Through this process the subject learns to identify with
vocational roles, gender roles, and more abstract ethnic, national, and political roles, before acquiring a sense of practical identity.

The self for Mead, then, is entirely socially constituted and sociality is
posited as the precondition for the self and ontogenetic development. Both
the notions of role-taking and of gestural communication provide the basis of
the ontogenetic account of the socialization of the individual. In Mead's
ontogenetic account, children are understood to internalize the functionaliz-

ing or 'normalizing' behavior of social institutions in the process of success-ful self-formation and to take on the perspective of the 'generalized other' whereby they learn to apply the behavioral expectations of all members of society.[78]

Honneth argues that Mead's notion of taking on the perspective of the generalized other can be directly translated into a theory of recognition and he interprets the internalization of the generalized other in strictly normative rather than functional terms:

> If it is the case that one becomes a socially accepted member of one's commu-nity by learning to appropriate the social norms of the 'generalized other,' then it makes sense to use the concept of 'recognition' for this intersubjective relationship: to the extent that growing children recognize their interaction partners by way of an internalization of their normative attitudes, they can know themselves to be members of their social context of cooperation. [79]

Although Honneth may be taking some liberty in portraying Mead's social psychology as a theory of recognition, there are undoubtedly some scattered remarks throughout Mead's later lectures where he employs the term 'recog-nition' to convey this reciprocal pattern of perspective-taking and the depen-dency of the subject on the social context for self-formation: "It is that self," he says, "which is able to maintain itself in the community, that is recognized in the community in so far as it recognizes others."[80]

It is, however, very difficult to argue that Mead conceives his theory of reciprocal perspective-taking as a more general theory of *mutual* recognition. Although it is possible to retrieve passages in Mead's work in which he uses the term 'recognition,' one can just as easily single out passages that indicate Mead had in mind a notion of 'social control' or the functional integration of individuals into society on the basis of internalized perspectives of the gener-alized other.[81] The interaction between the 'generalized other' and the indi-vidual is also not strictly one of mutuality nor an intersubjective one between individual subjects. In this sense, Honneth both over-extends his reading of Mead and also overlooks the productive form of normalization and power at play here: that subjects are also potentially constituted by 'normalizing' modes of conduct that ensure social control and the functional coordination of actions; that recognition understood in Mead's terms is also a function of power.

Honneth extends the parallels between Mead's and Hegel's work even further in regard to what he considers to be their shared notions of recogni-tion. In particular, he seeks to draw from Mead's work the means to recon-ceptualize the three forms of intersubjective relation he identified in the young Hegel—love, rights, and solidarity (later achievement)—and to devel-op three corresponding forms of self-relation—self-confidence, self-respect, and self-esteem. He admits, however, that Mead makes no mention anywhere in his work of the type of mutual recognition that was identified with love in his reconstruction of Hegel's work. Instead Mead provides a more functionally orientated account that emphasizes the importance of early interactive processes and role-taking for the successful formation of self and for providing the basis for all mature forms of social interaction and integration. In this respect, for Honneth, Hegel's notion of 'love' stands as the quintessential basis of the theory of recognition, which as we shall discuss below, he instead augments with the insights of object-relations theory in order to more fully develop a corresponding account of a practical relation-to-self that can ensure self-confidence through the early caring relations of significant others.

However, for Honneth there is a closer affinity between Hegel's notion of recognition relations of 'right' and Mead's notion of the 'generalized other.' For Honneth, Mead's work offers a way of both amending and substantively deepening the second form of recognition in terms of legal relations.[82] In basic terms, Honneth finds in Mead the general notion of a practical relation-to-self, which is developed only by the recognition of the subject as a right-bearing member of the community. The concept of 'right' underpins Mead's notion of the reciprocal behavioral obligations that all members of a given society can expect from one another. By taking the perspective of the 'generalized other,' subjects are also understood to be internalizing the rights that members of a society are expected to accord one-another: "Rights are the claims ... about which I can be sure the generalized other [will] meet."[83] Moreover, this legally rendered generalized perspective is also the basis upon which the subject learns to view herself as a legal person, a person with dignity and self-respect. Honneth suggests one can find in Mead the idea that the experience of being recognized as a legal person, a person endowed with rights, "ensures that one can develop a positive attitude towards oneself. For in realizing that they are obliged to respect one's rights, [the members of the community] ascribe to one the quality of morally responsible agency."[84]

Honneth argues that like Hegel, Mead grounds the general notion of recognition on property rights. As with Hegel, the mutual respect of property ownership or possession is viewed as the basis of community membership; mutual respect is ensured by reciprocal perspective-taking, whereby in relation to property: "taking the attitude of the others guarantees to [the subject] the recognition of his own rights."[85] In this way, Honneth suggests, in taking the attitude of the other towards myself, I understand myself to be "a particular type of person"; I apply a positive attitude to myself, as a person worthy of self-respect.[86] This form of legal recognition has a universalistic basis and is granted on the basis of attributes that all members of the community share with one another. It provides a concept of practical self-relation that concerns only the 'me' of subjective identity; that phase of the self that takes on the shared normative expectations of all other members of a given society.

As was the case with the epistemic self-relation, in Honneth's reconstruction, the creative impulsiveness of the practical-self reacts to the normative controls of the generalized other in a way that is understood to challenge the organized and institutionalized 'me,' the institutionalized norms enshrined in rights. The practical responses of the 'I' in this context, are viewed by Honneth more in terms of the subject's own moral responses to the institutionalized 'me.' The 'me' is the conservative moment of selfhood that places limits on the impulsiveness of the 'I' from the perspective of a social 'we.'[87] Thus, both the 'I' of practical identity formation and the cognitive 'I' of self-knowledge can never be 'grasped directly.'[88] It is only in memory that the subject becomes aware of the 'I.' The 'I' is the agent of our spontaneous actions but because we cannot have direct access to it, we are constantly surprising ourselves with our own responses: we can never be "fully aware of what we are... It is [only] as we act that we are aware of ourselves."[89]

Honneth therefore suggests:

> This is why ... the concept of the 'I' ... has something unclear and ambiguous about it. What it stands for is the sudden experience of a surge of inner impulses, and it is never immediately clear whether they stem from pre-social drives, the creative imagination, or the moral sensibility of one's own self.[90]

Honneth is right to point out that the status of the 'I' is unclear; however, he overlooks the fact that this lack of clarity is also the source of many problems in Mead's work and that it might be open to quite different interpretative possibilities. As Whitebook argues, the problem with leaving the content of the 'I' so unspecified is that it lends itself to "a strong conventionalist interpretation of [Mead's] theory, in which self-formation becomes a process of imprinting, in which the standpoint of the other—that is the demands of society—is stamped on a relatively indeterminate 'I.'"[91]

Furthermore, much of this theory of subject-formation can also be attributed to the functional genesis of the 'I' in the early cognitive account of problem-solving. In contrast to Honneth's reading, if Mead's concept is traced throughout his work, it is clear that he consistently views the 'I' as the functional source of positive solutions to problems, whether they be moral problems or cognitive ones, and as the functional integration of socialized individuals into the social group. The subject's impulsive reactions to the organized attitudes of the group are viewed by Mead as alternative forms of reorganization of group attitudes rather than forms of moral protest arising from inadequately recognized subjects. In this sense, he continues to see the 'I' as the source of the solution to problems encountered in action or a new presentation of the various perspectives internalized by the 'me.' It is also significant that Mead only ever conceptualizes conflict encountered in action in a positive light as providing a solution to problems encountered in action.

As Aboulafia suggests, throughout his work, Mead never accounts for forms of psychological conflict that cannot be attributed solely to problem-solving.[92] Like Mead, it seems in his own reconstruction, Honneth views the conflict between the 'I' and 'me' only in positive or constructive terms. The 'I,' as Honneth represents it in his analysis, forces the 'me' to find a solution to problems experienced in the context of intersubjectively rigid or conventional norms of a society.

This is particularly a problem for the model of subject-formation that is propounded in Mead's work and which Honneth seems to uncritically accept. In particular, as authors such as McNay and Allen have suggested, in the model of recognition that Honneth develops in *The Struggle for Recognition*, subject-formation appears to consist of the unreflective internalization of norms with no way of discriminating between norms that might also be constituted by power relations or that reproduce social inequalities or 'subordinating ideologies.'[93] In this sense, Honneth's own adoption of Mead's theory of socialization reproduces this problem because subject-formation is theorized without taking adequate account of power relations or ideologically structured forms of recognition.[94] Honneth invests so heavily in the normative character of internalizing the other's perspective that his theory of subject-formation cannot take account of the constitutive effects of power, which remains 'secondary' to the mutuality of primary forms of recognition.

Moreover, as Aboulafia suggests, this problem is also a product of the way in which Mead conceives of the subject as 'split' between the 'I' and 'me.' As discussed above, the 'I' cannot know itself; the 'me' is the only aspect of the self that can be known as such. The 'I' can only enter consciousness once it is filtered into the 'me'—in other words, once it becomes a social object. For Mead, only the 'me' has the capacity for self-reflection as an "object of the generalized other."[95]

However, this begs the question: how can the subject self-consciously determine her own self-formation in a manner that is not over-determined by norms and values if she can never be aware of her own 'I'-impulses or resistance to the socialized 'me'? This is not to deny the importance of novelty or spontaneity in Mead's account of the 'I,' rather to question whether, according to Mead's overly socialized account, the self can self-consciously shape the content of her own 'I'-impulses. As Aboulafia explains:

> The novel happens to the 'me.' The self cannot decide to incorporate the novel, nor can the 'I,' which can act in a spontaneous and novel fashion, by itself reflect on how it will act ... The self is found already constituted, and through the manner in which it is constituted must play a part in what the 'I' does, it cannot direct or determine the 'I.' There is no place in Mead's model ... for self-conscious selection of who or what one is to become, the conscious making of the self or person by the self.[96]

To avoid being no more than a passive internalization of the generalized other, the subject needs to have autonomous and critically reflexive purchase over the changes that shape the self as a product of both the 'I' and the 'me.' According to Mead's account, though, we can only ever be cognitively aware of any impulses or creative 'deviations' from the perspective of the 'me.' As Aboulafia suggests, the problem with Mead's work is that he posits an irresolvable dualism not only between the 'I' and 'me' but also between reflective and non-reflective experience, and this seems to leave no mediating point from which a (self-)consciousness can process novel experiences as they occur.[97]

As Whitebook also notes, this problem can be attributed to Mead's failure to adequately consider the existence of a pre-reflexive self.[98] Mead's very notion of 'taking on the role of the other,' Whitebook argues, "assumes the existence of a pre-reflexive agent, however minimal, capable of doing the taking on." Mead's model of socialization is so totalizing that he posits a self that does not exist prior to taking on the perspective of the other.[99] Although he attempted to militate against the effects of this problem with the concept of the 'I,' as we have seen, the category is not robust enough to perform the task and instead leads to a dualism between the 'I' and 'me,' "an infinite regress regarding self-knowledge."[100] In contrast to Honneth's reading, then, it can be argued that for Mead the subject does not develop in conflict with the other in terms of a strict *intersubjective* interaction *per se*, rather the subject is a product of the internalization of *generalized* perspectives and role-taking. The conflict that Mead conceptualizes does not occur between subjects but is internal to the individual herself.[101] In other words, conflict is located at the level of the individual psyche between the 'I' and 'me' but is not literally a process of (intersubjective) social struggle.

Honneth uncritically transposes Mead's notion of the 'I's' response to the 'me' as a notion of social conflict that is seamless or integrative. He assumes that the 'I-impulses' force the 'me' to struggle to achieve more inclusive forms of social recognition. This immediately raises two issues. Firstly, this reading renders conflict and power in overly functionalized terms and 'struggle' is therefore only ever articulated within the context of an already internalized moral-social vocabulary. As discussed previously, conflict and power are therefore not theorized as co-constitutive but merely restricted to the context of a secondary 'reaction' within the context of already existing norms. Secondly, by basing the notion of conflict on Mead's distinction between the 'I' and 'me,' Honneth seems to assume there is a seamless flow between internal psychic and external social worlds. This assumes not only that psychic impulses can be readily expressed and translated into an external moral-social discourse but also that the psyche is totally socially determined in the first place.

Instead, of considering the above-mentioned problems, Honneth centers his discussion on the critical importance of the 'I' and 'me' as the basis for explaining social conflict: "this inner friction between the 'I' and 'me' represents the outline of the conflict that is supposed to be able to explain moral development of both individuals and society."[102] Honneth argues that it is this further expansion of the conceptual distinction of the 'I' and 'me' in relation to normative behavioral expectations that pushes Mead's work in a social psychological direction unable to be taken by Hegel. Firstly, for Honneth, this aspect of Mead's work indicates that the form of 'mutual recognition' associated with rights cannot adequately account for the unique particularities that differentiate individual citizens in any society. Secondly, Honneth contends that the conflictual interplay between the 'I' and 'me' enables Mead to address the impression that the subject is merely passively constituted by the norms and perspectives of the generalized other. He argues that the function of the 'I' and 'me' in this context enables Mead not only to account for the 'normative control of one's conduct' but the "creative deviations with which, in our everyday action, we ordinarily react to social obligations."[103]

The crux of Honneth's reinterpretation of Mead lies in the explanatory potential embodied in this conceptual distinction. The main aspect of Mead's work that for Honneth extends Hegel's original theory of recognition is the conflict potential contained in the expanded concept of the 'I' and 'me,' which serves to explain the motivational source for the 'struggle for recognition.' In this sense, Mead is seen to offer Honneth a social psychological account of Hegel's dialectic between dependence and independence: a theory of social development that is fundamentally based on the intersubjective constitution of the subject but one that accounts for a dynamic element of conflict when individual possibilities for identity-formation are denied. Moreover, the psychological conflict between the 'me' as perspective-taker, and the 'I' who reacts to these social attitudes and moral expectations, also provides Honneth with the notion of social change more generally—the crucial notion of the 'struggle for recognition.' The creative impulses of the 'I' call into question the identity of the 'me' as the internalized perspective of one's partners in interaction. The demands of the 'I' call out for expanded forms of intersubjective recognition to accommodate aspects of individual identity that are not currently being met.

To resolve this moral conflict and 'realize' the demands of the 'I,' Honneth argues that the only recourse the subject has is to address her claims for 'recognition' to a future anticipated society in which norms and attitudes are expanded to such an extent that the subject's idealized claims for recognition can be met.[104] Mead conceives of a progressive democratization of society built into the individualizing demands of the 'I,' particularly in terms of an expansion to individual rights and freedom from 'conventions' and 'given laws.' As Honneth presents it there is an internal dynamic inherent to Mead's account of moral conflict that generates normative progress within any given society.[105] Honneth contends that Mead's account of moral conflict constitutes a theory of social development that "provides a social-psychological basis for the Hegelian idea of a 'struggle for recognition.'"[106] For Honneth, Mead's work is invaluable not only because it provides a model of social development that can be understood as a process of the 'struggle for recognition' but more importantly, he is able to explain its motivational basis—the crucial factor that was missing in Hegel's account.[107]

This is the central premise of Honneth's later reading of Mead. He considers Mead is able to provide a social-psychological explanation for the 'struggle for recognition' as the form of 'social praxis' that drives social change. Somewhat problematically, in my view, Honneth therefore takes up the idea that individual psychological processes can be joined in a kind of 'network' of demands or "moral deviations which blanket the social life-process."[108] These 'I-demands' are then combined to form a 'single historical force' or supra-individual agent for social change; a form of social change that in every instance is read as a demand for and response to inadequate forms of recognition. In other words, Honneth equates psychic conflict with social conflict, when the two, it might be argued, are of a very different order. In Honneth's view there is a contestation within an existing moral-social universe in which subjects are already immersed. Moreover, leaving to one side *intra*-psychic conflict, Honneth misses the point of Foucault's more genealogical notion of power where power is understood as a series of conflicts over interpretation and perspectives, rather than integration into or participation in shared conflict within a pre-existing moral order.

It is evident, therefore, that between the works of 1980 and 1992, Honneth's interpretation of Mead is quite radically altered in line with his turn to a theory of recognition. The notion of 'practical intersubjectivity' that structures his early work, with its implications for a broadly conceived theory of intersubjectivity and philosophical anthropology, is replaced by a social-psychological theory of subject-formation and explanation of Hegel's 'struggle for recognition,' which is based on the conflict between the 'I' and 'me' generated by the demands of individuation. Honneth works this thesis into a theory of social development that is grounded on the expectation that expanded recognition-relations will be the inevitable outcome of all forms of conflictual social interaction.

In recent work, however, Honneth has significantly re-assessed Mead's work and critically rejected it as the central reference for developing a theory of recognition. Honneth no longer considers that Mead's social psychology provides an adequate explanation for the 'struggle for recognition.' In fact, he now problematizes some of the functional tendencies of Mead's theory of socialization and social integration in terms of reciprocal perspective-taking discussed above. He precisely acknowledges that the problem with Mead's psychological explanation is that it appears to operate on a supra-individual level, "developing independently of the reactive behavior of the two partici-pants."[109] As a consequence he acknowledges that Mead does not adequately distinguish between the forms of action that might be considered normative by the criteria of mutual recognition.

Moreover, Honneth has now abandoned any attempt to structure the mod-el of the 'struggle for recognition' on the internal psychological conflict of the 'I' and 'me.' He now views the concept of the 'I' as an inadequate model for explaining the locus of all forms of moral rebellion and as the catalyst for social development more generally. Likewise, Mead's model of subject-for-mation has been critically scrutinized and abandoned due to the functional model of internalized behavioral expectations on which it is based.[110] Honneth therefore instead turns to object-relations psychoanalysis to under-take an empirical reconstruction of the primary forms of intersubjectivity and self-formation. This reorientation towards object-relations theory constitutes a major reformulation of the theory of recognition that has become central to Honneth's project and the fundament upon which his later work is based.

Chapter Nine

Intersubjectivity or Primary Affectivity?

Honneth's Reading of Winnicott

Honneth's theory of recognition is fundamentally based on the notion of the intersubjective constitution of the subject. If self-formation is a product of everyday interactions with others, then the form these interactions take is central both to self-formation and the capacity to become a reciprocating partner in interaction. Although Honneth initially reconstructs an account of subject-formation with recourse to Mead's notion of the internalization of perspectives, he moves to extend this analysis by drawing on object-relations theory in the context of enumerating the pattern of recognition confirmed through relations of love.

For Honneth, love, or 'primary affectivity,' represents not just the first stage of mutual recognition but is also its structural core.[1] Through love, subjects mutually confirm each other with regard to the concrete nature of their needs and in the reciprocal experience of loving care, come to know themselves as needy beings who are permanently dependent on their relations with others. In this context, Honneth defines love relationships as normatively guided emotional attachments between caregivers and children, as well as adult relations of friendship and love.[2] Relations of love are fundamental to Honneth's account of subjectivity and subject-formation, and for the development of subjective capacities required for participation in public life. His argument is that because infants establish their identities in relationships with certain significant others, the nature of these relationships structures the formation of identity, and more mature forms of relationality. For Honneth, the primary relationships of infants are crucial if they are to successfully construct a sense of self-confidence in their bodies as reliable sources of expression for their emotions, feelings, and needs. One becomes a subject and learns to recognize, offer, and demand respect in the context of emotional attachments to a primary caregiver, who cares for the total embodied and psychological needs of the infant and recognizes the subject in her 'vulnerability and sovereignty.'[3]

In order to construct this model of recognition, Honneth initially emphasized the compatibility of Mead's and Winnicott's accounts of individualization through socialization. For Honneth, both are originally understood to hold similar views about the subject's psychic organization as a process of internalization of the communicative patterns of interaction partners.[4] With recourse to object-relations theory, Honneth's original intention in *The Struggle for Recognition* was to extend Mead's intersubjective account of socialization beyond the internalization of moral consciousness to the centrality of primary affectivity for successful subject-formation. For Honneth, this also meant further developing Mead's notion of the 'I' in psychoanalytic terms, seeking to explain it as a pre-conscious source of innovation by which new claims to identity emerge and are asserted. Accordingly, an individual's future ability for the articulation of his or her needs and desires is understood to be dependent on conditions of support and care from significant others. Only with a particular quality of primary care can the individual be confident enough to allow for the creative exploration of his or her inner impulses without fear of being abandoned. This emotional, body-related sense of security provides an underlying layer that forms the psychological prerequisite for the development of all further attitudes of self-respect. Attacks on this core sense of physical and emotional integrity, such as torture, rape, neglect, or lack of engagement, tear at this confidence in self, damaging a sense of self/other boundaries.

To explain the precarious balance between independence and attachment in primary affective relationships, Honneth turns to the interactionist psychoanalytic theories of both Donald Winnicott and Jessica Benjamin, which emphasize the lasting significance of prelinguistic interactive experiences for subject-formation. In Honneth's view, Winnicott's work, in particular, makes it possible to reconceptualize Hegel's notion of love as a form of recognition or 'being oneself in another' in empirically verifiable terms and provides a more robust means of theorizing recognition than Mead's social psychology.

Rather than being based on the intrapsychic processes of the subject, as in the orthodox Freudian tradition of psychoanalysis, Winnicott's object-relations theory begins from the premise that early affective attachments and interactions with significant others are fundamental for successful ego-development. In comparison, Freudian psychoanalysis is based on a subject-centered model, dealing with the subject-object relation only from the view of the subject in terms of libidinal energies directed towards the object, and the model of relationality between the mother and infant is given a much less significant role. As Honneth suggests, significant others in this schema are viewed only as the "objects of libidinal charges stemming from the intra-psychic conflict between unconscious instinctual demands and gradually emerging ego-controls."[5] The object-relational model of psychoanalysis therefore posits a radically different anthropology to that of Freudian psycho-analysis, attempting to portray, as Whitebook suggests, "a less conflictual and more mutualistic" or "more sociable picture of human nature"; an anthropological premise that suggests human infants are already primed for intersubjectivity.[6]

For Honneth, object-relations theory furnishes him with two fundamental criteria in the development of a theory of recognition. Firstly, it provides him with the central category of 'symbiosis,' which becomes the defining feature of what he terms a theory of 'primary intersubjectivity.' In Honneth's view, the care with which significant others attend to the infant in the first few months of life "is not added to the child's behavior as something secondary but is rather merged with the child in such a way that one can plausibly assume that every human life begins with a phase of undifferentiated inter-subjectivity, that is, of symbiosis."[7] Secondly, Honneth views object-rela-tions theory as providing a more empirically oriented account of Hegel's dialectic between dependence and independence, now recast as the struggle to find a balance between mergence and separation in early childhood. In this respect, Honneth argues, that object-relations theory is especially suited to a 'phenomenology of recognition' because "it can convincingly portray love as a particular form of recognition only owing to the specific way in which it makes the success of affectional bonds dependent on the capacity, acquired in early childhood, to strike a balance between symbiosis and self-asser-tion."[8]

It should be noted that while in *The Struggle for Recognition* Honneth views the object-relations theory of Winnicott as particularly amenable to extending the intersubjective insights and account of self-realization first provided by Hegel and Mead, in subsequent work Winnicott's object-rela-tions theory, particularly his account of subject-formation and primary affec-tivity, comes to replace Mead's social psychology entirely.[9] It is possible to argue that Honneth's reconstruction of Winnicott's work around the central concepts of symbiosis and primary affective relations has now become one of the primary reference points for the theory of recognition, and also antici-pates the turn to an ontology of affective attunement in his more recent work *Reification*. In what follows, therefore, Honneth's interpretation of Winnicott will be reconstructed in some detail to elucidate this genealogy and highlight both the importance and problems with this interpretation for his current position.

In Honneth's reading, Winnicott's work is initially central to the articulation of a theory of socialization that emphasizes the importance of early primary relations for securing the necessary balance between attachment and independence that is fundamental for both successful self-development and the basis for all future forms of recognition relations. As mentioned above, central to Honneth's interpretation is the concept of 'symbiosis' or the infant's primary mergence with the mother, which Winnicott refers to in various ways, as either the 'holding phase,' the primary 'mother-baby unit,' or the phase of 'primary maternal preoccupation.'[10] This symbiotic phase is understood to begin *in utero* and is maintained into the first few months of life. Although the concept of symbiosis has its origins in the Freudian notion of 'primary narcissism' or the infant's original state of omnipotence, Honneth is keen to stress the alternative meaning given to it by Winnicott.[11] Through his own clinical and observational research, Winnicott is understood to reorientate the notion of primary narcissism in particularly 'relational' terms. This is famously captured in his claim: "There is no such thing as a baby."[12] With this astonishing announcement, Winnicott challenges the classical notion of the subject and posits an originary 'intersubjective' or mergent state, suggesting we cannot refer to the infant in isolation but only in an undifferentiated state with the mother. For Winnicott, then, it is not appropriate to speak of the infant as an individual, rather only of a mother-infant dyad or "environment-individual set-up."[13] According to this thesis, therefore, we cannot presuppose that the individual precedes an ontological affective state of fusion with the mother.

It might immediately be contested, however, that strictly speaking this is not an instance of intersubjectivity at all because in fact it describes a position in which neither mother nor infant is conceived as a subject in their own right. As Whitebook has argued, although we might be able to refer to this 'early dyadic activity' as interactive, it cannot properly be termed 'intersubjective.' In Daniel Stern's terms, it might be more appropriate to characterize this early phase as a form of 'interaffectivity' rather than 'intersubjectivity.'[14] Although working from very different perspectives, both Stern and Whitebook argue that the concept of 'intersubjectivity' is only applicable to a later stage of development when it is possible to speak of a more fully developed sense of subjectivity. For Whitebook, intersubjectivity more properly refers to the developmental phase when "self-reflection and symbolization are in place"; for Stern, intersubjectivity is preverbal but refers to a form of relatedness based on a "shared framework of meaning and means of communication such as gesture, posture, or facial expression."[15]

Both Whitebook and Stern make the important point that intersubjectivity should not be conceptualized as an originary phenomenon but instead understood as an emergent capacity that develops out of earlier phases of interaction. This argument has extremely far-reaching consequences for the inter-

subjective paradigm. Moreover, in this context, it already allows us to identify a tension that arises out of Honneth's particular reading of Winnicott.
Honneth wants to posit both an undifferentiated stage which precedes subjectivity of any kind and yet also conceptualize this symbiotic phase as a primary form of intersubjectivity.[16] This is a very difficult balance to maintain.
The question is, can he have it both ways?

It is clear, however, that Honneth explicitly reconstructs Winnicott's account of original mergence in thoroughly intersubjective-theoretic terms. The
key to understanding Honneth's theory of recognition is found in the detail of
his reading of Winnicott's theory of the primary mother-infant bond or affective ontological state.

For Winnicott, ego-development and the development of the self only
occur in a mother-infant unit.[17] The capacity for independence and the 'capacity to be alone,' paradoxically, can only develop in the presence of the
mother and as a result of her continuous existence and care.[18] In Winnicott's
terms, the individual can only come-into-being, become a 'me' as compared
to a 'not-me' because "there exists an environment which is protective; the
protective environment is in fact the mother preoccupied with her own infant
and oriented to the infant's ego requirements through her identification with
her own infant."[19] The 'presence' of the mother is crucial for the later ability
of the individual to have self-confidence in her embodied self and to creatively explore her own needs without fear of being abandoned. The presence
of the mother is also the facilitating factor in the infant being able to experience reality, and eventually distinguish between internal reality and external
world.

Winnicott conceptualizes the individual's psychological development as
moving through three phases, from a phase of 'absolute dependence' to
'relative dependence,' and finally 'towards independence.' The third stage of
development, 'towards independence,' is so termed to indicate that the attempt to achieve independence is an ongoing life-process that is constantly
navigated in adult life.[20]

The key term for Winnicott to describe the earliest stages of life is 'dependence.' He holds that human infants cannot even begin to exist—'to
be'—in the sense of becoming a distinct human being in their own right,
unless satisfactory conditions of maternal care, such as 'holding' are provided. According to this view, one only becomes an individual *after* an
originary mergent or symbiotic state with the mother. In this period of absolute dependence, Winnicott explains: "The important thing is that *I am* means
nothing unless *I* at the beginning *am along with another human being* who
has not yet been differentiated off. For this reason it is more true to talk about
being than to use the words *I am* [to explain the earliest stages of human
life.]"[21] Winnicott therefore makes a distinction between an initial stage of
'absolute dependence' or the 'holding phase,' which refers not only to physi-

cal holding but to total environmental, physiological, and psychological care, and the concept of 'living with.' The awareness of 'living with' an other can only occur when mother and infant finally emerge from an originary state of symbiosis and begin to differentiate themselves from one another. In Honneth's view, during the first few months of life associated with 'absolute dependence,' "the child is incapable of differentiating between self and environment, and moves within a horizon of experience, the continuity of which can only be assured by the supplemental assistance of a partner in interaction."[22] During this time, the infant also has no specific awareness of the maternal care being provided and no control over the quality of care or the nature of the maturational environment.[23] In other words, for Winnicott, the human infant does not enter the world with a distinct sense of self, not even of a pre-reflexive kind, but is instead conceptualised in an undifferentiated state with his or her external environment.

'Good-enough' mothering and the 'holding' the infant receives from the mother, particularly in terms of his or her bodily care, is vital for the development of the ego. Ego-support provided by the maternal environment enables the infant to gradually integrate experiences into a whole 'unit,' or what Winnicott refers to as the 'personality.'[24] The development of the ego is, however, also dependent on the integration of motor and sensory functions into a single body-scheme.[25] If all goes well during this period of affective care, the infant "starts to be linked with the body and the body-functions" and becomes aware of the surface of the skin as a "limiting membrane."[26] The development of a body-scheme is fundamental to the infant's ability to integrate psyche and soma and to eventually distinguish between 'me' and 'not-me.'[27] A reliable holding environment is therefore necessary for the infant to establish a 'continuity-of-being' and to develop from a primary unintegrated state to a form of structured integration or organization.[28]

It is important to note that for Winnicott, the 'facilitating environment' is optimally provided by the biological mother. Although he acknowledges the importance of paternal care, he tends to conceptualize this as care given to the mother-infant unit, particularly support for the mother, whom he describes as being in a vulnerable state herself. For Winnicott, this period of intense affectivity or "primary maternal preoccupation" indicates a *psychological* condition or state of "heightened sensitivity" on the part of the mother, which is increased towards the end of pregnancy and lasts for a matter of weeks or months after the birth of the child. He likens this to a "withdrawn" or "dissociated state," "almost an illness" from which a mother usually recovers.[29] It indicates an intense period of identification or total preoccupation with the infant to the exclusion of all other persons and interests.

As a consequence Winnicott's model of primary affective care is conceptualized in particularly gendered terms.[30] He views this intensely merged state as a normal although temporary phase, which is vital for the successful ego-development of the infant.[31] This kind of care, or what Winnicott refers to as 'good-enough' mothering, provides both a secure and reliable physiological and psychological environment that is empathetic to the particular needs of the infant. The mother is therefore the infant's first environment or 'facilitating environment,' and this 'being-together' of mother and infant is responsible for the emotional health and development of the infant.[32]

Honneth certainly does not endorse this gendered view of primary relations of love and care, and is careful to emphasize that the role of the primary caregiver can be fulfilled by any loving significant other, and is not necessarily the child's biological mother. However, like Winnicott, Honneth does conceptualize the primary state of symbiosis as experienced to the same *degree of intensity* by both mother and child.[33] In Honneth's view, "the concepts that Winnicott uses to characterize the individual phases are always at the same time descriptions not merely of one participant—the child—but rather of each of the states of the relationship between the 'mother' and the child."[34] Moreover, as the following passage makes clear, Honneth remarkably interprets the initial relationship of symbiosis as one equally identifiable for both 'mother' and infant: "Here, both partners to interaction are *entirely* dependent on each other for the satisfaction of their needs and are *incapable* of individually demarcating themselves from each other."[35] This depiction of the equal dependency of the mother on the child not only problematically assumes the equal status of both partners in the mergent state, but also suggests that both are affected in the same way and that the mother is somehow completely dependent on the infant for the fulfillment of her own needs.

Several theorists, including Iris Marion Young, Amy Allen, and Johanna Meehan, have rightly criticized Honneth's overly idealized and romanticized notion of love and the mother-infant unit upon which his theory of recognition is founded.[36] Both Allen and Meehan have argued that Honneth's presupposition that the mother experiences a period of 'symbiotic intoxication' to the same degree as her infant is highly implausible, and reject the idea that the mother is absolutely dependent on her infant to meet her own needs. In fact, as Meehan remarks, even if an exclusive symbiotic unity between mother and child were desirable, it is highly improbable because women are often juggling not only the needs of the newborn infant but also the needs of other children or family members, and a variety of tasks including returning to paid employment.[37] A mother may experience some period of intense bonding; however, this does not mean that she loses her own autonomy or independence—she is and remains a subject in her own right.[38]

Moreover, as both Young and Allen contend, Honneth's model of affective care as a relation of mutual recognition overlooks the fact that the mother-infant relation is in fact structured by "asymmetries of power, dependence and unreciprocated labor."[39] As Allen enumerates, even though the primary relation between parent and child might be constituted by love, it is also inevitably an asymmetrical power relationship. Although mothers are not "necessarily oppressive and dominating toward their babies—though unfortunately they may act in these ways ... they are certainly able to exercise a great deal of power over their infants, power that the infant is not in any position to reciprocate."[40] Moreover, as Young points out, according to the terms of Honneth's account, mutuality and symmetrical reciprocity cannot be equally applied in the context of relations of care because the principle of care is conceptualized as "recognizing the needs of individuals in their particularity."[41] Subjecting care to the measure of symmetrical reciprocity or equality implied in the concept of mutual recognition immediately undermines the idea of recognizing and attending to the particularity of individual needs. Although, in theory, relations between caregivers and receivers, particularly parents and children, may be reciprocated over a lifetime, during the period of childhood such relations are inevitably uni-directional and asymmetrical, and cannot be reciprocated in the same way.[42] Young argues that, as it stands, Honneth's model of love and care cannot adequately account for relations of power that also exist between parents and children nor is it clear what 'mutual recognition' in care relations actually means when such relations are structured asymmetrically.[43]

However, Honneth has continued to defend a concept of care defined as an "original modus [of care that] represents a reciprocal, symmetrical relation such as is familiar to us in the context of friendship or intimate relationships" while maintaining that "one-sided care and devotion represent a special case of asymmetrical care."[44] As Allen has identified, however, this division between two types of symmetrical and asymmetrical care only seems to make Honneth's position more ambiguous, as it is unclear whether the *original* mode of symmetrical care is meant to apply to the *originary* human relation between the primary care-giver and child or only the more mature love relation between friends and partners.[45] Either way, his conception one-sidedly characterizes relations between the primary caregiver and infant in exclusively normative terms.

In spite of these difficulties, the somewhat idealized presumption of a primary state of symbiosis remains central to Honneth's model of recognition. For him, the main problem that arises from this primary dependent state is not the asymmetrical relations of power, nor *merely* the experience of symbiotic oneness but the problem of achieving a dialectical interplay between fusion and separation that enables both mother and infant to demarcate themselves from one another. For Honneth, the central question that arises from the concept of 'primary intersubjectivity' found in Winnicott's work is: "how are we to conceive of the interactional process by which 'mother' and child are able to detach themselves from a state of undifferentiated oneness in such a way that, in the end, they learn to accept and love each other as independent persons?"[46] In this respect, there appears to be a conflation in

Honneth's formulation of intersubjectivity that occurs precisely at this point. It is unclear whether the notion of 'primary intersubjectivity' is meant to refer to the symbiotic state or only to the post-symbiotic experience of detachment, where intersubjectivity can be conceptualized as the interaction between two individuals who exist as subjects.

It is this gradual process of demarcation that Winnicott theorizes with the concept 'relative dependence.' It is assumed by both Honneth and Winnicott that the initial moves to independence can only be made once the mother begins to 'de-adapt' from her "primary, bodily identification with the infant," and begins to reorient her attention to a wider social circle, especially other family members and friends, and to resume some version of her routine prior to the birth of the child.[47] In contrast to the stage of 'absolute dependence,' the mother no longer ministers to the infant's needs as if they were an extension of her own and her attention is not directed toward the infant with the same degree of intensity. In the stage of 'relative dependence,' the infant now begins to become painfully aware of his dependence on the mother as she begins to leave him alone for longer periods of time; he now "*feels* a need for the mother."[48] At the same time as the mother is said to 'recover' from her state of complete identification with the infant, the child's intellectual capacities begin to develop, enabling the child to differentiate between self and environment, internal reality and external world.[49]

In this phase of gradual 'de-adaptation,' which occurs between six months and two years of age, the external world is gradually presented to the infant and the mother increasingly leaves the infant for longer periods of time. However, the shock of reality produces anxiety, hatred, and disillusionment, and with the mother's increasing absence, the infant learns that his or her mother "is outside his or her omnipotent control."[50] As a response to the mother's apparently new-found autonomy and diminished identification, the infant begins to undertake destructive acts towards her. With the impingement of external reality and loss of omnipotence, the child directs his or her aggression towards the mother as a means of testing this newly imposed reality.[51] It is crucial that the mother is able to both survive and resist these aggressive acts without punishment so that the child is able to perceive the mother as an independent subject in her own right but also to know that her love has not been withdrawn. It is only in the struggle to integrate his or her own aggressive impulses, in the context of this new form of relationality, that the infant in turn learns to love the mother.[52]

It is significant, then, that up until this point, the infant is not conceptualized as being a distinct subject or separate being with his or her own sense of self. Following Winnicott, Honneth assumes that a subject or self only develops as a secondary state arising out of the original phase of symbiosis. Within the terms of Honneth's analysis, the primary affective state is understood precisely as an ontologically merged, subjectless state and the premise of original symbiosis and the subsequent process of gradual independence continue to be fundamental to his theory of recognition. Honneth assumes that it is only as a secondary experience that subject-formation is conceptualized arising from the gradual and painful separation of mother and infant. Moreover, it is this original tension between attachment and separation that also provides him with a psychoanalytically derived account of an originary form of struggle and conflict.

In *The Struggle for Recognition*, Honneth interprets the infant's aggressive acts towards the mother not only as the first expressions of reality-testing but also, drawing on Jessica Benjamin's relational-psychoanalytic theory, interprets the process of separation or detachment as a 'struggle for recognition.'[53] Honneth argues that the process of detachment, which is often displayed in aggressive or destructive form, can be understood as a struggle for recognition that leads to the infant's realization of his or her dependence on "the loving care of an independently existing person with claims of her own."[54] The dialectic of dependence and independence reconstructed through object-relations theory, therefore, becomes the core of Honneth's theory of the struggle for recognition and the basis for explaining not only the ongoing human capacity to continually strive for recognition but also equally to deny recognition of the other.

The success of this primary recognitive process results in a mutually independent loving relation between (m)other and child rather than symbiosis. However, the success of this first form of recognition also depends on the ability of the mother to 'de-adapt' or separate from the initial mergent state with the infant. The mother's inability to facilitate this separation is as equally harmful to the infant as the failure of adequate 'holding' in the primary phase of 'absolute dependence.' The child is therefore equally reliant on the mother's recognition of his or her independence.

The process of 'mutual demarcation' is also facilitated by an additional coping mechanism that Winnicott terms 'transitional objects' or 'transitional phenomena.'[55] With this concept, Winnicott is referring to the first significant objects that infants become affectively attached to beyond the attachment with the mother, whether this is a toy, a piece of cloth, or the child's own thumb which the child passionately clings to or sucks on. Winnicott argues that such objects demonstrate much more than oral stimulation or satisfaction, providing the infant with a transitional object or first "not-me possession."[56] It is not the object *per se* that is important but the fact that the object is the child's first possession and provides an "intermediate area between the subjective and what is objectively perceived."[57] In other words, the transitional object enables the infant to make use of empirical objects in his or her environment that facilitate the transition from a state of mergence with the external world to one of 'relative independence.'

However, the important point is that the transitional object is neither an internal nor an external object but a creative act on the part of the infant, which Winnicott traces back to the capacity for creative play acquired through the phase of good-enough mothering. By adapting to the infant's needs in the symbiotic stage, the mother "gives the illusion that there is an external reality that corresponds to the infant's own capacity to create."[58] The transitional object must therefore also seem to provide some kind of comfort to the infant or 'reality of its own' during the phase of separation from the mother. The transitional object stands in for a substitute love-object and is the recipient of both the infant's intense affectivity as well as her attempts to destroy and mutilate it. It is crucial, then, that the transitional object never changes and that it survives the infant's intense love, hate, and aggression. Most significantly, the right of the infant to possess the object is never challenged, nor is it ever questioned whether the object is conceived from within or presented from without. Moreover, the transitional object is intensely linked with the capacities for playing and creativity, and to the use of illusion, symbols, and objects that continues through into adult life.[59] The suggestion Honneth takes from Winnicott is, therefore, that reality testing is a lifelong task and that transitional objects are repeatedly used to bridge the gap between inner and outer reality.[60] This constant mediation between internal imaginary and external worlds in adult life is filled by cultural objectivations, for example, art and religion, which Winnicott conceives as a continuation of the originary process of play and creativity and as examples of the continuing function of illusion.[61]

It is precisely this intersubjectively developed capacity to be alone and play creatively that Honneth posits as the central characteristic of love as a form of recognition. The trust that the child experiences in the continuity and quality of the 'mother's care' provides not only the model for all future forms of successful affective intersubjectivity but also the ability for the individual to form a positive self-relation. For Honneth: "...it is only this symbiotically nourished bond, which emerges through mutually desired demarcation, that produces the degree of basic self-confidence indispensable for autonomous participation in public life."[62]

From his reconstruction of Winnicott's work in *The Struggle for Recognition*, Honneth draws far-reaching conclusions not only about the structure of mutual recognition but also what he identifies as a 'latent interest' or the ontological source for the constant human 'struggle for recognition.' It is the precarious balance between symbiotic fusion and individuation experienced in infancy that provides the foundation for a permanent tension and struggle for recognition.[63] In Honneth's view, therefore:

> We can then proceed from the hypothesis that all love relationships are driven by the unconscious recollection of the original experience of merging that

characterized the first months of life for 'mother' and child. The inner state of symbiotic oneness so radically shapes the experiential scheme of complete satisfaction that it keeps alive, behind the back of the subject and throughout the subject's life, the desire to be merged with another person.[64]

Honneth points out that the desire for mergence is only transformed into a relation of mutual recognition once separation has been achieved enabling each partner to be acknowledged as an independent person in his or her own right. For Honneth, it is the early developmental process of achieving independence that colors and shapes intrapsychic life even in adulthood. Ultimately, then, in Honneth's view, love represents "a symbiosis refracted by mutual individuation."[65] In other words, at its core, the concept of subjectivity being defined here is understood as a ruptured symbiosis, and characterized by a perpetual tension between independence, on the one hand, and the pull to re-experience the original undifferentiated state between mother and infant, on the other. Consequently, pathologies of recognition in love relations can also be attributed to unsuccessful attempts at separation between mother and infant. Importantly, for Honneth, Winnicott's psychoanalytically derived anthropological model provides a normative ideal of both subject-formation and intersubjectivity that represents the structural core of recognition, and a theory of love or primary affectivity that is posited as the precursor, both conceptually and genetically, to all other forms of recognition.[66]

The concept of subjectivity as a form of ruptured symbiosis is one that Honneth also extends in work written subsequent to *The Struggle for Recognition*. In "Postmodern Identity and Object Relations Theory," Honneth posits the "primordial experience of symbiosis" as an anthropological and ontological condition, which the subject is continually compelled to replicate and re-experience throughout her life. The traumatic experience of demarcation from an original undifferentiated state with the mother structures the psychic life of the individual to such an extent that she is continually motivated to repeat and re-experience the original state of fusion via the use of transitional space between herself and other subjects that replicates the original fusion between internal and external reality. As a response to postmodern challenges to the psychoanalytically derived notion of the subject, Honneth now refers to the process of the "communicative liquefaction of the ego" to explain the attempt by the individual subject to constantly enter a transgressive space between inner and outer reality in order to creatively explore new aspects of her identity.[67] In other words, with recourse to Winnicott's notion of transitional phenomena, Honneth suggests the individual must be able to periodically collapse the boundaries between ego demarcation and mergence to creatively explore, by way of an internalized communicative dialogue with her interaction partners, an inner pluralization of subjective possibilities.

Honneth proposes that a communicative notion of subjectivity can therefore accommodate the postmodern challenge of the multiple characteristics of identity, based on the notion of an "intrapsychic capacity for dialogue."[68] Drawing on the work of Hans Loewald, Honneth also attempts to extend this interactionist notion of subjectivity to account for an intersubjectivist concept of the drives. This reconceptualized theory of the drives eschews the Freudian model of the drives as a destructive force, replacing it with an intersubjective account that posits the drives as the capacity to structure or organize the internalization of "external patterns of interaction."[69] The energy of the drive is also understood to facilitate the process of differentiation and integrates the child's psychic life once the original symbiotic state with the mother has been broken. Using an alternative object-relations model, Honneth argues it is possible to refute the Freudian model of ego-development as a process of gradual ego-strength in which the claims of the id are understood to be brought under the rational control of the ego. Instead, it is replaced with a model of ego-development as a communicative process of internalizations that create an internal psychic capacity for dialogue, enabling the subject to integrate multiple forms of experience and identity. Honneth connects the capacity of the infant to be able to organize his or her psychic forces in terms of a pattern of internalization, as the result of the early care and holding provided by the significant other. He contends that this process can only arise if it is "preceded by a stage of experienced unity, of the absence of difference between subject and reality."[70] The argument here is based on the premise that the process of internalization can only succeed if the infant has first experienced his or her own urges and drives as merged with those of the mother.

As McNay has observed, this renewed engagement with object-relations theory seems to indicate Honneth's attempt to produce a more complex and dynamic, socialized account of the psyche that avoids some of the deterministic tendencies of his earlier account based on Mead's work. However, as McNay argues, the capacity for conflict and dissonance, or forms of unsociable sociability, continues to be underplayed in his account of the subject. McNay warrants that: "The idea that, in response to the heterogeneity of social life, individuals develop an ever-refined capacity for the liquefaction of the self is a questionably normative account of action. In emphasizing the individual's accommodative capacities, it underplays the likelihood of negative and aggressive responses to difference."[71] Moreover, it seems the more Honneth moves towards the category of a primordial state of affective recognition, the more the notion of struggle becomes de-emphasized in his work, and he underplays the conflictual and negative responses to primary interaction as well as the forms of power that structure primary relations. As McNay contends, this bestows a transcendental status to affective forms of recognition that "can only be assured by underplaying the negative effects of power upon subjectivity, by construing them as secondary distortions extrinsic to a primordial dynamic of mutuality."[72]

The problem is, that beginning with an originary *undifferentiated* state between mother and infant also means *failing to differentiate* between forms of relationality, between power relations and forms of normative interaction, that structure the process of subject-formation. This tends to immunize primary forms of affectivity from any effects of power. Conceptualizing the development of the subject as a rupture of an original whole or oneness assumes that the subject originates in a context free from power and is primarily primed for affective and normative intersubjective relations as a result of an originary existential experience. This sets up a dualism between forms of interaction, between power and affectivity, whereby all other forms of relationality are posited as secondary to or as a deviation from original forms of normative interaction or social sociability.

In further work on object-relations theory, however, Honneth has continued to emphatically defend the thesis of an original symbiosis and corresponding theory of the subject, maintaining that the early attempt to achieve independence out of an original undifferentiated state constitutes a profound "contribution to the modern understanding of the subject."[73] On the basis of this contention, Honneth at times has been surprisingly at odds with interactionist and intersubjectively oriented infant research, notably the work of Daniel Stern, whom he singles out for criticism. With particular reference to Stern's work, Honneth argues emphatically that "a lot of effort ought to go into refuting the empirical objections raised today against the assumption of a primordial state of symbiosis."[74] Stern, and other infant researchers such as Beatrice Beebe and Frank Lachmann, concur with Winnicott's basic premise that "the organization of behavior should be viewed as the property of the mother-infant system rather than the property of the individual."[75] However, the fundamental difference between them is that neither Stern nor Beebe and Lachmann begin from the premise of an undifferentiated state or fusion between mother and infant. Rather, they begin from the premise that two individuals comprise the mother-infant dyad, and understand infant development as a dynamic interplay between "both self-regulation and interactive-regulation processes."[76] Beebe and Lachmann point to research that demonstrates the capacities of newborn infants to discriminate between their own vocalizations and those of others within the first day of life, thereby indicating the awareness of at least some primary sense of self and capacity to organize their own experiences.[77] Along with Stern, they therefore conclude "that there is no original perceptual confusion between organism and environment."[78]

Even more significantly, Beebe and Lachmann refute the notion of internalization as a means for understanding the way in which the child learns to organize inner life and the ability to distinguish between 'me' and 'not-me.'

The argument here is that the model of internalization is suggestive of a large degree of social conformity or total socialization of the psyche. Rather, they suggest that the inner organization of the infant's internal world should be understood as co-constructed, not merely externally imposed or communicated. In this respect, according to the interactionist models of Stern and Beebe and Lachmann, ego development is understood as a dynamic process by which self-regulation and interactions with significant others proceed at the same time. According to this model, interactive regulations are not merely internalized into self-regulations, rather "existing self-regulations are altered by, as well as alter, interactive regulations."[79] Beebe and Lachmann maintain that the infant begins life with his own agency, an agency that potentially conflicts with the mother's agency rather than passively internalizes her interactive behavior and expectations. Therefore, rather than positing a primary symbiotic state, these theorists fundamentally begin from an interactive stance which assumes there is already some form of ego present. However, Beebe and Lachmann strenuously argue that the primary capacity for interaction does not simply imply either mutuality or symmetry, nor does it ascribe a positive value to primary interaction, nor a necessary causality. Rather, it assumes that each subject is affected by her own self-regulation as well as by interaction partners but this may include conflict as much as it might mean mutually adjusting to one another.

As a response to such concerns, articulated, for example, by Joel Whitebook, Honneth's use of the concept of symbiosis as a primary intersubjective category has come under scrutiny. Whitebook argues that the existence of at least some form of 'pre-reflexive proto-self' is difficult to deny as it is evident that infants "bring much to infant-mother interaction that is specifically their own." Moreover, the development of a body-scheme presupposes the existence of a least a 'bodily ego' which is constituted by "the infant's distinct physiologically determined repertoire of dispositional states." This in turn, "becomes the fundament upon which more elaborated and reflective forms of selfhood are constructed."[80] The work of both Stern and Whitebook poses questions about accounting for the complex genesis of the subject, and about what the nature of the 'inter' of intersubjectivity actually refers to. In those exchanges, Honneth is urged to consider whether the category of symbiosis can do the work required and whether it can be conceptualized in the manner he originally intended. His recent work on psychoanalysis and object-relations is framed with the feasibility of the central category of symbiosis in mind but seems to constitute a series of qualifications rather than any significant modification to his original position.

In his response to Whitebook, Honneth now concedes that even in the first few months of life, infants have an "elementary sense of self." In this context, drawing more comprehensively on Stern's work, Honneth appears to acknowledge that infants "have a rudimentary capacity for distinguishing between self and other and for perceiving the intentionality of the other."[81] However, far from diminishing the intersubjective stance, Honneth considers this qualification potentially enhances intersubjectivism and the importance of early caregiver and child interaction. In this sense, too, he clarifies that his initial employment of the term 'primary intersubjectivity' to explain the notion of an early symbiotic state between 'mother' and child was somewhat misleading, in the sense that this primary phase is not strictly speaking "an encounter between two self-aware, independent subjects…"[82]

However, the acknowledgement of the existence of an early 'elementary sense of self' also has significant ramifications for the notion of an original symbiotic unity that was central to Honneth's account in *The Struggle for Recognition*. Quoting Stern, who draws on recent empirical and clinical investigations, Honneth now also seems to conclude: "…that the capacity to have merger- or fusion-like experiences … is secondary to and dependent upon an already existing sense of self and other."[83] As a consequence, Honneth argues, we can no longer understand the notion of symbiosis as an all-encompassing stage that begins *in utero* and continues into the first months of life. Rather, intense moments of cuddling, feeding, and holding between caregivers and infants create 'sporadic' or 'episodic moments' of fusion or symbiosis that individuals seek to recreate throughout their lives. In this sense, symbiosis is now considered to be an 'interim period' in which the actions of caregivers are momentarily experienced as an extension of the infant's needs, rather than a totalizing undifferentiated state. Honneth suggests that symbiotic experience, therefore, represents the 'zero-point' of recognition, an experience which compels individuals to strive for forms of reciprocal recognition in which both partners in a relationship are sufficiently differentiated in more mature relations.[84] Such qualifications raise a series of open questions in regard to Honneth's intersubjective approach, most notably, how the notion of an elementary or pre-existing sense of self might be conceptualized and how this might impact upon a theory of intersubjectivity and subject-constitution.

Nonetheless, in recent work, Honneth continues to maintain the notion of symbiosis as the basis of a theory of recognition while also reconsidering the way in which the motivation for the struggle for recognition is conceptualized. It is the early trauma or rupture of the primary symbiotic experience that compels "the subject to rebel again and again against the experience of not having the other at our disposal."[85] Honneth clarifies his most recent position in the following terms:

> I now assume that the impulse to rebel against established forms of recognition can be traced to a deep-seated need to deny the independence of those with whom one interacts and to have them, 'omnipotently,' at one's disposal. We would then have to say that the permanence of the 'struggle' for recognition

stems not from an unsocializable ego's drive for realization but rather from the anti-social striving for independence that leads each subject to deny, again and again, the other's difference.[86]

Honneth admits that this explanation constitutes a shift away from his earlier thesis that the 'struggle for recognition' is motivated by a particular kind of *moral* experience that stems from negative feelings of being unjustly or inadequately recognized. Rather, the thesis he now proposes is that struggle or conflict be understood as a response to an *anthropologically posited human need to recreate the experience of symbiosis and thereby negate the independence of the other.* In other words, the traumatic experience of the rupture of early states of mergence constitutes Honneth's version of 'the work of negativity.'[87] It is this primary negative experience that compels subjects to seek to deny the independence or recognition of the other but also, he suggests, to recreate a mergent state, for example, in love relations or by seeking security in a homogeneous community when feeling threatened. Honneth argues that the bridge between the anthropological need for mergence and the moral claims of recognition is based on the premise that "the individual tendency to deny that others are not at one's disposal would merely be the flip-side of the human interest in having essential components of *who one is* be socially recognized."[88]

However, there is now an indecision on Honneth's part about how to account for the fact that negative anti-social impulses may compel struggles for recognition as much as morally motivated ones. As Honneth suggests, these impulses often sit in tension with one another and it is not clear how they can be reconciled and understood entirely as 'moral experiences' motivated by a lack of recognition.[89] As Bankovsky suggests, Honneth's equivocation in regard to the problem of integrating both "negative and positive dimensions of recognition should encourage an approach to the ideal of mutual recognition that is not simply affirmative but also critical of its orientation and content. His preference for the positive version prevents Honneth from bringing a sufficiently critical perspective to his own account." From the perspective of this study, this would require a consideration of the interplay of both positive and negative forms of intersubjectivity, or as Bankovsky suggests, acknowledging "the imbrication of positive and negative forces" and the ways in which relations between caregivers and infants, as well as mature relations of love, may equally consist of love and care as well as 'possessive' and 'appropriative' impulses.[90]

However, rather than pursue this path, in more recent work on object-relations theory, the primary concept of 'affective recognition' has been brought to the fore and has begun to emerge as an ontological category. Honneth now continuously emphasizes that the primary experience of symbiosis is purely an affective category rather than being a cognitive process or one of moral experience.[91] In other words, it is only by experiencing a primary affective relation, whereby the infant is first attached to and 'affected' by a primary caregiver, that she can in a secondary process begin to internalize the normative expectations and viewpoints of her interaction partners and begin to develop a sense of self.[92] This primordial sense of recognition is understood to provide a sense of affirmation that is confirmed in expressive and affective gestures towards the other, according them social validity.[93]

Honneth though increasingly develops a position which posits a primordial form of affectivity as the fundamental ontological basis of the theory of recognition. He has also extended this theoretical stance in developing a 'moral epistemology of recognition' with affective and expressive affirmation at its core. For Honneth, recognition means much more than merely 'perceiving,' 'identifying,' or 'cognizing' the other in terms of acknowledging the other's identity. Rather, as he has clarified more recently, 'recognition precedes cognition'; it refers to an affirmative affective stance towards the world that precedes all forms of interaction or recognition.[94]

In this sense, there are a number of gradual and implicit conflations that occur in Honneth's work across various writings. In his earliest works he begins with a broad-based theory of intersubjectivity that is narrowed to a theory of recognition, and from a notion of recognition there is a shift to a notion of primary affective interdependence, which has now become the basis for the theory of recognition *per se*. However, the social processes Honneth conceptualizes in the terms of a theory of recognition require a more complex understanding of the interplay between intersubjectivity, subjectivity, conflict, and power that cannot be accounted for by his theory of recognition as it stands. As Whitebook has argued, for example, even interdependent affectivity or affective intersubjectivity presumes a proto-subjectivity, and as Allen, Young, and McNay have noted, conditions of symmetrical reciprocity cannot be conceived in isolation from conditions of asymmetrical reciprocity, where power subtly works either in social and structural ways, or noticeably in psychological ones. In this respect, there is a profound narrowing of the theory of intersubjectivity and anthropology that underpins Honneth's project, and as we shall discuss in the final chapter, this has a significant impact on the parameters of his critical social theory including his ability to provide an adequate 'critique of power.'

5

Anthropology, Recognition, and Critique

Chapter Ten

A Critical Theory of Recognition

Anthropological, Historical, or Ontological Justification?

This philosophical reconstruction sheds light on Honneth's defense of anthropological arguments in terms of the intersubjectivity of recognition and the construction of a form of ethical life that is derived immanently from within the structure of recognition relations. In keeping with this conceptual approach, Honneth also explains processes of social change in relation to the structural interconnection between the three patterns of recognition. According to Honneth, it is the deep-seated normative demands intrinsic to the structure of recognition-relations that compels individuals and groups to struggle for expanded forms of recognition and new forms of social organization.[1]

In *The Struggle for Recognition*, Honneth attempts to define a model of critical social theory that can account for both an immanent basis for critique and context-transcending validity with reference to a 'formal concept of ethical life' or *Sittlichkeit*. The three intersubjective patterns of recognition constitute Honneth's version of a good or ethical life in the sense that they provide the conditions for successful identity-formation or development of an 'ethical personality.'[2] The three spheres of love, law, and achievement, which are roughly equivalent to Hegel's divisions between family, state, and civil society, are central to the development of three corresponding forms of practical self-relation. The formal concept of ethical life is to be understood as a normative ideal in which specific patterns of recognition enable individuals to acquire the self-confidence, self-respect, and self-esteem necessary for full self-realization. Honneth wants to suggest that this ideal is not merely a theoretical construct but that it is pre-scientifically located in the structure of intersubjective social relations and can offer an evaluative framework from which to critically assess the general conditions for successful subject-formation within existing forms of social organization.

Such an orientation towards ethical values is, however, not intended to provide a substantive notion of the 'good life.' Rather, Honneth wants to account for a notion of ethical life in formal terms only: the three interdependent patterns of recognition are intended to account for successful self-realization in an abstract manner in an effort to avoid embodying particular visions of the good life. The anthropological structures of recognition are intended to provide a context-transcending claim to validity that is universally applicable regardless of historical or socio-cultural context. The forms of recognition associated with love, rights, and achievement as Honneth presents them, therefore, "do not represent established institutional structures but only general patterns of behaviour, they can be distilled, as structural elements, from the concrete totality of forms of life."[3] Honneth suggests such a theoretical proposal cannot expect to determine once and for all which values might constitute an ethical life. The development of substantive values must be left open to historical change and to the future of social struggles.[4] He therefore also attempts to justify the context-immanent features of recognition by leaving the model open enough to account for the particularity of socio-cultural and historical contexts in which recognitive identity claims are made. Nonetheless, he posits that the content of the three conditions of recognition is thick enough to offer normative criteria for successful identity-formation that extends normative theory beyond the scope of deontological or Kantian approaches that are based on self-determination and moral autonomy alone. In contrast to communitarian approaches, however, Honneth attempts to account for ethical criteria without returning to a relativistic option that would seem to offer no way of distinguishing between better or worse notions of the good life.

Honneth's means of articulating the necessary structural conditions for a formal concept of ethical life is provided by the connection he makes between the necessary experience of the three forms of intersubjective recognition, the three corresponding forms of self-relation, and the forms of social organization required to ensure successful self-realization.[5] This structural recognition-complex is grounded on "an anthropological conception that can explain the normative presuppositions of social interaction."[6] For Honneth, there is a developmental logic between the three forms of self-relation that a subject acquires through processes of socialization. Firstly, a subject must acquire basic self-confidence attained through loving relationships in which she has the capacity to express her own embodied needs and know they will be met by the care of significant others. Secondly, this basic self-confidence is a prerequisite for the subject to be able to secure a positive feeling towards herself as a person worthy of self-respect because she is considered a morally responsible and autonomous being equal to all others in the context of legal relations. Thirdly, this principle of equality before the law subsequently provides the capacities required to experience oneself as an individual who is valued for her contribution to society as well as deriving a sense of self-worth in the knowledge that she is integrated into a shared value-community.[7] In Honneth's view, the three forms of recognitive relations "represent normative perspectives with reference to which subjects can reasonably argue that existing forms of recognition are inadequate or insufficient and need to be expanded."[8] Hence, in Honneth's view, the three patterns of recognition constitute standards for 'healthy' forms of social relations against which 'pathologies' or 'misdevelopments' of social life can be identified and potentially transformed.

In his more recent work, Honneth has sought to delineate more strongly the conditions of social recognition that are open to historical change and normative progress, and those that are deep-seated human constants.[9] Although the historicist dimension was present in *The Struggle for Recognition*, notably, it was confined to only two of the recognitive conditions—law and achievement—which Honneth conceptualized as being open to progressive change.[10] Significantly, in *The Struggle for Recognition*, Honneth exempts love from the potential for normative development, arguing that only relations of law and achievement are open to the possibility for historical change. There, love is still conceptualized in the following anthropological terms: "the experience of love, whatever historical form it takes, represents the inner-most core of all forms of life that qualify as 'ethical.' Because it does not admit of the potential for normative development, the integration of love into the intersubjective network of a post-traditional form of ethical life does not change its fundamental character."[11] Moreover, because love is understood to provide "the basic prerequisite for every type of self-realization," and is considered the core of ethical life, this constructs the entire recognition model in fundamentally anthropological terms.

In *Redistribution or Recognition?*, Honneth reassesses these early formulations and attempts to add an historicist dimension to his analysis of the development of the three spheres of recognition and accompanying forms of practical self-relation. It is only once the family becomes a distinctly privatized and separate sphere, and when we can speak of the emergence of a distinct phase of 'childhood' in which a specific model of primary care is fostered with the concurrent development of a modern notion of love, that it is possible to conceptualize 'love' as a specific form of recognition-relation that is crucial for self-confidence and the expression of embodied needs;[12] it is only once rights become universalized and disaggregated from forms of status and privilege that it is possible to speak of a form of self-respect that is attributed to all individuals on the basis of their status as an autonomous human being accorded equal rights; and this, in turn, requires that rights be separated from status. In this way, the contribution individuals make to society enabling them to feel esteemed for their contribution becomes further individualized and 'meritocratized,' as well as open to contestation in regard to the values that determine the recognition of individual achievement. [13]

Significantly, Honneth now argues that moral expectations of social recognition cannot be *exclusively* justified with reference to an anthropological model: "Rather, such expectations are the product of the social formation of a deep-seated claim-making potential in the sense that they always owe their normative justification to principles institutionally anchored in the historically established recognition order." Moreover, he now specifically attributes the "differentiation of the three spheres of recognition" to the historical development of "bourgeois-capitalist society," and emphasizes the profound normative structural transformation that emerges with modernity as initiating the shift to a social-recognition-order. [14] In this sense, too, he now gives far greater credence to the role modern institutions play in ensuring the reproduction of recognitive norms and values, as well as conceiving institutions as the embodiment of recognition relations achieved as the result of social-historical contestation. Honneth has therefore more recently acknowledged that the anthropological structures of social recognition alone cannot adequately provide justification for grounding a critical social theory. He now more strenuously attempts to maintain a form/content distinction, suggesting that only the *form* of moral expectations of recognition represents an invariant anthropological feature whereas their *content* depends on the different ways in which they become institutionalized and differentiated within in any given society. [15]

In order to more fully justify a context-immanent perspective, Honneth now claims that the moral expectations of recognition must be understood in relation to the specific structural transformation that occurs with the historical development of bourgeois-capitalist society. [16] For Honneth, this recent introduction of a 'temporal element' demonstrates that the "structure of the required recognition conditions continues to change with the historical process." [17] In his more recent work, Honneth attempts to make a more convincing link between normative principles, social theory, and critique. On the one hand, he continues to maintain that his proposal proceeds "social anthropologically from a core of expectations of recognition that all subjects bring to social interaction." On the other hand, however, he also adds a historicizing dimension, arguing that 'recognition needs' are not predetermined according to an anthropological model, rather it is only the structure of recognition relations that act as an anthropological constant. [18]

Furthermore, Honneth argues that the three patterns of recognition also contain 'internal normative principles' against which it is possible to evaluate existing forms of recognition and make normative claims regarding the need for further expansion. [19] The three forms of recognition are characterized by three fundamental features to which subjects can appeal when they believe their entitlement to any one form is not being met: in relations of love, subjects can appeal to the 'neediness principle'; in legal relations the 'equality principle'; and in 'cooperative relations' they can refer to the 'achievement principle.' The three recognition principles constitute the normativity inherent in social relations to which subjects can refer in instances where recognition is inadequately institutionalized in any given socio-cultural context and does not adequately reflect deep-seated moral expectations. The three recognition principles therefore act as counterfactual ideals against which currently institutionalized norms of recognition can be measured.

Furthermore, in order to sustain a basis for critique, Honneth now incorporates a notion of "validity surplus" which he suggests is internal to the three forms of recognition, arguing that: "...each principle of recognition has a specific surplus of validity whose normative significance is expressed by the constant struggle over its appropriate application and interpretation."[20] All forms of recognition, including love, therefore are now conceptualized as containing an internal conflict dynamic that ensures each is open to permanent contestation and development with regard to the way in which they are applied, institutionalized, and interpreted.[21] However, for Honneth, socially institutionalized forms of recognition never exhaust their normative potential, rather each form of recognition has a surplus of validity that is never fulfilled and that is open to the promise of continual expansion and the potential for ongoing learning processes.[22] The content and mode of institutionalization of each form of recognition is therefore permanently open to rational debate and dispute and subject to publicly reasoned forms of justification.[23] This aspect of subjecting recognition to 'the space of public reason' is an element that Honneth has also begun to emphasize more strongly in recent work.[24]

In this context, Honneth has also sought to define the concept of recognition more definitively, seeking to distinguish between recognition as a 'receptive' or as an 'attributive' act, and in so doing institutes significant conceptual clarifications. As an 'attributive' act, recognition is understood as the ascription of new qualities upon the subject from the position of the recognizer, whereas a 'receptive' act of recognition is defined in terms of 'correctly perceiving' the qualities that a subject already possesses and therefore only "reinforcing or manifesting them secondarily."[25] For Honneth, then, 'attributive' acts of recognition are 'constitutive' of identity, whereas 'perceptive' acts of recognition are 'reproductive,' whereby "the status or positive qualities possessed by a person or social group are ... simply reproduced in a meaningful way."[26]

Not surprisingly, Honneth prefers the 'perception' or 'reception' model of recognition because he argues that it "permits us to account better for our intuition that recognition must be motivated by practical reasons: we thereby react in a correct or appropriate way to the reasons contained in the evaluative qualities that human beings possess in different respects."[27] In this sense, Honneth suggests recognition does not construct or create individual features or qualities but merely actualizes pre-existing capacities that are "already present as potentialities in order to then be realized." Recognition, then, is understood by Honneth to be an 'unambiguously positive' act that facilitates the subject's self-identification with qualities or capacities that she already possesses.[28] It is therefore only 'indirectly' constituting in terms of building the capacities required for developing a positive self-relation and such capacities are built up through patterns of affirmative interaction or evaluative recognition.

Honneth acknowledges, however, that both the 'attributive' and 'reception' models are faced with the threat of relativism in that evaluative features appear to be based on values that are dependent on the institutionalized norms in any given social-historical context or lifeworld. Nonetheless, he believes that the receptivity or response model is better equipped to address the problem of relativism once a notion of moral progress is applied to the forms of evaluation in any given society.[29] Honneth's concern with the attribution model is that it corresponds with a certain form of 'value relativism' thereby making it difficult to ascertain the ethical validity of attributive qualities or to determine whether such qualities are only relative to the recognizer. In Honneth's view, the constitution model contains no context-transcending criterion against which forms of attributive recognition can be adequately assessed or critiqued.

In this respect, Honneth leans on a certain form of 'value realism' to bolster his claim that evaluative qualities can be 'correctly perceived' according to forms of recognition that are 'motivated by reasons,' evaluative reasons that although given in any particular lifeworld are open to historical change and re-evaluation.[30] The notion of moral progress that Honneth builds in is understood to provide a context-transcending form of validity by ensuring that 'responsive' forms of recognition meet the universal criteria of promoting the capacity for autonomy and undistorted forms of self-realization.

The notion of moral progress and of validity surplus, however, does not just apply separately to each of the three forms of self-relation or three spheres of recognition; it also applies to the general development of social relations of recognition overall. Honneth now argues more definitively that in order to justify a form of context-transcending validity that extends beyond a particular social context, the notion of a surplus of normative validity needs to be complemented by a general theory of moral progress. For Honneth, "the normative expansion of the three spheres of recognition—can be interpreted as indicators of moral progress in the sense that they can inform us about the desirability of processes of social change."[31]

Honneth's assessment of the need for a concept of moral progress particularly arises in the context of justifying the basis of a recognition-theoretical concept of justice in his debate with Nancy Fraser in *Redistribution or Recognition?* There, Honneth addresses the problem of identifying a pre-theoretical basis for critique that does not merely entrench prevailing social conditions. As he had already identified in *The Struggle for Recognition*, the issue is to be able to differentiate between progressive or reactionary forms of social struggle and to be able to critically assess "the developmental direction [of] present-day social conflicts."[32] In Honneth's view, a theory of progress is required in order to avoid a form of ethical perspectivism or a form of justification that gives new social movements a privileged or elitist status.[33] The idealization of new social movements, in Honneth's view, "risks precipitously affirming the prevailing level of political-moral conflict in a given society."[34] In this sense, it is problematic for a critical social theory to base its critique *only* on those normative claims that have been articulated by new social movements whose moral demands have reached the level of the public sphere. Honneth's argument is that the critical social theorist must be able to evaluate the moral claims of contemporary social struggles from the perspective of "future possibilities."[35]

In outlining a theory of moral progress, Honneth begins with the assumption that the structural transformation of the three recognition spheres that occurs with modernity constitutes a morally superior form of social integration. Central to the criteria for evaluating the level of social integration achieved are the two concepts of social inclusiveness and individualization. Accordingly, an expansion of social recognition can be measured in terms of the increases in both the number of persons included into the recognition relations of any given society, and by the opportunities available for individuals to develop and express aspects of their personality in the context of mutual recognition.[36] Honneth argues that these normative criteria make it possible to evaluate the moral demands of contemporary social struggles according to whether their claims are aimed at short-term change or long-term increases in forms of social recognition.[37] Moral progress is therefore evaluated in terms of the three principles of neediness, equality, and achievement and according to the criteria of increased individualization and inclusiveness that indicate an increase in the level of social integration.[38]

However, despite the inclusion of this historicizing dimension, it is unclear whether the notion of moral progress, based as it is on the two criteria of increased individuality and inclusivity adequately addresses the necessary justificatory requirements for the task of critique. The question is whether Honneth's approach still privileges a particular form of the 'good life' in maintaining a connection between the value-order of recognition and the notion of individuality and inclusiveness? As interlocutors such as Cooke and Zurn have suggested, the criteria which form the basis of Honneth's model of critical social theory could just as easily apply to other models of ethical life.[39] The same criteria, for example, could just as easily be used to describe Foucault's account of increasing individualization and inclusion, but as a process of subjectivation in the context of institutionalized practices and norms that are the historical outcome of disciplinary practices and power relations.[40]

This raises another major problem for Honneth's model of self-realization as dependent upon social relations of recognition. The more recent designation of recognition as an attributive rather than constitutive act seems to further reinstitute a dualism between action types and sits in tension with the more dynamic notion of intersubjective subject constitution indicated in earlier work. As will be discussed further in the following chapter, given that Honneth's model is largely based on an understanding of power as domination, he does not adequately account for relations of power that are constitutive of subject-formation and social relations more generally, or that may be co-constitutive of increasing individualization and integration, even in conditions of autonomy and freedom. He therefore does not adequately consider the ways in which, as Forst notes, relations of power can be *inherent* to certain forms of recognition or that norms of recognition may contribute to the reinforcement of subordinating forms of subject-formation.[41]

Furthermore, despite Honneth's attempts to provide a 'formal' concept of ethical life on the basis of enduring recognitive structures of self-realization, as Zurn has suggested, the problem still remains how "to show that the telos of self-realization itself should be the governing ideal of social organization."[42] Zurn questions whether the 'telos of self-realization' underpinning Honneth's account of ethical life holds the kind of context-transcending validity that Honneth requires to justify his project of critique.[43] Zurn argues that Honneth's:

> appeal to the actual structure of identity development [cannot] answer to challengers who might ask: Why self-realization and not pious self-abregation, or virtuous subservience to communal ends, or righteous obedience to the moral law, or maximization of the pleasure of others, etc.? All of these alternatives and more are live options in ethical theory today, and if one concedes that human nature is malleable, then one cannot simply appeal to the mere universality of structures of identity development in order to ground the telos of self-realization as *the* proper focus of social organization.[44]

As both Cooke and Zurn demonstrate, Honneth still needs to do more to justify why the notion of a social recognition-order constitutes a framework of ethical criteria that is more convincing than alternative models currently provided by a range of other critical social theorists.[45] As Bankovsky also suggests, it is not entirely clear that the three forms of positive self-relation central to Honneth's model are the only, or the most important, forms of self-relation subjects might require for successful self-formation and human flourishing.[46]

Moreover, it might be argued that in many ways Honneth's attempts to historicize recognition as an achievement of modernity in an effort to provide a more convincing context-immanent basis of justification has only introduced a significant tension into his work between the historicist dimensions, now read as a quasi-philosophy of history, and anthropological forms of justification that now operate within his theory. Although Honneth's attempt at historicization represents a progressive amendment to his project of critical social theory, it seems that rather than addressing the core problems of justification, it represents an indecision on his part. In fact, it might be argued that Honneth wants to have a 'bet both ways,' so to speak. For, although he complements his conception of the three spheres of recognition with an historical analysis, there is no shift in the underlying premise regarding the primary model of recognition, only a re-conceptualization of the social-theoretical ways in which it has developed into three differentiated spheres. This 'bet both ways' is evident in the following passage from *Redistribution or Recognition?* when Honneth claims:

> The *distinctively human dependence on intersubjective recognition* is always shaped by the particular manner in which the mutual granting of recognition is institutionalized within a society. From a methodological point of view, this consideration has the consequence that subjective expectations of recognition cannot *simply be derived from an anthropological theory* of the person. To the contrary, it is the most highly differentiated recognition spheres that provide the key for retrospective speculation on the particularity of the intersubjective 'nature' of human beings. Accordingly, the practical self-relation of human beings—the capacity made possible by recognition, to reflexively assure themselves of their own competences and rights—is not something given once and for all; like subjective recognition expectations, this ability expands with the number of spheres that are differentiated in the course of social development for socially recognising specific components of the personality.[47]

In this sense, Honneth reconfirms a commitment to the primary anthropological claim in terms of his recourse to a 'distinctively human dependence on intersubjective recognition' and the conditions for self-realization that this entails. However, he now also specifies that such a model cannot be based entirely on invariant anthropological features but must be supplemented by an empirical analysis of the institutionalization of recognition in any given social-historical context. However, it is very difficult for Honneth to maintain both these forms of justification without begging the question of whether recognition itself, and the notion of intact forms of self-realization, provide the form of context-transcending validity that his critical social theory requires. The introduction of a historicist dimension seems to challenge the very need to maintain an anthropological basis for normative critique. This tension has been heightened further by the fact that in certain writings since *Redistribution or Recognition?*, Honneth has only reconfirmed his commitment to an anthropological-ontology of recognition.

In this respect, Honneth's model still ultimately continues to be grounded in an anthropological and ontological account; the historical instantiations simply provide a means to add detail to this initial anthropological proposal at the level of social-theoretical analysis. In his recent work *Reification*, Honneth moves to further develop a notion of primary affectivity as the ontological basis for a theory of recognition. These recent developments produce a tension in Honneth's work between the attempt to historicize the three institutionalized forms of recognition, on the one hand, and yet reinforce an anthropological-ontology of primary intersubjective relations, on the other, indicating a dilemma in terms of the form of justification used to ground his critical social theory.

PRIMARY AFFECTIVITY AS ONTOLOGY OF RECOGNITION

In his work *Reification*, Honneth extends the affective concept of recognition in a manner that signifies a significant reconfiguration of the category. There Honneth posits an affective form of recognition as a primary, existential mode of relatedness or 'being-in-the-world' that is prior to all other forms of human relation. He also explicitly refers to this originary affectivity as a 'transcendental condition' that is prior to the three normatively oriented forms of mutual recognition previously outlined in *The Struggle for Recognition*.[48] In other words, Honneth now posits a two-level order of recognition: recognition refers, firstly, to an elementary form of recognition at a social-ontological level and, secondly, to the three normatively and historically derived forms of recognition—love, law, and achievement—conceived in terms of a formal notion of ethical life. In a move that recalls his early insights into a notion of 'practical intersubjectivity,' Honneth develops an ontological notion that designates our 'practical involvement' in the world. Incorporating insights from both Sartre and Lukács in relation to an existential or practical, rather than epistemic stance to others and the world, Honneth develops an "'existential' mode of recognition [that] provides a foundation for all other more substantial forms of recognition in which the affirmation of other persons' specific characteristics is at issue."[49]

Honneth compares this primordial form of 'recognition' with Heidegger's notion of 'care' or 'attunement,' Lukács' notion of 'engaged praxis,' Dewey's notion of 'practical involvement,' and Cavell's notion of 'acknowledgement.' As discussed in chapter 2, in order to construct this elementary notion of recognition, Honneth reconstructs what he perceives to be a second, 'unofficial' reading of Lukács' analysis of reification in *History and Class Consciousness*, where reification is understood as a deviation from a 'correct' or 'genuine' mode of relating to the world. According to Honneth, reification can be understood as the temporary loss, concealment, or 'forgetfulness' of an elementary form of recognition. In Honneth's view, therefore, Lukács' concept of reification presupposes "a more primordial and genuine form of praxis, in which humans take up an empathetic and engaged relationship towards themselves and their surroundings."[50]

In this reconceptualization, the notion of recognition is substituted for Lukács' conception of engaged praxis to identify "the structure of a specifically human mode of existence."[51] This existential form of recognition as 'involvement' or 'attunement' designates an affective and engaged mode of interaction with the world. Moreover, Honneth contends that this recognition stance indicates an "empathetic engagement in the world, arising from the world's significance and value, [that] is prior to our acts of detached cognition." Recognition here indicates that in our interactions with the world, we do not primarily take a contemplative, detached, or cognitive stance but rather assume a positive or affirmative practical engagement, an existentially conceived notion of "caring comportment."[52]

Honneth critically contrasts this ontological conception of recognition with 'communicative' or 'intentional' stances. In this later work he notably argues that Mead's notion of perspective-taking is inadequate because it lacks an account of the antecedent emotional attachment that is required before subjects can learn to take the perspective of the other.[53] Honneth now argues that reciprocal perspective-taking is a "kind of intersubjective stance [which] is always already connected with an element of positive affirmation and emotional inclination, which is not sufficiently expressed in the attribution of rational motives."[54] The internalization of perspectives, therefore, must assume a form of recognition that is prior to conceptualization and linguistic articulation.

In *Reification*, Honneth also extends the stance taken in his earlier essay "Invisibility," where he outlined an 'epistemology of recognition,' claiming that recognition precedes cognition. In this context, a lack of recognition is understood to constitute a form of 'invisibility,' that does not designate the neglect to perceive a subject in a literal sense, but rather that he or she has been actively or intentionally ignored or 'looked through' in a social sense. In "Invisibility," Honneth argues that recognition is not merely a form of cognition but an intentionally expressive act that overwhelmingly confers "the positive meaning of an affirmation." The absence of such forms of 'social' perception indicates that a subject (or group) is not visible in a figurative sense for the other; in other words, they are not granted social validity. In this sense, though, recognition is also conceived as a distinctly action-theoretic concept, in which a subject can 'force' another into actions

that affirm her existence by 'striking back' or contesting her social invisibility.[55]

In *Reification,* Honneth transforms the 'epistemology of recognition' into
a more broadly conceived *a priori* notion of affective attunement, which in
many ways loses its overtly action-theoretic character. In the later work,
recognition refers to a pre-cognitive affirmative stance not only towards
others, but also the self and the world, and is the very condition of rational
thought and all further moral or ethical orientations.

In order to legitimate this primordial recognition stance, Honneth also
once again emphasizes the fundamental importance of affectivity in ontogenetic development. Drawing on developmental psychology, particularly the
research of Peter Hobson and Michael Tomasello, Honneth highlights the
child's affective attachment to a significant caregiver as fundamental to his
or her ability to adopt the perspective of a second person. Developmentally, a
child requires emotional or affective receptivity to another before the capacity for cognition and the ability to take a decentered perspective is acquired.
Thus, it is only "a kind of existential, even affective sympathy towards other
persons that allows children to experience their perspectives on the world for
the first time as having significance."[56] Leaning on Adorno's notion of 'libidinal cathexis,' Honneth contends that an openness or receptivity to the
world and an ability to perceive an external reality requires an originary
attachment to a concrete other that is oriented by love. He also assumes that it
is only through this primary affective attachment that subjects learn to take a
'recognitional' stance to non-human objects. By imitating the meaning given
to an object by a significant other, the child also internalizes the value that
object has for another subject.[57] Honneth therefore takes up Adorno's idea
that the "human mind arises out of an early imitation of a loved figure of
attachment."[58] In Adorno's work, these early mimetic experiences, "in which
our thinking develops through love," also "have a continued existence as
trace memories," despite the instrumentalizing effects of the capitalist life
form that compels social conformity and restricts critical capacities. It is
these early trace memories of non-instrumentalized relations of love and care
that carry an emancipatory interest that points beyond reified forms of existence. In this later essay, then, Honneth draws together his work on object-
relations psychoanalysis with an account of Adorno's notion of mimetic
reason to substantiate primary affectivity as a foundational category.[59]

As several commentators have noted, this reconstruction of the theory of
recognition places an enormous conceptual load on the category of recognition.[60] Moreover, from the perspective of this study, Honneth's turn to a
social-ontology of recognition raises a number of substantial questions. In
particular, there has been a shift from a theory of intersubjectivity understood
in action-theoretic terms to an ontology of affective attunement, and this
raises the question of the status of a more dynamically conceived notion of

intersubjectivity based on multifarious patterns of interaction. Moreover, there seems to be a lack of clarity between conceptual categories, now theorized in terms of both a theory of intersubjectivity in interpersonal affective terms, and a social ontology of 'caring comportment' towards the world.

This problem is further exacerbated in *Reification*, where Honneth conceptualizes 'intersubjectivity' in terms of the child's primary identification with or imitation of a significant other. Once again, it can be argued that an affective attachment or imitation between infant and significant other does not constitute an intersubjective relation. This elision of conceptual categories is evident when Honneth moves seamlessly between a social-ontological conception of recognition drawn from Heidegger's notion of care and Lukács' notion of empathetic engagement, to a discussion of developmental psychology and an ontogenetic account of primary affective intersubjectivity. In the first case, with reference to Heidegger and Lukács, Honneth is referring to a non-cognitive, affective means of relating to the world in social ontological terms. In the second case he is primarily concerned with an 'intersubjective' theory of acknowledgement and the temporal acquisition of affective or emotional receptivity and attachment to a significant other as the prerequisite for cognition and symbolization. Honneth himself acknowledges that there is a difference between the notion of 'fundamental existential care' and the ontogenetic account of affective intersubjective relations with a significant other but resolutely defends the idea that the ontogenetic account supports his claim for the social-ontological foundation of recognition.

Once again a substantial slippage can be detected here between the normative theory of intersubjectivity and subject-formation, and an ontology of recognition. The way in which Honneth reconstructs the notion of recognition as a transcendental category, in many places in *Reification*, again restates recognition in a way that has distinctly normative implications. Within the terms of this account, Honneth attempts to separate out the normative theory of recognition from the foundational premise of an ontology of affective recognition. However, in some passages, recognition is portrayed as an elementary form of relatedness that is always already 'positive' and 'affirmative' and this gives the distinct impression that aggression, power, hatred, and violence are all secondary deviations to a primary form of 'affectivity' or 'care.'[61]

In response to critics, Honneth has attempted to modify his claims and to defend his recent social-ontological stance, arguing it is possible to separate out the second-order normative orientation of recognition, understood in terms of a formal concept of ethical life, from a more ontological notion of recognition understood as an 'affectedness' or 'antecedent identification' towards others, our self, and nature. The normatively oriented forms of recognition represented by love, law, and achievement are then considered to be normative extensions of this elementary form of recognition that are "filled out" historically.[62] Honneth clarifies that he means to argue that the ontological notion of recognition refers merely to a primary 'receptivity' or 'affective engagement' that is a precursor to all other forms of human action or interaction but does not determine the particular stance taken towards another person. In terms of the social-ontological notion of recognition he holds that: "Love and hate, ambivalence and coldness, can all be expressions of this elementary recognition as long as they can be seen to be modes of existential affectedness."[63]

In some ways, this more recent attempt by Honneth to separate out primary forms of 'affective' relationality from normative stances potentially opens up future possibilities to address some of the issues that have been identified throughout this study. However, in order to be fruitful and prevent an overburdening of the concept of recognition the ontological notion of affectedness towards the world may need to be separated from the intersubjective notion of recognition. As Varga argues, if Honneth wants to avoid the perception that he posits an overly positive and normative anthropology, he needs to refrain from referring to a primordial form of relatedness as 'recognition' and replace it with a term such as 'affective attunement.'[64] This might prevent the fusion between first- and second-order categories and the slippages between the normative and anthropological meanings of the term. Moreover, the notion of 'affective attunement' might be separated from the reading of Lukács' account of reification in order to avoid the aforementioned problems of seeming to posit a 'positive' or one-dimensionalized account of relationality that seems to separate it from other modalities of interaction. In this sense, forms of relationality cannot be posited *a priori* as positive or normative, and this would enable the development of a more multi-dimensional theory of relationality or intersubjectivity, understood as a constant interplay between 'positive' and 'negative' forms of affectedness.

Nonetheless, despite these qualifications, perhaps one of the most striking shifts in the work on reification is the move from the more explicit action-theoretic stance of Honneth's earlier work to a notion of primary affect. As a consequence of this transition, the agonistic notions of conflict and struggle that were so central to Honneth's early work have become de-emphasized in the move to posit a primary ontological form of affective recognition. Moreover, Honneth's tendency to posit a 'genuine' or 'correct' mode of relating to the world with the category of affective recognition screens out the possibility of identifying a more complex philosophical anthropology that can account for a variety of modalities of specifically human interaction and the importance of understanding the way in which different modalities of relatedness condition one another. This overburdening of the category of recognition as both anthropological-ontology and tripartite normative theory has resulted in a retreat from the early dynamic and broad-based approach to both philosophical anthropology and intersubjectivity that were evident in his early work.

Chapter Eleven

The Power of Critique

The previous chapters have provided an immanent reconstruction of the philosophical anthropology and theory of intersubjectivity upon which Honneth attempts to ground a normative critical theory. The argument in the foregoing discussion has been that the works of Habermas, Marx, Foucault, Hegel, Mead, and Winnicott are central to understanding Honneth's attempt to re-conceptualize the intersubjective paradigm and the anthropological basis for his project of critique. However, the above reconstruction has also elucidated the problems associated with this anthropological foundation, particularly in regard to constructing a normative theory of intersubjectivity and the consideration of the 'critique of power.' The major question that arises from this study is, what consequences does Honneth's anthropological and intersubjectivist approach have for his attempt to construct a critical social theory? This final chapter will attempt to consider precisely this question. The aim here is to consider the vicissitudes of Honneth's accounts of intersubjectivity and power in the context of attempting to ground a normative theory on an anthropological basis. In what follows, then, a reconstruction of Honneth's version of social philosophy and critical theory will be critically discussed in comparison to alternative versions of critical social theory. This discussion aims to reveal the problems associated with Honneth's approach that result from his attempt to bring the central elements of anthropology, normativity, and critique together as the defining features of his project.

The key to understanding Honneth's approach is the connection he makes between anthropology, social philosophy, and the diagnoses of social pathologies which is central to his method of critical social theory. In his reconstruction of the tradition of social philosophy, Honneth identifies the 'diagnosis of social pathologies,' as one of the defining characteristics of the discipline, a method which is intended to elucidate forms of social suffering

183

or 'abnormal' forms of social development that inhibit full human flourishing.[1] As Honneth identifies, in the history of the tradition this has tended to mean that a critical perspective is constructed in negative terms by naming pervasive social ills or deformations in social reproduction and integration. Such a conception, however, also presupposes there is a "conception of normality" against which, to use a medical analogy, the 'health' of societies can be measured.[2]

This reliance on a 'paradigm of social normality' assumes that the critical social theorist has already posited an ideal about what it means to live a good, 'healthy,' or well-lived life. In this sense, what distinguishes social philosophy from both moral and political philosophy is that it fundamentally "relies upon criteria of an ethical nature."[3] It is worth noting here that Honneth uses the term 'social philosophy' almost interchangeably with 'critical social theory' but there are some differences between the two, and these will be discussed further below. In comparison to political philosophy, which is based on an analysis of the formation and maintenance of political order, or moral philosophy which is concerned with issues of right or just action, social philosophy, in Honneth's terms, is concerned with the limitations imposed on recognitively structured individual self-realization as a result of the radical changes to forms of social relation that arise with the advent of modernity.[4]

For Honneth, the emergence of social philosophy as a specific form of critique first arises with the work of Rousseau, whose analysis of capitalist modernization and the rise of civil society, specifically a distinct bourgeois public sphere, highlighted the negative effects of a distinctly new, modern form of social life. As Honneth points out, in comparison to Hobbes, Rousseau is not concerned with questions of justice nor the founding of a political order, but rather with underlying social conditions and the effects of modernity that lead to social deformations.[5] Honneth argues that Rousseau can be considered the founder of the discipline because of the way in which he conceptualizes the course of civilization or modern social development as 'pathological' and evaluates this misdevelopment against an ethical framework. In Rousseau's case, this is conceptualized as a diremption from an original natural condition or anthropologically defined form of self-relation.[6] In comparison to Hobbes, the history of social philosophy, then, begins with Rousseau's alternative conception of the transition from a "state of nature" to the "civil condition" and the inherent problems and difficulties this new form of collective life entails.[7]

As a consequence of the newly emerging sphere of civil society, a new sphere of analysis is designated. It is no longer the state that is considered the main guarantor of conditions for self-realization but instead the sphere of the social that has become differentiated from the state. In Honneth's view, it is in this context "that social philosophy emerged as a representative of an ethical perspective in the unknown territory of a gradually emerging society."[8] Thus, social philosophy can be described as the study of a distinct domain that arises "from the collision of social or political order and individual subjects." As Martin Saar usefully defines it: "the theoretical domain of social philosophy is thus located in an intermediate space, or a space of interference, namely the space between, or at the intersection of, society and subjectivity."[9] It is only once the construction and reproduction of society comes to be understood as a fundamentally human responsibility that 'society' becomes a distinct order of inquiry. As Saar argues, "it is only in the course of the early modern view of the fundamental self-createdness or fundamental constructivity of human society that the independent character of social-philosophical questions arises: because sociality has no basis outside itself, society becomes a project and a problem."[10]

From this new complex of problems epitomized in Rousseau's pioneering work, Honneth traces the genealogy of social philosophy through the works of Hegel and Marx, to Nietzsche's radical reformulations, through to its sociological 'turn' with Weber, Durkheim, Tönnies, and Simmel, and then to its more contemporary manifestation with Lukács, the first generation of the Frankfurt School, and beyond that to the work of Arendt, Habermas, and Foucault. As Saar points out, each of these theorists confronts the ambiguities of modern freedom, equality, and sociality, and attempts to address the consequences of alienated forms of modern social relations in a variety of ways. Mostly they attempt to resolve these ambiguities "with ambitious projects of natural 'reconciliation' or merely diagnose … a tragic and irreconcilable tension."[11] Each identifies social pathologies that deform or distort the potential for self-realization, whether they are conceptualized in terms of alienation, reification, nihilism, bifurcation, atomization, demystification, or commercialization. Moreover, each constructs a diagnosis of modern life that both reveals social mis-developments and posits a conception of ethical life against which these deformations can be evaluated.

For Honneth, this particular genealogy of social philosophy has several important methodological implications and challenges. Firstly, the impact of the sociological reformulation of social-philosophical approaches in the nineteenth-century resulted in the development of a distinct interdisciplinary perspective.[12] In Honneth's view, the founders of sociology can all be distinguished by their commitment to a diagnosis of social pathologies that also continues to be based on distinctly ethical criteria. However, they also bring an empirical dimension to bear on their analyses that had hitherto been missing from social-philosophical approaches. Honneth argues that from this point onwards, the tradition of social philosophy was therefore "compelled to ground its claims on the results of empirical research."[13] It was no longer adequate to base the critical assessment of existing social relations on grand theory alone.

However, perhaps the most fundamental challenge to social philosophy is posed by Nietzsche's genealogical method, which caused a radical reconsideration of the forms of justification used to normatively ground critical social theory.[14] As Honneth notes, just like other social philosophers before him, Nietzsche bases his genealogical analysis on a notion of the good life which serves as the means for critically evaluating an ideal "cultural form of life." However, unlike his predecessors, who typically derived this evaluative framework from a form of anthropological theory understood to represent universal human features, Nietzsche applies a form of ethical particularism to his cultural-historical analyses that immediately appeared to undermine social philosophy's claim to represent a universalistic normative position.[15] This form of perspectivism seriously challenges the credibility not only of universalistic approaches but also the possibility of grounding normative social critique in a way that has context-transcending validity. For as Honneth notes, Nietzsche's particularism made it "suddenly clear that, behind every ethical universalism, a set of values and convictions expressing merely one particular world view might be concealed."[16]

Henceforth, every social philosophy or critical social theory is confronted with the challenge of justifying the normative basis for critique in a way that avoids merely representing a particularistic version of the good life. It could no longer be taken for granted that the evaluative framework used to diagnose social pathologies could be said to be applicable across different historical or social-cultural contexts.

In order to address this fundamental issue, Honneth argues that social philosophy tended to take one of two different methodological approaches as a means of justifying the basis for critique: either an anthropological or historical-philosophical one.[17] Both models were aimed at avoiding cultural perspectivism and distinguished by the means by which they attempted to justify their universalistic applicability: "While philosophical anthropology sought to gain a general concept of the human form of life by going back to its natural starting point, the philosophy of history deduced such a concept from human development's inevitable goal."[18] Anthropological approaches are characterized by the way in which they derive their normativity from general human features that are taken to be basic preconditions for successful forms of self-realization. For Honneth, Rousseau, and as has been noted above, the German tradition of philosophical anthropology are considered to have made major contributions to the articulation of this model.

In the case of historical-philosophical approaches, it is a matter of articulating a prospective end-state to which the course of history or the historical bearer of revolutionary potential would necessarily lead.[19] The second position is exemplified by Hegel's conceptualization of a rational progression of human history and Lukács' *History and Class Consciousness*.[20] In this light Honneth also singles out Horkheimer and Adorno's *Dialectic of Enlighten-*

ment as fatefully adopting a form of negativistic historical-philosophical reconstruction that limited their approach to the depiction of the mis-development of the historical process. As a result, the ethical criteria that form the basis against which their critique can be generated fades from view, and they screen out any democratic potential or possibility for an ethical form of life.[21] For Honneth, once Lukács' philosophy of history had become discredited and the proletariat could no longer be considered the bearer of an 'emancipatory interest' and agent for historical change, and Horkheimer and Adorno's response in *Dialectic of Enlightenment* tumbles into a negativistic downward-spiral leaving no space for conceptualizing normative advancements at all, social philosophy is forced to look in another direction to ascertain how it can justify the basis for critically assessing the social pathologies of modern social life.[22]

For Honneth, it is therefore Arendt, and following her Habermas, Castoriadis, and Taylor, who are once again able to identify an emancipatory potential within social reality and provide a renewed basis for reconceptualizing the project of critique. It is of course, as discussed above, Habermas' intersubjectivism that in Honneth's view provides the best way to proceed. Habermas' theory of communicative action is not only able to identify an immanent reference point in social reality but more importantly can demonstrate that such an emancipatory potential expresses "the unmet demands of humanity at large."[23] Moreover, Habermas is able to reconstruct Critical Theory's dialectical method in a way that can justify a form of context-transcending normativity by re-legitimating a concept of social—or communicative—rationalization that had previously been constructed in overly negative terms by the first generation of the Frankfurt School.[24]

However, Honneth acknowledges that Foucault's Nietzschean-inspired genealogical studies once again re-ignited the question of the legitimacy of universalism and the notion of context-transcending validity in contemporary social philosophy. Foucault's perspectivism has raised a permanent methodological concern for social philosophy and critical social theory. In Honneth's view, critical theory is now compelled to incorporate some form of genealogical method that can verify the empirical application of moral norms and the validity of truth claims within any given social-historical context.[25]

In response to the set of challenges raised by Foucault's work, Honneth identifies three possible approaches that he suggests social-philosophers might adopt in order to address these problems: (1) a form of procedural ethics; (2) a formal anthropological model; (3) a historically relativized form of ethics. Honneth emphatically supports only the second of these approaches as the only viable option for defending a form of context-transcending validity that he considers to be one of the central aims of social philosophy. In Honneth's view, "the survival of social philosophy ... depends on the success with which the claim of a weak, formal anthropology can be justified in the future."[26] As discussed above, Honneth's commitment has always been to defend an anthropological justification for normative critique, and despite some modifications in his recent work with the introduction of an historical dimension, he continues to fundamentally support this basic presupposition.

As indicated in the foregoing discussion, though, Foucault's work also explicitly brings the question of power to the center of social-philosophical concerns. The force of Foucault's argument, as Honneth himself acknowledges, is to challenge the "thesis that every context-transcending norm—and especially every reference to human nature—merely conceals a power-related construction."[27] As discussed above, however, in his own reconstruction Honneth does not adequately consider the way in which the conceptualization of power has been a defining component of the social-philosophical tradition. What Honneth seems to overlook, in Martin Saar's terms, is that "sociality is in itself a question of power," and that power is an essential dimension of the critical perspective of social philosophy that needs to be made more explicit.[28]

In this context, it is instructive to compare Saar's alternative reconstruction of the tradition of social philosophy that offers a counter-interpretation of the task of critique. Although agreeing with Honneth's basic outline of the genealogy of social philosophy as a distinct discipline, Saar argues that it can alternatively be reconstructed as a 'critique of power,' which can be traced along two different lines of thought in the history of philosophy. Most importantly, as he argues, the very project of critique fundamentally depends on the notion of power that operates within any critical social theory.[29] Saar identifies two main concepts of power that can be traced through the history of social philosophy: (1) a domination-theoretic one, and (2) an ontological version that denotes a constitutive version of power. These two different concepts of power can both be identified in Aristotle's practical philosophy in the notion of *dynamis*, which to begin with has an ontological meaning, denoting the "forces or powers that are intrinsic to a person, a thing or even a divine being." In addition, the notion of *dynamis* also retains what Saar refers to as an 'action-related' connotation, signifying an external influence over individual action, or the power of one will over another. In the history of social and political thought, this complex notion of power has become separated into two quite distinct concepts of power, as either *potestas*, which Saar suggests carries 'action-theoretic' connotations, or *potentia*, which retains ontological or constitutive dimensions.[30]

In the history of social philosophy, the first notion of power can be identified in the work of Hobbes, and traced through the work of theorists such as Weber, who reconceptualized it in terms of domination, to Marx, and to contemporary theorists such as Habermas, and we could also add Honneth, where it has become the dominant concept of power employed in social-theoretical analysis. This domination-theoretic view of power is individualistic, instrumentalist, and hierarchical, and understands power as the subjugation of one will by another or by an external authority. It treats power as a property of subjects or a scarce resource that is held by some individuals and not others, and which places external limitation upon the capacities and actions of individuals and social groups.[31]

According to this standard 'action-theoretic' view, associated with thinkers such as Weber, "someone 'has' power to the extent to which the other does not ... and 'having power' thus means being able to determine actions and determine others to act."[32] In the Weberian conceptual framework, power is thus understood as a form of domination or subjugation, and the task becomes determining the legitimacy of power in which the will of the individual is subjugated to the political order. This view reduces power to questions of 'sovereignty' or the centralization of power in the state, and therefore to issues of authority and legitimacy in relation to an existing legal or political order.[33]

The second ontological or constitutive version of power can be traced via Spinoza, is reformulated in different ways by philosophers such as Nietzsche and Arendt, and is re-examined by figures such as Deleuze and Foucault. This form of power is defined in terms of the ontological concept of *potentia*, referring to the very capacities or potentiality of a person or thing, or the very forces or dynamics that constitute persons or things. Importantly, though, this alternative concept of power is not individualistic but relational; it operates as a network or "radius of possible effects and actions in relation to other persons and things" and is the "basis for all possible actions and interactions." Thus understood, power is not a resource or characteristic that can be acquired or possessed, rather as discussed in relation to Foucault's work, it is a "constitutive principle."[34] As Saar suggests, this notion of power has anthropological connotations—it is not a separate feature a person acquires but is part of their constitution—and brought together with broader questions in regard to the social or political order, it carries ontological connotations. Power, then, is conceptualized as intrinsic to the human condition; it conditions the common space of action and the 'web of human affairs' and relations.[35]

As Saar argues, these two very different concepts of power, one as domination and one a constitutive form, provide two very different platforms for critique. According to the logic of the first position, the task of critique will be framed in terms of an analysis and critique of domination. As Saar perceptively argues, based on a domination-theoretic notion of power, critique will always be based on an analysis of power "where action is determined externally, and power operates only in the absence of freedom." The critique of power, then, will always be based on a dualism between types of action, between forms of power that are legitimate and illegitimate, and between forms of action that are conducted from a position of freedom and those that are subject to power. Significantly, this form of power is only ever conceptualized as the opposite to freedom, and as incompatible with the normative basis of concepts of freedom and autonomy. Thus, as Saar argues, the critique of power as a critique of domination continues to posit a dualism between freedom and power, and is "conceptualized in terms of a defense against incursion, repression and subjugation, and its general principle remains coercion."[36]

In contrast, the constitutive notion of power begins from an understanding that power is intrinsic to social relations and constitutive of subject-formation. As discussed in relation to Foucault's work, power is therefore understood as enabling and productive, not coercive nor prohibitory; it does not stand opposed to freedom but in fact may be the very condition of the possibility of freedom, autonomy, and individuality.[37] This alternative conception of power as "a general constitutive principle" has major ramifications for the project of critique. For as Saar suggests, following Foucault, if there is no 'absolute outside' of power, then it is no longer possible to simply divide forms of action into those that are legitimate and illegitimate, or those that are subject to power and those that are conditioned by freedom.[38]

If social philosophy and critical theory are understood as being a critique of power in this more complex sense, Saar argues that the task of critique can only proceed by unearthing the complex interplay of power and normativity in social relations, and by tracing the specific history of relations of power as they pertain to the development of social institutions, norms, and identities, forms of individuation and social life. It also means applying the same critical stance to one's own critical-theoretical position in order to interrogate the co-implication of power and normative criteria in the values that form the basis for critique.[39] It could be suggested, then, that a 'genealogical proviso' might be directed not only towards the application of norms in any given society but also to the construction of normative categories as well.[40]

Taking into account these distinctions, it is possible to conclude that Honneth largely employs an action-theoretic notion of power throughout his work. However, the argument developed here is that in his early work, Honneth began to conceptualize an alternative action-theoretic account of power that did not merely reproduce a standard Weberian or Marxian account of power. Honneth therefore avoided reducing the analysis of power to questions of legitimacy or authority, or to either an individualistic or systems-theoretic account, or one concerned with the centralization of power. Rather, drawing on Foucault, Honneth contributes to a conception of power in intersubjective or relational terms, depicting it as a form of strategic intersubjectivity or as an open field of struggle. Honneth therefore claimed that power should not be conceptualized at the level of systems, but as a form of 'micro-power' that is operative at the level of everyday life. He therefore brings into relief an important distinction between systems-theoretic and action-theoretic accounts of power, a distinction that is not adequately captured by Saar's categories outlined above. In this respect, it can be argued that in his early work, Honneth brings important insights to the analysis of power, particularly in terms of the potential for a more Foucaultian inspired 'action-theoretic' account that has largely been overlooked in later work. [41]

The question is, then, what happens to the analysis of power in Honneth's subsequent development of a theory of recognition?

From the beginning, Honneth's theory of recognition has undeniably been concerned with a critique of power and domination, as his focus on social suffering and distorted individual self-realization implies. However, it could be argued that in *The Struggle for Recognition*, Honneth reverts to a fairly standard action-theoretic view of power along the lines outlined by Saar, whereby the analysis of power is subsumed to the notion of class struggle, or understood as an instrument that one individual or group wields over another in terms of the power to withhold or grant claims for recognition. Moreover, as Saar's analysis reveals, even in his early interpretation of Foucault, Honneth neglects to consider ontological or constitutive forms of power, whereby power is understood as a potential or enabling capacity rather than only a form of action expressed through social conflict and struggle.

Consequently, Honneth's reconstruction of the tasks of social philosophy and critical theory has largely resulted in the reduction of critique to an analysis of domination-theoretic forms of power that prevent or prohibit individuals from achieving full self-realization. As a result, Honneth has tended to overlook the complexity of the constitutive dimensions of power, not only in regard to intersubjective relations and subject-formation, but he also narrows the scope in which we might understand the way power conditions the field of the social more generally. In this sense, he perpetuates an action-theoretic stance in which power is conceived as operating only in the absence of freedom, and therefore does not consider the potential interplay between power and recognition in any comprehensive manner.

RECOGNITION, POWER, AND CRITIQUE

In his more recent work, however, Honneth re-engages with the problem of power as it pertains to the theory of recognition. In the essay "Recognition as Ideology," he acknowledges that recognition can take ideological forms and notes that power can operate in ways that are productive of identity. Gesturing towards Foucault, Honneth argues that ideological forms of recognition cannot be considered repressive nor on the face of it do they appear irrational, as subjects must be motivated by good reasons to identify with the evalua-

tive qualities being addressed to them. Honneth's analysis in the essay largely proceeds, however, with a critical examination of Althusser's notion of
ideology and with the question of how "recognition can ... also operate as a
conformist ideology ... without employing methods of repression."[42] In other words, how do individuals take on board certain subject-esteeming values
that appear rationally justified and freedom-enhancing but which, in fact,
produce a diminishment of autonomy and reproduce forms of social domination?

In contrast to his earlier account of power, which was intrinsically related
to the notion of social struggle, in this latest work, Honneth attempts to
address the fact that ideological forms of recognition may operate so 'seamlessly' that they do not engender any struggle or resistance from subjects at
all.[43] If ideological forms of recognition are accepted willingly and they
secure a subject's compliance to dominating social norms passively and
without conflict or resistance, then as Honneth concedes, it is very difficult to
distinguish between ideological and normative forms of recognition.
Honneth suggests the willingness of subjects to comply with subordinating
forms of recognition can be explained with reference to several main features
they must exhibit in order to be experienced as credible. To be effective,
ideological forms of recognition must be overwhelmingly positive and subjects must be able to accept such forms of evaluation on the basis of good
reasons; in other words, they cannot be overtly injurious, such as forms of
racism or misogyny. To be credible, then, ideological forms of evaluation
must also be convincing in the light of historical progress and accepted in
terms of the prevailing norms and values of any given society. Moreover,
ideological forms of recognition must enable a subject to relate to herself
affirmatively and must be experienced as autonomy-enhancing rather than
prohibitive. Finally, such forms of recognition must be seen to create or
express new qualities or values such that they motivate subjects to identify
with them because they represent a new distinguishing feature or form of
achievement. Thus, all told, ideological forms of recognition can be said to
operate entirely within "an historical space of reasons" because they display
features that are "positive, credible and contrastive."[44] Ideological forms of
recognition, then, cannot be understood as an 'irrational system of beliefs' or
a form of 'false consciousness' in the conventional sense, but nonetheless
they do create a 'disconnect' between first-order experiences of social domination and second-order reflexive capacities for 'correctly' identifying the
causes or explanations for those social conditions.[45]

The task as Honneth sees it, then, is to be able to distinguish between
forms of recognition that merely evoke social conformity and reproduce
forms of domination, from normative forms of recognition that achieve more
than just symbolic expression. Honneth suggests, therefore, that the only way
to distinguish between ideological and non-ideological forms of recognition

is on the basis of evidence of their material fulfillment. Ideological or 'false' forms of recognition may hold out an evaluative promise of recognition; however, they are not backed-up or 'expressed' by equivalent material responses or institutional practices that 'truly' meet the justified demands of recognition. For Honneth, then, ideological forms of recognition appear credible and rational, in the sense that they meet the evaluative criteria of recognition; however, such recognition is demonstrated only at a symbolic level and lacks material instantiation. This reveals the 'irrational core' of ideological forms of recognition, which for Honneth is demonstrated when an unjustifiable gap between symbolic and material or institutional substantiation is revealed.

In attempting to work through these issues, Honneth firstly seeks to clarify more forcefully the meaning and definition of recognition, and in so doing, reiterates the distinction between its 'constitutive' and 'attributive' forms. As discussed in the preceding chapter, Honneth makes a distinction between recognition as either 'constitutive' in the sense that it generates qualities or features of a subject for the first time; or, recognition as 'responsive,' which merely refers to the actualization of pre-existing qualities or capacities that are understood to have already been present or that subjects already possess. In this second case, qualities are conceived as potentialities that are actualized only through acts of recognition, which enable subjects to identify with their own capacities by developing a positive relation-to-self. Honneth, therefore, endorses only an 'identificatory' model of intersubjective constitution, in the sense that individual features are already present as potentialities but subjects are only able to identify with them once they are confirmed by others.[46] Following Laitinen, Honneth seems to endorse the suggestion that recognition is only 'initially' constitutive in the sense of ensuring that subjects develop the capacities for developing a positive self-relation, which in a second step, is required for identifying with their own evaluative qualities. In other words, a practical identity "does not consist of [a subject] simply having features, but rather [of her] having features that [she *identifies*] with."[47] Honneth understands this model as a 'middle position' between forms of constructivism and representationalism but it seems clear that he understands the connection between recognition and identity, then, to be a matter of enabling a pre-existing identity to be actualized in social conditions which prevent its distortion. In this context, it seems that Honneth's preference for a 'receptive' model of recognition might also be associated with the attempt to avoid recognition being associated with power at the level of normative intersubjective relations; that is, to maintain that recognition be maintained as a moral category by not being defined as directly constitutive of identity.

There are two major sets of issues that arise in the context of this latest work on recognition, ideology, and power. The first set of issues arises as a result of the distinctions Honneth makes between recognition as a responsive rather than a constitutive act. If recognition is only understood as a receptive act in this manner, it therefore follows that acts of recognition are understood to refer to an act of 'perceiving' or 'receiving' forms of identity that already exist or that have *already been constituted*. Honneth admits this when he suggests that in the model he adopts, we can only understand recognition as constitutive of subjects in an 'indirect' not a 'direct' sense—it does not construct particular features or qualities but merely facilitates the actualization of pre-existing ones. Recognition therefore refers to an act, or claim for action, from recognizee to recognizer to 'correctly' perceive a pre-constituted form of subjectivity. In terms of the analysis of power, the consequence of this position seems to be that it is only possible *post facto* to recognize more or less dominating forms of subjectivity. In other words, it does not rule out that subjects might also be constituted in relations of power or that they might internalize negative patterns of interaction in the process of subject-formation.

If this is the case, though, what does recognition-theory actually then tell us about subject-constitution or subject-formation in a more comprehensive sense?

Although Honneth correctly avoids identifying recognition as purely a form of social constructivism, there seem to be several potential implications of trying to maintain this strict separation between 'constitution' and 'affirmation.' Firstly, this stance seems to dampen the more dynamic intersubjective notion of subject-formation that is suggested by Honneth's earlier work with reference to Mead and Winnicott, where both the process of the internalization of others' perspectives, the conflict between the 'I' and 'me,' and the early childhood process of attachment and separation, lend themselves to the idea of a more 'directly' constituting process of intersubjective formation. Secondly, it also seems very difficult to maintain this strict separation in practice, whereby recognition is understood to be only 'indirectly' constitutive by being restricted to the creation of a positive relation-to-self.

As Honneth explains in his more psychoanalytically orientated essays, the idea of a "subject's relation-to-self—represents a process in which children gradually internalize patterns of interaction they learn in their successive encounters with their mother, father, siblings and, finally, peers. The organization of the psyche thus occurs as an interactive process in which the maturing subject learns to recognize the independence of objectively existing relations of interaction only by mirroring them intrapsychically, in order to give rise to a variety of different internal agencies."[48] It is fair to suggest, that even these early patterns of interaction will reflect both positive and negative forms, and will be both relations of love and care, as well as power, asymmetricality and at times ambivalence, and these are all patterns of interaction that might be internalized and mirrored intrapsychically. Maintaining that recognition is only constitutive in the sense of developing a (positive) rela-tion-to-self does not then address the issue of the constitution of the subject where both positive and negative patterns of interaction might be intercon-nected. The argument that recognition is only a response to the value of features that subjects already possess does not seem to adequately address or account for the negative or conflictual forms of subject constitution. In other words, understood only as a response to features identified as 'positive' might ably defend the normativity of recognition itself, but it is unclear how it directly addresses negative, ambivalent, or power-saturated forms of sub-ject-constitution.

This more dynamic picture of subject-formation also indicates the need to account for both positive and negative forms of interaction and intersubjec-tivity. As we discussed above, Honneth himself admits there are two compet-ing accounts of recognition that circulate in his work: one driven by 'anti-social impulses' that, for him, arise from the ongoing desire of the subject to recreate the original symbiotic state with the mother and thereby deny the other's difference; the other by emancipatory impulses, where the subject is morally motivated to make recognition claims. As Honneth suggests, these impulses often sit in tension with one another and it is not clear how they can be reconciled and understood entirely as 'moral experiences' motivated by a lack of recognition.[49] This seems to suggest the need to account for the co-constitution of the subject in the context of both positive and negative forces and forms of intersubjectivity, many of which may be internalized and mir-rored intrapsychically and which ensure that claims for recognition are never easily determined as emanating entirely from moral sources. In this sense, as Bankovsky suggests, Honneth's claim that by receiving constant affirmative recognition subjects develop an 'undistorted authentic identity' seems to miss the need for a more critical approach towards subjectivity and subject-formation.[50]

In a similar vein, it might also be argued that it is necessary to consider a more complex notion of productive power in relation to subject-formation, one that does not reduce it simply to a mode of domination nor form of ideology. This brings us back to the notion of power discussed above, where power is understood as both constitutive and as a form of action; where intersubjectivity might simultaneously be relational, enabling, and asymmet-rical. As Wartenberg suggests, in this sense relations of power can be double-sided. For example, parenting is an example of power that can be transforma-tive in the sense of 'empowering' another "by increasing the other's re-sources, capabilities, effectiveness and ability to act."[51] He suggests such relations of power are not simply asymmetrical and focused on the restriction of action but rather on the enablement of certain capacities and relations-to-self. In this sense, power is understood as 'constitutive' rather than simply action-theoretic, as both a form of 'power over' others as well as the 'power to' act or become, but crucially it is also not conflated with or reduced to a notion of domination.[52] In this sense, although some forms of productive power might be more benign that others, power is understood to be a form of asymmetricality that is open-ended, one which enables a reciprocal interplay between power and freedom.[53] As Foucault observed, 'relations of power' are distinguishable from forms of domination in the sense that they are always "changeable, reversible and unstable." It is only when such an interplay between power and freedom, or power and the *potential* for resistance becomes congealed, in the sense that it becomes 'invariable' and prevents all 'reversibility of movement' in a relationship, that we can aptly speak of a 'state of domination.'[54]

It seems, however, that Honneth's analysis of power cannot account for this more complex understanding of power. In the schema he has constructed, power seems either to be associated with a form of open-ended struggle or strategic action between individuals and groups, represented in his earlier work; or as a form of domination understood at the level of institutions to be 'productive' in the sense of creating evaluative features that are *ideologically* imposed and with which subjects themselves passively identify. As Amy Allen has suggested though, forms of productive power are not simply forms of domination; rather power in a constitutive, enabling sense must be understood as "a broader concept than *domination*."[55] The divide Honneth institutes between domination as constitutive of evaluative features at the level of institutions, and power as an action-theoretic notion of struggle and conflict between different groups, seems to miss all the possible states in between. It does not countenance a broader understanding of power as constitutive of the field of the social, nor the reciprocal interplay of power and freedom as an intrinsic feature of intersubjective relations and subject-formation.

Secondly, in this latest analysis of power, Honneth seems to (re)institute a distinction in the analysis of power between the level of intersubjective recognition and the level of institutions. By employing the notion of ideology, Honneth introduces a distinction between "...transformations of consciousness or evaluative systems of statements whose source lies not in intersubjective behavior, but in institutionalized rules and arrangements."[56] Thus, he suggests, we need to shift from an analysis of recognition and power at the level of intersubjective relations to the level of institutionally guaranteed forms of recognition. Moreover, he contends that the relation between recognition and institutions is, in turn, affected by the way in which institutions are constituted in the first place.

It should be made clear at this point that Honneth generally maintains an action-theoretic stance in relation to institutions, thereby avoiding a systems-theoretic analysis. In this sense, for Honneth, institutions are understood as the embodiment or crystallizations of certain forms or patterns of recognition rather than understood in purely functionalist or systemic terms. For example, as a modern institution, the family is representative of the embodiment of the recognition of individual needs, whereas modern legal institutions embody the principle of recognitive equality and respect. As Honneth suggests, institutions should therefore be understood as embodying forms of recognition that are the result of social-historical struggles; even if they do not ever fully realize their normative potential, modern institutions contain the 'promise' of social freedom embodied in institutionalized recognition relations. For example, the way in which certain institutions are regulated to protect workers in terms of safety or health care is understood to reflect "sediments of practices of recognition in the lifeworld"; in other words, institutions are 'expressions' of recognition.[57] This action-theoretic stance also concurs with Honneth's emphasis on 'social' rather than 'system' integration, in the sense that even the economic market and state are conceived as relying upon underlying normative 'constraints' or "depend at least on [the] tacit consent" of the social subjects in any given society.[58] However, he also suggests that where institutions are not 'expressive' of patterns of recognition that are directly claimed by subjects or groups themselves, they may be implicated in perpetuating ideological forms of recognition. Such ideological forms create or ascribe new aspects of identity and are therefore responsible for "the emergence of illusory or fictionalizing beliefs," which encourage subjects "to freely subordinate themselves to the prevailing system of rules and expectations."[59]

It is unclear, then, whether Honneth is conceding that institutions might also be the embodiment of intersubjective forms of *power* as much as they might be crystallizations of patterns of *recognition*.[60] If this was indeed the case, it would represent an extension of the action-theoretic stance towards power that was reflected in earlier insights, and brought together with a constitutive notion of power, would be closer to the interplay between action and constitution in the analysis of power that is being argued for here, as well as indicating an acknowledgment of the co-constitutive dimensions of both power and recognition, at least in regard to institutions.

Nonetheless, despite generally maintaining an action-theoretic stance in relation to institutions, it is evident that Honneth also introduces a theoretical divide between intersubjective relations and institutions in terms of the critique of power. Although this does not equate to a separation between action and systems-theoretic versions of power, it does constitute a separation in the analysis of power understood as *domination* at the level of institutions and leaves under-theorized the forms of *productive power* at the level of intersubjective relations and constitutive of social life more broadly. In this sense, Honneth's analysis implies that only institutional forms of power as domination are productive or constitutive in the sense that they enable subjects to apply new forms of evaluation to themselves in ways that reproduce social domination without struggle or conflict. Not only does this introduce a distinction in the analysis of power at the level of institutions that suppresses the original action-theoretic stance but it also reinstates a domination-theoretic approach to the analysis of power rather than maintaining the intersubjective and action-theoretic approach to power articulated in his early work.

Moreover, Honneth's employment of the notion of 'ideology' to examine the notion of 'productive' power seems to lose the complexity of Foucault's analysis. Foucault's own analysis of 'productive' power and the 'paradox of individualization,' as McNay suggests, captures the more "ambivalent effects of individualizing governmentality," and his genealogical studies point to the difficulty of neatly separating morally justified and power-saturated forms of interaction or subject-formation.[61] In an explicit critique of Althusser and structuralist accounts of power, in his later work, Foucault develops a more agonistic and action-theoretic notion of power that emphasizes the ongoing interplay between power and freedom. In this respect, Foucault does not conceive of a 'radical disconnect' between first-order experiences of social domination and second-order reflexive capacities for 'correctly' identifying the causes or explanations of these social conditions. The task for Foucault is not to be able to disclose beliefs as distorted, erroneous, or false, nor to reveal a more rational or underlying 'truth' or authentic core of social reality. Rather, the more action-theoretic current in Foucault's work emphasizes the ongoing connection between truth and power, and the perpetual struggle over meaning and the production of knowledge. In this sense, Foucault envisaged a more agonistic play of forces and contestation over the construction of meaning rather than either monocausal explanations or unidirectional forms of power.

Honneth's original critique of Foucault in *The Critique of Power* seemed to suggest an extension of this action-theoretic account of power in regard to institutions. In other words, it suggested that institutions be understood as sites of action and interaction, ones which also represent the embodiment of power relations and the outcome of strategic struggles between different social actors. These patterns of action are, in turn, reflected in the institutional practices and values enacted between individuals and institutions; they are forms of power that 'act upon the actions' of others and which condition the field of social interaction. However, this suggests a more dynamic role for social actors, where there is a constant reciprocal interplay between social subjects and institutions, thereby avoiding a structuralizing or functionalist approach.[62] It might be argued that in Honneth's later work, there seems to be a tension between institutions as producing ideological practices and forms of evaluation, in contrast to the more struggle-theoretic notion of the constitution of institutions. Once constituted, it seems that institutions lose any sense of an internally contestatory character in terms of the interactions between the subjects who inhabit those institutions and in the application of norms and evaluative forms of recognition.

In this latest work, then, Honneth ends up making several problematic distinctions between interpersonal and institutional levels of analysis, and between constitutive and responsive forms of recognition, and this has consequences for the 'critique of power.'[63] Restricted to a critique of pathologies as ideological or institutionally imposed forms of power, the theory of recognition does not fully address the broader problem of constitutive forms of power and reinstitutes a separation of action types, between norm-free and power-free forms of action. It does not yet adequately provide the resources to address power as productive of subjects, identities, and institutions, ones that might be produced simultaneously in relations of power as well as relations of recognition.

We have come full circle, then, returning to the problem that first inspired Honneth to reconsider the grounds of a robust 'critique of power' in his first monograph. However, the argument traced throughout this book is that a continuing series of reductions in Honneth's anthropological model has resulted in his reproducing a dualism between types of intersubjectivity and interaction, which was the very problem he sought to avoid in his original study of power and reconstruction of the intersubjective paradigm. These are issues, however, that Honneth needs to more fully address in order for his model of critical social theory to be up to the task of establishing both the basis for a complex 'critique of power' and a normative theory of recognition.

Although Honneth has remained remarkably open to a variety of traditions, his articulation of an anthropology of intersubjectivity has continued to narrow since his early works *Social Action and Human Nature* and *The Critique of Power*, from a broad-based theory of intersubjectivity to an ontology of affectivity in his latest work *Reification*. This has had the effect of narrowing and idealizing his analysis of the human condition, in terms of both a theory of intersubjectivity and a theory of subject-formation. Moreover, it overlooks the complexity of the critique of power and this in turn has profound ramifications for the way in which Honneth attempts to justify the project of critical social theory.

Furthermore, it might be argued that despite acknowledging the importance of Foucault's genealogical approach in his reconstruction of social philosophy, Honneth has not fully taken account of the challenge his work poses for the attempt to conceptualize a form of context-transcending validity for a critical social theory.[64] As discussed above, he neglects to adequately consider the potential specificity of recognitive forms of self-relation and the notion of self-realization to a particular historical and social-cultural context. Moreover, as Saar's work attests, Honneth has not fully considered the constitutive dimension of power in articulating the diagnostic aims of a critical social theory. In this sense, Honneth also overlooks the effects of power as constitutive of both social relations of recognition and forms of self-formation, and this also has methodological implications in terms of the way in which normative claims are justified. In this sense, despite his original intention, Honneth repeats the same error he accuses Habermas of making. Although Honneth is critical of Habermas' dualistic model of types of interaction, and the separation of normative integration from forms of system integration characterized by money and power, Honneth also unwittingly institutes a separation of forms of interaction between relations of power and relations of recognition, as if the two can be neatly untangled. One of the arguments proposed here is that Honneth needs to take account of power more fully both at the level of his social-theoretical diagnoses, and anthropologically as a persistent co-constitutive dimension of social relations. To begin with a multivarious or complex anthropology enables the critical social theorist to equally take account of both forms of power and normative social relations as features of sociality and intersubjectivity.

Honneth's reconceptualization of intersubjectivity as recognition has not only limited the scope for an analysis of power but also narrowed the philosophical anthropology underpinning his work. This reduction also shapes the way in which Honneth seeks to ground the project of critique on the basis of normative anthropological features structured into primary recognitive relations. However, the conceptualization of a more complex anthropology reveals the problem of deriving a normative theory directly from anthropological structures *per se*. As this reconstruction has sought to demonstrate, the articulation of a more complex anthropology indicates that normative features may not justifiably be taken as an anthropological given. Instead, normative values may need to be acknowledged as being of a secondary order; values which might be determined and agreed upon intersubjectively according to a shared ethical framework but that cannot be guaranteed anthropologically. Normative theory might therefore be informed by anthropological possibilities but not directly derived from them. The argument proposed here is that both power and normative forms of relationality need to be theorized simultaneously as forms of social relations that mutually and continually condition one another, and that in constructing the basis for a critical social theory both forms of social relation need to be fully taken into account. This means that we cannot simply posit a critical vantage point 'beyond power' relations and that we must find ways to ground critique that can account for the enduring human capacity for both normative and power-based forms of intersubjectivity.

Notes

INTRODUCTION

1. Honneth describes the project of critical theory in these terms in Axel Honneth, *The Fragmented World of the Social*, ed. Charles W. Wright, Albany, SUNY Press, 1995, pp. xii-xiii; see also Axel Honneth, *The Critique of Power: Reflective Stages in a Critical Social Theory*, trans. K. Baynes, Cambridge MA, & London, The MIT Press, 1991, p. xiv.

2. Max Horkheimer, "Traditional and Critical Theory," in *Critical Theory: Selected Essays*, New York, Seabury Press, 1972, pp. 188-243.

3. See Joel Anderson, "Situating Axel Honneth in the Frankfurt School Tradition," in ed. D. Petherbridge, *Axel Honneth: Critical Essays*, Boston & Leiden, Brill, 2011, pp. 46. Although Honneth undertook his dissertation at the Free University of Berlin with Urs Jaeggi, he also spent some time at Starnberg with Habermas from 1982-83. Honneth was also assistant professor to Habermas in Frankfurt between 1983-89. After positions in Berlin and Konstanz he was appointed to the chair of Social Philosophy at the Wolfgang-Goethe University in Frankfurt in 1996 and became director of the Institute for Social Research in 2001.

4. In 2011, Honneth became Jack C. Weinstein Professor in Humanities in the Department of Philosophy at Columbia University, sharing his time between the University of Frankfurt and Columbia University. Horkheimer and Adorno fled Germany with the rise of Nazism in 1933 and arrived via different routes to New York, where they were affiliated with the department of Sociology at Columbia University. See Thomas Wheatland, *The Frankfurt School in Exile*, University of Minnesota Press, Minnesota, 2009; Rolf Wiggerhaus, *The Frankfurt School: Its History, Theories and Political Significance*, trans. M. Robertson, Cambridge, MA, MIT Press, 1994; Martin Jay, *Marxism and Totality: The Adventures of a Concept from Lukács to Habermas*, Berkeley, University of California Press, 1984.

5. See for example the essays on Sartre, Merleau-Ponty and Castoriadis in Axel Honneth, *The Fragmented World of the Social*, 1995; on Derrida and Levinas, see "The Other of Justice: Habermas and the Ethical Challenge of Postmodernism," in *Disrespect: The Normative Foundations of Critical Theory*, Cambridge, Polity Press, 2007, pp. 99-128; on Foucault, *The Critique of Power*, 1991.

6. See Axel Honneth, interview with Miriam Bankovsky, "The Relevance of Contemporary French Philosophy for a Theory of Recognition, in *Recognition Theory and Contemporary French Moral and Political Philosophy: Reopening the Dialogue*, eds. Miriam Bankovsky and Alice Le Goff, Manchester, Manchester University Press, 2012, pp. 23-38. In this sense, for example, Honneth credits Sartre for drawing attention to the existential rather than merely epistemic stance to others and the world; he takes up Derrida's and Levinas' insights in regard

to the asymmetricality of ethical relations and unconditional responsibility to the other (which he applies to the sphere of intimate relations in his theory of recognition); and acknowledges the important contribution of both Sartre and Foucault in identifying the more conflictual and negative dimensions of intersubjective and social relations.

7. Axel Honneth, "Recognition and Critical Theory Today: An Interview with Axel Honneth," Gonçalo Marcelo, *Philosophy and Social Criticism*, vol. 39, no. 2, pp. 209-221, 2013; Joel Anderson, "Situating Axel Honneth in the Frankfurt School Tradition," in ed. D. Petherbridge, *Axel Honneth: Critical Essays*, Boston & Leiden, Brill, 2011.

8. See Honneth, "Recognition and Critical Theory Today: An Interview with Axel Honneth," Gonçalo Marcelo, *Philosophy and Social Criticism*, vol. 39, no. 2, pp. 209-221, 2013.

9. See Joel Anderson, "Situating Axel Honneth in the Frankfurt School Tradition," p. 34.

10. See Joel Anderson, "Situating Axel Honneth in the Frankfurt School Tradition," pp. 34 and 53.

11. Although as Honneth notes, this interdisciplinary work of the Institute for Social Research is not represented in Horkheimer and Adorno's *Dialectic of Enlightenment* and further recedes as they turn more completely to philosophical resources in works such as *Negative Dialectics* and the *Eclipse of Reason*. See Honneth, "Critical Theory" in *The Fragmented World of the Social: Essays in Social and Political Philosophy*, trans. C. W. Wright, Albany, SUNY Press, 1995, pp. 61-91.

12. In fact, in early work Honneth cited interest in the more 'peripheral' members of the Frankfurt School such as Neumann and Kirchheimer in the sense that they provided more fruitful insights towards an empirically orientated theory of society, which was lacking in the work of Adorno, Horkheimer, and Marcuse. See Axel Honneth, "Critical Theory" in *The Fragmented World of the Social: Essays in Social and Political Philosophy*, trans. C. W. Wright, Albany, SUNY Press, 1995, pp. 61-91.

13. See Honneth, *The Critique of Power*, Chapters 1-3.

14. Theodor Adorno, *Negative Dialectics*, trans. E.B. Ashton, London, Routledge, 1973; Axel Honneth, "The Social Dynamics of Disrespect: On the Location of Critical Theory Today," in *Disrespect: The Normative Foundations of Critical Theory*, Cambridge, Polity Press, 2007, pp. 64-5. In this respect, in his early work Honneth is somewhat critical of Adorno's work and largely assumes Habermas' more critical stance towards Horkheimer and Adorno (see, for example, *The Critique of Power*.) However, in his later work, Honneth provides a much more sympathetic and renewed engagement with Adorno's work. See, for example, Axel Honneth, "The Possibility of a Disclosing Critique of Society: The Dialectic of Enlightenment in Light of Current Debates in Social Criticism," in *Disrespect: The Normative Foundations of Critical Theory*, Cambridge, Polity Press, 2007, pp. 49-62; "A Physiognomy of the Capitalist Form of Life: A Sketch of Adorno's Social Theory," and "Performing Justice: Adorno's Introduction to Negative Dialectics," in *Pathologies of Reason: On the Legacy of Critical Theory*, trans. James Ingram et al. New York, Columbia University Press, 2009.

15. Fraser and Honneth, *Redistribution or Recognition?*, p. 240. See Jürgen Habermas, *Knowledge and Human Interests*, Beacon Press, Boston, 1971.

16. Fraser and Honneth, *Redistribution or Recognition?*, p. 137.

17. See Fraser and Honneth, *Redistribution or Recognition?*, p. 244.

18. See also Roger Foster, "Recognition & Resistance: Axel Honneth's Critical Social Theory," *Radical Philosophy*, vol. 94, March/April, 1999, pp. 6-18.

19. See, for example, Axel Honneth, *Suffering from Indeterminacy: An Attempt at a Reactualisation of Hegel's Philosophy of Right*, Assen, Van Gorcum, 2000; *Pathologies of Individual Freedom: Hegel's Social Theory*, Princeton, Princeton University Press, 2010; *Das Recht Der Freiheit: Grundriß einer Demokratischen Sittlichkeit*, Berlin, Suhrkamp Verlag, 2011.

20. See also Carl-Göran Heidegren, "Anthropology, Social Theory, and Politics: Axel Honneth's Theory of Recognition," *Inquiry*, vol. 45, 2002, pp. 433-46.

21. This is the task laid out in Honneth, *The Critique of Power*.

1. THE INTERSUBJECTIVE GROUNDS OF CRITIQUE

1. See Honneth's reconstruction of social philosophy in "Pathologies of the Social: The Past and Present of Social Philosophy," in *Disrespect: The Normative Foundations of Critical Theory*, Cambridge, Polity Press, 2007, where he constructs the methodological concerns of critical social theory in these terms. See also Honneth, *Redistribution or Recognition?*, p. 240.

2. Nancy Fraser and Axel Honneth, *Redistribution or Recognition?: A Political-Philosophical Exchange*, London & New York, Verso, 2003, pp. 238-9.

3. See, for example, Horkheimer "Traditional and Critical Theory." See Honneth's essays "A Social Pathology of Reason: On the Intellectual Legacy of Critical Theory" and "Reconstructive Social Criticism with a Genealogical Proviso: On the Idea of 'Critique' in the Frankfurt School," both in Axel Honneth, *Pathologies of Reason: On the Legacy of Critical Theory*, trans. James Ingram, New York, Columbia University Press, 2009.

4. Axel Honneth, "Critical Theory," in *The Fragmented World of the Social*, ed. Charles W. Wright, Albany, SUNY Press, 1995, p. 86; *The Critique of Power*, especially chapters 1 & 2.

5. Honneth, "Reconstructive Social Criticism with a Genealogical Proviso: On the Idea of 'Critique' in the Frankfurt School," *Pathologies of Reason: On the Legacy of Critical Theory*, trans. James Ingram, New York, Columbia University Press, 2009, p. 45.

6. Axel Honneth, "Critical Theory," p. 74. See, in particular, Theodor W. Adorno & Max Horkheimer, *The Dialectic of Enlightenment*, London & New York, Verso, 1992.

7. Honneth, "Reconstructive Social Criticism with a Genealogical Proviso," p. 44.

8. Honneth, "Critical Theory," pp. 61-91.

9. Honneth, "Reconstructive Social Criticism with a Genealogical Proviso," p. 44.

10. Fraser and Honneth, *Redistribution or Recognition?*, pp. 239; 242.

11. See Honneth's discussion in Axel Honneth, "Reconstructive Social Criticism with a Genealogical Proviso," pp. 43- 53, where he outlines the risk of a 'strong' context-transcending form of critique as representing either an elitist or paternalistic viewpoint, or worse being a form of despotism (p. 44).

12. Fraser and Honneth, *Redistribution or Recognition?*, p. 240.

13. Honneth, *Redistribution or Recognition?*, in Nancy Fraser and Axel Honneth, *Redistribution or Recognition?: A Political-Philosophical Exchange*, London & New York, Verso, 2003, p. 242.

14. Honneth, *Redistribution or Recognition?*, p. 244.

15. Honneth, *Redistribution or Recognition?*, p. 245.

16. Honneth, *Redistribution or Recognition?*, p. 246.

17. Axel Honneth and Hans Joas, *Social Action and Human Nature*, trans. Raymond Meyer, Cambridge, Cambridge University Press, 1988 (1980), p. 85. See their discussion of Habermas' critique of Plessner's account of expressiveness.

18. Honneth, *Redistribution or Recognition?*

19. Honneth and Joas, *Social Action and Human Nature*.

20. Jürgen Habermas, *Knowledge and Human Interests*, Beacon Press, Boston, 1971, p. 284.

21. Seyla Benhabib, "The Generalized and the Concrete Other: The Kohlberg-Gilligan Controversy," *Praxis International*, vol. 5, no. 4, 1985.

22. See William Rehg, *Insight and Solidarity: A Study in the Discourse Ethics of Jürgen Habermas*, Berkeley, Los Angeles, London, University of California Press, 1994 esp. ch. 4, p. 95.

23. Jay M. Bernstein, *Recovering Ethical Life: Jürgen Habermas and the Future of Critical Theory*, Routledge, London & New York, 1995.

24. Jürgen Habermas, *Philosophical-Political Profiles*, Cambridge, MA, The MIT Press, 1983, p. 158.

25. A. Honneth, "The Other of Justice: Habermas and the Ethical Challenge of Postmodernism," in *The Cambridge Companion to Habermas*, ed. S. White, Cambridge, MA: Cambridge University Press, 1995.

26. Honneth, *The Struggle for Recognition: The Moral Grammar of Social Conflicts*, trans., Joel Anderson, Cambridge, Polity Press, 1995 (1992).

27. See S. Benhabib, *Critique, Norm and Utopia: A Study of the Foundations of Critical Theory*, New York, Columbia University Press, 1986, pp. 320-21. Also Johanna Meehan, "Autonomy, Recognition, and Respect: Habermas, Benjamin, and Honneth," *in Feminists Read Habermas: Gendering the Subject of Discourse*, ed. Johanna Meehan, New York & London, Routledge, 1995.

28. Axel Honneth, The Social Dynamics of Disrespect: Situating Critical Theory Today," in *Habermas: A Critical Reader*, ed. Peter Dews, Oxford, Blackwell Publishers, 1999, p. 331.

29. See A. Honneth, *The Fragmented World of the Social: Essays in Social and Political Philosophy*, ed. Charles Wright, Albany, State University of New York Press, 1995. See specifically the chapter, "Work and Instrumental Action: On the Normative Basis of Critical Theory," pp. 15-49.

30. Jay M. Bernstein, "Suffering Injustice: Misrecognition as Moral Injury in Critical Theory," *International Journal of Philosophical Studies*, vol. 13, no. 3, 2005, p. 307.

31. Bernstein, "Suffering Injustice," p. 308.

32. Honneth, "Social Dynamics of Disrespect," p. 331. Also see Honneth, "Moral Consciousness and Class Domination: Some Problems in the Analysis of Hidden Morality," *The Fragmented World of the Social*.

2. READING MARX AFTER HABERMAS

1. Honneth, "Domination & Moral Struggle: The Philosophical Heritage of Marxism Reviewed," *The Fragmented World of the Social*, pp. 3-14.

2. Honneth, "Domination & Moral Struggle."

3. See also Löwith's interpretation to which Honneth's is indebted. Karl Löwith, *From Hegel to Nietzsche: The Revolution in Nineteenth-Century Thought*, trans. David Green, New York, Columbia University Press, 1991 (1964), p. 265.

4. Honneth, "Domination & Moral Struggle."

5. George Márkus, *Marxism and Anthropology: The Concept of 'Human Essence' in the Philosophy of Marx*, trans. E. de Laczay and G. Márkus, Assen, The Netherlands, Van Gorcum, 1978; "Alienation and Reification in Marx and Lukács," *Thesis Eleven*, nos. 5-6, 1982, pp. 139-161.

6. Markus, "Alienation and Reification in Marx and Lukács."

7. Karl Marx, *The Economic and Philosophical Manuscripts of 1844*, ed. Dirk J. Struik, trans. Martin Milligan, New York, International Publishers, 1973, p. 331.

8. Honneth, "Domination & Moral Struggle."

9. See Márkus, *Marxism and Anthropology*; "Alienation and Reification in Marx and Lukács," *Thesis Eleven*, nos. 5-6, 1982, pp. 139-161.

10. Honneth, "Work and Instrumental Action," in *The Fragmented World of the Social*, ff. 58, p. 283.

11. See for example Jürgen Habermas, *Knowledge and Human Interests*, Part 1; "Labor and Interaction: Remarks on Hegel's Jena Philosophy of Mind," in *Theory and Practice*, trans. John Viertel, London, Heinemann, 1974.

12. Honneth, "Work and Instrumental Action," *Thesis Eleven*, nos. 5-6, 1982. Honneth argues, however, that this problematic does not begin with Habermas but has a rather long history, as typified in the work, for example, of Arendt and Scheler. In the history of critical Marxism, Lukács, Adorno, and Horkheimer also share in common the loss of the critical potential of the individual working subject that Marx had conceptualized with the concrete notion of work in his early writings.

13. The first version of Honneth's essay, "Work and Instrumental Action," was published in *Thesis Eleven*, 1982. A revised and expanded version is published in Honneth, *The Fragmented World of the Social*, 1995.

14. Markus, *Marxism and Anthropology*.

15. I'm referring here to Honneth, "Work and Instrumental Action," *Thesis Eleven*, 1982.

16. Honneth, "Work and Instrumental Action," *Thesis Eleven*, p.175.

17. Honneth, "Work and Instrumental Action," *Thesis Eleven*, p. 175.

18. Honneth, "Work and Instrumental Action," *Thesis Eleven*, p. 176.

19. Honneth, "Work and Instrumental Action," *Thesis Eleven*, p. 177.

20. Honneth, "Work and Instrumental Action," *Thesis Eleven*, p. 178.

21. Habermas, *Theory of Communicative Action*, vol. 2, p. 340; see also Tom Rockmore on this point in *Habermas on Historical Materialism*, Bloomington & Indianapolis, Indiana University Press, 1989.

22. A. Honneth, *Reification: A New Look at an Old Idea*, ed. Martin Jay, with Judith Butler, Raymond Geuss, & Jonathan Lear, Oxford & New York, Oxford University Press, 2008. As Lukács himself later acknowledges, logically there must need to be a non-alienating form of objectification, otherwise, the 'transcendence' or elimination or alienation would mean the 'end of objective reality.' See Georg Lukács, "Preface," *History and Class Consciousness: Studies in Marxist Dialectics*, trans. Rodney Livingstone, London, Merlin Press, 1971, p. xxiv.

23. Honneth, *Reification*, p. 55.

24. Honneth, *Reification*, p. 55.

25. Honneth, *Reification*, pp. 36-7.

26. Roger Foster, "Recognition and Resistance: Axel Honneth's Critical Social Theory," *Radical Philosophy*, vol. 94, March/April, 1999, p. 8.

27. Honneth, "Work and Instrumental Action," *Thesis Eleven,* p. 180.

28. See Habermas' response to similar criticisms made by Agnes Heller, in "Reply to my Critics" in *Habermas: Critical Dates*, eds. John Thompson & David Held (London & Basingstoke, The Macmillan Press, 1982) where he employs Honneth's own arguments in defense of his position, but also dismisses Honneth's attempt to construct a critical concept of work. p. 225; 312 ff. 11.

29. A. Honneth, *The Critique of Power: Reflective Stages in a Critical Social Theory*, trans. K. Baynes, Cambridge MA & London, The MIT Press, 1991, p. 202.

30. See Honneth, *The Critique of Power*, p. 248. This is most evident in Jürgen Habermas, "Technology and Science as 'Ideology'," in *Toward a Rational Society: Student Protest, Science, and Politics,* trans. Jeremy J. Shapiro, London, Heinemann, 1971.

31. Honneth, *The Critique of Power*, p. 269. Although, as Honneth notes, this notion is only consistently articulated in Marx's historical investigations. See Habermas, *Knowledge and Human Interests*, pp. 51-2.

32. Habermas, *Knowledge and Human Interests*, p. 54.

33. Habermas, *Knowledge and Human Interests*, p. 61. In the interpretation of Marx developed in *Knowledge and Human Interests*, Habermas also suggests that Hegel's Jena *Philosophy of Mind* might have been used as the model upon which the movement of history compelled by the conflict between social classes might have been understood as a 'dialectic of moral life.' See *Knowledge and Human Interests*, pp. 58-9.

34. Honneth, *The Critique of Power*, p. 276.

35. Honneth, *The Critique of Power*, p. 274. However, in "Toward a Reconstruction of Historical Materialism," Habermas argues that only an *analytic* answer can explain social development in terms of a directional 'logic,' and he emphatically dismisses class struggle and social conflict as the paradigm of the social change on the grounds that it is only a descriptive interpretation.

36. Honneth, *The Critique of Power*, p. 284.

37. Honneth, *The Critique of Power*, p. 273 (my emphasis).

38. Honneth, *The Critique of Power*, p. 274.

39. Honneth, *The Critique of Power*, pp. 269, 279; Habermas, *Knowledge and Human Interests*, p. 54.

40. Honneth, *The Critique of Power*, p. 270. However, see B. Gregg, "Axel Honneth, *Kritik der Macht*," *New German Critique*, no. 47, Spring/Summer, 1989, pp. 183-188, for a critique of Honneth's insistence of maintaining the model of *class* struggle.

41. See also Axel Honneth, "Domination and Moral Struggle," in *The Fragmented World of the Social*.

42. Honneth, "Domination and Moral Struggle," ff.54.
43. Honneth, *The Critique of Power*, p. 270.
44. Honneth, *The Critique of Power*, p. 270.
45. Honneth, *The Critique of Power*, pp. 270-1 (my emphasis).
46. See Jay M. Bernstein, Jay M., "Suffering Injustice: Misrecognition as Moral Injury in Critical Theory," *International Journal of Philosophical Studies*, vol. 13 (3), 2005, pp. 303-324.
47. Bernstein, "Suffering Injustice," p. 317; see Theodor W. Adorno, "Progress" in *Critical Models: Interventions and Catchwords*, trans. Henry W. Pickford, New York, Columbia University Press, 1998, p. 152.
48. Bernstein, "Suffering Injustice," p. 305.

3. THE SOCIAL AS A FIELD OF STRUGGLE

1. Notably, this is the subtitle of *The Critique of Power*. See A. Honneth, *The Critique of Power: Reflective Stages in a Critical Social Theory*, trans. Kenneth Baynes, The MIT Press, Cambridge, MA, & London, 1991 (1988; 1985).
2. See A. Honneth, "Afterword to the Second German Edition (1988)," in *The Critique of Power*, especially pp. xiii; xv-xvi. For an insightful critical review see Richard J. Bernstein, "*The Critique of Power*, in *Political Theory*, August, 1992, pp. 523-527.
3. Honneth, *The Critique of Power*, p. xiv.
4. Honneth, *The Critique of Power*.
5. In this sense, Honneth offers an especially original reconstruction of Foucault's work that also attempts to construct a productive dialogue between Critical Theory and French post-structuralism that both predates and distinguishes it from Habermas' more dismissive treatment in *The Philosophical Discourse of Modernity*. See Honneth, *The Critique of Power*, p. 101-2. See also Robert Sinnerbrink, "Power, Recognition, and Care: Honneth's Critique of Poststructuralist Social Philosophy," in *Axel Honneth: Critical Essays*, ed. D. Petherbridge, Leiden & Boston, Brill, 2011.
6. See Robert Sinnerbrink, "Power, Recognition, and Care: Honneth's Critique of Post-structuralist Social Philosophy,"; Bert van den Brink, "Recognition, Pluralism, and the Expectation of Harmony: Against the Ideal of an Ethical Life 'Free from Pain'," in *Axel Honneth: Critical Essays*, ed. D. Petherbridge, Leiden & Boston, Brill, 2011.
7. See N. Crossley, *The Politics of Subjectivity: Between Foucault and Merleau-Ponty*, Aldershot, Avebury, 1994, for an alternative attempt to combine Foucault's notion of power into a theory of intersubjectivity as a 'phenomenology of power.'
8. Note, however, that Foucault denied the association with structuralism on many occasions. See, for example, the conclusion to *The Archaeology of Knowledge*, London, Tavistock Publications, 1972, notably pp. 200-201. See also H. Dreyfus and P. Rabinow, *Michel Foucault: Beyond Structuralism and Hermeneutics*, Chicago, Chicago University Press, 1982.
9. Honneth's reconstruction of three phases does not take into account the final two volumes of *The History of Sexuality: The Use of Pleasure: Volume 2* (1985) and *The Care of the Self: Volume 3* (1985), which he would not have had access to at the time of writing *The Critique of Power* as both were published around the same time as Honneth's book was published in German (1985). Thus, the three phases Honneth identifies differ from later interpretations that also reconstruct Foucault's work into three distinct phases according to archaeology, genealogy, and the 'history of subjectivity' or 'care of the self.' For an alternative reading see B. Han, *Foucault's Critical Project: Between the Transcendental and the Historical*, Stanford, Stanford University Press, 2002.
10. See D. Couzens Hoy, *Foucault: A Critical Reader*, p. 130; see Honneth, *The Critique of Power*, p. 154.
11. Honneth, *The Critique of Power*, p. 156.

12. M. Foucault, *Discipline and Punish: The Birth of the Prison*, Middlesex, Penguin Books, 1979 (1975); M. Foucault, *The History of Sexuality: Volume 1* [*La Volonté de savoir*], London, Penguin Books, 1978.

13. B. Hanssen, *The Critique of Violence: Between Poststructuralism and Critical Theory*, London & New York, Routledge 2001, p. 112. See Foucault, "Nietzsche, Genealogy, History," in P. Rabinow, *The Foucault Reader*, London, Penguin Books, 1984.

14. Hanssen, *The Critique of Violence*, p. 112.

15. Hanssen, *The Critique of Violence*, p. 113.

16. See Michel Foucault, *The Archaeology of Knowledge*, London, Tavistock Publications, 1972, p. 150.

17. See also Lois McNay, *Foucault and Feminism: Power, Gender and the Self*, Boston, Northeastern University Press, 1992, p. 27.

18. Michel Foucault, *Discipline and Punish: The Birth of the Prison*, Middlesex, Penguin Books, 1979 (1975), p. 27.

19. The reorientation towards social *relations* of power in Foucault's work is also compelled by the events of May 1968. See, for example, "Truth and Power," in M. Foucault, *Power/Knowledge: Selected Interviews and Other Writings, 1972-1977*, ed. Colin Gordon, New York, Pantheon Books, 1980, p. 111. See Honneth, *The Critique of Power*, p. 152.

20. See also M. Kelly, "Foucault, Habermas, and the Self-Referentiality of Critique" in *Critique and Power: Recasting the Foucault/Habermas Debate*, ed. Michael Kelly, Cambridge, MA & London, The MIT Press, 1994, p. 367; see also M. Foucault, "The Art of Telling the Truth" in *Critique and Power*.

21. M. Foucault, "Truth and Power," in *Power/Knowledge: Selected Interviews and Other Writings, 1972-1977*, ed. Colin Gordon, New York, Pantheon Books, 1980, p. 114. It is also within this context, in a of reversal Clausewitz's assertion, that Foucault argues that politics must be understood as 'war carried on by other means' ("Two Lectures," p. 90). See M. Foucault, *Society Must be Defended*, trans. D. Macey, London, Allen Lane, Penguin Books, 2003.

22. Hanssen, *The Critique of Violence*, p. 108. See Foucault's more explicit discussion of the polymorphous nature of social struggle in *Society Must be Defended*. Also see Benjamin Gregg, "Kritik der Macht," *New German Critique*, no. 47, Spring-Summer, 1989, pp. 183-188); Bernstein, "*The Critique of Power*."

23. Foucault, "Truth and Power," p. 116.

24. Foucault, "Truth and Power," p. 121.

25. M. Foucault, "Two Lectures," in *Power/Knowledge*, p. 88. Also see M. Foucault, *Society Must be Defended*, London, Allen Lane, Penguin Books, 2003.

26. Foucault, *Society Must be Defended*, p. 13. See also M. Foucault, "Two Lectures," in *Power/Knowledge*, p. 88.

27. Foucault, *Society Must be Defended*, p. 13.

28. Foucault, *Society Must be Defended*, p. 35.

29. Foucault, "Truth and Power," p. 122; Honneth, *The Critique of Power*, p. 154.

30. McNay, *Foucault and Feminism*, p. 25.

31. Foucault, *Society Must be Defended*, p. 14.

32. Cited in (eds.) Fontana & Bertani, "Situating the Lectures," in Foucault, *Society Must be Defended*.

33. Foucault, *Society Must be Defended*.

34. Honneth, *The Critique of Power*, p. 154; p. 322, ff. 9.

35. Honneth, *The Critique of Power*, p. 322. ff. 9.

36. Honneth, *The Critique of Power*, p. 155.

37. Foucault, *Society Must be Defended*, p. 168. See also Michel Foucault, *The History of Sexuality: Volume 1* [*La Volonté de savoir*], London, Penguin Books, 1978, p. 95.

38. Foucault, *Society Must be Defended*, p. 168-9.

39. See Foucault, *The History of Sexuality: Volume 1*; Honneth, *The Critique of Power*, p. 155.

40. Honneth, *The Critique of Power*, p. 155.

41. Foucault, *Society Must be Defended*, p. 169.

42. Honneth, *The Critique of Power*, p. 155.

43. See Foucault, *The History of Sexuality: Volume 1*, p. 94-7; Honneth, *The Critique of Power*, p. 160.

44. Foucault, *The History of Sexuality: Volume 1*, p. 92.

45. Honneth, *The Critique of Power*, p. 156.

46. Honneth, *The Critique of Power*, p. 157.

47. See also N. Crossley, *The Politics of Subjectivity*, for an analysis along similar lines, p. 133.

48. Also see M. Foucault "The Ethic of Care of the Self as a Practice of Freedom" in *The Final Foucault*, eds. J. Bernauer and D. Rasmussen, Cambridge MA, The MIT Press, 1988; Kelly, "Foucault, Habermas, and the Self-Referentiality of Critique," p. 391, ff. 2.

49. M. Foucault, "The Subject and Power," in H. L. Dreyfus and P. Rabinow, *Michel Foucault: Beyond Structuralism and Hermeneutics*, Chicago, Chicago University Press, 1982, p. 219.

50. Foucault, "The Subject and Power" (my emphasis). The later essay also makes it clear that Foucault does take into account the role of social groups, something Honneth critiques in regard to Foucault's earlier work.

51. Foucault, "The Subject and Power," p. 217.

52. It is worth noting that Honneth nowhere refers to "The Subject and Power" essay but appears not to have had access to it at the time of writing *The Critique of Power*.

53. Foucault, "The Subject and Power," p. 211.

54. Foucault, *The History of Sexuality, Vol. 1*, p. 95.

55. See Kelly's argument that Foucault's later insistence that freedom is a constitutive feature of modernity therefore offers a means to counter critics who accuse him of lacking a normative basis. Kelly, "Foucault, Habermas, and the Self-Referentiality of Critique," p. 382.

56. Foucault had already outlined the inextricable link between power and resistance in the earlier interviews contained in *Power/Knowledge* and *The History of Sexuality, Volume 1*. See in particular the six hypotheses on power in "Power and Strategies" in *Power/Knowledge*, p. 142, where he clearly states "that there are no relations of power without resistances..."; See *The History of Sexuality, Volume 1*, esp. pp. 94-96. However, as Richard Bernstein also suggests, this is an aspect of Foucault's work that Honneth notably neglects in his interpretation. See Bernstein, "Review of *The Critique of Power*," p. 527.

57. Foucault, "The Subject and Power," pp. 221-2.

58. See also Hanssen, *The Critique of Violence*, p. 154.

59. Foucault, "The Subject and Power," p. 220 (my emphasis).

60. Foucault, "The Subject and Power," p. 220 (my emphasis).

61. Foucault, "The Subject and Power," pp. 210-11.

62. Honneth, *The Critique of Power*, ff. 9, p. 322.

63. Hanssen, *The Critique of Violence*, p. 155.

64. Foucault, "The Subject and Power," pp. 222-3.

65. Foucault, "The Subject and Power," p. 211; pp. 217-8.

66. Hanssen, *The Critique of Violence*, p. 149.

67. M. Foucault, "Politics and Ethics: An Interview," in P. Rabinow, *The Foucault Reader*, pp. 377-9. See also Hannah Arendt, *The Human Condition*, Chicago & London, The University of Chicago Press, 1958; *On Violence*, New York, Harcourt, Brace & World, 1970; *On Revolution*, London, Penguin Books, 1990 (1963). Also see J. Habermas, "Hannah Arendt: On the Concept of Power," in *Philosophical-Political Profiles*, trans. F. Lawerence, Cambridge, MA, The MIT Press, 1983, pp. 171-187. See also David Ingram's discussion of the comparisons between the concept of power in the work of Habermas, following Arendt, and Foucault. D. Ingram, "Foucault and Habermas," in *The Cambridge Companion to Foucault*, Second Edition, ed. Gary Gutting, Cambridge, Cambridge University Press, 2005, esp. pp. 262-266.

68. Hanssen, *The Critique of Violence*, p. 152; Ingram, "Foucault and Habermas," p. 264, 265; Foucault, "The Subject and Power," p. 220.

69. Foucault, "The Subject and Power," pp. 219-20 (my emphasis).

70. Foucault, "The Subject and Power," p. 221.

71. Foucault, "The Subject and Power," p. 212 (my emphasis).

4. REGIMES OF DISCIPLINE

1. Honneth, *The Critique of Power*, p. 160.

2. Michel Foucault, *Discipline and Punish: The Birth of the Prison*, Middlesex, Penguin Books, 1977, p. 27.

3. Honneth, *The Critique of Power*, p. 156-7.

4. Honneth, *The Critique of Power*, p. 159.

5. Honneth, *The Critique of Power*, p. 158; 160.

6. Honneth, *The Critique of Power*, p. 158.

7. Honneth, *The Critique of Power*, p. 161.

8. Honneth, *The Critique of Power*, p. 162.

9. Honneth, *The Critique of Power*, p. 162. See also Nancy Fraser, "Foucault on Modern Power: Empirical Insights and Normative Confusions," in *Unruly Practices: Power, Discourse and Gender in Contemporary Social Theory*, Minneapolis, The University of Minnesota Press, 1989; J. Habermas, "Some Questions Concerning the Theory of Power: Foucault Again," in *The Philosophical Discourse of Modernity*, trans. F. Lawrence, Cambridge, MA, The MIT Press, 1995.

10. Foucault, *The History of Sexuality: Volume 1*, p. 85.

11. Honneth, *The Critique of Power*, p. 165-6.

12. Honneth, *The Critique of Power*.

13. Honneth, *The Critique of Power*, p. 166; 167-8.

14. Honneth, *The Critique of Power*, p. 167.

15. Honneth, *The Critique of Power*, p. 168.

16. Honneth, *The Critique of Power*, p. 168.

17. See Foucault's discussion of 'govermentality' in "Governmentality," eds. G. Burchell, C. Gordon, and P. Miller, *The Foucault Effect: Studies in Governmentality*, London, Harvester Wheatsheaf, 1991.

18. See Foucault, *The History of Sexuality: Volume 1*, pp. 140-1; 143-4.

19. See Foucault, *The History of Sexuality: Volume 1*, final section "Right of Death and Power over Life"; Honneth, *The Critique of Power*, p. 169.

20. See Foucault, *The History of Sexuality: Volume 1*, p. 139, where he brings these two strands together.

21. See Foucault, *The History of Sexuality: Volume 1*, final section "Right of Death and Power over Life"; Honneth, *The Critique of Power*, p. 169.

22. M. Foucault, "The Art of Telling the Truth," in *Critique and Power*, ed. Michael Kelly, p. 148. See Han, *Foucault's Critical Project*, p. 111. Also see Hanssen, "Between Kant and Nietzsche: Foucault's Critique," in *Critique of Violence* and "Critical Theory and Poststructuralism: Habermas and Foucault" in *The Cambridge Companion to Critical Theory*, ed. Fred Rush, Cambridge, Cambridge University Press, 2004. See also "What is Enlightenment?" in Rabinow, *The Foucault Reader*. See Foucault, "Critical Theory/Intellectual History," Kelly, *Critique and Power*, p. 117, where Foucault explicitly self-identifies with the Frankfurt School.

23. See, for example, B. Han, *Foucault's Critical Project*, p. 111. Also see Peter Dews discussion in *The Logics of Disintegration: Post-Structuralist Thought and the Claims of Critical Theory*, London & New York, Verso, 1987, esp. chapters 5 & 6; see also Charles Taylor, "Foucault on Freedom and Truth," in *Foucault: A Critical Reader*, ed. David Couzens Hoy, Oxford, Basil Blackwell.

24. See Colin Hearfield, *Adorno and the Modern Ethos of Freedom*, Aldershot, Ashgate, 2004, p. 99.

25. Honneth, *The Critique of Power*, p. 170.

26. McNay, *Foucault and Feminism*, p. 25; Honneth, *The Critique of Power*.

27. Foucault, "Truth and Power," p. 118.

28. Honneth, *The Critique of Power*, p. 172.

29. Honneth, *The Critique of Power*, p. 173.

30. McNay, *Foucault and Feminism*, p. 38-9.

31. Honneth, *The Critique of Power*, p. 174.

32. Foucault therefore seems to purposely play on the double meaning of the French verb *conduire*, which as the translator of "The Subject and Power" notes, can mean 'to lead or to drive' or 'to behave or conduct oneself.' See Translator's Note, "The Subject and Power," p. 221.
33. Honneth, *The Critique of Power*, p. 175.
34. Honneth, *The Critique of Power*, p. 175.
35. See Ingram, "Foucault and Habermas," in *The Cambridge Companion to Foucault*, p. 247.
36. Foucault, *Discipline and Punish*, p. 222.
37. Foucault, *Discipline and Punish*, p. 222.
38. A. Honneth, "Foucault and Adorno: Two Forms of The Critique of Modernity," in *The Fragmented World of the Social: Essays in Social and Political Philosophy*, ed. C. W. Wright, Albany, SUNY Press, 1995 p. 122-2.
39. Honneth, *The Critique of Power*, p. 192.
40. Honneth, *The Critique of Power*, p. 194.
41. Cf. Michael Kelly, "Foucault, Habermas, and the Self-Referentiality of Critique."
42. Honneth, *The Critique of Power*, p. 195.
43. T. Adorno and M. Horkheimer, *The Dialectic of Enlightenment*, London & New York, Verso, 1992 (1972), p. 231.
44. Honneth, "Foucault and Adorno," p. 122.
45. Honneth, "Foucault and Adorno," p. 126.
46. See Adorno and Horkheimer, *The Dialectic of Enlightenment*.
47. Honneth, *The Critique of Power*, p. 199.
48. Honneth, "Foucault and Adorno," p. 123.
49. A. Honneth, "A Social Pathology of Reason: On the Intellectual Legacy of Critical Theory," in *The Cambridge Companion to Critical Theory*, ed. Fred Rush, Cambridge, Cambridge University Press, 2004. However, as his work on psychiatric and prison experience reveals, it can be argued that Foucault also has a notion of 'suffering' operating as a motivating force for critical questioning, even if it is not one based on psychic tensions in the same manner as Adorno.
50. Honneth, "Foucault and Adorno," p. 130.
51. Adorno and Horkheimer, *The Dialectic of Enlightenment*, p. 232.
52. Honneth is quoting from Theodor W. Adorno, *Negative Dialectics*, trans. E. B. Ashton, London, Routledge, 1973, p. 203.
53. Honneth, "A Social Pathology of Reason: On the Intellectual Legacy of Critical Theory," p. 352. See also Jay Bernstein's excellent discussion of Adorno's view of social suffering as the source for the need for critical reflection in "Suffering Injustice: Misrecognition as Moral Injury in Critical Theory," *International Journal of Philosophical Studies*, vol. 13 (3), 2005 pp. 303-324.
54. Honneth, "Foucault and Adorno," p. 131.
55. To be sure, Honneth would not have access to some of Foucault's later writings such as "What is Critique?" at the time of writing *The Critique of Power*. See D. Nikolinkas, "Foucault's Ethical Quandary" in *Michel Foucault: Critical Assessments: Volume 3*, ed. B. Smart, London & New York, Routledge, 1994, pp. 348-362, for a good discussion of the normative dimension evident in Foucault's later work.
56. See the discussion by R. Coles, *Self/Power/Other: Political Theory and Dialogical Ethics*, Ithaca & London, Cornell University Press, 1992, p. 84.
57. M. Foucault, "What is Enlightenment?", pp. 42, 44.
58. Foucault, "What is Enlightenment?", pp. 45, 39. Michael Kelly suggests that what becomes more evident in the later work is that Foucault shares a common problem with the tradition of Critical Theory, a common concern that is drawn together in their respective attempts to address the problem: "how to practice modern critique in a philosophical manner given its self-referentiality." For Honneth, as for Habermas, this 'critical attitude' is the question of modernity creating normativity out of itself; for Foucault, it is a permanent critique of our present. Kelly, "Foucault, Habermas, and the Self-Referentiality of Critique," p. 382.
59. Foucault, "What is Enlightenment?", pp. 41; 47.

60. Honneth & Joas, *Social Action and Human Nature*, p. 137.

5. INTERSUBJECTIVITY IN THE CONDITION OF POWER

1. See Honneth & Joas, "Preface," *Social Action and Human Nature*, p. x.
2. Honneth & Joas, *Social Action and Human Nature*, p. 11.
3. Honneth & Joas, *Social Action and Human Nature*, p. 7.
4. Honneth & Joas, *Social Action and Human Nature*, p. 7.
5. See Elias, *What is Sociology?*, chapter 4, on this point.
6. Wayne Hudson, "Appendix II: European Philosophical Anthropology," *The Reform of Utopia*, Aldershot, Ashgate, 2003, p. 121.
7. Honneth & Joas, *Social Action and Human Nature*, p. 37.
8. Honneth & Joas, *Social Action and Human Nature*, p. 15.
9. Honneth & Joas, *Social Action and Human Nature*, p. 26 (my emphasis).
10. Honneth & Joas, *Social Action and Human Nature*, p. 118.
11. Honneth & Joas, *Social Action and Human Nature*, p. 118.
12. See also Martin Jay, *Marxism and Totality: The Adventure of a Concept from Lukács to Habermas*, Cambridge, Polity Press, 1984, pp. 46-47.
13. Michel Foucault, "Nietzsche, Genealogy, History," in *The Foucault Reader*, pp. 87-8.
14. Foucault, "Nietzsche, Genealogy, History," p. 83.
15. Foucault, "Nietzsche, Genealogy, History," p. 86.
16. Foucault, "Nietzsche, Genealogy, History," p. 81; Colin Hearfield, *Adorno and the Modern Ethos of Freedom*, Aldershot, Ashgate, p. 104; Barry Smart, *Foucault, Marxism and Critique*, London & New York, 1983, p. 76.
17. Foucault, "Nietzsche, Genealogy, History," pp. 88; 86. Also see Barry Smart, *Foucault, Marxism and Critique*, pp. 75-7; Hearfield, *Adorno and the Modern Ethos of Freedom*, pp. 103-4.
18. Foucault, "Nietzsche, Genealogy, History," p. 81.
19. Foucault, "Nietzsche, Genealogy, History," p. 83.
20. Judith Butler, "Foucault and the Paradox of Bodily Inscriptions," *The Journal of Philosophy*, Eighty-Sixth Annual Meeting of the American Philosophical Association (Eastern Division), vol. 86, no. 11, November, 1989, p. 601; Hearfield, *Adorno and the Modern Ethos of Freedom*, pp. 103-105.
21. Butler, "Foucault and the Paradox of Bodily Inscriptions," p. 602. Butler in fact further suggests that despite Foucault's repeatedly denying the 'materiality' of the body, the ambiguous terms of his analysis suggest not only that there might be 'a body which is external to its construction,' a materiality 'preconditional to history,' but also that "the body … must therefore logically represent a dynamic locus of resistance to culture per se." (p. 602). Also see Butler's discussion of Foucault in *The Psychic Life of Power: Theories in Subjection*, Stanford, Stanford University Press, 1997. In this vein, Hearfield further argues that without the notion of a body external to its construction, a body prior to discursive inscriptions, to speak of the perpetual character of *struggle* would have no significance (Hearfield, *Adorno and the Modern Ethos of Freedom*, p. 104).
22. Foucault, "Nietzsche, Genealogy, History," p. 85.
23. Foucault, "Nietzsche, Genealogy, History," p. 83.
24. Foucault, "Nietzsche, Genealogy, History," pp. 83-4.
25. Hanssen, *The Critique of Violence*.
26. Foucault, "Nietzsche, Genealogy, History," p. 84.
27. Foucault, "Nietzsche, Genealogy, History," p. 76.
28. Foucault, "Nietzsche, Genealogy, History," p. 85.
29. McNay, *Feminism and Foucault*, p. 188.
30. In this respect, Honneth's predominant focus on *Discipline and Punish* in his critique of Foucault's work is akin to Habermas' interpretation in *The Philosophical Discourse of Modernity*.

31. Foucault, "Nietzsche, Genealogy, History," p. 79.

32. Foucault, "Nietzsche, Genealogy, History," p. 89.

33. Foucault, "Nietzsche, Genealogy, History," p. 93.

34. Foucault, "The Ethic of Care for the Self as a Practice of Freedom," in *The Final Foucault*, p. 13.

35. Hanssen, *The Critique of Violence*, p. 154.

36. Foucault engages directly with Kant's essay on at least three occasions in his later work, "What is Enlightenment?" in *The Foucault Reader: An Introduction to Foucault's Thought*, ed. P. Rabinow, London, Penguin Books, 1984; "What is Critique?" trans. Kevin Paul Geiman in *What is Enlightenment? Eighteenth-Century Answers and Twentieth Century Questions*, ed. James Schmidt, Berkeley, Los Angeles & London, University of California Press, 1996; "Kant on Enlightenment and Revolution," *Economy and Society*, 15, no. 1, 1986, pp. 88-96.

37. However, this interest in Kant can be traced back to Foucault's doctoral dissertation on Kant published as Michel Foucault, *Introduction to Kant's Anthropology*, ed. Roberto Nigro, trans. Reoberto Nigro & Kate Briggs, Los Angeles, Semiotext(e), CA, 2008.

38. See M. Foucault, "What is Enlightenment?", in *The Foucault Reader: An Introduction to Foucault's Thought*, ed. P. Rabinow, London, Penguin Books, 1984, p. 35.

39. Foucault, "What is Critique?" in ed. James Schmidt, *What is Enlightenment?* pp. 386-7; See also M. Foucault, "What is Enlightenment?", in *The Foucault Reader: An Introduction to Foucault's Thought*, ed. P. Rabinow, London, Penguin Books, 1984, esp. pp. 32-36, for a similar discussion.

40. Foucault, "What is Critique?", p. 395.

41. Foucault, "What is Critique?", p. 397.

42. Foucault, "What is Critique?", p. 397.

43. Foucault, "What is Critique?", p. 396.

44. Foucault, "What is Critique?", p. 397.

45. M. Foucault, "The Ethic of Care for the Self as a Practice of Freedom," in *The Final Foucault*, p. 19.

46. See, for example, M. Foucault, "What is Enlightenment?", pp. 47-48, where he clearly separates out and describes four elements in his analysis, of which strategic action, or 'a strategic side to these practices', is only one component.

47. Nicholas H. Smith, "Social Power and the Domination of Nature," *History of the Human Sciences*, vol. 6, no. 3, 1993, p. 108-109.

48. On Foucault's notion of the 'strategic intersubjectivity of struggle' in terms of 'social alignments', see Joesph Rouse, "Power/Knowledge" in *The Cambridge Companion to Foucault*, Second Edition, ed. Gary Gutting, Cambridge & New York, Cambridge University Press, 2005; Thomas Wartenberg, *The Forms of Power: From Domination to Transformation*, Philadelphia, Temple University Press, 1990, p. 150, cited in Rouse, "Power/Knowledge." On Elias' notion of 'figuration' see *What is Sociology?*. However, it is also important to note, that Elias' notion of 'figuration' has much more 'functionalist' overtones than Foucault's intersubjective-theoretic notion of power.

49. Foucault, "The Subject and Power," p. 221.

50. Ingram, "Foucault and Habermas" in *The Cambridge Companion to Foucault*, ed. Gary Gutting, p. 265. Ingram further argues that Foucault's notion of strategic action, if it comports with any model of gamesmanship at all, is more akin to "the model of 'play' that Gadamer has argued underlies all forms of consensual understanding" (Ingram, p. 264).

51. Schmidt and Wartenberg in Kelly, *Critique and Power*, p. 290.

52. Schmidt and Wartenberg in Kelly, *Critique and Power*, p. 304.

53. Schmidt and Wartenberg in Kelly, *Critique and Power*, p. 305.

54. M. Foucault, "What is Enlightenment?", in *The Foucault Reader*, ed. P. Rabinow, pp. 47-8.

55. David Ingram, "Foucault and Habermas," p. 267.

56. Michel Foucault, "What is Enlightenment?", p. 42.

57. Ingram, "Foucault and Habermas," p. 267.

58. Schmidt and Wartenberg in *Critique and Power*, ed. M. Kelly, p. 305.

59. Foucault, "What is Critique?", p. 392.

60. Foucault, "The Ethic of Care for the Self as a Practice of Freedom," in *The Final Foucault*, p. 2.

61. See Foucault, "The Ethic of Care for the Self as a Practice of Freedom."

62. Foucault, "The Ethic of Care for the Self as a Practice of Freedom," p. 11

63. Foucault, "The Ethic of Care for the Self as a Practice of Freedom," p. 11.

64. Foucault, "The Ethic of Care for the Self as a Practice of Freedom," pp. 19-20.

65. Foucault, "The Ethic of Care for the Self as a Practice of Freedom," p.20.

66. Cited in K. Racevskis, "Michel Foucault, Rameau's Nephew and the Question of Identity," in *The Final Foucault*, p. 29.

67. Foucault, "The Ethic of Care for the Self as a Practice of Freedom."

68. As the violent actions of the subject of Ralph Ellison's *Invisible Man* remind us. Honneth opens his more recent essay "Invisibility" with a discussion of Ellison's novel, *Invisible Man*, London, Penguin Books, 2001.

69. Foucault, "The Ethic of Care for the Self as a Practice of Freedom," p. 18.

70. Honneth, *The Critique of Power*, p. 303.

6. FROM THE CONTINGENCY OF STRUGGLE TO THE PRIMACY OF RECOGNITION

1. See responses by Butler et al. in Axel Honneth, *Reification: A New Look at an Old Idea*, with J. Butler, R. Geuss & J. Lear, ed. Martin Jay, New York, Oxford University Press, 2008, regarding the critique of Honneth's overly 'positive' anthropology. See also Maeve Cooke, *Representing the Good Society*, Cambridge, MA & London, The MIT Press, 2006, pp. 61-71, particularly pp. 70-71.

2. See also Robert R. Williams, *Recognition: Fichte and Hegel on the Other*, Albany, SUNY Press, 1992; *Hegel's Ethics of Recognition*, Berkeley, Los Angeles, London, 1997.

3. Axel Honneth, *The Struggle for Recognition: The Moral Grammar of Social Conflicts*, Cambridge, Polity Press, 1995, p. 29.

4. Honneth, *The Struggle for Recognition*, p. 5, my emphasis.

5. Honneth: "subjects [must] have already *positively* taken the other into account, before they engaged in hostilities. Both must, in fact, already have accepted the other in advance as a partner to interaction upon whom they are willing to allow their own activity to be dependent." Axel Honneth, *The Struggle for Recognition: The Moral Grammar of Social Conflicts*, Cambridge, Polity Press, 1995, p. 45. As will be discussed below, it seems that in his later work *Reification*, Honneth comes to acknowledge some of the problems ensuing from this original conflation and attempts to separate out original affective recognition from normativity, however, continues to refer to both the ontology of affective relations and normative intersubjectivity in terms of a theory of 'recognition.' See Honneth, *Reification*; also see S. Varga, "Critical Theory and the Two-Level Account of Recognition: Towards a New Foundation?", *Critical Horizons*, vol. 11, no. 1, 2010.

6. G.W.F. Hegel, *System of Ethical Life and First Philosophy of Spirit*, ed. & trans. H.S. Harris & T.M. Knox, Albany, SUNY Press, 1979 (*First Philosophy of Spirit* sometimes referred to as *Realphilosophie* 1); *Realphilosophie* (sometimes referred to as *Realphilosophie II*) translated into English as *Hegel and the Human Spirit: A Translation of the Jena Lectures on the Philosophy of Spirit (1805-6) with Commentary*, trans. & Intro. Leo Rauch, Detroit, Wayne State University Press, 1983. The translation of Honneth's, *The Struggle for Recognition* continues to refer to the latter text as *Realphilosophie* throughout; for consistency, I shall follow this usage in the body of the text; however, all translations refer to the English translation cited here.

7. See Axel Honneth, *Suffering From Indeterminacy: An Attempt at a Reactualisation of Hegel's Philosophy of Right*, Assen, Van Gorcum, 2000; Axel Honneth, *The Pathologies of Individual Freedom: Hegel's Social Theory*, Princeton, Princeton University Press, 2010; Honneth, *Das Recht Der Freiheit: Grundriß einer Demokratischen Sittlichkeit*, Berlin, Suhr-

kamp Verlag, 2011. This shift in Honneth's stance towards the *Philosophy of Right* is also influenced by more recent interpretations such as the work of Robert Williams who traces a theory of intersubjectivity through to the later *Philosophy of Right*; see Robert R. Williams, *Recognition: Fichte and Hegel on the Other*, Albany, SUNY Press, 1992; *Hegel's Ethics of Recognition*, Berkeley, Los Angeles, London, 1997.

8. See J. Habermas, "The Idea of the Theory of Knowledge as Social Theory," in *Knowledge and Human Interests*, 1972 (1968), p. 147. The discussion of Hegel in this essay is also later incorporated into Habermas' discussion of Hegel in "Labour and Interaction: Remarks on Hegel's Jena Philosophy of Mind," in *Theory and Practice*, 1974 (1971). However, despite their similar interpretations in the broader context of Hegel interpretation, Honneth's reading of Hegel can be distinguished from Habermas' quite clearly. Habermas is more insistent that particularly *The First Philosophy of Spirit*, and *Realphilosophie* (1803 and 1805, respectively) provide the more promising and developed theory of recognition as a theory of interaction or intersubjectivity, and a more differentiated and nuanced conceptualization of Spirit as constituted by the three mediums, language, labor and moral relations. For Habermas it is therefore the middle texts of the Jena period that are more constitutive of a theory of 'communicative action.' Honneth, however, clearly preferences the *System of Ethical Life* as the more promising for developing a primary theory of intersubjectivity.

9. Ludwig Siep, "The Struggle for Recognition: Hegel's Dispute with Hobbes in the Jena Writings," trans. C. Dudas, in John O'Neill *Hegel's Dialectic of Desire and Recognition: Text and Commentary*, Albany, SUNY Press, 1996.

10. Honneth, *The Struggle for Recognition*, p. 107 (my emphasis). Cf. Williams, Hegel's *Ethics of Recognition*, pp. 10-12; 19-20; Siep, "The Struggle for Recognition: Hegel's Dispute with Hobbes in the Jena Writings."

11. Honneth, *The Struggle for Recognition*, p. 107.

12. Honneth, *The Struggle for Recognition*, p. 15.

13. Honneth, *The Struggle for Recognition*, p. 13.

14. See, for example, Honneth, *The Struggle for Recognition*, p. 18, where he discusses the "organic relationship of ethical life."

15. Hegel for a brief period came to be heavily influenced by Schelling and the development of Hegel's 'organic worldview' at that time also partially incorporates Schelling's 'philosophy of nature,' which is in turn influenced by Spinoza. See F.W.J. Schelling, *Ideas for a Philosophy of Nature as Introduction to the Study of this Science*, 1797, Second Edition 1803, trans. Errol E. Harris & Peter Heath, Introduction by Robert Stern, Cambridge, Cambridge University Press, 1988; *First Outline of a System of the Philosophy of Nature*, 1799, including "Introduction to the Outline of a System of the Philosophy of Nature, or, On the Concept of Speculative Physics and the Internal Organization of a System of this Science" (1799), trans, & Introduction Keith R. Peterson, New York, SUNY Press, 2004. See also Frederick Beiser, *Hegel*, New York & London, Routledge, 2005, p. 87. In his first years in Jena, Hegel wrote his first direct engagement with Schelling's philosophy in his *The Difference between Fichte's and Schelling's System of Philosophy*, trans. H. S. Harris & W. Cerf, Albany, SUNY Press, 1977.

16. Dieter Henrich, *The Course of Remembrance and Other Essays on Hölderlin*, ed. E. Förster, Stanford, California, Stanford University Press, 1997.

17. See Williams, *Recognition: Fichte and Hegel on the Other*, p. 78; Jean Hypolitte, *Introduction to Hegel's First Philosophy of History*, trans. B. Harris & J.B. Spurlock, Gainesville, University Press of Florida, 1996, p. 39.

18. Dieter Henrich, *The Course of Remembrance and Other Essays on Hölderlin*, ed. E. Förster, Stanford, California, Stanford University Press, 1997, p. 124.

19. G.W.F. Hegel, *The Spirit of Christianity and Its Fate*, trans. T.M. Knox, Intro. R. Kroner, in *Early Theological Writings*, Philadelphia, University of Pennsylvania Press, 1948, p. 213.

20. Hegel, *The Spirit of Christianity and Its Fate*, p. 225.

21. This translation of Henrich quoted Williams, *Recognition: Fichte and Hegel on the Other*, p. 77; official translation Dieter Henrich, *The Course of Remembrance and Other Essays on Hölderlin*, ed. E. Förster, Stanford, California, Stanford University Press, 1997, p. 131.

22. Dieter Henrich, *The Course of Remembrance and Other Essays on Hölderlin*, ed. E. Förster, Stanford, California, Stanford University Press, 1997, p.131; See G.W.F. Hegel, "Preface," *Phenomenology of Spirit*, §17, 18, p. 10, trans. A. V. Miller, Oxford, Oxford University Press, 1977. This shift already occurs in the *Realphilosophie*, as precursor to *The Phenomenology*.

23. Dieter Henrich, *The Course of Remembrance and Other Essays on Hölderlin*, p. 139.

24. This translation of Henrich quoted Williams, *Recognition: Fichte and Hegel on the Other*, p. 77; official translation Dieter Henrich, *The Course of Remembrance and Other Essays on Hölderlin*, p. 137.

25. Henrich, *The Course of Remembrance and Other Essays on Hölderlin*, p. 132.

26. This translation of Henrich quoted Williams, *Recognition: Fichte and Hegel on the Other*, p. 78, my emphasis; official translation Dieter Henrich, *The Course of Remembrance and Other Essays on Hölderlin*.

27. Hegel, *Spirit of Christianity and Its Fate*.

28. See F.W.J. Schelling, *Ideas for a Philosophy of Nature as Introduction to the Study of this Science*, esp. pp. 51; 137-9; also see Robert Stern, "Introduction," pp. xxi-xxii: On Schelling's notion of *Potenzen*, see Schelling, *First Outline of a System of the Philosophy of Nature*, esp. pp. 193-232; and in relation to Hegel, Pinkard, *Hegel: A Biography*, Cambridge, Cambridge University Press, 2000, p. 130.

29. Hegel, *Natural Law: The Scientific Ways of Treating Natural Law, Its Place in Moral Philosophy, and Its Relation to the Positive Sciences of Law*, trans. T. M. Knox, Intro. H. B. Acton, Foreword, J. Silber, Philadelphia, University of Pennsylvania Press, 1975. See Harris, Introduction to *System of Ethical Life*, p. 3; Terry Pinkard, *Hegel: A Biography*.

30. Honneth, *The Struggle for Recognition*, p. 13.

31. Frederick Beiser, *Hegel*, New York & London, Routledge, 2005 p. 37.

32. Hegel, *Natural Law: The Scientific Ways of Treating Natural Law, Its Place in Moral Philosophy, and Its Relation to the Positive Sciences of Law*, pp. 112-113; also see Translator's note, p. 463.

33. Honneth, *The Struggle for Recognition*, p. 14.

34. Honneth, *The Struggle for Recognition*, p. 14; Hegel, *Natural Law*, p. 113.

35. Honneth, *The Struggle for Recognition*, p. 14 (my emphasis).

36. Honneth, *The Struggle for Recognition*, p. 16. See Fichte, *Foundations of Natural Right*, Cambridge, Cambridge University Press, 2000.

37. H.S. Harris, *Hegel's Development: Night Thoughts (Jena 1801-1806)*, Oxford, Clarendon Press, 1983, p. 70. See also H.S. Harris, "Introduction," *System of Ethical Life*, pp. 3-7.

38. Note: the official translation by Harris translates '*Potenzen*' as 'levels' throughout the text, or occasionally this is substituted by 'power.' See also, Pinkard, *Hegel*.

39. Hegel, *System of Ethical Life*, pp. 99-100.

40. Harris, "Introduction," *System of Ethical Life*, p. 101, ff. 2.

41. Hegel, *System of Ethical Life*, p. 102.

42. F.W. J. von Schelling, *First Outline of a System of the Philosophy of Nature*, trans. K. R. Peterson, Albany, SUNY Press, 2004.

43. Hegel, *System of Ethical Life*, pp. 104-5.

44. Hegel, *System of Ethical Life*, p. 107.

45. Hegel, *System of Ethical Life*; Pinkard, *Hegel*, p. 172.

46. Hegel, *System of Ethical Life*, §424-5, pp. 109-110.

47. Whitebook, "First and Second Nature in Hegel and Psychoanalysis," *Constellations*, vol. 15, no. 3, 2008, p. 383. Whitebook's analysis refers only to the *Phenomenology*, which is an oversight in relation to the critique of Honneth's work. However, his analysis can also be applied to the *System of Ethical Life*.

48. Whitebook, "First and Second Nature in Hegel and Psychoanalysis," pp. 384; 383.

49. See Honneth, *The Struggle for Recognition*, p. 185, ff. 24. Also see Gillian Rose, *Hegel Contra Sociology*, London, Athlone; New Jersey, Humanities Press, 1981.

50. Honneth, *The Struggle for Recognition*, p. 18.

51. Hegel, *System of Ethical Life*, p. 110.

52. Hegel, *System of Ethical Life*, p. 110.

53. Hegel, *System of Ethical Life*, p. 112.

54. H.S. Harris, "The Concept of Recognition in Hegel's Jena Manuscripts," in John O'Neill *Hegel's Dialectic of Desire and Recognition: Text and Commentary*, Albany, SUNY Press, 1996, p. 237.

55. Hegel, *System of Ethical Life*, p. 112.

56. See Hegel, "Two Fragments on Love," trans. H.S. Harris, *CLIO*, vol. 8.2, 1979, esp. p. 263; "Love" in *Early Theological Writings*, trans. T. M. Knox, Intro. R. Kroner, Philadelphia, University of Pennsylvania Press, 1948.

57. Honneth, *The Struggle for Recognition*, p. 18.

58. See Hegel, *System of Ethical Life*, pp. 121-122. Hegel recognized early the incompatibility between the 'private' relations of the family and 'property' and economic relations, in other words, relations in what he would later come to call 'civil society.'

59. Honneth, *The Struggle for Recognition*, p. 19.

60. Honneth, *The Struggle for Recognition*, p. 19.

61. Hegel, *System of Ethical Life*, pp. 123-4.

62. Hegel, *System of Ethical Life*, p. 124.

63. Hegel, *System of Ethical Life*, pp. 124-5.

64. Hegel, *System of Ethical Life*, p. 125.

65. Hegel, *System of Ethical Life*, p. 125.

66. Hegel, *System of Ethical Life*, pp. 125-6. See also H.S. Harris, *Hegel's Development: Night Thoughts (Jena 1801-1806)*, Oxford, Clarendon Press, 1983, p. 121.

67. Hegel, *System of Ethical Life*, p. 127.

68. Honneth, *The Struggle for Recognition*, p. 26.

69. Hegel, *System of Ethical Life*, §442, p. 125.

70. Honneth, *The Struggle for Recognition*, p. 20.

71. Honneth, *The Struggle for Recognition*, p. 20.

72. Honneth, *The Struggle for Recognition*, p. 23.

73. Honneth, *The Struggle for Recognition*, p. 21.

74. Honneth, *The Struggle for Recognition*, p. 21.

75. See Hegel, *System of Ethical Life*, §452-454, pp. 134-136.

76. It is not yet 'universal' as it will later become in the third level of Absolute Ethical Life in the State. See Honneth, *The Struggle for Recognition*, p. 21.

77. Honneth, *The Struggle for Recognition*, p. 21.

78. Siep, "The Struggle for Recognition: Hegel's Dispute with Hobbes in the Jena Writings," trans. C. Dudas, in John O'Neill, *Hegel's Dialectic of Desire and Recognition: Text and Commentary*, Albany, SUNY Press, 1996, pp. 275-6; Siep in Williams, *Hegel's Ethics of Recognition*, Berkeley, Los Angeles, London, 1997.

79. See Honneth, *The Struggle for Recognition*, Ch. 2; Hegel, *System of Ethical Life*, in *System of Ethical Life and First Philosophy of Spirit*, ed. & trans. H.S. Harris & T.M. Knox, Albany, SUNY Press, 1979.

80. Hegel, *System of Ethical Life*, §455, pp. 137-138.

81. Honneth, *The Struggle for Recognition*, p. 22.

82. Honneth, *The Struggle for Recognition*, p. 23.

83. Honneth, *The Struggle for Recognition*, p. 23.

84. Honneth, *The Struggle for Recognition*, p. 24; ff. 40, p. 186.

85. See Jean-Philippe Deranty, *Beyond Communication: A Critical Study of Axel Honneth's Social Philosophy*, Leiden & Boston, Brill, 2009.

86. Honneth, *The Struggle for Recognition*, p. 23.

87. Honneth, *The Struggle for Recognition*, p. 23.

88. Honneth, *The Struggle for Recognition*, p. 19.

89. Alexandre Kojève, *Introduction to the Reading of Hegel: Lectures on The Phenomenology of Spirit*, ed. A. Bloom, trans. J. H. Nichols, Ithaca & London, Cornell University Press, 1969, pp. 9; 11; 43; 243-4: "Man was born and History began with the first Fight that ended in the appearance of a Master and a Slave," p. 43.

90. Honneth, *The Struggle for Recognition*, p. 25.

91. See Honneth, *The Struggle for Recognition*, p. 25.

92. Honneth, *The Struggle for Recognition*, p. 26: "...the moment of struggle within the movement of recognition [is] granted only a negative, transitional function" but not yet a "positive (that is, consciousness-forming function)."

7. THE NORMATIVE GROUND OF CONFLICT AND SOCIALITY

1. G.W.F. Hegel, *System of Ethical Life and First Philosophy of Spirit*, ed. & trans. H.S. Harris & T.M. Knox, Albany, SUNY Press, 1979; see Honneth, *The Struggle for Recognition*, pp. 27-30.

2. Pinkard, *Hegel*, p. 173.

3. Honneth, *The Struggle for Recognition*, p. 28 (my emphasis).

4. Siep, "The Struggle for Recognition: Hegel's Dispute with Hobbes in the Jena Writings," in John O'Neill, *Hegel's Dialectic of Desire and Recognition*, Albany, SUNY Press, 1996 p. 278.

5. G.W.F. Hegel, *Realphilosophie*, translated into English as *Hegel and the Human Spirit: A Translation of the Jena Lectures on the Philosophy of Spirit (1805-6) with Commentary*, trans. & Intro. Leo Rauch, Detroit, Wayne State University Press, 1983. I will continue to refer to this text as *Realphilosophie* to remain consistent with Honneth's usage in *The Struggle for Recognition*.

6. See Honneth, *The Struggle for Recognition*, p. 29.

7. Honneth, *The Struggle for Recognition*, p. 33.

8. Honneth, *The Struggle for Recognition*, p. 33.

9. Honneth, *The Struggle for Recognition*, p. 34.

10. Hegel, *Realphilosophie*, p. 85-90; *Hegel's Development: Night Thoughts (Jena 1801-1806)*, p. 478.

11. Hegel, *Realphilosophie*, p. 97.

12. See Leo Rauch, "Introduction," in Hegel, *Realphilosophie*, p. 19.

13. With remarkable insight, in this reconstruction, Hegel also alludes to the 'othersided-ness' of language, represented by the faculty of the imagination that is both creative and unpredictable, drawing on unconscious imagery that is not immediately present to consciousness. In describing the faculty of the imagination, Hegel conceptualizes the human being as the 'Night': "...the interior of [human] nature, existing here—pure Self—[and] in phantasmagoric representations it is night everywhere....We see this Night when we look a human being in the eye, looking into a Night which turns terrifying." The self then, is "a frightening vacuity" that is not fully accessible to intersubjective understanding and reason; it is "free arbitrariness—[able] to dismember images and to reconnect them in the most dissociated manner." This is one of Hegel's admissions of the *un*taken-for-granted 'nature' of the human being. Instead of beginning with the ethical certainty and primacy of intersubjectivity as in the *System of Ethical Life*, in the later text, Hegel begins with the 'pure Self' and the interiority of the human being. This is in stark contrast to the more relationally oriented philosophical analysis in the *System of Ethical Life*, and indicates a move away from the earlier suggestion of intersubjective primacy. See Hegel, *Realphilosophie*, p. 87; Rauch, "Introduction," in Hegel, *Realphilosophie*, p. 19.

14. Hegel, *Realphilosophie*, p. 99.

15. Hegel, *Realphilosophie*, p. 99.

16. Hegel, *Realphilosophie*, p. 102.

17. Hegel, *Realphilosophie*, p. 103.

18. Honneth, *The Struggle for Recognition*, p. 35.

19. Hegel, *Realphilosophie*, p. 104.

20. Hegel, *Realphilosophie*, p. 103.

21. Hegel, *Realphilosophie*, p. 106.

22. Honneth argues that this conceptualization is the result of the problems that Hegel encounters in trying to reconcile and introduce an intersubjective dimension of the will within the monological framework of the philosophy of consciousness. See Honneth, *The Struggle for Recognition*, p. 36.

23. Hegel, *Realphilosophie*, p. 106.

24. Honneth, *The Struggle for Recognition*, p. 36.

25. Honneth, *The Struggle for Recognition*, pp. 36-7.

26. Hegel, *Realphilosophie*, p. 107.

27. Honneth, *The Struggle for Recognition*, p. 37.

28. Honneth, *The Struggle for Recognition*, p. 39.

29. Honneth surmises that Hegel's intention here is to indicate a shift away from his earlier position in the *Theological Writings* where 'love' is conceptualized as the form of relationality that is generalized to theorize social bonds in the community more generally.

30. Honneth, *The Struggle for Recognition*, pp. 37-8.

31. Honneth, *The Struggle for Recognition*, pp. 38-9.

32. Hegel, *Realphilosophie*, p. 110. Honneth remarks that in this sense, 'Hegel is entirely a classical theoretician of the bourgeois family' (Honneth, *The Struggle for Recognition*, p. 39). Iris Marion Young has criticized Honneth for uncritically adopting Hegel's overly idealized notion of love in *The Struggle for Recognition*, thereby assuming both its inherent normativity and unchanging nature. Honneth more explicitly attempts to historicize love in later work and acknowledges that the sphere of love requires some intervention from the sphere of law to protect against pathological forms of love relations. See Iris Marion Young, "Recognition of Love's Labor: Considering Axel Honneth's Feminism," in eds. Bert van den Brink and David Owen, *Recognition and Power: Axel Honneth and the Tradition of Critical Social Theory*, Cambridge, Cambridge University Press, 2007, pp. 189-212; Axel Honneth, "Between Justice and Affection: The Family as a Field of Moral Disputes," in *Privacies: Philosophical Evaluations*, ed. Beate Rössler, Stanford, CA, Stanford University Press, 2004, pp. 142-162.

33. See Hegel, *First Philosophy of Spirit*, §303, p. 233; Hegel, *Realphilosophie*, p. 110.

34. Hegel, *First Philosophy of Spirit*, §303-304, p. 233.

35. See Hegel, *First Philosophy of Spirit*, §325, p. 249.

36. Hegel: "...for in possession there lies the contradiction that something external, a thing, a universal [moment] of the earth, should be under the control of a single [man], which is contrary to the nature of the thing as an outward universal." Hegel, *First Philosophy of Spirit*, §309, p. 238.

37. Hegel, *First Philosophy of Spirit*, §308, p. 237.

38. Siep, "The Struggle for Recognition: Hegel's Dispute with Hobbes in the Jena Writings," p. 281.

39. Hegel, *First Philosophy of Spirit*, §310, p. 239.

40. Hegel, *First Philosophy of Spirit*, §313, p. 241; Hegel further states that 'singularity must be superseded' because ultimately "...consciousness only is the gaining of recognition from another." Hegel, *First Philosophy of Spirit*, §311, p. 240.

41. Honneth, *The Struggle for Recognition*, p. 40.

42. Paul Ricoeur, *The Course of Recognition*, trans. D. Pellauer, Cambridge, MA & London, Harvard University Press, 2005 p. 162

43. Ricoeur, *The Course of Recognition*, p. 163-7; Hobbes, *Leviathan*.

44. Hegel, *Realphilosophie*, p. 110-111.

45. Ricoeur, *The Course of Recognition*, p. 163; Honneth, *The Struggle for Recognition*, p. 41-2.

46. Hegel, *Realphilosophie*, p. 111 (emphasis partly mine).

47. Honneth, *The Struggle for Recognition*, pp. 41-2.

48. Hegel, *Realphilosophie*, p. 111.

49. Honneth, *The Struggle for Recognition*, p. 43 (my emphasis).

50. Honneth, *The Struggle for Recognition*, p. 42 (my emphasis).

51. Honneth, *The Struggle for Recognition*, p. 42 (my emphasis).

52. Honneth, *The Struggle for Recognition*, p. 43.

53. Honneth, *The Struggle for Recognition*, p. 43.

54. Honneth, *The Struggle for Recognition*, p. 44 (my emphasis).

55. Honneth, *The Struggle for Recognition*, p. 45 (my emphasis).

56. These are precisely the kind of separation of action types that Honneth originally sought to avoid as indicated by his critique of Habermas' separation of action spheres.

57. Honneth, *The Struggle for Recognition*, pp. 45-46.
58. Honneth, *The Struggle for Recognition*, p. 47; 48.
59. Honneth, *The Struggle for Recognition*, p. 47.
60. See one of Honneth's few engagements with the concept of recognition as it is presented in the *Phenomenology* in Axel Honneth, "From Desire to Recognition: Hegel's Account of Human Sociality," in *Hegel's Phenomenology of Spirit: A Critical Guide*, Cambridge, Cambridge University Press, 2008, pp. 76-90. See also Joel Whitebook's critique of Honneth in this regard. Whitebook argues that Honneth's preference for the early Hegel as opposed to the Hegel of the *Phenomenology*, and his subsequent use of Mead instead of Freud in an attempt at a re-actualization of Hegel's idea, results in a denial of the radically conflictual nature of both the individual's psychic and social life (Joel Whitebook, "Mutual Recognition and the Work of the Negative," in *Pluralism and the Pragmatic Turn: The Transformation of Critical Theory*, Cambridge, MA & London, The MIT Press, 2001, pp. 257-291).
61. However, in comparison Levinas establishes an intersubjectivist interpretation that shifts the focus away from the monological fear and preoccupation of the subject with her own death to a concern with the death of the other, and this in turn reveals not only mutual vulnerability but also the possibility of a shared co-existence. In this sense, Honneth and Levinas share the idea that intersubjective relations possess a normative content and primary ethicality. However, where Honneth emphasizes the symmetricality and reciprocity of intersubjectivity as mutual recognition, Levinas emphasizes the asymmetricality and inequality of ethical intersubjectivity, or what he terms the '*curvature of intersubjective space.*' In contrast, Honneth only applies the notion of asymmetrical ethical intersubjectivity to the first sphere of recognition, in relations of love and care between caregivers and children. The differences between Levinas' non-dialectical approach and Honneth's Hegelian-inspired dialectical theory of recognitive intersubjectivity are illuminating, and point to further work that cannot be explored here. See Levinas, *Totality and Infinity: An Essay on Exteriority*, trans. Alphonso Lingis, Dordrecht, Boston, London, Kluwer Academic Publishers, 1991, p. 215-6; 291. Also see Eva Erman, "Reconciling Communicative Action with Recognition: Thickening the 'Inter' of Intersubjectivity," *Philosophy and Social Criticism*, vol. 32, no. 3, 2006, pp. 377-400. See Honneth's sympathetic discussion of both Derrida and Levinas in Axel Honneth, "The Other of Justice: Habermas and the Ethical Challenge of Postmodernism," in *The Cambridge Companion to Habermas*, ed. Stephen K. White, Cambridge, Cambridge University Press, 1995, pp. 289-323.
62. Honneth, *The Struggle for Recognition*, p. 52.
63. Honneth, *The Struggle for Recognition*, p. 53.
64. Honneth, *The Struggle for Recognition*, pp. 53-4.
65. Honneth, *The Struggle for Recognition*, pp. 56-7.
66. Honneth, *The Struggle for Recognition*, p. 24.
67. Honneth, *The Struggle for Recognition*, p. 57.
68. Honneth, *The Struggle for Recognition*, pp. 57-8.
69. Honneth, *The Struggle for Recognition*, p. 59.
70. See also Williams' discussion of Theuinissen's work in *Hegel's Ethics of Recognition*, p. 17.
71. Theunissen, "The Repressed Intersubjectivity in Hegel's Philosophy of Right," in *Hegel and Legal Theory*, eds. Drucilla Cornell, Michel Rosenfeld & David Gray Carlson, New York & London, Routledge, 1991, pp. 10-13; Williams, *Hegel's Ethics of Recognition*, pp. 16-19.
72. Michael Theunissen, "The Repressed Intersubjectivity in Hegel's Philosophy of Right," pp. 10-12.
73. Axel Honneth, *Suffering from Indeterminacy: An Attempt at a Reactualization of Hegel's Philosophy of Right*, Assen, Van Gorcum, 2000; Honneth, *The Pathologies of Individual Freedom: Hegel's Social Theory*, Princeton, Princeton University Press, 2010; Honneth, *Das Recht Der Freiheit: Grundriß einer Demokratischen Sittlichkeit*, Berlin, Suhrkamp Verlag, 2011; English translation: Axel Honneth, *Freedom's Right: The Social Foundations of Democratic Life*, New York, Columbia University Press, 2014 (forthcoming). It is beyond the scope of this current study to discuss *Das Recht Der Freiheit* in any detail, which was published after this project was completed. The focus of this project is specifically on Honneth's early attempt to develop an anthropological ground to the theory of recognition and the reconstruction of the

intersubjective paradigm as the basis of a critical theory and framework for analysing power and domination. Although the later work develops a more explicitly historical approach and substantially extends Honneth's reconsideration of the role of institutions as it pertains to the theory of recognition, it does not alter the main argument developed here in regard to the original reorientation of the intersubjective paradigm and loss of insights in regard to a philosophical anthropology and theory of power. My contention is that the arguments developed here also pertain to the later work, which is underpinned by the same intersubjective stance developed in the early work.

74. See in particular Robert Williams, *Hegel's Ethics of Recognition.*

75. See Honneth, *Suffering from Indeterminacy*, p. 21.

76. Theunissen, "The Repressed Intersubjectivity in Hegel's Philosophy of Right," p. 8; p. 3.

77. Honneth, *The Pathologies of Individual Freedom: Hegel's Social Theory*, Princeton, Princeton University Press, 2010.

78. Honneth, *The Pathologies of Individual Freedom,* 2010; Honneth, *Das Recht Der Freiheit,* 2011; Frederick Neuhouser, *Foundations of Hegel's Social Theory: Actualizing Freedom*, Cambridge, MA, & London, Harvard University Press, 2000.

79. Cf. G.W.F. Hegel, *Philosophy of Right*, trans. T.M. Knox, London, Oxford, New York, Oxford University Press, 1979 (1952). Honneth also ignores the categories of the Logic in his reconstruction of the *Philosophy of Right*. See G.W.F. Hegel, *Science of Logic*, trans. A.V. Miller, Foreword J. N. Findlay, New York, Humanity Books, 1999.

80. Honneth, *Suffering from Indeterminacy*, p. 56.

81. Emmanuel Renault, "The Theory of Recognition and Critique of Institutions," in *Axel Honneth: Critical Essays*, ed. Danielle Petherbridge, Leiden & Boston, Brill, 2011. Also see Jean-Philippe Deranty, *Beyond Communication: A Critical Study of Axel Honneth's Social Philosophy*, Leiden & Boston, Brill, 2009, p. 231.

82. Deranty, *Beyond Communication*, p. 231; Renault, "The Theory of Recognition and Critique of Institutions."

83. This is more akin to the concept that Honneth later goes on to attempt to develop in *Reification*; however, as shall be discussed further below, he does so in a manner that continues to constitute primary relations in terms of the concept of recognition.

8. PRACTICAL INTERSUBJECTIVITY AND SOCIALITY IN MEAD

1. Axel Honneth & Hans Joas, *Social Action and Human Nature*, trans. Raymond Meyer, Cambridge, Cambridge University Press, 1988 (1980), p. 26; see also Carl-Göran Heidegren, "Anthropology, Social Theory, Politics: Axel Honneth's Theory of Recognition," in *Inquiry*, 45, 2002, pp. 433-46, here p. 434.

2. See J. Habermas, "Individuation through Socialization: On George Herbert Mead's Theory of Subjectivity," in *Postmetaphysical Thinking*, trans. W.H. Hohengarten, Cambridge, Polity Press, 1992; see on Habermas Peter Dews, *The Limits of Disenchantment: Essays on Contemporary European Philosophy*, London & New York, Verso, 1995, p. 174.

3. See J-P Deranty's study, *Beyond Communication*, which draws out these aspects of Honneth's work.

4. See Hans Joas, *G. H. Mead: A Contemporary Re-examination of his Thought*, Cambridge, Polity Press, 1985 (1980).

5. Honneth & Joas, *Social Action and Human Nature*, p. 10.

6. Honneth & Joas, *Social Action and Human Nature*, p. 10.

7. Honneth & Joas, *Social Action and Human Nature*, p. 61.

8. Honneth & Joas, *Social Action and Human Nature*, pp. 61-62.

9. Honneth & Joas, *Social Action and Human Nature*, p. 62. See for example, Mead's essays on Fichte and Hegel in G. H. Mead, *Movements of Thought in the Nineteenth Century*, ed. Merritt H. Moore, Chicago, University of Chicago Press, 1936. Also see Joas, *G. H. Mead*, chapter 3.

10. Honneth & Joas, *Social Action and Human Nature*, p. 60-62; also see John Dewey's prefatory remarks to 1932 publication of Mead's *The Philosophy of the Present*, Chicago & London, Open Court Publishing House, 1932; also see Gary A. Cook, "The Development of G. H. Mead's Social Psychology," in *Philosophy, Social Theory, and the Thought of George Herbert Mead*, ed. Mitchell Aboulafia, Albany, SUNY, 1991, pp. 89-107, here p. 89.

11. G. H. Mead, *The Individual and the Social Self*, ed. David Miller, Chicago & London, The University of Chicago Press, 1982 p. 49.

12. Cook, "The Development of G. H. Mead's Social Psychology," p. 90.

13. Mead, *The Individual and the Social Self*, p. 46.

14. G. H. Mead, "Social Psychology as Counterpart to Physiological Psychology," in *Selected Writings*, ed. Andrew J. Reck, Chicago & London, The University of Chicago Press, 1964, p. 103.

15. Habermas, "Individuation through Socialization."

16. Joas, *G. H. Mead*, p. 152.

17. Honneth & Joas, *Social Action and Human Nature*, p. 60.

18. Honneth & Joas, *Social Action and Human Nature*, p. 60.

19. G. H. Mead, *Mind, Self, and Society from the Standpoint of a Social Behaviorist*, ed. Charles W. Morris, Chicago & London, The University of Chicago Press, 1934, pp. 7-8.

20. Mead, *Selected Writings*. Mead's early essays are important for understanding the genesis of his basic anthropology and the way in which these three strands of his thought are finally brought together. The essays from 1900 onwards, which were published in Mead's lifetime, outline the pragmatist and action-theoretic approach he applied to basic psychological and philosophical problems. In particular, Mead's early essay "The Definition of the Psychical" (1903) is important for outlining the beginnings of his intersubjectivistic approach to the subject matter of psychology and the functionalist foundations of both his theory of action and self-consciousness, a functionalism that Honneth later unwittingly incorporates into his own recognition theory. See Joas, *G. H. Mead*; Cook, "The Development of G. H. Mead's Social Psychology."

21. Mead, in Joas, *G. H. Mead*, pp. 6-8; Cook, "The Development of G. H. Mead's Social Psychology," p. 90.

22. Cook, "The Development of G. H. Mead's Social Psychology" pp. 90-1. John Dewey, "The Reflex Arc Concept in Psychology," (1896) reprinted in John Dewey, *Philosophy, Psychology, and Social Practice*, ed. Joseph Ratner, New York, Capricorn Books, 1965, quoted in Cook, "The Development of G. H. Mead's Social Psychology," p. 90.

23. Cook, "The Development of G. H. Mead's Social Psychology," pp. 90-91.

24. In essays such as "Suggestions Toward a Theory of the Philosophical Disciplines" and "The Definition of the Psychical," Mead begins outlining a theory of 'subjectivity,' or what Mead terms the 'psychical' or 'consciousness.'

25. Mead, "Suggestions Toward a Theory of the Philosophical Disciplines" in *Selected Writings*, p. 12.

26. See Cook, "The Development of G. H. Mead's Social Psychology," p. 93.

27. Mead, "The Definition of the Psychical" in *Selected Writings*, p. 46.

28. Cook, "The Development of G. H. Mead's Social Psychology," p. 93.

29. Mead, "The Definition of the Psychical" in *Selected Writings*, p. 52.

30. Mead states: "if the psychical is functional and the consciousness of the individual at the same time, it is hard to avoid the conclusion that this phase of our consciousness—or in other words, the individual qua individual—is functional in the same sense." (Mead, "The Definition of the Psychical" in *Selected Writings*, p. 46.)

31. Habermas, "Individuation through Socialization," p. 158.

32. Habermas, "Individuation through Socialization," p. 158; Cook, "The Development of G. H. Mead's Social Psychology," p. 95.

33. Mead, "The Definition of the Psychical" in *Selected Writings*, p. 46 & 55.

34. Cook, "The Development of G. H. Mead's Social Psychology," p. 95; Mead, "The Definition of the Psychical" in *Selected Writings*, p. 47.

35. Joas, *G. H. Mead*, p. 83; see Mead, "The Definition of the Psychical" in *Selected Writings*, p. 55.

36. See Mead, "The Definition of the Psychical" in *Selected Writings*, p. 53.

37. Mead, "The Definition of the Psychical" in *Selected Writings*, pp. 52-54; also see Cook, "The Development of G. H. Mead's Social Psychology," p. 95.

38. Cook, "The Development of G. H. Mead's Social Psychology," pp. 93-95.

39. Joas, *G. H. Mead*, pp. 79 & 81.

40. Mead, *The Individual and the Social Self*, p. 156. See also G. H. Mead, *Mind, Self, and Society from the Standpoint of a Social Behaviorist*, ed. Charles W. Morris, Chicago & London, The University of Chicago Press, 1934; Honneth & Joas, *Social Action and Human Nature*, pp. 62-3.

41. See Charles Morris, "Introduction," G. H. Mead, *The Philosophy of the Act*, ed. Charles Morris, Chicago & London, The University of Chicago Press, 1938, pp. xli-xlii. G. H. Mead; also important is *The Philosophy of the Present*, Chicago & London, Open Court Publishing House, 1932.

42. Honneth & Joas, *Social Action and Human Nature*, p. 67.

43. Honneth & Joas, *Social Action and Human Nature*, p. 68.

44. Honneth & Joas, *Social Action and Human Nature*, pp. 68-9.

45. For Mead the fundamental difference between human and non-human perception, which is facilitated by the evolution of the human hand, is the capacity for the manipulation of objects in instrumental action. See Mead, *The Philosophy of the Act*, p. 141. See Joas, *G. H. Mead*, p. 148.

46. Honneth & Joas, *Social Action and Human Nature*, pp. 68-9.

47. Mead, *The Philosophy of the Act*, pp. 143-144.

48. Mead, "Miscellaneous Fragments," *The Philosophy of the Act*, p. 654.

49. Honneth & Joas, *Social Action and Human Nature*, p. 70.

50. Honneth & Joas, *Social Action and Human Nature*, p. 70.

51. Joas, *G. H. Mead*, p. 14.

52. Joas, *G. H. Mead*, p. 14.

53. Honneth & Joas, *Social Action and Human Nature*, p. 69.

54. Prominent in this regard is the work by Jean-Philippe Deranty, *Beyond Communication*.

55. Honneth, *The Struggle for Recognition*, p. 71.

56. Honneth, *The Struggle for Recognition*, pp. 71-72.

57. Honneth, *The Struggle for Recognition*, p. 72.

58. In contrast to the study in *Social Action and Human Nature*, however, here Honneth does not dwell on the significance of gestural communication nor emphasize its significance for embodied forms of intersubjectivity. Rather, more in line with Habermas' interpretation of Mead, Honneth focuses primarily on the significance of the 'vocal gesture' and linguistic interaction as the fundamentally significant human form of communication.

59. Honneth, *The Struggle for Recognition*, p. 73.

60. Mead, "The Social Self," p. 145. See also Karen Hanson, *The Self Imagined: Philosophical Reflections on the Social Character of Psyche*, New York, Routledge & Kegan Paul, 1986.

61. Mead, "The Social Self," p. 143.

62. Jürgen Habermas, *The Theory of Communicative Action: Lifeworld and System: A Critique of Functionalist Reason*, Volume 2, trans. Thomas McCarthy, Boston, Beacon Press, 1987 (1981), p. 41.

63. Mead, *Mind, Self, and Society*, p. 196.

64. Mead, *Mind, Self, and Society*, p. 196.

65. Mitchell Aboulafia, *The Mediating Self: Mead, Sartre, and Self-Determination*, New Haven & London, Yale University Press, 1986, p. 13.

66. Honneth, *The Struggle for Recognition*, p. 75.

67. Honneth, *The Struggle for Recognition*, p. 76.

68. Habermas, "Individuation through Socialization," p. 178; ff. 49, p. 202.

69. Habermas, "Individuation through Socialization," p. 178.

70. Honneth, *The Struggle for Recognition*, p. 76.

71. Honneth, *The Struggle for Recognition*, p. 76.

72. Habermas, "Individuation through Socialization," p. 179.

73. Habermas, "Individuation through Socialization," p. 180.

74. This refers to the series of articles published in Mead's lifetime republished in Mead, *Selected Writings*, 1964.
75. Mead, "The Social Self," p. 146; quoted in Honneth, *The Struggle for Recognition*, p. 76.
76. Honneth, *The Struggle for Recognition*, p. 77.
77. Honneth, *The Struggle for Recognition*, p. 77.
78. Honneth, *The Struggle for Recognition*, p. 78.
79. Honneth, *The Struggle for Recognition*, p. 78.
80. Mead, *Mind, Self, and Society*, p. 196.
81. See, for example, Mead's published essay "The Genesis of the Self and Social Control" in *Selected Writings*, where Mead states: "Social control depends, then, upon the degree to which the individuals in society are able to assume the attitudes of the others [in the social group] ...all of the institutions...serve to control individuals who find in them the organization of their own social responses" (p. 291). Here Mead is clearly not talking about norms of mutual recognition but functional cooperation of members of a given society. In particular, he is also pointing to the institutionalized dimension of internalized perspectives, which Honneth does not take into full consideration. By 'norms' Mead mostly refers to 'norms of conduct' as a form of 'social control'—meaning 'control of conduct' by which individuals conform to the rules and conventions of behavior in a given society. However, Honneth's definition of 'normativity' is much thicker. He understands normative interaction as a form of mutual recognition by which one can make objective judgements about forms of interaction; that is, whether they are autonomous and mutually enhance individual flourishing or reinforce inequalities and forms of suffering.
82. Honneth, *The Struggle for Recognition*, p. 80.
83. Honneth, *The Struggle for Recognition*, p. 79.
84. Honneth, *The Struggle for Recognition*, p. 79; 80.
85. Mead, *Mind, Self, and Society*, p. 199.
86. Honneth, *The Struggle for Recognition*, p. 79.
87. Habermas, "Individuation through Socialization," p. 180.
88. Honneth, *The Struggle for Recognition*, p. 81.
89. Mead, *Mind, Self, and Society*, p. 174.
90. Honneth, *The Struggle for Recognition*, p. 81.
91. Joel Whitebook, "First Nature and Second Nature in Hegel and Psychoanalysis," *Constellations*, Volume 15, No. 3, 2008, pp. 382-389, here p. 386.
92. Mitchell Aboulafia, "Self-Consciousness and the Quasi-Epic of the Master," in (ed.) Mitchell Aboulafia, *Philosophy, Social Theory, and the Thought of George Herbert Mead*, Albany, SUNY Press, 1991, pp. 223- 24, here p. 233.
93. Amy Allen, "Recognizing Domination: Recognition and Power in Honneth's Critical Theory," *Journal of Power*, Vol. 3, No. 1, April 2010, pp. 27-8.
94. Amy Allen, "Recognizing Domination," pp. 27-8. Allen's case of Elizabeth demonstrates how even in recognitive relations of love, authority figures, especially parents, may unwittingly transmit norms to children that are power-saturated and reproduce subordinating ideologies, in this case regarding gender. As children have not yet developed critical-reflexive capacities or resistance mechanisms they tend to be unable to critically respond and may in fact become attached to the very forms of 'recognition' that reinforce social inequalities. Also see "A Conversation between Axel Honneth, Amy Allen, and Maeve Cooke, Frankfurt am Main, 12 April 2010," *Journal of Power*, Vol. 3, No. 2. August, 2010, pp. 153-170; Lois McNay, *Against Recognition*, Cambridge, Polity Press, 2008, pp. 8-9.
95. Aboulafia, *The Mediating Self*, p. 61.
96. Aboulafia, *The Mediating Self*, p. 58.
97. Aboulafia, *The Mediating Self*, p. 65.
98. Whitebook "First Nature and Second Nature in Hegel and Psychoanalysis"; also see Aboulafia, *The Mediating Self*; also see Peter Dews, *The Limits of Disenchantment*, pp. 178-9, who makes a similar critique of Habermas' reading of Mead in relation to the necessary presupposition of a 'rudimentary self-awareness.'

99. Whitebook, "First Nature and Second Nature in Hegel and Psychoanalysis," pp. 385-6. See also Joel Whitebook, "Mutual Recognition and the Work of the Negative," in *Pluralism and the Pragmatic Turn: The Transformation of Critical Theory*, *Essays in Honor of Thomas McCarthy*, ed. William Rehg & James Bohman, Cambridge, MA. & London, The MIT Press, 2001.

100. Aboulafia, *The Mediating Self*, p. 57.

101. Also see Deranty, *Beyond Communication*, on this point, although for an argument that draws very different conclusions from the ones articulated here.

102. Honneth, *The Struggle for Recognition*, p. 82.

103. Honneth, *The Struggle for Recognition*, p. 81.

104. Honneth, *The Struggle for Recognition*, pp. 82-3.

105. Honneth, *The Struggle for Recognition*, p. 83.

106. Honneth, *The Struggle for Recognition*, pp. 83-4.

107. Honneth draws a direct comparison between Hegel and Mead on this count: "Like Hegel, Mead considers the motor of those directed changes to be a struggle in which subjects continually strive to expand the range of their intersubjectively guaranteed rights and, in so doing, to raise the level of their personal autonomy. For both thinkers, then, the historical liberation of individuality occurs in the form of a long-term struggle for recognition." Honneth, *The Struggle for Recognition* , p. 84.

108. Honneth, *The Struggle for Recognition*, p. 83.

109. Axel Honneth, "Grounding Recognition: A Rejoinder to Critical Questions," trans. Joel Anderson, *Inquiry*, 45, 2002, pp. 499-520; here p. 502.

110. See Honneth, "Grounding Recognition"; Heidegren, "Anthropology, Social Theory, and Politics," p. 438.

9. INTERSUBJECTIVITY OR PRIMARY AFFECTIVITY?

1. Honneth, *The Struggle for Recognition*, p. 107.

2. Honneth, *The Struggle for Recognition*, p. 95.

3. Johanna Meehan, "Autonomy, Recognition, and Respect: Habermas, Benjamin, and Honneth" in ed. Johanna Meehan, *Feminists Read Habermas: Gendering the Subject of Discourse*, New York & London, Routledge, 1995, p. 243.

4. Axel Honneth, "Postmodern Identity and Object-Relations Theory: On the Seeming Obsolescence of Psychoanalysis," *Philosophical Explorations*, no. 3, September, 1999, pp. 225-242, here p. 231.

5. Honneth, *The Struggle for Recognition*, p. 96.

6. Whitebook, "First Nature and Second Nature in Hegel and Psychoanalysis," p. 382.

7. Honneth, *The Struggle for Recognition*, p. 98.

8. Honneth, *The Struggle for Recognition*, p. 98.

9. The increasing importance of object-relations theory for Honneth's project, and the replacement of Mead with Winnicott's interactionist psychoanalytic perspective is evident in the following works: Honneth, "Grounding Recognition"; Axel Honneth, "Facets of the Presocial Self: Rejoinder to Joel Whitebook," in *The I in We: Studies in the Theory of Recognition*, Cambridge, Polity Press, 2012, pp. 217-231; "The Work of Negativity: The Psychoanalytic Revision of the Theory of Recognition," in eds. Jean-Philippe Deranty, Danielle Petherbridge, John Rundell, & Robert Sinnerbrink, *Recognition, Work, Politics: New Directions in French Critical Theory*, Leiden & Boston, Brill, 2007, reprinted in *The I in We: Studies in the Theory of Recognition*, Cambridge, Polity Press, 2012, pp. 293-200.

10. See Donald W. Winnicott, "Primary Maternal Preoccupation" in *Through Paediatrics to Psychoanalysis*, London, Karnac Books, 2007 (1958); "From Dependence Towards Independence in the Development of the Individual" (1963); "The Theory of the Parent-Infant Relationship" (1960) in *The Maturational Processes and the Facilitating Environment*, London, Karnac Books, 1990 (1965).

11. Winnicott rarely uses the term 'primary narcissism' but instead refers to this primary state interchangeably as either the 'holding phase,' 'absolute dependence,' or 'primary maternal preoccupation.' See Jan Abram, *The Language of Winnicott* (Second Edition), London, Karnac Books, 2007, p. 70.

12. Donald W. Winnicott, "Anxiety Associated with Insecurity" (1952) in *Through Paediatrics to Psychoanalysis*, London, Karnac Books, 2007 (1958), p. 99.

13. Winnicott, "Anxiety Associated with Insecurity," p. 99.

14. Daniel N. Stern, *The Interpersonal World of the Infant: A View from Psychoanalysis and Developmental Psychology*, London & New York, Karnac Books, 1985, p. 132; see Whitebook, "First Nature and Second Nature in Hegel and Psychoanalysis," p. 385.

15. Whitebook, "First Nature and Second Nature in Hegel and Psychoanalysis," p. 385; Stern, *The Interpersonal World of the Infant*, p. 125.

16. Whitebook, "Mutual Recognition and the Work of the Negative," p. 279.

17. For Winnicott the 'holding environment' is preferably provided by one caregiver and in his early work he tends to suggest this is best done by the biological mother. However, the holding environment also includes the father and society in general as an ongoing necessity. For further discussion see Jan Abram, *The Language of Winnicott* (Second Edition), London, Karnac Books, 2007, pp. 193-4.

18. Donald W. Winnicott, "The Capacity to be Alone" (1958) in *The Maturational Processes and the Facilitating Environment*, London, Karnac Books, 1990 (1965) p. 30; 33.

19. Winnicott, "The Capacity to be Alone," p. 33.

20. See Donald W. Winnicott, "From Dependence Towards Independence in the Development of the Individual" (1963) & "The Theory of the Parent-Infant Relationship" (1960) in *The Maturational Processes and the Facilitating Environment*, London, Karnac Books, 1990 (1965).

21. Donald W. Winnicott, "The Ordinary Devoted Mother and her Baby," *Nine Broadcast Talks*, republished in *The Child and the Family*, London, Tavistock Publications, 1957, quoted in Jan Abram, *The Language of Winnicott* (Second Edition), London, Karnac Books, 2007, p. 70.

22. Honneth, *The Struggle for Recognition*, p. 99.

23. Winnicott, "The Theory of the Parent-Infant Relationship," p. 46.

24. Jan Abram, *The Language of Winnicott* (Second Edition), London, Karnac Books, 2007, p. 159.

25. Honneth, *The Struggle for Recognition*, p. 99.

26. Donald W. Winnicott, "Ego Integration in Child Development" (1962) in *The Maturational Processes and the Facilitating Environment*, London, Karnac Books, 1990 (1965), p. 59.

27. Winnicott, "The Theory of the Parent-Infant Relationship," pp. 44-5.

28. Winnicott, "The Theory of the Parent-Infant Relationship," p. 44.

29. Donald W. Winnicott, "Primary Maternal Preoccupation" in *Through Paediatrics to Psychoanalysis*, London, Karnac Books, 2007 (1958), pp. 300-305. Winnicott himself prefers not to use the term 'symbiosis' and tends to refer to the term 'mergence' or 'primary maternal preoccupation' to describe this phase.

30. Winnicott suggests, however, that in good enough circumstances an adoptive mother can fulfill this role. In his early work he tends to theorize the role of the mother in gendered terms but does acknowledge the role of paternal care in the general sense of caring for the mother-infant unit.

31. Winnicott, "Primary Maternal Preoccupation," p. 301. Winnicott does, however, acknowledge the psychological differences between the mother's identification with the infant and the infant's dependence on the mother, which does not involve identification.

32. Abram, *The Language of Winnicott*, p. 164.

33. Johanna Meehan, "Recognition and the Dynamics of Intersubjectivity," in ed. D. Petherbridge, *Axel Honneth: Critical Essays,* Boston & Leiden, Brill, 2011.

34. Honneth, *The Struggle for Recognition*, p. 99.

35. Honneth, *The Struggle for Recognition*, p. 99 (my emphasis).

36. See Iris Marion Young, "Recognition of Love's Labor: Considering Axel Honneth's Feminism," in eds. Bert van den Brink and David Owen, *Recognition and Power: Axel*

Honneth and the Tradition of Critical Social Theory, Cambridge, Cambridge University Press, 2007, pp. 189-212; Amy Allen, "Recognizing Domination: Recognition and Power in Honneth's Critical Theory," *Journal of Power*, Vol. 3, No. 1, April 2010, pp. 21-32; Johanna Meehan, "Recognition and the Dynamics of Intersubjectivity," in ed. D. Petherbridge, *Axel Honneth: Critical Essays,* Boston & Leiden, Brill, 2011.

37. Meehan, "Recognition and the Dynamics of Intersubjectivity."
38. Allen, "Recognizing Domination," p. 24.
39. Young, "Recognition of Love's Labor," p. 207.
40. Allen, "Recognizing Domination," p. 24.
41. Young, "Recognition of Love's Labor," p. 206.
42. Young, "Recognition of Love's Labor," p. 207.
43. Young, "Recognition of Love's Labor," p. 206; 207.
44. Axel Honneth, "Rejoinder," in eds. Bert van den Brink and David Owen, *Recognition and Power: Axel Honneth and the Tradition of Critical Social Theory*, Cambridge, Cambridge University Press, 2007, p. 362. However, in a recent interview, Honneth has acknowledged that he failed to consider a more differentiated model of love and care, and admits that the problem has been his tendency to use a formulation of love and care that is 'neutral in content.' See Axel Honneth, Amy Allen, and Maeve Cooke, "A Conversation between Axel Honneth, Amy Allen, and Maeve Cooke, Frankfurt am Main, 12 April 2010," *Journal of Power*, Vol. 3, No. 2. August, 2010, pp. 157-8.
45. Allen, "Recognizing Domination," pp. 24-5.
46. Honneth, *The Struggle for Recognition*, p. 98.
47. Honneth, *The Struggle for Recognition*, p. 100.
48. Donald W. Winnicott, "From Dependence Towards Independence in the Development of the Individual" (1963) in *The Maturational Processes and the Facilitating Environment*, London, Karnac Books, 1990 (1965), p. 88.
49. Honneth, *The Struggle for Recognition*, p. 100. See Winnicott, "From Dependence Towards Independence in the Development of the Individual," pp. 87-8.
50. Honneth, *The Struggle for Recognition*, p. 100.
51. For Winnicott, unlike the Freudian model, these destructive acts do not represent an attempt to cope negatively with frustrations but are rather a means of testing a reality that is now outside his/her control.
52. Honneth, *The Struggle for Recognition*, p. 101.
53. Honneth, *The Struggle for Recognition*, p. 101, drawing on Jessica Benjamin, *The Bonds of Love: Psychoanalysis, Feminism, and the Problem of Domination*, London, Virago Press, 1990 (1988).
54. Honneth, *The Struggle for Recognition*, p. 101.
55. Donald D. Winnicott, "Transitional Objects and Transitional Phenomena" (1951) in *Through Paediatrics to Psychoanalysis*, London, Karnac Books, 2007 (1958); Honneth, *The Struggle for Recognition*, p. 102.
56. Winnicott, "Transitional Objects and Transitional Phenomena," p. 229.
57. Winnicott, "Transitional Objects and Transitional Phenomena," p. 231.
58. Winnicott, "Transitional Objects and Transitional Phenomena," p. 239.
59. Winnicott, "Transitional Objects and Transitional Phenomena," pp. 231-3; Abram, *The Language of Winnicott*, p. 337.
60. Honneth, *The Struggle for Recognition*, p. 103.
61. Winnicott, "Transitional Objects and Transitional Phenomena," p. 230. For further discussion see André Green, *Play and Reflection in Donald Winnicott's Writings*, London, Karnac, 2005.
62. Honneth, *The Struggle for Recognition*, p. 107.
63. See Honneth, *The Struggle for Recognition* & Honneth "Grounding Recognition," p. 503.
64. Honneth, *The Struggle for Recognition*, p. 105.
65. Honneth, *The Struggle for Recognition*, p. 107.
66. Honneth, *The Struggle for Recognition*, pp. 106-7.
67. Honneth, "Postmodern Identity and Object-Relations Theory," p. 240.

68. Honneth, "Postmodern Identity and Object-Relations Theory," p. 235.

69. Honneth, "Postmodern Identity and Object-Relations Theory," p. 238.

70. Honneth, "Postmodern Identity and Object-Relations Theory," p. 233.

71. McNay, *Against Recognition*, p. 143.

72. McNay, *Against Recognition*, p. 143.

73. Honneth, "Postmodern Identity and Object-Relations Theory," p. 233.

74. Honneth, "Postmodern Identity and Object-Relations Theory," p. 233; see also White-book, "Mutual Recognition and the Work of the Negative," p. 278.

75. Beatrice Beebe and Frank M., Lachmann, *Infant Research and Adult Treatment: Co-constructing Interactions*, Hillsdale, NJ, The Analytic Press, 2002, p. 67.

76. Beebe and Lachmann, *Infant Research and Adult Treatment*, p. 67. See Stern in André Green and Daniel N. Stern et al., *Clinical and Observational Psychoanalytic Research: Roots of a Controversy*, eds. Joseph Sandler, Anne-Marie Sandler, & Rosemary Davies, London, H. Kamac Books, 2000, p. 88; Stern, *The Interpersonal World of the Infant*.

77. Beebe and Lachmann, *Infant Research and Adult Treatment*, p. 69. See Stern in André Green and Daniel N. Stern et al., *Clinical and Observational Psychoanalytic Research*," p. 88; Stern, *The Interpersonal World of the Infant*.

78. Beebe and Lachmann, *Infant Research and Adult Treatment*, p. 69; Stern, *The Interpersonal World of the Infant*.

79. Beebe and Lachmann, *Infant Research and Adult Treatment*, p. 182.

80. Joel Whitebook, "First Nature and Second Nature in Hegel and Psychoanalysis," *Constellations*, Volume 15, no. 3, 2008, pp. 386-7.

81. Axel Honneth, "Facets of the Presocial Self: Rejoinder to Joel Whitebook," in *The I in We: Studies in the Theory of Recognition*, Cambridge, Polity Press, 2012, p. 222.

82. Honneth, "Facets of the Presocial Self," p. 227. Honneth, however, detects significant ambiguities in Whitebook's argument. For example, with reference to the debate between Habermas and Henrich, he points out the difference between an early 'pre-reflexive intuition of self' and an 'initial capacity for reflection,' or indeed, consciousness. Honneth also argues that it is contradictory to maintain an argument for primary narcissism or omnipotence in which infants are unable to separate themselves from their surroundings, while simultaneously arguing for the existence of a core, pre-social sense of self.

83. Honneth, "Facets of the Presocial Self," p. 222, quoting Stern, *The Interpersonal World of the Infant*, p. 70.

84. Honneth, "Facets of the Presocial Self," p. 229.

85. Axel Honneth, "Grounding Recognition: A Rejoinder to Critical Questions," in Symposium on Axel Honneth and Recognition, *Inquiry*, no. 45, 2002, p. 504.

86. Honneth, "Grounding Recognition," p. 504.

87. See Honneth's alternative discussion in "The Work of Negativity: The Psychoanalytic Revision of the Theory of Recognition," in eds. Jean-Philippe Deranty, Danielle Petherbridge, John Rundell, & Robert Sinnerbrink, *Recognition, Work, Politics: New Directions in French Critical Theory*, Leiden & Boston, Brill, 2007, reprinted in *The I in We: Studies in the Theory of Recognition*, Cambridge, Polity Press, 2012, pp. 193-200.

88. Honneth, "Grounding Recognition," p. 504. In a more recent essay, Honneth seeks to revisit this problematic via a more sympathetic engagement with Freud, and reclaims a specific reading of his work for an intersubjective theory of the subject, explaining the condition of a ruptured symbiosis in terms of the negation or repression of an original separation anxiety from the lost love object. See Axel Honneth, "Appropriating Freedom: Freud's Conception of Individual Self-Relation," in Axel Honneth, *Pathologies of Reason: On the Legacy of Critical Theory*, trans. James Ingram, New York, Columbia University Press, 2009, pp. 126-145.

89. See Honneth, "Grounding Recognition," p. 504.

90. Miriam Bankovsky, *Perfecting Justice in Rawls, Habermas and Honneth: A Deconstructive Perspective*, London & New York, Continuum Books, 2012, p. 195.

91. See Honneth, "Postmodern Identity and Object-Relations Theory," p. 234.

92. See Honneth, *Reification*, p. 42.

93. Axel Honneth, "Invisibility: On the Epistemology of 'Recognition,'" in *Recognition*, Axel Honneth & Avishai Margalit, Supplement of the Aristotelian Society, no. 75, 2001, pp.

116-119. Here Honneth draws on Daniel Stern's work in *The First Relationship: Infant and Mother* (Cambridge, MA, Harvard University Press, 1977), to establish a performative and preverbal notion of recognition based on the early infant interactions between caregiver and infant, although without taking on board Stern's theory of intersubjectivity or his objections to the notion of originary symbiosis.

94. Honneth, "Invisibility: On the Epistemology of 'Recognition,'" p. 126.

10. A CRITICAL THEORY OF RECOGNITION

1. See Christopher Zurn, "Anthropology and Normativity: A Critique of Axel Honneth's 'Formal Conception of Ethical Life,'" *Philosophy and Social Criticism*, vol. 26, no.1, 2000, p. 115.

2. Fraser and Honneth, *Redistribution or Recognition?*, pp. 136-7.

3. Honneth, *The Struggle for Recognition*, p. 174.

4. Honneth, *The Struggle for Recognition*, p. 179.

5. See Honneth, *The Struggle for Recognition*, p. 173; Christopher Zurn, "Anthropology and Normativity: A Critique of Axel Honneth's 'Formal Conception of Ethical Life,'" *Philosophy and Social Criticism*, vol. 26, no. 1, 2000, p. 115.

6. Honneth, "The Social Dynamics of Disrespect," p. 72.

7. Honneth, *The Struggle for Recognition*, pp. 173-4.

8. Fraser and Honneth, *Redistribution or Recognition?*, p. 143.

9. It should be noted in this context that Honneth also employs a very specific account of modernity in the articulation of his social-theoretical model. Honneth leans more heavily on a notion of 'social' rather than 'system' integration and is concerned with the 'moral constraints' underlying all forms of integration and reproduction in modern, capitalist societies. In contrast to Luhmann and Habermas, Honneth argues that even systems such as the economy are abstract forms of social exchange that are underpinned by a tacit normative agreement or a shared value-system. For Honneth, then, there are no norm-free spheres of interaction or forms of integration that have become decoupled from normative social life-worlds. Rather, all institutionalized spheres of social life are open to normative improvement. See Fraser and Honneth, *Redistribution or Recognition?*, p. 249; Honneth, "The Social Dynamics of Disrespect," p. 72.

10. Honneth, *The Struggle for Recognition*, pp. 174-5.

11. Honneth, *The Struggle for Recognition*, p. 176.

12. See also Axel Honneth, "Love and Morality: On the Moral Content of Emotional Ties," in *Disrespect: The Normative Foundations of Critical Theory*, Cambridge, Polity Press, 2007; and Honneth's discussion of love and friendship in *Das Recht Der Freiheit: Grundriß einer Demokratischen Sittlichkeit*, Berlin, Suhrkamp Verlag, 2011.

13. Fraser and Honneth, *Redistribution or Recognition?*, pp. 139-141.

14. Fraser and Honneth, *Redistribution or Recognition?*, p. 137; 142. Honneth acknowledges, however, that this 'revolution' of the social recognition-order occurred with "class- and gender-specific delays" (p. 142).

15. Fraser and Honneth, *Redistribution or Recognition?*, p. 174. See also *Das Recht Der Freiheit* for the development towards a more explicitly historical perspective.

16. Fraser and Honneth, *Redistribution or Recognition?*, p. 137.

17. Fraser and Honneth, *Redistribution or Recognition?*, p. 181.

18. Fraser and Honneth, *Redistribution or Recognition?*, p. 247

19. Fraser and Honneth, *Redistribution or Recognition?*, p. 143.

20. Fraser and Honneth, *Redistribution or Recognition?*, p. 186.

21. In this sense, Honneth attempts to amend the view proposed in *The Struggle for Recognition*, that love does not have the potential for normative development. He is now convinced that love also possesses a surplus of normative validity that emerges and expands as a result of interpretative conflicts. See Fraser and Honneth, *Redistribution or Recognition?*, ff. 35, p. 192.

22. Fraser and Honneth, *Redistribution or Recognition?*, p. 186.

23. Fraser and Honneth, *Redistribution or Recognition?*, p. 145.

24. See Fraser and Honneth, *Redistribution or Recognition?*; Axel Honneth, "Recognition as Ideology: The Connection between Morality and Power," in *The I in We: Studies in the Theory of Recognition*, Cambridge, Polity Press, 2012, pp. 75-97.

25. Axel Honneth, "Recognition as Ideology," p. 81.

26. Honneth, "Recognition as Ideology," p. 81

27. Honneth, "Recognition as Ideology," p. 81.

28. Axel Honneth, "Grounding Recognition: A Rejoinder to Critical Questions," in 'Symposium on Axel Honneth and Recognition,' *Inquiry*, no. 45, 2002, pp. 509-510.

29. Honneth, "Grounding Recognition," p. 508.

30. Honneth, "Recognition as Ideology," p. 82.

31. Fraser and Honneth, *Redistribution or Recognition?*, p. 263.

32. Fraser and Honneth, *Redistribution or Recognition?*, pp. 182-3.

33. Fraser and Honneth, *Redistribution or Recognition?*, p. 116; Axel Honneth, "Reconstructive Social Criticism with a Genealogical Proviso: On the Idea of 'Critique' in the Frankfurt School," in *Pathologies of Reason: On the Legacy of Critical Theory*, trans. James Ingram, New York, Columbia University Press, 2009.

34. Fraser and Honneth, *Redistribution or Recognition?*, p. 115.

35. Fraser and Honneth, *Redistribution or Recognition?*, p. 183.

36. Fraser and Honneth, *Redistribution or Recognition?*, pp. 184-6.

37. Fraser and Honneth, *Redistribution or Recognition?*, pp. 183-5.

38. Fraser and Honneth, *Redistribution or Recognition?*, p. 187.

39. See also Cooke, *Re-Presenting the Good Society*, p. 67.

40. Christopher Zurn, "Anthropology and Normativity: A Critique of Axel Honneth's 'formal conception of Ethical Life,'" *Philosophy and Social Criticism*, vol. 26, no. 1, 2000, p. 119.

41. Rainer Forst, "To Tolerate Means to Insult": Toleration, Recognition and Emancipation, in eds. Bert van den Brink and David Owen, *Recognition and Power: Axel Honneth and the Tradition of Critical Social Theory*, Cambridge, Cambridge University Press, 2007. p. 216; see also Allen, "Recognizing Domination" for further discussion in relation to this point.

42. Zurn, "Anthropology and Normativity," p. 121.

43. Zurn, "Anthropology and Normativity, p. 119. See Cooke, *Re-Presenting the Good Society*, pp. 66-7.

44. Zurn, "Anthropology and Normativity," p. 121.

45. Cooke, *Re-Presenting the Good Society*, p. 67; Zurn, "Anthropology and Normativity."

46. Miriam Bankovsky, *Perfecting Justice in Rawls, Habermas and Honneth: A Deconstructive Perspective*, London & New York, Continuum, 2012, p. 189.

47. Fraser and Honneth, *Redistribution or Recognition?*, p. 138 (my emphasis).

48. Honneth, *Reification*, p. 152.

49. Honneth, *Reification*, p. 90, ff. 70. See Honneth discussions of Sartre in "The Struggle for Recognition: On Sartre's Theory of Intersubjectivity," in *The Fragmented World of the Social*, pp. 158-167; *The Struggle for Recognition*, Chapter 7. See also "The Relevance of Contemporary French Philosophy for a Theory of Recognition: An Interview" in Miriam Bankovsky & Le Goff, Alice, *Recognition Theory and Contemporary French Moral and Political Philosophy: Reopening the Dialogue*, Manchester, Manchester University Press, 2012, pp. 23-38.

50. Honneth, *Reification*, p. 27.

51. Honneth, *Reification*, p. 32.

52. Honneth, *Reification*, p. 38.

53. Honneth, *Reification*, p. 42.

54. Honneth, *Reification*, p. 35

55. Axel Honneth, "Invisibility: On the Epistemology of 'Recognition,'" in *Recognition*, Axel Honneth & Avishai Margalit, *Supplement of the Aristotelian Society*, no. 75, 2001, pp. 114-5.

56. Honneth, *Reification*, p. 45.

57. Honneth, *Reification*, p. 63. It should be noted, though, that Honneth effectively continues to maintain an intersubjective stance in relation to non-human objects. Moreover, as Deranty suggests, although Honneth develops a 'libidinal' account of recognition in this context, "he

230 *Notes*

still maintains his intersubjectivist reading of affective attachments, which prevents him from giving full weight to the organic nature of the subject." See Jean-Philippe Deranty, "The Theory of Social Action in Merleau-Ponty and Honneth," in *Recognition Theory and Contemporary French Moral and Political Philosophy: Reopening the Dialogue*, eds. Miriam Bankovsky and Alice Le Goff, Manchester, Manchester University Press, 2012, p. 124; ff. 13, p. 126.

58. Honneth, *Reification*, p. 44. Here Honneth cites Adorno's aphorism 99 in *Minima Moralia* to the effect that "a human being only becomes human at all by imitating other human beings." Theodor Adorno, *Minima Moralia: Reflections on a Damaged Life*, London & New York, Verso, 2005, p. 154.

59. Axel Honneth, "A Physiognomy of the Capitalistic Lifeform: A Sketch of Adorno's Social Theory," in *Pathologies of Reason: On the Legacy of Critical Theory*, New York, Columbia University Press, 2009, p. 70. See also Deranty, *Beyond Communication*, p. 461. Honneth's later essays also represent a renewed engagement with Adorno's work, especially with regard to the notion of mimesis.

60. Somogy Varga, "Critical Theory and the Two-Level Account of Recognition—Towards a New Foundation?", *Critical Horizons*, vol. 11, no. 1, 2010, pp. 19-33; Deranty, *Beyond Communication*, p. 262-3; 468.

61. See Judith Butler, "Taking Another's View: Ambivalent Implications," in Axel Honneth, *Reification: A New Look at an Old Idea*, ed. Martin Jay, Oxford & New York, Oxford University Press, 2008, pp. 97-119.

62. Honneth, *Reification*, p. 152.

63. Honneth, *Reification*, pp. 151-2.

64. Varga, "Critical Theory and the Two-Level Account of Recognition," p. 23.

11. THE POWER OF CRITIQUE

1. See Axel Honneth, "Pathologies of the Social: The Past and Present of Social Philosophy" in *Disrespect: The Normative Foundations of Critical Theory*, Cambridge, Polity Press, 2007, pp. 3-48.

2. Honneth, "Pathologies of the Social," p. 34.

3. Honneth, "Pathologies of the Social," p. 4.

4. Honneth, "Pathologies of the Social," p. 5.

5. Honneth, "Pathologies of the Social," p. 5.

6. Honneth, "Pathologies of the Social," p. 17.

7. Martin Saar, "Power and Critique," *Journal of Power*, vol. 3, no. 1, April 2010, p. 8.

8. Honneth, "Pathologies of the Social," p. 33.

9. Saar, "Power and Critique," p. 7. Saar acknowledges that although some of these concerns can be traced back much further in the history of philosophy, for example, to the works of Plato and Aristotle, the difference is that in their works "they remain tied to principles of order that are still located beyond the social itself."

10. Saar, "Power and Critique," p. 8.

11. Saar, "Power and Critique," p. 8.

12. Saar, "Power and Critique," p. 7.

13. Honneth, "Pathologies of the Social," p. 4.

14. Honneth, "Pathologies of the Social," p. 17.

15. Honneth, "Pathologies of the Social," p. 17.

16. Honneth, "Pathologies of the Social," p. 17.

17. Honneth, "Pathologies of the Social," pp. 22-3.

18. Honneth, "Pathologies of the Social," p. 22.

19. Honneth, "Pathologies of the Social," pp. 22-3.

20. Honneth, "Pathologies of the Social," p. 26.

21. Honneth, "Pathologies of the Social," p. 30.

22. Honneth, "Pathologies of the Social," p. 33.

23. Fraser and Honneth, *Redistribution or Recognition?*, pp. 243-4.

24. See also Honneth's discussion of the centrality of the social rationalization thesis to the project of Critical Theory in "A Social Pathology of Reason: On the Intellectual Legacy of Critical Theory," in *Pathologies of Reason: On the Legacy of Critical Theory*, trans. James Ingram, New York, Columbia University Press, 2009.

25. Honneth, "Reconstructive Social Criticism with a Genealogical Proviso," p. 52; "Pathologies of the Social," p. 40.

26. Honneth, "Pathologies of the Social," p. 42. In Honneth's opinion, the other two approaches undermine the project of social philosophy by, in the case of procedural ethics, making the project of social philosophy redundant by leaving the evaluation of social pathologies and development to be determined by the members of a particular social order; or in the case of a historically relativized ethical framework, basing critical analysis on a historically contingent mode of reflection and relative forms of ethical life.

27. Honneth, "Pathologies of the Social," p. 40.

28. Saar, "Power and Critique," p. 9.

29. Saar, "Power and Critique," p. 7.

30. Saar, "Power and Critique," p. 9; see also Hannah Arendt, *The Human Condition*, Chicago & London, The University of Chicago Press, 1958, pp. 199-207. Saar's reference here to an 'action-related' form of power must be sharply distinguished from my use of the term of an 'action-theoretic' notion of power in my discussion of Foucault's work above. My use of the term is intended to designate an intersubjective, relational notion of power that can be detected in Foucault's work, whereas Saar's use of the term refers to a form of power as domination and an individualistic notion of power. To avoid confusion, when discussing Saar's conceptualization, I prefer to use the term 'domination-theoretic.'

31. Saar, "Power and Critique," p. 9.

32. Saar, "Power and Critique," p. 10.

33. Notably, some elements of this conception are reproduced in Habermas' earlier work, where the notion of power is conceptualized predominantly in terms of its centralization in state bureaucracy, and the 'critique of power' becomes a question of legitimation. See, for example, Habermas, *The Theory of Communicative Action*. However, in *Between Facts and Norms*, Habermas extends and elaborates the notion of communicative power and re-engages with the notion of power inspired by Arendt. See Jürgen Habermas, *Between Facts and Norms*: *Contributions to a Discourse Theory of Law and Democracy*, trans. William Rehg, Cambridge, Polity Press, 1996.

34. Saar, "Power and Critique," p. 11.

35. Arendt, *The Human Condition*, p. 200; 204.

36. Saar, "Power and Critique," pp. 13-14.

37. Saar, "Power and Critique," pp. 15-16.

38. Saar, "Power and Critique," p. 16; Foucault, *The History of Sexuality*, Vol. 1, p. 95.

39. Saar, "Power and Critique," p. 15. See also Amy Allen, *The Politics of Our Selves: Power, Autonomy and Gender in Contemporary Critical Theory*, New York, Columbia University Press, 2008.

40. See Axel Honneth, "Reconstructive Criticism with a Genealogical Proviso: On the Idea of 'Critique' in the Frankfurt School," in *Pathologies of Reason: On the Legacy of Critical Theory*, trans. James Ingram et al., New York, Columbia University Press, 2009, pp. 43-53. Notably, Honneth only refers to the need to subject the *application* of norms to genealogical critique, not the underlying normative category itself.

41. In this sense, the notion of power developed here seeks to elaborate the connections between the ontological or constitutive and 'action-theoretic' dimensions of power with reference to Foucault's work.

42. Axel Honneth, "Recognition as Ideology: The Connection between Morality and Power," in *The I in We: Studies in the Theory of Recognition*, Cambridge, Polity Press, 2012, pp. 75-97; p. 77. In this essay, Honneth's analysis is largely focused on the problem of the third kind of recognition and the creation of values of esteem that might be ideological.

43. Amy Allen, "Recognising Domination: Recognition and Power in Honneth's Critical Theory," *Journal of Power*, vol. 3, no. 1, April, 2010, p. 22.

44. Honneth, "Recognition as Ideology," pp. 86-88.

45. Christopher Zurn, "Social Pathologies as Second-Order Disorders," in *Axel Honneth: Critical Essays*, ed. D. Petherbridge, Leiden & Boston, Brill, 2011, pp. 348-9.

46. See Honneth, "Grounding Recognition," p. 510.

47. Arto Laitinen, "Interpersonal Recognition: A Response to Value or a Precondition of Personhood?" in *Inquiry: An Interdisciplinary Journal of Philosophy*," vol. 45, 2002, p. 474. Also see Radu Neculau, "Being Oneself in Another: Recognition and the Culturalist Deformation of Identity," *Inquiry*, vol. 55, no. 2, April, 2012, pp. 148-170.

48. Axel Honneth, "The Work of the Negativity: A Recognition-Theoretical Revision of Psychoanalysis," in *The I in We: Studies in the Theory of Recognition*, Cambridge, Polity Press, p. 198.

49. Honneth, "Grounding Recognition."

50. Bankovsky, *Perfecting Justice in Rawls, Habermas and Honneth*, p. 195.

51. Thomas Wartenberg, *The Forms of Power: From Domination to Transformation*, Philadelphia, PA, Temple University Press, 1990, here quoting Jean Baker Miller, "Colloquium: Women and Power," *Stone Center for Developmental Services and Studies Work in Progress*, no. 882-01, 1982, p. 2.

52. Thomas Wartenberg, *The Forms of Power: From Domination to Transformation*, Philadelphia, PA, Temple University Press, 1990 esp. ch. 9 & 10; quoted in Steven Lukes, *Power: A Radical View*, Basingstoke & New York, Second Edition, 2005, p. 84. Wartenberg also suggests therapy and teaching might also be considered forms of productive power that are asymmetrical yet enabling in a positive sense.

53. In contrast, drawing on Levinas, Honneth conceptualizes 'asymmetrical' relations of love and care between parents and children as a special case of asymmetrical recognition, which foregrounds the 'ethical relevance' of such relations rather than conceiving of them simultaneously as a form of power. See Honneth's discussion of Levinas and Derrida in this regard in Axel Honneth, "The Other of Justice: Habermas and the Ethical Relevance of Postmodernism," in *Disrespect: The Normative Foundations of Critical Theory*, Cambridge, Polity Press, 2007, pp. 99-128; Honneth, The Relevance of Contemporary French Philosophy for a Theory of Recognition: An Interview" with Miriam Bankovsky, pp. 29-30.

54. Foucault, "The Ethic of Care of the Self as a Practice of Freedom," p. 3; 12.

55. Amy Allen, *The Power of Feminist Theory: Domination, Resistance, Solidarity*, Boulder, CO, Westview Press, 1999, see esp. ch. 5, p. 125; Lukes, *Power: A Radical View*, p. 84.

56. Honneth, "Recognition as Ideology," p. 84.

57. Honneth, "Recognition as Ideology," p. 84. See also Honneth's response to Emmanuel Renault in his "Rejoinder" in *Axel Honneth: Critical Essays*, ed. D. Petherbridge, Leiden and Boston, Brill, 2011, pp. 391-422.

58. Honneth, *Recognition or Redistribution?*, pp. 249-250.

59. Honneth, "Recognition as Ideology," pp. 84; 85.

60. Cf. Habermas' incorporation of a notion of communicative power as 'productive' of institutions in Jürgen Habermas, *Between Facts and Norms: Contributions to a Discourse Theory of Law and Democracy*, trans. William Rehg, Cambridge, Polity Press, 1996. Although this represents an advance from the theory of power outlined in *The Theory of Communicative Action*, in the sense that Habermas elaborates a notion of communicative power that extends his analysis of power beyond its earlier circumscription in terms of systems theory, it also does not adequately conceptualize the interplay between power and freedom nor the notion of constitutive power in the Foucaultian sense. See also Amy Allen, "The Unforced Force of the Better Argument: Reason and Power in Habermas' Political Theory," *Constellations*, vol. 19, no. 3, 2012, pp. 353-368.

61. Lois McNay, "The Politics of Suffering and Recognition: Foucault contra Honneth," in *Recognition Theory and Contemporary French Moral Philosophy: Reopening the Dialogue*, eds. Miriam Bankovsky & Alice Le Goff, Manchester, Manchester University Press, p. 66.

62. See Jean-Philippe Deranty, "The Theory of Social Action in Merleau-Ponty and Honneth," in *Recognition Theory and Contemporary French Moral Philosophy: Reopening the Dialogue*, eds. Miriam Bankovsky & Alice Le Goff, Manchester, Manchester University Press, p. 118.

63. See also McNay, "The Politics of Suffering and Recognition"; Allen, "Recognising Domination: Recognition and Power in Honneth's Critical Theory."

64. See also Honneth, "Reconstructive Social Criticism with a Genealogical Proviso."

Bibliography

Aboulafia, Mitchell, *The Mediating Self: Mead, Sartre, and Self-Determination*, New Haven & London, Yale University Press, 1986.

Aboulafia, Mitchell, *Philosophy, Social Theory, and the Thought of George Herbert Mead*, Albany, SUNY Press, 1991.

Aboulafia, Mitchell, "Self-Consciousness and the Quasi-Epic of the Master," in ed. Mitchell Aboulafia, *Philosophy, Social Theory, and the Thought of George Herbert Mead*, Albany, SUNY Press, 1991, pp. 223-24.

Abram, Jan, *The Language of Winnicott* (Second Edition), London, Karnac Books, 2007.

Adorno, Theodor W., *Negative Dialectics*, trans. E.B. Ashton, London, Routledge, 1973.

Adorno, Theodor W., & Horkheimer, Max, *The Dialectic of Enlightenment*, London & New York, Verso, 1992 (1972.)

Adorno, Theodor W., *Critical Models: Interventions and Catchwords*, trans. Henry W. Pickford, New York, Columbia University Press, 1998.

Adorno, Theodor W., *Minima Moralia: Reflections on a Damaged Life*, London & New York, Verso, 2005, p. 154.

Alexander, Jeffrey & Lara, Maria Pia, "Honneth's New Critical Theory of Recognition," *New Left Review*, vol. 220, 1996.

Allen, Amy, *The Power of Feminist Theory: Domination, Resistance, Solidarity*, Boulder, CO, Westview Press, 1999.

Allen, Amy, *The Politics of Our Selves: Power, Autonomy, and Gender in Contemporary Critical Theory*, New York, Columbia University Press, 2008.

Allen, Amy, "Recognizing Domination: Recognition and Power in Honneth's Critical Theory," *Journal of Power*, vol. 3, no. 1, April 2010, pp. 21-32.

Allen, Amy, "The Unforced Force of the Better Argument: Reason and Power in Habermas' Political Theory," in *Constellations*, vol. 19, no. 3, 2012, pp. 353-368.

Alway, Joan, *Critical Theory and Political Possibilities: Conceptions of Emancipatory Politics in the Works of Horkheimer, Adorno, Marcuse and Habermas*, Connecticut & London, Greenwood Press, 1995.

Anderson, Joel, "Situating Axel Honneth in the Frankfurt School Tradition," in ed. D. Petherbridge, *Axel Honneth: Critical Essays*, Boston & Leiden, Brill, 2011.

Arendt, Hannah, *The Human Condition*, Chicago & London, The University of Chicago Press, 1958.

Armstrong, Timothy J., trans., *Michel Foucault: Philosopher*, New York & London, Harvester Wheatsheaf, 1992.

Aristotle, *The Basic Works of Aristotle*, ed. Richard McKeon, New York, The Modern Library, 2001.

Bankovsky, Miriam, *Perfecting Justice in Rawls, Habermas and Honneth*, London & New York, Continuum Books, 2012.

Bankovsky, Miriam & Le Goff, Alice, *Recognition Theory and Contemporary French Moral and Political Philosophy: Reopening the Dialogue*, Manchester, Manchester University Press, 2012.

Barry, A., Osborne, T. & Rose, N., *Foucault and Political Reason: Liberalism, Neo-liberalism and Rationalities of Government*, eds. London, UCL Press, 1996.

Beebe, Beatrice & Lachmann, Frank, M., *Infant Research and Adult Treatment: Co-constructing Interactions*, Hillsdale, NJ, The Analytic Press, 2002.

Beiser, Frederick, *Hegel*, New York & London, Routledge, 2005.

Benhabib, Seyla, "The Generalised and the Concrete Other: The Kohlberg-Gilligan Controversy," *Praxis International*, vol. 5, no. 4, 1985.

Benhabib, Seyla, *Critique, Norm and Utopia: A Study of the Foundations of Critical Theory*, New York, Columbia University Press, 1986.

Benjamin, Jessica, *The Bonds of Love: Psychoanalysis, Feminism, and the Problem of Domination*, London, Virago Press, 1988.

Bernstein, Jay M., *Recovering Ethical Life: Jürgen Habermas and the Future of Critical Theory*, Routledge, London & New York, 1995.

Bernstein, Jay M., "Suffering Injustice: Misrecognition as Moral Injury in Critical Theory," *International Journal of Philosophical Studies*, vol. 13 (3), 2005, pp. 303-324.

Bernstein, Richard J., "*The Critique of Power*," in *Political Theory*, August, 1992, pp. 523-527.

Best, Steven, *The Politics of Historical Vision: Marx, Foucault, Habermas*, New York & London, The Guilford Press, 1995.

Bowlby, John, *Attachment and Loss: Volume 1, Attachment*, London, The Hogarth Press, 1970.

Bowlby, John, *The Making and Breaking of Affectional Bonds*, London, Tavistock, 1979.

Butler, Judith, "Foucault and the Paradox of Bodily Inscriptions," *The Journal of Philosophy*, Eighty-Sixth Annual Meeting of the American Philosophical Association (Eastern Division), vol. 86, no. 11, November, 1989, pp. 601-607.

Butler, Judith, *The Psychic Life of Power: Theories in Subjection*, Stanford, Stanford University Press, 1997.

Cannon, Bob, *Rethinking the Normative Content of Critical Theory: Marx, Habermas and Beyond*, Hampshire & New York, Palgrave, 2001.

Coles, R., *Self/Power/Other: Political Theory and Dialogical Ethics*, Ithaca & London, Cornell University Press, 1992.

Cook, Gary A., "The Development of G. H. Mead's Social Psychology," in *Philosophy, Social Theory and the Thought of George Herbert Mead*, Albany, SUNY Press, 1991, pp. 89-107.

Cooke, Maeve, *Re-presenting the Good Society*, Cambridge, M.A. & London, The MIT Press, 2006.

Cornell, Drucilla, Rosenfeld, Michael, & Gray Carlson, David, *Hegel and Legal Theory*, New York & London, Routledge, 1991.

Critchley, Simon & Bernasconi, Robert, eds, *The Cambridge Companion to Levinas*, Cambridge, Cambridge University Press, 2002, p.14-15.

Critchley, Simon, *Infinitely Demanding: Ethics of Commitment, Politics of Resistance*, London & New York, Verso, 2007.

Crossley, Nick, *The Politics of Subjectivity: Between Foucault and Merleau-Ponty*, Aldershot, Avebury, 1994.

Crossley, Nick, *Intersubjectivity: The Fabric of Social Becoming*, London, SAGE Publications, 1996.

Deranty, Jean-Philippe, "Conceptualising Social Inequality: Redistribution of Recognition," *Social Inequality Today: Refereed Conference Proceedings*, Centre for Research on Social Inclusion, Macquarie University, Sydney, 2003.

Deranty, Jean-Philippe, "Injustice, Violence and Social Struggle. The Critical Potential of Honneth's Theory of Recognition," in *Contemporary Perspectives in Critical and Social Philosophy*, eds. Rundell, J., Petherbridge, D., Bryant, J., Hewitt, J., Smith, J., Leiden, Brill, 2004.

Deranty, Jean-Philippe, *Beyond Communication: A Critical Study of Axel Honneth's Social Philosophy*, Leiden & Boston, Brill, 2009.

Dewey, John, "Prefatory Remarks" in G. H. Mead, *The Philosophy of the Present*, Chicago & London, Open Court Publishing House, 1932.

Dewey, John, "The Reflex Arc Concept in Psychology" (1896) in John Dewey, *Philosophy, Psychology, and Social Practice*, ed. Joseph Ratner, New York, Capricorn Books, 1965.

Dews, Peter, *Logics of Disintegration: Post-structuralist Thought and the Claims of Critical Theory*, London & New York, Verso, 1988 (1987).

Dews, Peter, *The Limits of Disenchantment: Essays on Contemporary European Philosophy*, London & New York, Verso, 1995, p. 174.

Dreyfus, H. and Rabinow, P., *Michel Foucault: Beyond Structuralism and Hermeneutics*, Chicago, Chicago University Press, 1982.

Dubiel, Helmut, *Theory and Politics: Studies in the Development of Critical Theory*, trans. B. Gregg, Cambridge, MA & London, The MIT Press, 1985.

Eagle, Morris, N. *Recent Developments in Psychoanalysis: A Critical Evaluation*, New York, McGraw-Hill Book Company, 1984.

Elias, Norbert, *What is Sociology?* trans. Stephen Mennell & Grace Morrissey, New York, Columbia University Press, 1970.

Ellison, Ralph, *Invisible Man*, London, Penguin Books, 2001.

Erman, Eva, "Reconciling Communicative Action with Recognition: Thickening the 'Inter' of Intersubjectivity," *Philosophy and Social Criticism*, vol. 32, 3, 2006, pp. 377-400.

Falzon, C., *Foucault and Social Dialogue: Beyond Fragmentation*, London & New York, Routledge, 1998.

Fichte, J. G., *The Science of Knowledge*, ed. & trans. Peter Heath & John Lachs, Cambridge University Press, Cambridge, 1982 (1970).

Fichte, J.G., *Foundations of Transcendental Philosophy (Wissenshaftslehre, Novo Methodo, 1796/99)*, ed. & trans. Daniel Breazeale, Cornell, University Press, Ithaca & London, 1992.

Fichte, J.G., *Foundations of Natural Right*, ed. Frederick Neuhouser, trans. Michael Baur, Cambridge, Cambridge University Press, 2000.

Forst, Rainer, "'To Tolerate Means to Insult': Toleration, Recognition, and Emancipation," in eds. Bert van den Brink and David Owen, *Recognition and Power: Axel Honneth and the Tradition of Critical Social Theory*, Cambridge, Cambridge University Press, 2007, pp. 215-237

Foster, Roger, "Recognition and Resistance: Axel Honneth's Critical Social Theory," *Radical Philosophy*, vol. 94, March/April, 1999, pp. 6-18.

Foucault, Michel, *The Birth of the Clinic: An Archaeology of Medical Perception*, trans. A. M. Sheridan, New York, Vintage Books, 1973.

Foucault, Michel, *The Archaeology of Knowledge*, London, Tavistock Publications, 1972.

Foucault, Michel, "Critical Theory/Intellectual History," in Kelly, *Critique and Power: Recasting the Foucault/Habermas Debate*, Cambridge, MA, & London, The MIT Press, 1994.

Foucault, Michel, *Discipline and Punish: The Birth of the Prison*, Middlesex, Penguin Books, 1979 (1975).

Foucault, Michel, *The History of Sexuality: Volume 1* [*La Volonté de savoir*], London, Penguin Books, 1978.

Foucault, Michel, "Truth and Power," in *Power/Knowledge: Selected Interviews and Other Writings, 1972-1977*, New York, Pantheon Books, 1980.

Foucault, Michel, "The Subject and Power," in H. L. Dreyfus and P. Rabinow, *Michel Foucault: Beyond Structuralism and Hermeneutics*, Chicago, Chicago University Press, 1982.

Foucault, Michel, "Nietzsche, Genealogy, History," in P. Rabinow, *The Foucault Reader*, London, Penguin Books, 1984.

Foucault, Michel, *The Order of Things: An Archaeology of the Human Sciences*, London, Routledge, 1989.

Foucault, Michel, *Madness and Civilization: A History of Insanity in the Age of Reason*, trans. Richard Howard, London, Routledge, 1989.

Foucault, Michel, *The History of Sexuality: The Use of Pleasure, Volume 2*, trans. Robert Hurley, New York, Vintage Books, 1985.

Foucault, Michel, *The History of Sexuality: The Care of the Self, Volume 3*, trans. Robert Hurley, London Penguin Books, 1990 (1984).

Foucault, Michel, *Society Must be Defended*, eds. Fontana & Bertani, London, Allen Lane, Penguin Books, 2003.

Foucault, Michel, "Governmentality," in eds. G. Burchell, C. Gordon, and P. Miller, *The Foucault Effect: Studies in Governmentality*, London, Harvester Wheatsheaf, 1991.

Foucault, Michel, "Critical Theory/Intellectual History," in Kelly, *Critique and Power: Recasting the Foucault/Habermas Debate*, Cambridge, MA, & London, The MIT Press, 1994.

Foucault, Michel, "What is Enlightenment," in P. Rabinow, *The Foucault Reader*, London, Penguin Books, 1984.

Foucault, Michel, "Kant on Enlightenment and Revolution," *Economy and Society*, vol. 15, no. 1, 1986, pp. 88-96.

Foucault, Michel, "The Ethic of Care for the Self as a Practice of Freedom." An interview with Michel Foucault on January 20, 1984, with Raúl Fornet-Betancourt, Helmut Becker, & Alfredo Gomez-Müller, trans. J. D. Gauthier s.j., in *The Final Foucault*, eds. James Bernauer & David Rasmussen, The MIT Press, Cambridge, MA, & London, 1988.

Foucault, Michel, "The Art of Telling the Truth," in *Critique and Power: Recasting the Foucault/Habermas Debate*, ed. Michael Kelly, Cambridge, MA, & London, The MIT Press, 1994.

Foucault, Michel, "What is Critique?" in *What is Enlightenment? Eighteenth-Century Answers and Twentieth Century Questions*, ed. James Schmidt, Berkeley, LA & London, University of California Press, 1996.

Foucault, Michel, *Introduction to Kant's Anthropology*, ed. Roberto Nigro, trans. Roberto Nigro & Kate Briggs, Los Angeles, Semiotext(e), CA, 2008.

Fraser, Nancy, "Foucault on Modern Power: Empirical Insights and Normative Confusions," in *Unruly Practices: Power, Discourse and Gender in Contemporary Social Theory*, Minneapolis, The University of Minnesota Press, 1989.

Fraser, Nancy and Honneth, Axel, *Redistribution or Recognition?: A Political-Philosophical Exchange*, London & New York, Verso, 2003.

Gehlen, Arnold, *Man, His Nature and Place in the World*, trans. C. McMillan & K. Pillemer, New York, Columbia University Press, 1988.

Gregg, B., "Axel Honneth, *Kritik der Macht*," *New German Critique*, no. 47, Spring/Summer, 1989, pp. 183-188.

Green, André, *The Work of the Negative*, trans. Andrew Weller, London & New York, Free Association Books, 1999.

Green, André, *The Fabric of Affect in Psychoanalytic Discourse*, trans. Alan Sheridan, London & New York, Routledge, 1999 (1973).

Green, André and Daniel N. Stern et al., *Clinical and Observational Psychoanalytic Research: Roots of a Controversy*, eds. Joseph Sandler, Anne-Marie Sandler, & Rosemary Davies, London, H. Karnac Books, 2000.

Green, André, *Play and Reflection in Donald Winnicott's Writings*, London, Karnac, 2005.

Gutting, Gary, ed., *The Cambridge Companion to Foucault*, Second Edition, Cambridge & New York, Cambridge University Press, 2005.

Habermas, Jürgen, *Toward a Rational Society: Student Protest, Science and Politics*, trans. Jeremy J. Shapiro, London, Heinemann, 1971.

Habermas, Jürgen, *Knowledge and Human Interests*, trans. Jeremy Shapiro, London, Heinemann, 1972.

Habermas, Jürgen, *Theory and Practice*, trans. John Viertel, London, Heinemann, 1974.

Habermas, Jürgen, *Communication and the Evolution of Society*, trans. Thomas McCarthy, Boston, Beacon Press, 1979.

Habermas, Jürgen, "Reply to my Critics" in *Habermas: Critical Dates*, eds. John Thompson & David Held, London & Basingstoke, The Macmillan Press, 1982.

Habermas, Jürgen, *Philosophical-Political Profiles*, Cambridge, MA, 1983.

Habermas, Jürgen, *The Theory of Communicative Action. Volume One. Reason and the Rationalisation of Society*, trans. Thomas McCarthy, Boston, Beacon Press, 1984.

Habermas, Jürgen, *The Theory of Communicative Action. Volume Two. Lifeworld and System: A Critique of Functionalist Reason*, trans. Thomas McCarthy, Boston, Beacon Press, 1987.

Habermas, Jürgen, *Postmetaphysical Thinking*, Cambridge, Polity Press, 1995 (1988).

Habermas, Jürgen, *The Philosophical Discourse of Modernity*, trans. Frederick G. Lawrence, Cambridge, MA, The MIT Press, 1995.

Habermas, Jürgen, *Between Facts and Norms: Contributions to a Discourse Theory of Law and Democracy*, trans. William Rehg, Cambridge, Polity Press, 1996.

Han, B., *Foucault's Critical Project: Between the Transcendental and the Historical*, Stanford, Stanford University Press, 2002.

Hanson, Karen, *The Self Imagined: Philosophical Reflections on the Social Character of Psyche*, New York, Routledge & Kegan Paul, 1986.

Hanssen, Beatrice, *The Critique of Violence: Between Poststructuralism and Critical Theory*, London & New York, Routledge, 2000.

Harris, Henry S., *Hegel's Development: Toward the Sunlight, 1770-1801*, Oxford, The Clarendon Press, 1972.

Harris, Henry, S., *Hegel's Development: Night Thoughts (Jena 1801-1806)*, Oxford, Clarendon Press, 1983.

Hartmann, Martin and Honneth, Axel, "Paradoxes of Capitalism," *Constellations*, vol. 13, no. 1, 2006, pp. 41-58.

Haugaard, Mark, *Power*, Manchester and New York, Manchester University Press, 2002.

Hearfield, Colin, *Adorno and the Modern Ethos of Freedom*, Aldershot, Ashgate, 2004.

Hegel, G. W. F., *Early Theological Writings*, trans. T. M. Knox, Introduction and Fragments translated by Richard Kroner, Philadelphia, University of Pennsylvania Press, 1948.

Hegel, G. W. F., *Two Fragments on Love*, CLIO Vol. 8, Number, 2, 1979.

Hegel, G. W. F., *The Difference Between Fichte's and Schelling's System of Philosophy*, trans. H. S. Harris & W. Cerf, Albany, SUNY Press, 1977.

Hegel, G. W. F., *Natural Law: The Scientific Ways of Treating Natural Law, Its Place in Moral Philosophy, and its Relation to the Positive Sciences of Law*, trans. T. M. Knox, Intro. H. B. Acton, Foreword, J. Silber, Philadelphia, University of Pennsylvania Press, 1975.

Hegel, G.W.F., *System of Ethical Life and First Philosophy of Spirit*, ed. & trans. H.S. Harris & T.M. Knox, Albany, SUNY Press, 1979.

Hegel, G.W.F., *Realphilosophie* translated into English as *Hegel and the Human Spirit: A Translation of the Jena Lectures on the Philosophy of Spirit (1805-6) with Commentary*, trans. & Intro. Leo Rauch, Detroit, Wayne State University Press, 1983.

Hegel, G.W.F., *Phenomenology of Spirit*, trans. A.V. Miller, Foreword, J.N. Findlay, Oxford, Oxford University Press, 1977.

Hegel, G.W.F., *Philosophy of Right*, trans. T.M. Knox, London, Oxford, New York, Oxford University Press, 1979 (1952).

Hegel, G.W.F., *Science of Logic*, trans. A.V. Miller, Foreword J. N. Findlay, New York, Humanity Books, 1999.

Hegel, G.W.F., *The Logic of Hegel: Translated from the Encyclopaedia of the Philosophical Sciences*, trans. William Wallace, Oxford, Clarendon Press, 1892.

Hegel, G.W.F., *The Spirit of Christianity and Its Fate*, trans. T.M. Knox, intro. R. Kroner, in *Early Theological Writings*, Philadelphia, University of Pennsylvania Press, 1948.

Hegel, G.W.F. *Philosophy of Mind, Being Part Three of the Encyclopaedia of the Philosophical Sciences* (1830), translated by William Wallace, together with the *Zusätze* in Boumann's Text (1845), translated by A.V. Miller, with Foreword by J.N. Findlay, Oxford, Oxford at the Clarendon Press, 1971.

Heidegger, Martin, *Being and Time*, trans. Joan Stambaugh, Albany, SUNY Press, 1996 (1953).

Heidegren, Carl-Göran, "Anthropology, Social Theory, and Politics: Axel Honneth's Theory of Recognition," in Symposium on Axel Honneth and Recognition, *Inquiry*, no. 45, 2002, pp. 433-446.

Heller, Agnes, *The Theory of Need in Marx*, London, Allison & Busby, Spokesman Books, 1976.

Heller, Agnes "Habermas and Marxism," in eds. J. Thompson, & D. Held, *Habermas: Critical Debates*, London & Basingstoke, The Macmillan Press, 1982, pp. 21-41.

Heller, Agnes, ed. *Lukács Revalued*, Oxford, Basil Blackwell, 1983.

Henrich, Dieter, *The Course of Remembrance and Other Essays on Hölderlin*, ed. E. Förster, Stanford, California, Stanford University Press, 1997.

Henrich, Dieter, *Between Kant and Hegel: Lectures on German Idealism*, ed. David S. Pacini, Cambridge, MA. & London, Harvard University Press, 2003.

Hobbes, Thomas, *Leviathan*, ed. R. Tuck, Cambridge, Cambridge University Press, 1996.

Hohendahl, Peter Uwe and Fisher, Jaimey, *Critical Theory: Current State and Future Prospects*, New York and Oxford, Berghahn, 2001.

Hohendahl, Peter Uwe, *Reappraisals: Shifting Alignments in Postwar Critical Theory*, Ithaca & London, Cornell University Press, 1991.

Honneth, Axel & Joas, Hans, *Social Action and Human Nature*, trans. Raymond Meyer, Cambridge, Cambridge University Press, 1988.

Honneth, Axel, *The Critique of Power: Reflective Stages in a Critical Social Theory*, trans. Kenneth Baynes, Cambridge, Mass., & London, The MIT Press, 1991.

Honneth, Axel, interviewed by Peter Osborne and Stale Finke, "Critical Theory in Germany Today: An Interview with Axel Honneth," *Radical Philosophy* 65, Autumn, 1993.

Honneth, Axel "The Other of Justice: Habermas and the Ethical Challenge of Postmodernism," in *The Cambridge Companion to Habermas*, ed. Stephen K. White, Cambridge, Cambridge University Press, 1995.

Honneth, Axel, *The Fragmented World of the Social: Essays in Social and Political Philosophy*, ed. Charles Wright, Albany, State University of New York Press, 1995.

Honneth, Axel, "Foucault and Adorno: Two Forms of The Critique of Modernity," in *The Fragmented World of the Social: Essays in Social and Political Philosophy*, ed. C. W. Wright, Albany, SUNY Press, 1995.

Honneth, Axel, *The Struggle for Recognition: The Moral Grammar of Social Conflicts*, trans., Joel Anderson, Cambridge, Polity Press, 1995 (1992).

Honneth, Axel, "Pathologies of the Social: The Past and Present of Social Philosophy," trans. James Swindal, in *Handbook of Critical Theory*, ed. David Rasmussen, Oxford & Cambridge, Mass., Blackwell Publishers, 1996.

Honneth, Axel, "Democracy as Reflexive Cooperation: John Dewey and the Theory of Democracy Today," *Political Theory*, vol. 26, no. 6, Dec. 1998, pp. 763-783.

Honneth, Axel, "The Social Dynamics of Disrespect: Situating Critical Theory Today," in *Habermas: A Critical Reader*, ed. Peter Dews, Oxford, Blackwell Publishers, 1999.

Honneth, Axel, "Postmodern Identity and Object-Relations Theory: On the Seeming Obsolescence of Psychoanalysis, *Philosophical Explorations*, no. 3, September, 1999, pp. 225-242.

Honneth, Axel, *Suffering From Indeterminacy: An Attempt at a Reactualisation of Hegel's Philosophy of Right*, Assen,Van Gorcum, 2000.

Honneth, Axel, "Recognition or Redistribution? Changing Perspectives on the Moral Order of Society," *Theory, Culture & Society*, vol. 18, nos. 2 & 3, 2001, pp. 43-55.

Honneth, Axel, "Invisibility: On the Epistemology of 'Recognition,'" in *Recognition*, Axel Honneth & Avishai Margalit, *Supplement of the Aristotelian Society*, no. 75, 2001, pp. 127-139.

Honneth, Axel, "The Logic of Fanaticism: Dewey's Archaeology of the German Mentality," in *Pluralism and the Pragmatic Turn: The Transformation of Critical Theory, Essays in Honor of Thomas McCarthy*, eds. William Rehg and James Bohman, Cambridge, Mass., & London, The MIT Press, 2001.

Honneth, Axel, "Grounding Recognition: A Rejoinder to Critical Questions," in Symposium on Axel Honneth and Recognition, *Inquiry*, no. 45, 2002, pp. 499-520.

Honneth, Axel, "Between Hermeneutics and Hegelianism: John McDowell and the Challenge of Moral Realism," in *Reading McDowell: On Mind and World*, ed. Nicholas H. Smith, London & New York, Routledge, 2002.

Honneth, Axel, "On the Destructive Power of the Third: Gadamer and Heidegger's Theory of Intersubjectivity," *Philosophy and Social Criticism*, vol. 29, no.1, 2003, pp. 5-21.

Honneth, Axel, "Between Justice and Affection: The Family as a Field of Moral Disputes," in *Privacies: Philosophical Evaluations*, ed. Beate Rössler, Stanford, CA, Stanford University Press, 2004, pp. 142-162.

Honneth, Axel, "Organized Self-Realization: Some Paradoxes of Individualization," *European Journal of Social Theory*, vol. 7, no. 4, 2004, pp. 463-478.

Honneth, Axel, "A Physiognomy of the Capitalistic Lifeform: A Sketch of Adorno's Social Theory," *Constellations*, vol. 12, no. 1, 2005, pp. 50-64.

Honneth, Axel, *Disrespect: The Normative Foundations of Critical Theory*, Cambridge, Polity Press, 2007.

Honneth, Axel, "From Desire to Recognition: Hegel's Account of Human Sociality," in *Hegel's Phenomenology of Spirit: A Critical Guide*, eds. Dean Moyar & Michael Quante, Cambridge, Cambridge University Press, 2008, pp. 76-90.

Honneth, Axel, *Reification: A New Look at an Old Idea*, ed. Martin Jay, Oxford & New York, Oxford University Press, 2008.

Honneth, Axel, *Pathologies of Reason: On the Legacy of Critical Theory*, trans. James Ingram, New York, Columbia University Press, 2009.

Honneth, Axel, "From Desire to Recognition: Hegel's Account of Human Sociality" in *Hegel's Phenomenology of Spirit: A Critical Guide*, eds. Dean Moyar & Michael Quante, Cambridge, Cambridge University Press, 2008.

Honneth, Axel, "Recognition as Ideology," *Recognition and Power: Axel Honneth and the Tradition of Critical Social Theory*, in eds. Bert van den Brink & David Owen, New York & Cambridge, Cambridge University Press, 2007, pp. 323-347.

Honneth, Axel, *The Pathologies of Individual Freedom: Hegel's Social Theory*, Princeton, Princeton University Press, 2010.

Honneth, Axel, Allen, Amy and Cooke, Maeve, "A Conversation between Axel Honneth, Amy Allen, and Maeve Cooke, Frankfurt am Main, 12 April 2010," *Journal of Power*, Vol. 3, No. 2, August, 2010, pp. 153-170.

Honneth, Axel, *Das Recht Der Freiheit: Grundriß einer Demokratischen Sittlichkeit*, Berlin, Suhrkamp Verlag, 2011; (English translation) *Freedom's Right: The Social Foundations of Democratic Life*, New York, Columbia University Press, 2014 (forthcoming).

Honneth, Axel, *The I in We: Studies in the Theory of Recognition*, Cambridge, Polity Press, 2012.

Honneth, Axel, "The Relevance of Contemporary French Philosophy for a Theory of Recognition: An Interview" in eds. Miriam Bankovsky & Alice Le Goff, *Recognition Theory and Contemporary French Moral and Political Philosophy: Reopening the Dialogue*, Manchester, Manchester University Press, 2012, pp. 23-38.

Honneth, Axel, "Recognition and Critical Theory Today: An Interview with Axel Honneth," Gonçalo Marcelo, *Philosophy and Social Criticism*, vol. 39, no. 2, 2013, pp. 209-221.

Horkheimer, Max, *The Eclipse of Reason*, New York, Oxford University Press, New York, 1947.

Horkheimer, Max, *Critical Theory*, trans. M. O'Connell, New York, The Seabury Press, 1972 (1968).

Horkheimer, Max, *Dawn and Decline: Notes 1926-1931 and 1950-1969*, trans. Michael Shaw, New York, The Seabury Press, 1978.

Horstmann, Rolf-Peter, "Hegel," in *Routledge Encyclopaedia of Philosophy*, Volume 2, ed. Edward Craig, pp. 259-80.

Hoy, David Couzens, *Foucault: A Critical Reader*, Oxford, Basil Blackwell, 1986.

Hudson, Wayne, *The Reform of Utopia*, Aldershot, Ashgate, 2003.

Hyppolite, Jean, *Studies on Hegel and Marx*, trans. & Intro. John O'Neill, New York & London, Basic Books, 1969.

Hyppolite, Jean, *Introduction to Hegel's Philosophy of History*, trans. B. Harris & J. Bouchard Spurlock, Gainesville, University Press of Florida, 1996.

Ignatieff, Michael, *The Needs of Strangers*, Chatto & Windus, The Hogarth Press, London, 1984.

Ikäheimo, Heikki, "On the Genus and Species of Recognition," *Inquiry*, no. 45, 2002, pp. 447-446.

Ikäheimo, Heikki, "Analysing Social Inclusion in Terms of Recognitive Attitudes, *Social Inequality Today: Refereed Conference Proceedings*, Centre for Research on Social Inclusion, Macquarie University, Sydney, 2003.

Ingram, David, "Foucault and Habermas," in *The Cambridge Companion to Foucault,* ed., Gary Gutting, Second Edition, Cambridge & New York, Cambridge University Press, 2005, pp. 240-283.

Jay, Martin, *The Dialectical Imagination: A History of the Frankfurt School and the Institute of Social Research 1923-50*, London, Heinemann, 1973.

Jay, Martin, *Marxism and Totality: The Adventures of a Concept from Lukács to Habermas*, Cambridge, Polity Press, 1984.

Joas, Hans, *G. H. Mead: A Contemporary Re-examination of his Thought*, Cambridge, Polity Press, 1985 (1980).

Kelly, Michael, ed. *Critique and Power: Recasting the Foucault/Habermas Debate*, Cambridge, MA, & London, The MIT Press, 1994.

Kelly, Michael, "Foucault, Habermas, and the Self-Referentiality of Critique," in Kelly, Michael, ed. *Critique and Power: Recasting the Foucault/Habermas Debate*, Cambridge, MA, & London, The MIT Press, 1994.

Kernberg, Otto, F. *Object-Relations Theory and Clinical Psychoanalysis*, New York, Jason Aronson Inc, 1984.

Kojève, Alexandre, *Introduction to the Reading of Hegel. Lectures on the Phenomenology of Spirit*, ed. A. Bloom, trans. J. Nichols, Jr., Ithaca & London, Cornell University Press, 1980 (1969).

Kompridis, Nikolas, "From Reason to Self-Realization? Axel Honneth and the 'Ethical Turn' in Critical Theory," in *Contemporary Perspectives in Critical and Social Philosophy*, eds. J. Rundell, D. Petherbridge, J. Bryant, J. Hewitt, J. Smith, & Leiden, Brill, 2004.

Laitinen, Arto, "Interpersonal Recognition: A Response to Value or a Precondition of Personhood, *Inquiry*, no. 45, 2002, pp. 463-478.

Laitinen, Arto, "Social Equality, Recognition and Preconditions of Good Life," *Social Inequality Today: Refereed Conference Proceedings*, Centre for Research on Social Inclusion, Macquarie University, Sydney, 2003.

Laplanche, Jean, and Pontalis, Jean-Bertrand, *The Language of Psychoanalysis*, London, Karnac Books, 2006 (1973).

Levinas, *Totality and Infinity: An Essay on Exteriority*, trans. Alphonso Lingis, Dordrecht, Boston, London, Kluwer Academic Publishers, 1991.

Löwith, Karl, *From Hegel to Nietzsche: The Revolution in Nineteenth-Century Thought*, trans. David Green, New York, Columbia University Press, 1991 (1964).

Lukács, Georg, *The Theory of the Novel. An Historico-philosphical Essay on the Forms of Great Epic Literature*, trans. Anna Bostock, London, Merlin Press, 1971.

Lukács, Georg, *History and Class Consciousness: Studies in Marxist Dialectics*, trans. Rodney Livingstone, London, Merlin Press, 1971.

Lukács, Georg, *Soul and Form*, Anna Bostock, trans., London, Merlin Press, 1974.

Lukács, Georg, *The Young Hegel: Studies in the Relations between Dialectics and Economics*, trans. R. Livingstone, London, Merlin Press, 1975.

Lukes, Steven, *Power: A Radical View*, Second Edition, Basingstoke & New York, Palgrave Macmillan, 2005.

MacKendrick, Kenneth G., *Discourse, Desire, and Fantasy in Jürgen Habermas' Critical Theory*, New York & London, Routledge, 2008.

Magala, Slawomir, "History and the Ways Out of It: Reflexions on Axel Honneth's *Kritik der Macht,*" *Thesis Eleven*, no. 20, 1988, pp. 119-128.

Margalit, Avishai, "Recognizing the Brother and the Other," in *Recognition*, Axel Honneth & Avishai Margalit, *Supplement of the Aristotelian Society*, no. 75, 2001, pp. 127-139.

Markell, Patchen, *Bound by Recognition*, Princeton & Oxford, Princeton University Press, 2003.

Márkus, György, *Marxism and Anthropology: The Concept of 'Human Essence' in the Philosophy of Marx*, trans. E. de Laczay and G. Márkus, Assen, The Netherlands, Van Gorcum, 1978.

Márkus, György, "Alienation and Reification in Marx and Lukács," *Thesis Eleven*, nos. 5/6, 1982, pp. 139-161.

Márkus, György, "Life and Soul: The Young Lukács and the Problem of Culture," in *Lukács Revalued*, ed. Agnes Heller, Oxford, Basil Blackwell, 1983.

Marx, Karl, *The Economic and Philosophic Manuscripts of 1844* (ed.) Dirk Struik, New York, International Publishers, 1973.

Mead, George Herbert, *The Philosophy of the Present*, ed. Arthur E. Murphy, with Prefatory Remarks by John Dewey, Chicago & London, Open Court Publishing Company, 1932.

Mead, George Herbert, *Mind, Self, and Society from the Standpoint of a Social Behaviorist*, ed. Charles W. Morris, Chicago & London, The University of Chicago Press, 1934.

Mead, George Herbert, *Movements of Thought in the Nineteenth Century*, ed. Merritt H. Moore, Chicago, University of Chicago Press, 1936.

Mead, George Herbert, *The Philosophy of the Act*, ed. Charles W. Morris, Chicago & London, The University of Chicago Press, 1938.

Mead, George Herbert, *Selected Writings*, ed. Andrew J. Reck, Chicago & London, The University of Chicago Press, 1964.

Mead, George Herbert, *The Individual and the Social Self: Unpublished Work of George Herbert Mead*, ed. David L. Miller, Chicago & London, The University of Chicago Press, 1982.

Meehan, Johanna, "Autonomy, Recognition, and Respect: Habermas, Benjamin, and Honneth," in *Feminists Read Habermas: Gendering the Subject of Discourse*, ed. Johanna Meehan, New York & London, Routledge, 1995.

Meehan, Johanna, *Feminists Read Habermas: Gendering the Subject of Discourse*, ed. Johanna Meehan, New York & London, Routledge, 1995.

Meehan, Johanna, "Recognition and the Dynamics of Intersubjectivity," in *Axel Honneth: Critical Essays*, ed. Danielle Petherbridge, Leiden & Boston, Brill, 2011.

McNay, Lois, *Against Recognition*, Cambridge, Polity Press, 2008.

McNay, Lois, *Foucault and Feminism*, Boston, Northeastern University Press, 1992.

Moore, Barrington, *Injustice: The Social Bases of Obedience and Revolt*, London & Basingstoke, The MacMillan Press, 1978.

Moyar, Dean & Quante, Michael, eds. *Hegel's Phenomenology of Spirit: A Critical Guide*, Cambridge, Cambridge University Press, 2008.

Neculau, Radu, "Being Oneself in Another: Recognition and the Cultural Deformation of Identity," *Inquiry*, vol. 55, no. 2, April 2012, pp. 148-170.

Neuhouser, Frederick, *Foundations of Hegel's Social Theory: Actualizing Freedom*, Cambridge, MA, & London, Harvard University Press, 2000.

Nikolinkas, D., "Foucault's Ethical Quandary" in *Michel Foucault: Critical Assessments: Volume 3*, ed. B. Smart, London & New York, Routledge, 1994.

O'Neill, John, *Hegel's Dialectic of Desire and Recognition: Text and Commentary*, Albany, SUNY Press, 1996.

Owen, David, "Reification, Ideology and Power: Expression and Agency," *Journal of Power*, vol. 3, no. 1, 2010, pp. 97-109.

Pecora, Vincent. P., "Nietzsche, Genealogy, Critical Theory," *New German Critique*, no. 53, Spring-Summer, 1991, 104-130.

Pensky, Max, "Third Generation Critical Theory," in Critchley, Simon, & Schroeder, William, *A Companion to Continental Philosophy*, Malson, Mass. & Oxford, Blackwell Publishers, 1998.

Petherbridge, Danielle, ed., *Axel Honneth: Critical Essays*, Leiden & Boston, Brill, 2011.

Pinkard, Terry, *Hegel: A Biography*, Cambridge, Cambridge University Press, 2000.

Presbey, Gail, "The Struggle for Recognition in the Philosophy of Axel Honneth, Applied to the current South African Situation and its call for an 'African Renaissance,'" *Philosophy and Social Criticism*, vol. 29, no. 5, 2003, pp. 537-561.

Racevskis, K. "Michel Foucault, Rameau's Nephew and the Question of Identity," in *The Final Foucault*, eds. James Bernauer & David Rasmussen, The MIT Press, Cambridge, MA, & London, 1988.

Rasmussen, David, ed., *Handbook of Critical Theory*, Oxford & Cambridge, MA., Blackwell Publishers, 1996.

Redding, Paul, "Georg Wilhelm Friedrich Hegel," *Stanford Encyclopedia of Philosophy*, February 13 1997; revised June 26, 2006.

Rehg, William, *Insight and Solidarity: A Study in the Discourse Ethics of Jürgen Habermas*, Berkeley, Los Angeles, London, University of California Press, 1994.

Renault, Emmanuel, "The Theory of Recognition and Critique of Institutions," in *Axel Honneth: Critical Essays*, ed. Danielle Petherbridge, Leiden & Boston, Brill, 2011.

Ricoeur, Paul, *The Course of Recognition*, trans. D. Pellauer, Cambridge, MA & London, Harvard University Press, 2005.

Rockmore, Tom, *Habermas on Historical Materialism*, Bloomington & Indianapolis, Indiana University Press, 1989.

Rose, Gillian, *The Melancholy Science: An Introduction to the Thought of Theodor W. Adorno*, London & Basingstoke, The Macmillan Press, 1978.

Rose, Gillian, *Hegel Contra Sociology*, London, Athlone, & New Jersey, Humanities Press, 1981.

Rouse, Joesph, "Power/Knowledge," in *The Cambridge Companion to Foucault*, Second Edition, ed. Gary Gutting, Cambridge & New York, Cambridge University Press, 2005, pp. 95-122.

Rundell, John, *Origins of Modernity: The Origins of Modern Social Theory From Kant to Hegel to Marx*, Cambridge, Polity Press, 1987.

Rundell, John, "Imaginary Turns in Critical Theory: Imagining Subjects in Tension," in *Critical Theory after Habermas: Encounters and Departures*, eds. Dieter Freundlieb, Wayne Hudson, & John Rundell, Leiden & Boston, Brill, 2004.

Saar, Martin, "Power and Critique," *Journal of Power*, vol. 3, no. 1, 2010, pp. 7-20.

Sartre, Jean-Paul, *Being and Nothingness*, trans. H. E. Barnes, New York, Washington Square Press, 1993.

Schelling, F.W.J., *Ideas for a Philosophy of Nature as Introduction to the Study of this Science*, 1797, Second Edition 1803, trans. Errol E. Harris & Peter Heath, Introduction by Robert Stern, Cambridge, Cambridge University Press, 1988.

Schelling, F.W.J., *First Outline of a System of the Philosophy of Nature*, 1799, including "Introduction to the Outline of a System of the Philosophy of Nature, or, On the Concept of Speculative Physics and the Internal Organization of a System of this Science" (1799), trans. & Introduction Keith R. Peterson, New York, SUNY Press, 2004.

Schmid, Michael, "Habermas' Theory of Social Evolution," in *Habermas: Critical Debates*, eds. John Thompson & David Held, London & Basingstoke, The Macmillan Press, 1982, pp. 162-180.

Schmidt, James and Wartenberg, Thomas, "Foucault's Enlightenment: Critique, Revolution, and the Fashioning of the Self, " in *Critique and Power: Recasting the Foucault/Habermas Debate*, ed. Michael Kelly, Cambridge, MA, & London, The MIT Press, 1994.

Schmidt, James, ed., *What is Enlightenment? Eighteenth-Century Answers and Twentieth Century Questions*, Berkeley, LA, & London, University of California Press, 1996.

Sennett, Richard, *The Corrosion of Character. The Personal Consequences of Work in the New Capitalism*, New York & London, W.W. Norton & Company, 1998.

Siep, Ludwig, "The Struggle for Recognition: Hegel's Dispute with Hobbes in the Jena Writings," trans. C. Dudas, in John O'Neill *Hegel's Dialectic of Desire and Recognition: Text and Commentary*, Albany, SUNY Press, 1996.

Sinnerbrink, Robert, "Power, Recognition, and Care: Honneth's Critique of Poststructuralist Social Philosophy," in *Axel Honneth: Critical Essays*, ed. D.Petherbridge, Leiden & Boston, Brill, 2011.

Sinnerbrink, Robert, *Understanding Hegelianism*, London, Acumen, 2007.

Smart, Barry, *Foucault, Marxism and Critique*, London & Boston, Routledge and Kegan Paul, 1983.

Smart, Barry, ed., *Michel Foucault: Critical Assessments, Volume 3*, London & New York, Routledge, 1994.

Smith, Nicholas H., "Social Power and the Domination of Nature," *History of the Human Sciences*, vol. 6, no. 3, 1993.

Smith, Nicholas H., ed., *Reading McDowell: On Mind and World*, London & New York, Routledge, 2002.

Stern, Daniel, *The First Relationship: Infant and Mother*, Cambridge, MA & London, Harvard University Press, 2002.

Stern, Daniel, *The Interpersonal World of the Infant: A View From Psychoanalysis and Developmental Psychology*, London & New York, Karnac Books, 1985.

Taminiaux, Jacques, *Dialectic and Difference: Finitude in Modern Thought*, eds. James Decker & Robert Crease, New Jersey, The Macmillian, Humanities Press, 1985.

Tatranský, Tomáš, "A Reciprocal Asymmetry? Levinas's Ethics Reconsidered," in *Ethical Perspectives*, vol. 15, no. 3, 2008.

Taylor, Charles, *Hegel*, Cambridge, Cambridge University Press, 1975.

Taylor, Charles, *Sources of the Self: The Making of Modern Identity*, Cambridge, Cambridge University Press, 1989.

Theunissen, Michael, *The Other: Studies in the Social Ontology of Husserl, Heidegger, Sartre, and Buber*, trans. C. Macann, with an Introduction by F. Dallmayr, Cambridge, MA & London, The MIT Press, 1977.

Theunissen, Michael, "The Repressed Intersubjectivity in Hegel's Philosophy of Right," in *Hegel and Legal Theory*, Cornell, Drucilla, Rosenfeld, Michael, & Gray Carlson, David, New York & London, Routledge, 1991.

Thompson, E.P., *The Making of the English Working Class*, London, Victor Gollancz, 1980.

Thompson, J. & Held, D. eds., *Habermas: Critical Debates*, London & Basingstoke, The Macmillan Press, 1982.

Thompson, Simon, *The Political Theory of Recognition: A Critical Introduction*, Cambridge, Polity, 2006.

Todorov, Tzvetan, *Life in Common: An Essay in General Anthropology*, trans. Katherine Golson & Lucy Golsan, Lincoln & London, University of Nebraska Press, 2001.

Van den Brink, Bert & Owen, David, eds., *Recognition and Power: Axel Honneth and the Tradition of Critical Social Theory*, New York & Cambridge, Cambridge University Press, 2007.

Van den Brink, Bert "Recognition, Pluralism, and the Expectation of Harmony: Against the Ideal of an Ethical Life 'Free from Pain,'" in *Axel Honneth: Critical Essays*, ed. D. Petherbridge, Leiden & Boston, Brill, 2011.

Varga, Somogy, "Critical Theory and the Two-Level Account of Recognition: Towards a New Foundation?", *Critical Horizons*, vol. 11, no. 1, 2010, pp. 19-33.

Wartenberg, Thomas, *The Forms of Power: From Domination to Transformation*, Philadelphia, Temple University Press, 1990.

Wheatland, Thomas, *The Frankfurt School in Exile*, University of Minnesota Press, Minnesota, 2009.

Whitebook, Joel, *Perversion and Utopia: A Study in Psychoanalysis and Critical Theory*, Cambridge, MA. & London, The MIT Press, 1995.

Whitebook, Joel, "Mutual Recognition and the Work of the Negative," in *Pluralism and the Pragmatic Turn: The Transformation of Critical Theory, Essays in Honor of Thomas McCarthy*, eds. William Rehg and James Bohman, Cambridge, Mass., & London, The MIT Press, 2001.

Whitebook, Joel "First Nature and Second Nature in Hegel and Psychoanalysis," *Constellations*, Volume 15, No. 3, 2008, pp. 382-389.

Wiggerhaus, Rolf, *The Frankfurt School: Its History, Theories and Political Significance*, trans. M. Robertson, Cambridge, MA., MIT Press, 1994.

Williams, Robert R., *Recognition: Fichte and Hegel on the Other*, Albany, SUNY Press, 1992.

Williams, Robert R., *Hegel's Ethics of Recognition*, Berkeley, Los Angeles, London, 1997.

Winnicott, Donald W., *The Maturational Processes and the Facilitating Environment*, London, Karnac Books, 1990.

Winnicott, Donald, W., *Playing and Reality*, London & New York, Routledge, 1991 (1971).

Winnicott, Donald, W., *Through Paediatrics to Psychoanalysis: Collected Papers*, London, Karnac Books, 2007 (1958).

Winnicott, Donald, W., *The Family and Individual Development*, London & New York, Routledge, 2006 (1965).

Young, Iris Marion, "Recognition of Love's Labor: Considering Axel Honneth's Feminism," in eds. Bert van den Brink and David Owen, *Recognition and Power: Axel Honneth and the Tradition of Critical Social Theory*, Cambridge, Cambridge University Press, 2007, pp. 189-212.

Zurn, Christopher, "Anthropology and Normativity: A Critique of Axel Honneth's 'Formal Conception of Ethical Life,'" *Philosophy and Social Criticism*, vol. 26, no.1, 2000, pp. 115-124.

Zurn, Christopher, "Recognition, Redistribution, and Democracy: Dilemmas of Honneth's Critical Social Theory," *European Journal of Philosophy*, vol. 13, no. 1, 2005, pp. 89-126.

Zurn, Christopher, "Social Pathologies as Second-Order Disorders," in *Axel Honneth: Critical Essays*, ed. D. Petherbridge, Leiden & Boston, Brill, 2011.

Index

absolute dependence, 155, 156

Adorno, Theodor, 3, 31, 35, 178; conception of power and, 49; *The Dialectic of Enlightenment*, 54, 57, 59, 60, 186; modernity and, 54, 59, 60; *Negative Dialectics*, 61; philosophy of history and, 59; social action and, 50; suffering and, 59, 60

affective attachment, 148, 178, 179

agonism, 45, 99; alienation. *See also* theory of alienation; Habermas and, 22, 27; labor and, 21, 22, 23, 31; Marxian notion of, 26

Althusser, Louis, 198; ideological state apparatus and, 49; notion of ideology and, 192

anthropology: expressivist, 22; historical, 61, 64, 66, 67, 70; of action, 133, 134; of force and violence, 67; of intersubjectivity, 70; of sociable sociability, 63–67; of social action, 126, 133; of unsociable sociability, 67–70; normative, 64, 180; philosophical, 14, 18, 62, 63, 64–65, 66, 67, 81, 113, 126, 133, 135, 145, 183, 186; relation to alienation, 22

Arendt, Hannah, 185, 187; notion of power and, 46–47, 189

Aristotle, 85, 87, 188

autonomy, 13, 27, 172, 174, 190, 192; individual, 72; moral, 168; mothers and, 153, 155

Beebe, Beatrice, 160

Benjamin, Jessica, 148, 156

Bildung, 22, 24, 91

communicative action, conflict and power as modalities of, 28–32, 74

communicative rationalization, 30–31

conflict, 13, 17, 30, 56, 58, 68, 82, 83, 85, 86, 96–97, 98, 99, 101, 102, 106, 111, 114, 115, 116, 121, 138, 141, 143, 156, 159, 163, 164, 180, 196, 197; as modality of communicative action, 28–32; intra-psychic, 149; moral, 23, 29, 131, 144; psychic, 126, 145; psychological, 144; social, 3, 27, 49, 51, 97, 99, 100, 101, 104, 105, 106, 113, 114, 115–116, 143–144, 173, 198; strategic, 50, 55, 56

consciousness: individual, 107–108; moral, 148; philosophy of, 103, 105–106, 107–108, 109, 113, 118; psychical. *See* self-consciousness

crime, 95; recognition and, 96–104

critical social theory, 11, 187; communicative rationalization and, 30–31; economic meaning of labor and, 22; Honneth and, 5, 7, 11, 22, 35, 36–37, 78, 167, 173, 183, 199; normative, 77

247